THE INTERPLAY OF GLOBAL STANDARDS AND EU PHARMACEUTICAL REGULATION

This book analyses, and questions the impact and legitimacy of, the implementation of global pharmaceutical standards in the European risk regulation framework for pharmaceuticals.

Global standards increasingly shape risk regulation law and policy in the European Union, and the area of pharmaceuticals is no exception. As this book shows, global pharmaceutical standards set by the International Council for Harmonisation of Technical Requirements for the Registration of Pharmaceuticals for Human Use (ICH), after they are adopted through the European Medicines Agency (EMA), are an important feature of the regulatory framework for pharmaceuticals in the EU.

In addition to analysing the influence of these global standards in the EU, the book questions the legitimacy of the Union's reliance on global standards in terms of core administrative law principles of participation, transparency and independence of expertise. It also critically examines the accountability of the European Commission and the EMA, both as participants in global standard setting, and as the main gateway for global pharmaceutical standards being implemented in the European Union.

Hart Studies in Law and Health

Hart Studies in Law and Health aims to publish the best existing and upcoming voices in scholarship on law and health. Viewing law as a broad church, the series welcomes a range of methodologies from the doctrinal to the critical and including regulation and governance, and law and ethics approaches.

The Interplay of Global Standards and EU Pharmaceutical Regulation

The International Council for Harmonisation

Sabrina Röttger-Wirtz

•HART•
OXFORD • LONDON • NEW YORK • NEW DELHI • SYDNEY

HART PUBLISHING
Bloomsbury Publishing Plc
Kemp House, Chawley Park, Cumnor Hill, Oxford, OX2 9PH, UK
1385 Broadway, New York, NY 10018, USA
29 Earlsfort Terrace, Dublin 2, Ireland

First published in Great Britain 2021

A catalogue record for this book is available from the British Library.

Library of Congress Cataloging-in-Publication data

Names: Röttger-Wirtz, Sabrina, author.

Title: The interplay of global standards and EU Pharmaceutical Regulation : the International Council for Harmonisation / Sabrina Röettger-Wirtz.

Description: Oxford ; New York : Hart, 2021. | Series: Hart studies in law and health | Based on author's thesis (doctoral - Universiteit Maastricht, 2017). | Includes bibliographical references and index.

Identifiers: LCCN 2021017140 (print) | LCCN 2021017141 (ebook) | ISBN 9781509942992 (hardback) | ISBN 9781509943081 (paperback) | ISBN 9781509943012 (pdf) | ISBN 9781509943005 (pdf)

Subjects: LCSH: Drugs—Law and legislation—European Union countries. | International and municipal law—European Union countries. | ICH (Association)

Classification: LCC KJE6191 .R68 2021 (print) | LCC KJE6191 (ebook) | DDC 344.2404/233—dc23

LC record available at https://lccn.loc.gov/2021017140

LC ebook record available at https://lccn.loc.gov/2021017141

ISBN: HB: 978-1-50994-299-2
ePDF: 978-1-50994-301-2
ePub: 978-1-50994-300-5

Typeset by Compuscript Ltd, Shannon

Contents

Introduction

PHARMACEUTICALS HAVE BENEFITTED humanity, enhancing the quality of life and life expectancy, but their regulation is challenging, involving complex decisions over benefits and risk which require considerable expertise. The regulatory framework for pharmaceuticals has been placed in the spotlight by the recent Covid-19 pandemic which has shaken the European Union (EU) – together with the rest of the world – to its core.[1] With everyone anxiously awaiting treatments and vaccines, the question of how these products are regulated received a lot of public attention. In this context, the European Commission published its vaccine strategy in October 2020 stating that:

> The EU's regulatory framework, which set out high-standards and strict requirements, contains regulatory flexibilities to cater for urgencies. In this way, the development, authorisation and availability of vaccines can be accelerated while standards for vaccine quality, safety and efficacy remain strict. This is key to citizens' confidence.[2]

But who makes the standards that ensure the quality, safety and efficacy of pharmaceuticals on the EU market? And how are these rules determined? Which role do standards play within EU pharmaceutical law? The quote shows that the Commission views quality, safety and efficacy standards as central part of safeguarding a 'high level of health protection' in the EU, and the maintenance of a high level of protection is key to citizens' trust. This is true not only in the time of a pandemic. Therefore, the marketing authorisation that each medicinal product has to obtain before it can be placed on the internal market forms the core of the regulatory framework for medicinal products in the EU.[3] This book, written before the pandemic, makes the role of scientific and technical standards in the regulation of pharmaceuticals visible, focusing on the requirements of quality, safety and efficacy. The book reveals that the standards often are not set within the EU but rather on the global level. It shows the influence of global standards on EU pharmaceutical law and, rather than assessing the content of the standards, it raises questions regarding their legitimacy.

[1] On 11 March 2020, the WHO Director-General in the opening remarks at the media briefing declared the outbreak of Covid-19 to be a pandemic.

[2] European Commission, Communication – Preparedness for COVID-19 vaccination strategies and vaccine deployment, COM(2020) 680 final, 15 October 2020, 5.

[3] Directive 2001/83/EC, of the European Parliament and of the Council of 6 November 2001 on the Community code relating to medicinal products for human use, [2001] OJ L311/67, art 6; Regulation (EC) No 726/2004 laying down Community procedures for the authorisation and supervision of medicinal products for human and veterinary use and establishing a European Medicines Agency, [2004] OJ L136/1, art 3(1).

Within the EU, the regulation of risks for products, such as pharmaceuticals, food or chemicals, constitutes the largest source of regulation.[4] In these areas the EU has to strike a delicate balance between two Treaty objectives: (i) the free movement of goods, and (ii) the protection of public health, the environment and consumers.[5] Pharmaceutical regulation needs to balance protection of public health with the industry interests of obtaining marketing authorisations for their products and keeping the research and development phase as cost-effective as possible. As drug development is facing a 'productivity crisis',[6] with increasing costs for the development of new drugs and many failings in the development stage,[7] regulatory standards are of key interest for the pharmaceutical industry. Patients require safe medicines that effectively cure or treat their illness. In this setting, the regulation of pharmaceuticals is characterised by the interaction, competition and sometimes also collusion of the protection of public health, policies regarding the healthcare system, and industrial policy.[8]

I. EU PHARMACEUTICAL REGULATION IN A GLOBALISED MARKET

The process of globalisation with growing interrelation of markets, communication and traffic structures[9] has had an effect on risk regulation, which is now carried out at multiple levels – national, European and international – creating complicated and often interconnected structures of regulatory organisations and procedures.[10] These developments challenge the classical perception of regulators operating in a national administration, with powers confined to a single state.[11] Regulation in this regard is not limited to legislative measures, but is also carried out by means of the adoption of health, safety and quality

[4] A Alemanno, 'The Shaping of European Risk Regulation by Community Courts', Jean Monnet Working Paper 18/2008, (2008) 4.

[5] T Hervey and J McHale, *Health Law and the European Union* (Cambridge: Cambridge University Press, 2004) 287.

[6] F Pammolli, L Magazzini and M Riccaboni, 'The Productivity Crisis in Pharmaceutical R&D' (2011) 10 *Nature Reviews Drug Discovery* 428.

[7] J DiMasi, H Grabowski and R Hansen, 'Innovation in the pharmaceutical industry: New estimates of R&D costs' (2016) 47 *Journal of Health Economics* 20.

[8] G Permanand, *EU Pharmaceutical Regulation: The Politics of Policy-Making* (Manchester: Manchester University Press, 2006) 4; E Mossialos, M Mrazek and T Walley, 'Regulating Pharmaceuticals in Europe: An Overview', in E Mossialos, M Mrazek, and T Walley (eds), *Regulating Pharmaceuticals in Europe: Striving for Efficiency, Equity and Quality* (Maidenhead: Open University Press, 2004) 5.

[9] J Habermas, 'Die Postnationale Konstellation und die Zukunft der Demokratie', in J Habermas, *Die Postnationale Konstellation – Politische Essays* (Frankfurt am Main: Suhrkamp Verlag, 1998) 101.

[10] Ibid, 165.

[11] C Harlow, 'Composite Decision-Making and Accountability Networks: Some Deductions from a Saga' (2013) 32 *Yearbook of European Law* 3, 3.

standards for products and production processes.[12] Standards are voluntary, measurable criteria governing certain technical and/or scientific matters of a product or production process.[13]

Global standards implemented in the EU increasingly shape the regulation of risk in the Union. At the same time, the EU also shapes regulatory rules on a global level.[14] As the 2020 Pharmaceutical strategy for Europe states: 'The EU has an interest in working with its international partners towards more ambitious level of quality, efficacy and safety standards in international cooperation fora and organisations. **Common international standards** are a key tool. They facilitate the global development of pharmaceuticals.'[15] These types of measures are not given much attention in legal research due to their technical or scientific nature and non-binding form.[16] However, they are deeply intertwined with the legal frameworks.

As pharmaceuticals are 'global products' developed, tested, manufactured and marketed throughout different countries,[17] it is not surprising that regulatory power has shifted to the global level, driving a harmonisation of regulatory requirements in the form of technical and scientific standards for pharmaceuticals. These regulatory developments are epitomised in the International Council for Harmonisation of Technical Requirements for the Registration of Pharmaceuticals for Human Use (ICH).[18] The ICH and the impact of its standards on European pharmaceutical regulation will be critically examined in this book. The ICH consists of representatives of regulatory authorities as well

[12] C Scott, 'Standard-Setting in Regulatory Regimes', in R Baldwin, M Cave and M Lodge (eds), *The Oxford Handbook of Regulation* (Oxford: Oxford University Press, 2010).

[13] The definition of global standards will be discussed in Chapter 2.

[14] See in this regard especially the recent work of Joanne Scott: J Scott, 'The New EU "Extraterritoriality"' (2014a) 51 *Common Market Law Review* 1343; J Scott, 'Extraterritoriality and Territorial Extension in EU Law' (2014b) 62 *American Journal of Comparative Law* 87. With regard to pharmaceuticals, for example the EU's rule on clinical trials will affect trials carried out in third countries where the product will be marketed in the EU. See: M Flear, *Governing Public Health: EU Law, Regulation and Biopolitics* (Oxford: Hart Publishing, 2015); T Hervey and J McHale, *European Union Health Law – Themes and Implications* (Cambridge: Cambridge University Press, 2015) 506; T Hervey, 'The EU's (Emergent) Global Health Law', in T Hervey, C Young and L Bishop (eds), *Research Handbook on EU Health Law and Policy* (Cheltenham: Edward Elgar, 2017) 458.

[15] European Commission, Communication – Pharmaceutical Strategy for Europe, COM(2020) 761 final, 25 November 2020, 23 (emphasis in original).

[16] Some notable exceptions are: B Dorbeck-Jung, 'Challenges to the Legitimacy of International Regulation: The Case of Pharmaceuticals Standardisation', in A Føllesdal, R Wessel and J Wouters (eds), *Multilevel Regulation and the EU: The Interplay between Global, European and National Normative Processes* (Leiden: Martinus Nijhoff Publishers, 2008); N Hachez and J Wouters, 'A Glimpse at the Democratic Legitimacy of Private Standards: Assessing the Public Accountability of Global G.A.P.' (2011) 14 *Journal of International Economic Law* 677; H Röhl, 'Internationale Standardsetzung', in C Möllers, A Vosskuhle and C Walter (eds), *Internationales Verwaltungsrecht – Eine Analyse Anhand von Referenzgebieten* (Tübingen: Mohr Siebeck, 2007).

[17] Hervey and McHale (2015) 505.

[18] Before 2015 the ICH was known as the International Conference on Harmonisation of Technical Requirements for the Registration of Pharmaceuticals for Human Use.

as representatives of pharmaceutical industry associations and has established itself as the main standard-setting body in the field of pharmaceuticals.[19] Its standards shape the quality, safety and efficacy requirements that have to be complied with in the marketing authorisation procedures in the EU and worldwide.[20] Viewed in a broader context, the regulatory standards adopted by the ICH, together with other global hard and soft law such as human rights and global trade rules, form part of 'global health law'.[21]

II. GLOBAL STANDARDS: QUESTIONS OF LEGITIMACY

While increasingly risk regulation and health law are shaped on the international level, the required legitimation is not readily available where the confines of the nation states are left behind,[22] as global governance suffers from a democratic deficit.[23] Global regulatory initiatives have been criticised for taking place in a rather technocratic and closed setting, by regulators and representatives of the industry hiding from public scrutiny.[24] Often 'decision-making processes … tend to be elitist and opaque, with few participants and no agreed upon control'.[25] They suffer from a lack of representation of consumer interest or civil society participation in global standard-setting.[26] This entails the risk of establishing a system that fails to represent the interests of society at large.[27] In the context of global standard-setting, the regulated industry is an active player in the decision-making process, while accountability towards the public at large is often lacking.[28]

[19] In the context of the GCP see: Flear (2015) 222ff; M Flear, 'Charting a roadmap towards membership and formal voice in global bioethics standard-setting: Health research and the case of the International Council on Harmonisation' (2018) *Medical Law International* 157, 163.

[20] Hervey (2017) 458; Hervey and McHale (2015) 455.

[21] Hervey and McHale (2015) 433–532; Hervey (2017).

[22] C Joerges, 'Law, Science and the Management of Risks to Health at the National, European and International Level: Stories on Baby Dummies, Mad Cows and Hormones in Beef' (2001) 7 *Columbia Journal of European Law* 1, 3. See also: Habermas (1998), 94 and 109f. On the difficulty of achieving democratic legitimation on the international level: J Weiler, 'The Geology of International Law – Governance, Democracy and Legitimacy' (2004) 64 *Zeitschrift für ausländisches öffentliches Recht und Völkerrecht* 547. For a counterargument: G de Búrca, 'Developing Democracy Beyond the State' (2008) 46 *Columbia Journal of Transnational Law* 221.

[23] Hachez and Wouters (2011) 683.

[24] See eg: A Føllesdal, R Wessel and J Wouters (eds), *Multilevel Regulation and the EU: The Interplay between Global, European and National Normative Processes* (Leiden: Martinus Nijhoff Publishers, 2008); A Slaughter, 'The Accountability of Government Networks' (2001) 8 *Indiana Journal of Global Legal Studies* 347; de Búrca (2008) 224.

[25] M Shapiro, 'Administrative Law Unbounded: Reflections on Government and Governance' (2001) 8 *Indiana Journal of Legal Studies* 369, 374.

[26] Flear (2015).

[27] W Mattli, 'The Politics and Economics of Institutional Standards Setting: An Introduction' (2001) 8 *Journal of European Public Policy* 328, 331; J Mendes, 'EU Law and Global Regulatory Regimes: Hollowing Out Procedural Standards?' (2012) 10 *International Journal of Constitutional Law* 988.

[28] Scott (2010) 116.

Also the ICH has been criticised for a lack of transparency,[29] and decision-making confined within closed groups of experts, intertwining science with politics.[30] In the ICH's practice, the pharmaceutical industry is a privileged stakeholder in international standard-setting,[31] while input from patient and doctor associations is neglected.[32] Critics have even stated that 'the ICH process has permitted scientists from industry to renegotiate extensively the scientific standards that the regulatory agencies are supposed to be using to protect public health'.[33] In 2008, Dorbeck-Jung concluded in her analysis of the ICH that 'major challenges are to enhance the legitimacy of its standard-setting activities and to reveal the secrecy of its influence and powers in the regulatory practice'.[34] In essence, it is argued that the successes of the ICH thrive on a lack of transparency and participation of other interested parties.

Where standards are not only coordinating the interconnectability or compatibility of products like plugs or tubes, but govern the safety of products and guard public health,[35] as is the case for pharmaceuticals, such legitimacy questions are all the more compelling. Risk perception is 'unstable'[36] and regulatory responses are shaped by social and cultural context. The regulation of health risks, therefore, exceeds mere questions of technicalities, but contains political or normative choices that require a legitimate basis.[37] These concerns with regard to the ICH's legitimacy will be assessed in this book, also taking into account the substantial institutional reform the ICH has undergone since 2015.

III. THE CONTRIBUTION OF THIS BOOK: THE INFLUENCE OF GLOBAL STANDARDS THROUGH THE EU LENS

Concerns regarding the legitimacy of global standards will also affect the EU where it implements such standards into its regulatory framework. Where such

[29] C Hodgkin, 'International Harmonisation – The Need for Transparency' (1996) 9 *International Journal of Risk & Safety in Medicine* 195, 196.

[30] K Timmermans, 'Harmonization, Regulation, and Trade: Interactions in the Pharmaceutical Field' (2004) 34 *International Journal of Health Services* 651, 651.

[31] Hervey and McHale (2015) 441; M Rizzi, 'Non-Measurable Negotiations: The EU between Transnational Regulation of Pharmaceuticals and Private Law', in M Cremona and H Micklitz, *Private Law in the External Relations of the EU* (Oxford: Oxford University Press, 2016) 283; S Röttger-Wirtz, 'Independence under threat – the role of private actors in the setting of global pharmaceutical standards and resulting challenges for European public law' (2018a) 24 *European Public Law* 433.

[32] J Abraham and T Reed, 'Trading Risks For Markets: The International Harmonization of Pharmaceuticals Regulation' (2001) 1 *Health, Risk and Society* 113, 125. With regard to clinical trials see: Flear (2015) 220.

[33] J Abraham, 'The Pharmaceutical Industry as a Political Player' (2002) 360 *The Lancet* 1498, 1500.

[34] Dorbeck-Jung (2008) 71.

[35] Scott (2010) 116.

[36] J Black, 'The Role of Risk in Regulatory Processes', in R Baldwin, M Cave and M Lodge (eds), *The Oxford Handbook of Regulation* (Oxford: Oxford University Press, 2010) 321.

[37] Habermas (1998) 164f.

standards are relied on in the European framework, they may undermine the legitimacy of the European risk regulation framework if they do not fulfil the procedural requirements applicable to risk regulation in the EU. Although it is increasingly acknowledged that global standards influence policies and decisions in the EU,[38] an analysis of their implementation and an in-depth assessment of the influence these standards have on risk regulation in the EU is lacking.

Although the voluntary nature of standards may suggest that a legitimacy deficit on the global level is not problematic, it is argued in this book that their non-binding nature masks their substantial influence on European risk regulation. Even if the implementation of international standards is voluntary for the states participating in standard-setting, *de facto* states do implement global standards.[39] Once implemented, standards can lead to a shift in the requirements of proof for a regulated product.[40] After implementation, they have an impact on companies producing the regulated product but also the consumers of such products.[41] As will be shown, the ICH standards influence the whole pharmaceutical lifecycle.

The ICH standards shape the regulatory assessment of quality, safety and efficacy in the EU and, as argued by Hervey and McHale: '[a]ll of the EU's elaborate risk management processes that seek to ensure that pharmaceuticals and medical devices are safe as possible when reaching patients become irrelevant if the global context is ignored'.[42] This book, therefore, next to an analysis of the regulatory processes on the ICH level, sheds light on the influential role of ICH standards in EU pharmaceutical regulation and questions the legitimacy of their implementation. It will present recommendations to improve the global standard-setting process in the ICH, based on a comparison with procedural requirements in the EU, fully acknowledging that the procedural standards of EU risk regulation are not the only relevant benchmarks, given the multinational membership of the ICH. The book is not meant to depict European risk regulation as an ideal system, but rather to use the lessons learned in the European harmonisation process as inspiration for enhancing global harmonisation through standard-setting. Additionally, the book develops suggestions to improve the approach the EU takes as a legal system towards the integration of global standards.

[38] See eg: J Wouters and S Verhoeven, 'Regulation and Globalization: Interaction between International Standard-Setting Agencies and the European Union, in D Geradin, R Muñoz, and N Petit (eds), *Regulation Through Agencies in the EU: A New Paradigm of European Governance* (Cheltenham: Edward Elgar, 2006); J Mendes, 'Rule of Law and Participation: A Normative Analysis of Internationalized Rulemaking as Composite Procedures' (2014) 12 *International Journal of Constitutional Law* 370; Röhl (2007); P Müller-Graff, 'Das "Soft Law" der Europäischen Organisationen' (2012) 1 *Europarecht* 18.

[39] See also: D Kerwer, 'Rules that Many Use: Standards and Global Regulation' (2005) 18 *Governance* 611.

[40] Röhl (2007) 337f.

[41] Mendes (2012); Mendes (2014).

[42] Hervey and McHale (2015) 506.

Along with the study of legal doctrine and a variety of official documents, the research is supplemented by semi-structured qualitative interviews with officials involved in the ICH process from the European Commission, the European Federation of Pharmaceutical Industries and Associations (EFPIA) and the European Medicines Agency (EMA). A separate interview with officials of the EMA's Legal Department also took place.[43] An interview with an official from the German Federal Institute for Drugs and Medical Devices (Bfarm) was also conducted, in order to account for the perspective of EU Member States. These interviews were carried out in order to verify the insights obtained and to enquire whether the 'law in books' matched the 'law in action'.[44] In this regard, where references to such interviews are made, they should be regarded as a means to infuse the theoretical research with practical understanding.[45]

IV. THE STRUCTURE OF THIS BOOK

The book is divided in two parts: Part I, consisting of Chapters 1, 2, 3 and 4, is devoted to the in-depth study of the interaction of global pharmaceutical standards and the European regulatory framework for pharmaceuticals. Part II, consisting of Chapters 5, 6 and 7, is concerned with the legitimacy challenges arising from the interaction studied in Part I. The book ends with concluding remarks concerning the influence of ICH standards on the EU and the lessons learned from the analysis carried out in this book.

In Part I, Chapter 1 is devoted to an account of the history and the *status quo* of pharmaceutical regulation in the EU, closely examining the role of standards in the form of post-legislative guidance. Chapter 2 introduces the phenomenon of global standards and clarifies the complex institutional setting of global standard-setting bodies. Subsequently, Chapter 3 introduces the International Council for Harmonisation and its history, mandate and institutional structure, paying close attention to the role of the respective members in the standard-setting process. Chapter 4 analyses the ICH standards, the typology of guidelines and, finally, their legal nature. It then identifies the route through which ICH standards are implemented in the EU and how they affect the regulatory framework for pharmaceuticals.

In Part II, Chapter 5 establishes a framework for the legitimacy assessment of global standards and advocates that, concerning the question of sources of administrative law applicable to global standard-setting bodies,

[43] The footnotes make a distinction between 'EMA official' on the one hand and 'EMA Legal Department' on the other hand. This should only be seen as a reflection of the separate interviews and does not indicate a difference of position.

[44] R Pound, 'Law in Books and Law in Action' (1910) 44 *American Law Review* 12.

[45] J Baldwin and G Davis, 'Empirical Research in Law', in P Cane and M Tushnet (eds), *The Oxford Handbook of Legal Studies* (Oxford: Oxford University Press, 2003) 892.

European administrative law can provide inspiration for a global administrative law. Chapter 6 considers the legitimacy questions that ICH standards face by applying the procedural standards of participation, independence of expertise and transparency. With regard to each of these principles, European administrative law and specifically the procedural standards governing pharmaceutical regulation in Europe are applied to the ICH, testing the compatibility of the standard-setting process with European procedural norms. This analysis leads to suggestions for changes to the ICH process by 'uploading' European administrative law norms to the global level. Chapter 7 examines whether the legitimacy flaws carry over to the regulatory framework of the EU and whether they can be remedied within the EU by means of political and judicial accountability.

Part I

1

Regulating Pharmaceuticals in the European Union: Law and Administrative Rule-Making

THE EUROPEAN UNION can look back on over 50 years of pharmaceutical regulation, and today it is an important part of the 'patchwork'[1] of different policy domains that constitute EU health law,[2] constituting a central part of the Union's commitment to a 'high level of human health protection'.[3]

Pharmaceuticals, or 'medicinal products' as they are called in the EU legislation,[4] are defined with regard to their function and presentation,[5] as:

> (a) Any substance or combination of substances presented as having properties for treating or preventing disease in human beings; or
> (b) Any substance or combination of substances which may be used in or administered to human beings either with a view to restoring, correcting or modifying physiological functions by exerting a pharmacological, immunological or metabolic action, or to making a medical diagnosis.[6]

This chapter will introduce and analyse the regulatory framework, to provide the background for the following discussion of the impact of global standards on EU pharmaceutical regulation.

It will first examine the increasing regulatory harmonisation and subsequently discuss the *status quo*. In this chapter special attention is devoted to

[1] T Hervey and B Vanhercke, 'Health care and the EU: the law and policy patchwork', in E Mossialos, M Mrazek and T Walley (eds), *Regulating Pharmaceuticals in Europe: Striving for Efficiency, Equity and Quality* (Maidenhead: Open University Press, 2004).

[2] T Hervey and J McHale, *European Union Health Law – Themes and Implications* (Cambridge: Cambridge University Press, 2015); T Hervey, C Young and L Bishop (eds), *Research Handbook on EU Health Law and Policy* (Cheltenham: Edward Elgar, 2017).

[3] Art 168(1) TFEU.

[4] The terms pharmaceuticals, medicines and medicinal products are used interchangeably to enhance readability.

[5] See further: E Jackson, *Law and the Regulation of Medicines* (Oxford: Hart, 2012) 6.

[6] Directive 2001/83/EC, of the European Parliament and of the Council of 6 November 2001 on the Community code relating to medicinal products for human use, [2001] OJ L311/67, art 1(2).

the analysis of the marketing authorisation requirement.[7] Moreover, the chapter will highlight the role of non-binding administrative guidelines as forming an important cornerstone of pharmaceutical regulation.

I. EU PHARMACEUTICAL REGULATION: PAST AND PRESENT

Modern pharmaceutical regulation – placing an emphasis not only on the quality of the medicinal product, but also on safety and efficacy – is a relatively young phenomenon, as pharmaceuticals were not subject to governmental control until the 1960s in most countries.[8] This changed with the 1961 Thalidomide tragedy,[9] in response to which many European countries established regulatory bodies as well as systems of pre-marketing approval for medicines.[10] Also, the EU actively aimed for the regulation of pharmaceuticals and their related risks, in order to establish an internal market for medicinal products.

As in many areas of EU health law, the establishment and functioning of the internal market has been the key driving force in the development of EU pharmaceutical law.[11] As the free movement of goods on the internal market leads to deregulation by removing national legislation as obstacles to trade, harmonised regulatory measures are put in place to maintain safeguards for the protection of human health.[12] Thus, the core of EU pharmaceutical law – the marketing authorisation procedure with pharmaceutical standards governing the quality, safety and efficacy of medicinal products – is a form of risk regulation. Risk

[7] Directive 2001/83/EC, art 6; Regulation (EC) No 726/2004 laying down Community procedures for the authorisation and supervision of medicinal products for human and veterinary use and establishing a European Medicines Agency, [2004] OJ L136/1, art 3.

[8] Jackson (2012) 5; G Permanand, EU Pharmaceutical Regulation: The Politics of Policy–Making (Manchester: Manchester University Press, 2006) 1; J Abraham and G Lewis, *Regulating Medicines in Europe: Competition, Expertise and Public Health* (London: Routledge, 2000) 35–79. For an account of the development of pharmaceutical regulation see eg: J Lisman and Lekkerkerker, 'Four Decades of European Medicines Regulation: What Have They Brought Us?' (2005) 17 *International Journal of Risk & Safety in Medicine* 73; E Vos, Institutional Frameworks of Community Health and Safety Regulation – Committees, Agencies and Private Bodies (Oxford: Hart Publishing, 1999) 204ff.

[9] A drug prescribed to combat morning sickness in pregnant women led to serious malformations of the extremities of their newborn children. For further information on the Thalidomide crisis and its effects on pharmaceutical regulation see: S Krapohl, 'Thalidomide, BSE and the Single Market: An Historical-Institutionalist Approach to Regulatory Regimes in the EU' (2007) 46 *European Journal of Political Research* 25.

[10] Lisman and Lekkerkerker (2005) 73.

[11] A de Ruijter, *EU Health Law & Policy: The Expansion of EU Power in Public Health and Health Care* (Oxford: Oxford University Press, 2019) 65f; G Bache, M Flear and T Hervey, 'The Defining Features of the European Union's Approach to Regulating New Health Technologies', in M Flear, A Farrell, T Hervey and T Murphy (eds), *European Law and New Health Technologies* (Oxford: Oxford University Press, 2013).

[12] T Hervey and J McHale, *Health Law and the European Union* (Cambridge: Cambridge University Press, 2004) 90ff.

regulation aims to identify and prevent harm to human or animal health and the environment.[13] In the case of pharmaceuticals a large part of the regulation is aimed at making sure that medicinal products are safe to use for patients, while the harmonisation of those rules aims to facilitate the functioning of the internal market. As a result, pharmaceuticals are one of the most vigilantly regulated categories of goods in the EU.[14]

Nowadays, the EU's competence for regulatory actions in this area of pharmaceuticals is based on the shared competences of regulating the internal market (Article 4(2)(a) TFEU) and Article 4(2)(k) TFEU, covering 'common safety concerns in public health matters, for the aspects defined in this Treaty'. It should be noted that the protection and improvement of human health in general only provides the EU with a supportive competence according to Article 6(a) TFEU. In this regard, the public health mandate of the EU adopted in the Treaty of Maastricht, and currently enshrined in Article 168 TFEU, formalised the EU's growing health policies and at the same time delimited them.[15] Therefore, in field of pharmaceuticals the legal basis for EU measures is to be found in the provision on approximation of laws (Article 114 TFEU) in conjunction with Article 168(4) TFEU, which allows for EU legislative action in order to contribute to the achievement of public health objectives through '(m)easures setting high standards of quality and safety for medicinal products and devices for medical use'.

However, the extensive regulatory framework for medicinal products currently in place is the result of a history of European integration of pharmaceutical regulation that can be described as a rocky road of continuous reformation and step-by-step centralisation of decision-making power. The regulation of pharmaceuticals is politically sensitive and an important trait of national sovereignty, having an impact on health as well as industrial policies. Medicinal products proved to be a difficult case for the establishment of the internal market: the free movement of goods was not easily introduced for a product so thoroughly regulated on the national level, with nationally divergent policy approaches and interests.[16]

[13] Core literature on risk regulation: U Beck, *Risk Society: Towards a New Modernity* (London: Sage, 1992); O Renn, *Risk Governance – Coping with Uncertainty in a Complex World* (London: Routledge, 2008); C Hood, H Rothstein and R Baldwin, *The Government of Risk: Understanding Risk Regulation Regimes* (Oxford: Oxford University Press, 2003).

[14] Lisman and Lekkerkerker (2005) 78; A Cuvillier, 'The role of the European Medicines Evaluation Agency in the harmonization of pharmaceutical regulation', in R Goldberg and J Lonbay, *Pharmaceutical Medicine, Biotechnoloy and European Law* (Cambridge: Cambridge University Press, 2001) 142.

[15] de Ruijter (2019) 74.

[16] L Hancher, *Regulating for Competition – Government, Law and the Pharmaceutical Industry in the United Kingdom and France* (Alblasserdam: Haveka, 1989) 103ff; Vos (1999) 206–07; L Orzack, K Kaitin and L Lasagna, 'Pharmaceutical Regulation in the European Community: Barriers to Single Market Integration' (1992) 17 *Journal of Health Politics, Policy and Law* 847.

A. The Rocky Road to Harmonisation: The History of EU Pharmaceutical Regulation

The first pharmaceutical legislation adopted in the EU, Council Directive 65/65,[17] was adopted quite early in the history of EU law, predating any formal legal basis for EU health law.[18] The Treaty of Rome of 1957 only mentioned health as a potential restriction for free movement of goods and did not include a legal basis for health policy as such.[19] The Directive, in response to the Thalidomide tragedy, introduced a pre-marketing authorisation requirement based on the assessment of the criteria of quality, safety and efficacy for pharmaceuticals by national competent authorities.[20] This mandatory marketing authorisation requirement is still the 'fundamental principle'[21] of EU pharmaceutical regulation. At the time, the Council Directive provided a list of documentation including preclinical and clinical studies required for an application.[22] Although this was meant to pave the way for future mutual recognition of marketing authorisations, the implementation of these general requirements left considerable discretion to the Member States.[23]

Further harmonisation only took place 10 years later with the adoption of Council Directive 75/318/EEC, which provided more detail on the documentation required for applications to national authorities under Directive 65/65/EEC.[24] Its Annex contained detailed information on the trials required to prove the safety as well as efficacy of a medicine, and the data that needs to be provided by the applicant in a marketing authorisation procedure. This contributed to further harmonisation of the quality, safety and efficacy assessment, forming an important step towards the approximation of the regulatory systems of the Member States.[25]

[17] Council Directive 65/65/EEC of 26 January 1965, on the approximation of provisions laid down by law, regulation or administrative action relating to proprietary medicinal products, [1965] OJ Spec Ed Series I Volume 1965–1966, pp 20–24.

[18] T Hervey and A de Ruijter, 'The Dynamic Potential of European Union Health Law' (2020) *European Journal of Risk Regulation* 3.

[19] For an account of the development of EU health law over time see: M Guy and W Sauter, 'The history and scope of EU health law and policy', in T Hervey, C Young and L Bishop (eds), *Research Handbook on EU Health Law and Policy* (Cheltenham: Edward Elgar, 2017); Hervey and McHale (2015) 30–53.

[20] Council Directive 65/65/EEC, art 3. The requirement applied to proprietary medicinal products and not to generics.

[21] Hervey and McHale (2004) 289.

[22] Lisman and Lekkerkerker (2005) 75.

[23] J Feick, 'Learning and Interest Accommodation in Policy and Institutional Change: EC Risk Regulation in the Pharmaceutical Sector', ESCR Centre for Analysis of Risk and Regulation (CARR) Discussion Paper 25, (January 2005), 7.

[24] Council Directive 75/318/EEC of 20 May 1975 on the approximation of the laws of Member States relating to analytical, pharmaco-toxicological and clinical standards and protocols in respect of the testing of proprietary medicinal products, [1975] OJ L147/1.

[25] Lisman and Lekkerkerker (2005) 75; Cuvillier (2001) 139.

Additionally, the complementary Council Directive 75/319/EEC introduced the Community Procedure,[26] providing the opportunity for a company that had obtained marketing authorisation in one Member State, to apply for approval in at least five other Member States, which would take into account the evaluation of the first state.[27] This was a first step towards the proceduralisation of mutual recognition. The Directive established the Committee for Proprietary Medicinal Products (CPMP), composed of national representatives, set up in order to advise national authorities on the authorisation of medicinal products.[28] In case of an objection by a Member State to the authorisation of a product under the Community Procedure, the CPMP could pass an advisory opinion on the issue.[29] However, the procedure was not favoured by industry nor by the national authorities. In the eight years it operated, only 41 applications were filed.[30] Council Directive 83/570/EEC transformed it into the so-called Multistate Procedure with the number of receiving states required reduced to two.[31] However, also this change did not lead to greater success in terms of Member States accepting each other's assessments, and no procedure took place without an objection from the receiving states and discussion in the CPMP.[32]

The harmonisation of pharmaceuticals regulation gained new impetus due to the Single European Act and the envisaged goal of a Single Market by 1992.[33] As the harmonisation process was still severely hampered by persisting differences in the evaluation of the marketing authorisation applications and delay in the national procedures,[34] the introduction of the Concentration Procedure aimed to facilitate discussion of divergent views in the Member States.[35] An application had to be filed with a national authority as well as with the CPMP where the evaluation was subsequently discussed. Yet the procedure left the final decision on authorisation to the Member States individually,[36] and the CPMP opinion was not binding upon the Member States.[37] The procedure applied

[26] Second Council Directive 75/319/EEC on the approximation of provisions laid down by law, regulation or administrative action relating to proprietary medicinal products, [1975] OJ L147/13.

[27] Hancher (1989) 107.

[28] Second Council Directive 75/319/EEC, art 8.

[29] Ibid, art 11.

[30] European Commission, Report from the Commission to the Council on the Activities of the Committee for Proprietary Medicinal Products, COM(91)39 final, Brussels, 15 February 1991, p 14.

[31] Council Directive 83/570/EEC of 26 October 1983 amending Directives 65/65/EEC, 75/318/EEC and 75/319/EEC on the approximation of provisions laid down by law, regulation or administrative action relating to proprietary medicinal products, [1983] OJ L332/1.

[32] European Commission, COM(91)39 final, 16; Vos (1999) 209.

[33] Single European Act [1987] OJ L169/1.

[34] P Cecchini, *The European Challenge 1992 – Benefits of a Single Market* (Aldershot: Wildwood House, 1988) 68.

[35] Council Directive 87/22/EEC of 22 December 1986 on the approximation of national measures relating to the placing on the market of high-technology medicinal products, particularly those derived from biotechnology, [1987] OJ L15/38; Cuvillier (2001) 141.

[36] L Hancher, 'Creating the Internal Market for Pharmaceutical Medicines – An Echternach Jumping Procession?' (1991) 28 *Common Market Law Review* 824.

[37] Council Directive 87/22/EEC, art 4; Lisman and Lekkerkerker (2005) 76.

compulsorily for biotechnological medicines and optionally for other innovative or highly technological medicines. This procedure was more successful than previous attempts,[38] as the biotechnological products were subjected to a procedure that was different to 'normal' medicinal products and had a less extensive regulatory legacy.[39]

Finally, a thorough reform in 1993 established the system of pharmaceutical regulation that is essentially still operative today: the Mutual Recognition Procedure and the Centralised Procedure. Where a product is marketed in more than one Member State it can be authorised via the Mutual Recognition Procedure introduced by Council Directive 93/39/EC.[40] The reform additionally introduced the Centralised Procedure, with binding marketing authorisations on an EU level,[41] marking an important step from negative to positive integration. Additionally, the European Medicines Evaluation Agency (now the European Medicines Agency) was set up as a focal point in the marketing authorisation procedure. After an evaluation of the new procedures in October 2000,[42] the various Directives governing medicinal products were consolidated, which led to the adoption of the Community code relating to medicinal products for human use (Directive 2001/83/EC). Later, the legislation regarding the Centralised Procedure was also updated through the implementation of Regulation (EC) 726/2004. Moreover, the Mutual Recognition procedure was supplemented in 2004 with the Decentralised Procedure (DCP), which is a variation of the Mutual Recognition Procedure, used where marketing authorisation is sought in multiple Member States but where a national authorisation has not been issued.[43]

To conclude, the history of pharmaceutical regulation in the European Union is very much driven by the aim to establish the free movement of goods also for medicinal products. While direct mutual recognition of marketing authorisations between the Member States proved unobtainable, the marketing authorisation framework operating today is based on the harmonisation of regulatory requirements; the creation of mutual recognition procedures allowing for discussion and collaboration between the Member States, and a

[38] Hancher (1991) 824.

[39] Vos (1999) 209; National Institute for Public Health and the Environment (RVIM), 'Minds Open – Sustainability of the European Regulatory System for Medicinal Products', RVIM-Report 2014-0033, 17.

[40] Council Directive 93/39/EEC of 14 June 1993 amending Directives 65/65/EEC, 75/318/EEC and 75/319/EEC in respect of medicinal products, [1993] OJ L214/22.

[41] Council Regulation (EEC) No 2309/93 of 22 July 1993 laying down Community procedures for the authorisation and supervision of medicinal products for human and veterinary use and establishing a European Agency for the Evaluation of Medicinal Products, [1993] OJ L214/1.

[42] European Commission, Report from the Commission on the experience acquired as a result of the operation of the procedures for granting marketing authorisations for medicinal products laid down in Regulation (EEC) No 2309/93, in chapter III of directive 75/319/EEC and chapter IV of directive 81/851/EEC, COM(2001) 606 final, Brussels, 23 October 2001.

[43] Directive 2004/27/EC of the European Parliament, and of the Council of 31 March 2004 amending Directive 2001/83/EC, on the Community code relating to medicinal products for human use, [2004] OJ L136/34.

centralised, EU level procedure for innovative products; as well as the creation of bodies such as the European Medicines Agency (EMA) to facilitate the functioning of the procedures.[44] It is proof of the reluctance of Member States to trust the regulatory systems of other states in an area as politically sensitive as pharmaceuticals,[45] but at the same time a story of slowly increasing the mutual trust through regulatory cooperation.[46]

B. The *Status Quo* of EU Pharmaceutical Regulation: The Legislative Framework

Pharmaceuticals are subject to European regulation in all stages of the life-cycle from development through to use by the doctor or patient,[47] and this section can only provide an overview of the *status quo* of pharmaceutical regulation in the EU, rather than a complete picture of EU pharmaceutical law.[48] The two most important instruments of the EU's pharmaceutical legal framework are Directive 2001/83/EC, on the Community code relating to medicinal products, and Regulation (EC) 726/2004/EC, governing the centralised marketing authorisation procedure on the European level. These measures form the core of EU pharmaceutical law and introduce the marketing authorisation procedures which will be discussed in more detail in Section II. To supplement the harmonisation of the market access, subsequent changes to the marketing authorisation (so-called variations) also follow harmonised procedures.[49] In addition to the regulation of market access, the regulatory framework also contains rules dealing with labelling and packaging,[50] as well as wholesale[51] and advertising.[52] Of course, also horizontal policies such as competition law and the protection of intellectual property protection shape pharmaceutical law in the EU.[53]

[44] For a more detailed discussion of the evolution of the EU's pharmaceutical mutual recognition see: S Röttger-Wirtz, 'Mutual Recognition and the Ever-incomplete Internal Market for Pharmaceuticals' (2020a) 13 *Review of European Administrative Law* 61.

[45] Hancher (1989) 131; Feick (2005) 16ff.

[46] Feick (2005) 23; Vos (1999) 249.

[47] M Pilgerstorfer, 'EU law and policy on pharmaceuticals marketing and post-market control including product liability', in T Hervey, C Young and L Bishop (eds), *Research Handbook on EU Health Law and Policy* (Cheltenham: Edward Elgar, 2017) 156.

[48] For more detailed accounts of the EU's pharmaceutical regulatory framework see: Jackson (2012); S Shorthose, *Guide to European Pharmaceutical Regulatory Law* (Alphen aan den Rijn: Kluwer, 2013); M Manley and M Vickers (eds), *Navigating European Pharmaceutical Law* (Oxford: Oxford University Press, 2015).

[49] Commission Regulation (EC) No 1234/2008 concerning the examination of variations to the terms of marketing authorisations for medicinal products for human use and veterinary medicinal products, [2008] OJ L334/7.

[50] Directive 2001/83/EC, arts 54–69.

[51] Ibid, arts 76–85b.

[52] Ibid, arts 86–100.

[53] See generally: Hervey and McHale (2015) 341ff; L Hancher, 'The EU pharmaceuticals market: parameters and pathways', in E Mossialos, M Mrazek and T Walley (eds), *Regulating Pharmaceuticals in Europe: Striving for Efficiency, Equity and Quality* (Maidenhead: Open University Press, 2004).

The same is true for the product liability schemes, which are also applicable to medicinal products.[54]

Moreover, it should be emphasised that the regulation of the marketing authorisation procedures and the requirements to be fulfilled with regard to establishing quality, safety and efficacy of a medicinal products are connected directly to the pre-clinical and clinical research process.[55] The conditions that are put in place with regard to scientific data required for the authorisations shape the research and development process. In addition to this incidental regulatory effect, the EU has also explicitly regulated clinical trials since 2001,[56] subject to an in-depth reform in 2014,[57] addressing not only scientific but also ethical questions concerning clinical research.[58]

The main legislative framework for marketing authorisations has been supplemented through various other legislative measures regulating orphan medicinal products,[59] and for medicines for children,[60] herbal medicinal products,[61] and advanced therapy medicinal products.[62] In particular, the regulations for paediatric medicinal products and orphan medicinal products go further than the free movement and risk regulation logic of EU pharmaceutical law, as they establish incentives for development of medicinal products for otherwise often neglected consumer groups (ie children and patients with rare diseases).[63] These regulatory instruments thus aim to remedy market failures for the benefit of patients.[64]

Since 2010 extensive pharmacovigilance rules on the monitoring of the safety of medicinal products have also been put into place as part of the 'pharmaceuticals package' with proposed legislation on access to reliable

[54] See generally: Pilgerstorfer (2017).

[55] Bache, Flear and Hervey (2013) 23.

[56] Directive 2001/20/EC of the European Parliament and of the Council of 4 April 2001 on the approximation of the laws, regulations and administrative provisions of the Member States relating to the implementation of good clinical practice in the conduct of clinical trials on medicinal products for human use, [2001] OJ L121/34.

[57] Regulation (EU) No 536/2014 of the European Parliament and of the Council of 16 April 2014 on clinical trials on medicinal products for human use, and repealing Directive 2001/20/EC, [2014] OJ L158/1.

[58] See further: Hervey and McHale (2015) 292–321.

[59] Regulation (EC) No 141/2000 of the European Parliament and of the Council of 16 December 1999 on orphan medicinal products, [2000] OJ L18/1.

[60] Regulation (EC) No 1901/2006 of the European Parliament and of the Council of 12 December 2006 on medicinal products for paediatric use, [2006] OJ L378/1.

[61] Directive 2004/24/EC of the European Parliament and of the Council of 31 March 2004 amending, as regards traditional herbal medicinal products, Directive 2001/83/EC on the Community code relating to medicinal products for human use, [2004] OJ L136/85.

[62] Regulation (EC) No 1394/2007 of the European Parliament and of the Council of 13 November 2007 on advanced therapy medicinal products, [2007] OJ L324/12.

[63] Bache, Flear and Hervey (2013) 37f; K Seyett, 'Looking After the Orphans? Treatments for Rare Diseases, EU Law, and the Ethics of Costly Healthcare', in M Flear, A Farrell, T Hervey and T Murphy (eds), *European Law and New Health Technologies* (Oxford: Oxford University Press, 2013).

[64] Hervey and McHale (2015) 334–36.

information on medicines,[65] pharmacovigilance (safety monitoring)[66] and counterfeit medicines.[67] This is an important addition to the safety assessment at the point of marketing authorisation. As Jackson points out, a focus on the moment of marketing authorisation leads to a 'binary system … in which medicines are either safe or not safe, effective or ineffective',[68] whereas it is only a singular point in the lifecycle of a medicinal product. Therefore, pharmacovigilance is concerned with monitoring and remedying safety concerns in the post-authorisation stage.[69]

However, while overall pharmaceuticals are subject to extensive regulation in the EU, the very pronounced role of market values and risk regulation in EU pharmaceutical law leads to gaps that have been identified in the literature. EU health law has been criticised for falling short in the realisation of other non-market health values such as ethics or solidarity,[70] and pharmaceutical law is no exception to this. While the regulatory framework is very much concerned with ensuring safety for consumers and mitigation of risks, questions of comparative efficacy of a product or the assessment of its potential to meet the actual current health care needs are of lesser importance in the EU framework.[71] In this regard it should be stressed that questions of access to medicines in terms of price regulation and procurement remain a core competence of the Member States.[72] Only

[65] The proposals for the amendment of the Directive 2001/83/EC and Regulation (EC) 726/2004 as regards information to the general public on medicinal products were withdrawn in May 2014 (OJ C153/3).

[66] Adopted as: Directive 2010/84/EU of the European Parliament and of the Council of 15 December 2010 amending, as regards pharmacovigilance, Directive 2001/83/EC on the Community code relating to medicinal products for human use, [2010] OJ L348/74; Regulation (EU) No 1235/2010 of the European Parliament and of the Council of 15 December 2010 amending, as regards pharmacovigilance of medicinal products for human use, Regulation (EC) No 726/2004 laying down Community procedures for the authorisation and supervision of medicinal products for human and veterinary use and establishing a European Medicines Agency, and Regulation (EC) No 1394/2007 on advanced therapy medicinal products, [2010] OJ L348/1.

[67] Adopted as: Directive 2011/62/EU of the European Parliament and of the Council of 8 June 2011 amending Directive 2001/83/EC on the Community code relating to medicinal products for human use, as regards the prevention of the entry into the legal supply chain of falsified medicinal products, [2011] OJ L174/74.

[68] Jackson (2012) 73.

[69] In this context, the Urgent Union Procedure (arts 107i–107k Directive 2001/83/EC) was introduced. The aim of the procedure is to coordinate urgent responses to safety concerns and to ensure that the required level of expertise is involved in the decision-making. See further: M Chamon and S Wirtz, 'Complex procedures as hurdle to accountability: verticalization of pharmaceutical enforcement', in M Luchtman and M Scholten, *Law Enforcement by EU Authorities – Political and judicial accountability in a shared legal order* (Cheltenham: Edward Elgar, 2017).

[70] A de Ruijter, 'The impediment of health law's values in the constitutional setting of the EU', in T Hervey, C Young and L Bishop (eds), *Research Handbook on EU Health Law and Policy* (Cheltenham: Edward Elgar, 2017); T Hervey, C Young and L Bishop, 'Introduction', in T Hervey, C Young and L Bishop (eds), *Research Handbook on EU Health Law and Policy* (Cheltenham: Edward Elgar, 2017) 9ff.

[71] For a discussion of the risk focus see: Hervey and McHale (2015) 326; Jackson (2012) 77ff.

[72] de Ruijter (2019) 66.

the Patients' Rights Directive[73] and the Transparency Directive[74] have an – albeit limited – influence in this regard. The latest initiative in this context is Regulation on Health Technology Assessment which was proposed by the Commission in January 2018 and is currently in the legislative process.[75] In November 2020, during the Covid-19 pandemic, the European Commission presented its Pharmaceutical Strategy for Europe which deviated remarkably from the previous market- and risk-focused approach.[76] The Commission's proposed initiatives related mostly to issues of medicines accessibility for patients and opened up a debate surrounding the reallocation of incentives for pharmaceutical innovation towards unmet medical needs. The impact of this new strategy and whether the Member States agree to the increasing activity in this sector will be seen in the coming years.

C. The Institutional Framework: The EU's Pharmaceutical Executive

Together with its pursuit of policies regarding human health, the EU's institutional structure and capacity with regard to health law and policies has substantially grown.[77] For the regulation of pharmaceuticals, alongside the EU legislator (ie the Council and the European Parliament) the key actors in the day-to-day execution of regulation are the European Commission and the EMA, which are important contributors to the harmonisation process.[78]

The European Commission has a significant say in the formation of the content of European pharmaceutical regulation,[79] not only through the right of legislative initiative,[80] but also through the possibility to shape pharmaceutical policy through various soft law means.[81] It also monitors the correct application of legislation, especially in the Member States,[82] and takes binding decisions on marketing authorisations for pharmaceutical products.[83] Within

[73] Directive 2011/24/EU of the European Parliament and of the Council of 9 March 2011 on the application of patients' rights in cross-border healthcare, [2011] OJ L88/45.

[74] Council Directive 89/105/EEC of 21 December 1988 relating to the transparency of measures regulating the prices of medicinal products for human use and their inclusion in the scope of national health insurance systems, [1989] OJ L40/8.

[75] European Commission, Proposal for a Regulation of the European Parliament and of the Council on health technology assessment and amending Directive 2011/24/EU, COM(2018) 51 final, 31 January 2018.

[76] European Commission, Communication from the European Commission to the European Parliament, the Council, the Economic and Social Committee and the Committee of the Regions – Pharmaceutical Strategy for Europe, COM(2020) 761 final, Brussels, 25 November 2020.

[77] See especially: de Ruijter (2019).

[78] Cuvillier (2001).

[79] For an extensive analysis of the European Commission's role in EU health law see: de Ruijter (2019) 93ff.

[80] Art 17(2) TEU.

[81] See: Section III.

[82] Art 17(1) TEU.

[83] See: Section II A.

the Commission, the Directorate General for Health and Food Safety (DG SANTE) is responsible for pharmaceuticals.[84] Before that, the responsibility lay with the Directorate General Enterprise, a constellation that was criticised for facilitating the prioritisation of industrial concerns over public health issues.[85]

The EMA was set up as a 'culmination of thirty years of pharmaceutical legislation',[86] and became operational in January 1995.[87] It is one of the EU's 'non-majoritarian agencies'[88] created as 'satellite' bodies surrounding the executive, in order to infuse the decision-making process with independent scientific and technical expertise.[89] It has a central role in the marketing authorisation procedure and is tasked with the 'coordination of the scientific evaluation of the quality, safety and efficacy of medicinal products which are subject to Community marketing authorisation procedures' and the coordination of pharmacovigilance measures.[90] It coordinates the national agencies, making the EMA the centre of a large regulatory network of national regulatory authorities.[91] It includes the former Committee for Proprietary Medicinal Products (CPMP), which was renamed the Committee for Medicinal Products for Human Use (CHMP) in 2004, forming the EMA's main scientific committee.[92]

[84] The DG used to be called DG SANCO (for Health and Consumers), but was renamed during the Juncker Commission. For a discussion of the role of DG SANTE see: de Ruijter (2019) 97f; D Sindbjerg Martisen, 'Governing EU health law and policy – on governance and legislative politics', in T Hervey, C Young and L Bishop (eds), *Research Handbook on EU Health Law and Policy* (Cheltenham: Edward Elgar, 2017) 39ff.

[85] Permanand (2006) 38.

[86] M Groenleer, *The Autonomy of European Union Agencies – A Comparative Study of Institutional Developments* (Delft: Eburon, 2009) 143.

[87] The EMA was created through Council Regulation (EEC) No 2309/93. This Council Regulation was replaced by Regulation (EC) No 726/2004.

[88] The notion 'non-majoritarian agencies' is used to refer to the fact that although carrying out a public function, these bodies are independent from elected politicians. See: D Curtin, 'Delegation to EU Non-Majoritarian Agencies and Emerging Practices of Public Accountability', in D Geradin, R Munoz and N Petit (eds), *Regulation Through Agencies in the EU: A New Paradigm of European Governance* (Cheltenham: Edward Elgar, 2006) 92.

[89] D Curtin, *Executive Power of the European Union – Law, Practice and the Living Constitution* (Oxford: Oxford University Press, 2009) 52; de Ruijter (2019) 117–18. For further literature on European agencies and their role in the European Union see: M Chamon, *European Agencies – Legal and Political Limits to the Transformation of the EU Administration* (Oxford: Oxford University Press, 2016); M Everson, C Monda and E Vos (eds), *European Agencies in between Institutions and Member States* (Alphen aan den Rijn: Kluwer Law International, 2014); D Geradin, R Muñoz and N Petit (eds), *Regulation Through Agencies in the EU – A New Paradigm of European Governance* (Cheltenham: Edward Elgar, 2006).

[90] Regulation (EC) No 726/2004, art 57.

[91] For further detail on the network character of the EMA see: R Dehousse, 'Regulation by Networks in the European Community: The Role of European Agencies' (1997) 4 *Journal of European Public Policy* 246; Cuvillier (2001) 146; A Spina, 'The Regulation of Pharmaceuticals Beyond the State: EU and Global Administrative Systems', in E Chiti and B Mattarella (eds), *Global Administrative Law and EU Administrative Law* (Heidelberg: Springer, 2011).

[92] The other EMA Committees are: the Committee for Medicinal Products for Veterinary Use (CVMP), the Pharmacovigilance Risk Assessment Committee (PRAC), the Committee for Orphan Medicinal Products (COMP), the Committee on Herbal Medicinal Products (HMPC), the Committee for Advance Therapies (CAT) and the Paediatric Committee (PDCO).

Each of the Member States appoints a member and an alternate to form the scientific committees that carry out the assessments within the agency.[93]

II. THE CORE OF THE REGULATORY FRAMEWORK: THE MARKETING AUTHORISATION PROCEDURES

As became clear during the analysis of the history of EU pharmaceutical regulation earlier, the creation of the marketing authorisation procedures was a central pillar of the regulatory integration with regard to pharmaceuticals in the EU. Today, while no medicinal product may be placed on the market without obtaining prior marketing authorisation,[94] different routes to obtain a marketing authorisation are available: the Centralised Procedure, the Mutual Recognition and Decentralised Procedures, as well as national procedures.[95] The applicability of the procedures depends on the nature of the medicinal product in question and the targeted state market(s). This divergence in degree of integration and 'institutional layering'[96] in the regulation of one single type of product is certainly remarkable in the context of the internal market.

The procedures, apart from the national one, all entail a certain degree of collaboration between the national and EU authorities, and are, therefore, prime examples of the Union's composite administration.[97] The EU marketing authorisation procedures do not replace national ones, which are used where the product will be sold in one Member State only, and does not belong to the categories of products for which the centralised procedure is obligatory.[98] However, the requirements for the applicant to prove quality, safety and efficacy and the basic traits of the procedure are harmonised.[99] Still, the determination of the

[93] Regulation (EC) No 726/2004, art 61(1).

[94] Directive 2001/83/EC, art 6; Regulation (EC) No 726/2004, art 3.

[95] The marketing authorisation procedures are extensively discussed in literature. See eg: Feick (2005); B Collatz, *Die neuen europäischen Zulassungsverfahren für Arzneimittel* (Aulendorf: Editio-Cantor-Verlag, 1996); S Krapohl, *Risk Regulation in the Single European Market – The Governance of Pharmaceuticals and Foodstuffs in the European Union* (Basingstoke: Palgrave, 2008); G Permanand (2006) 49ff; Shorthose (2013) 105ff; Manley and Vickers (2015) 79 ff; Hervey and McHale (2015) 327–34ff; Pilgerstorfer (2017) 158–67.

[96] Feick (2005) 19.

[97] For more detail on the composite nature of the marketing authorisation procedures: M Eliantonio, 'Judicial Review in an Integrated Administration: the Case of "Composite Procedures"' (2014) 7 *Review of Administrative Law Journal* 65; S Röttger-Wirtz and M Eliantonio, 'From integration to exclusion – EU composite administration and gaps in judicial accountability in the authorisation of pharmaceuticals' (2019) 10 *European Journal of Risk Regulation* 393.

[98] For more information on the national procedure see: European Commission, "Notice to Applicants" Volume 2A – Procedures for marketing authorisation, Chapter 1 Marketing Authorisation, June 2018; Shorthose (2013)133 ff; Manley and Vickers (2015) 80–81.

[99] Regulation (EC) No 726/2004, arts 6, 17 and 18. See also: EMA, The European regulatory system for medicines and the European Medicines Agency – A consistent approach to medicines regulation across the European Union, (2014), EMA/437313/2014.

level – national or EU – where the marketing authorisation is granted is significant, as in every marketing authorisation a benefit-risk assessment is carried out, and the authority granting a marketing authorisation is ultimately deciding on the acceptable level of risk to human health.[100]

A. The Centralised Procedure

One route to obtaining a marketing authorisation is the Centralised Procedure, laid down in Regulation (EC) 726/2004,[101] carried out at the European level. It leads to an authorisation decision by the European Commission which is valid in the whole of the EU. The procedure is mandatory for certain biotechnology-derived and high-tech products, and optional for products with a new active substance or products offering a significant therapeutic, scientific or technical innovation.[102] The products for which it is mandatory are defined in the Annex as medicines for humans that are:[103] (i) biotechnologically developed pharmaceuticals; (ii) advanced therapy medicinal products as defined in Regulation 1394/2007; (iii) products with a new active substance (not authorised before the Regulation entered into force) for the treatment of certain diseases, such as for example cancer or autoimmune diseases; as well as (iv) orphan medicinal products. The procedure is optional for all other products with new active substances, as well as pharmaceuticals with a significant therapeutic, scientific or technical innovation, or where the authorisation is of interest at EU level.[104]

The company files a marketing authorisation application including the required documentation, the so-called dossier, with the EMA.[105] The benefit for the industry is that only one dossier has to be compiled for obtaining a marketing authorisation valid in all EU Member States.[106] The application is then assessed in the main scientific committee, the CHMP, which adopts either a favourable or an unfavourable opinion, if possible by consensus, but at least by absolute majority.[107] If the opinion is unfavourable, Article 9 of Regulation (EC) 726/2004 provides that the applicant is informed before and, the applicant can request a

[100] Hervey and McHale (2004) 282.
[101] For a discussion of the centralised procedure see: Manley and Vickers (2015) 89 ff; Shorthose (2013) 117 ff; Jackson (2012) 74; Pilgerstorfer (2017) 165ff.
[102] Regulation (EC) No 726/2004, art 3, Annex.
[103] Ibid, art 3(1).
[104] Ibid, art 3(2).
[105] Ibid, art 6.
[106] Hervey and McHale (2015) 329f.
[107] Committee for Medicinal Products for Human Use, Rules of Procedure, EMEA/45110/2007 Revised 23 March 2020, art 8. Additionally, Regulation (EC) No 726/2004 provides for the possibility of granting a conditional marketing authorisation (art 14(7)), reviewed annually, and a marketing authorisation under exceptional circumstances (art 14(8)), which contains certain obligations with regard to the safety of the product.

re-examination within 15 days upon receipt of the opinion.[108] After 210 days of the procedure, at the latest, the agency gives a favourable or an unfavourable opinion on the marketing authorisation and forwards it to the Commission.[109] The opinion is of advisory nature and the decision-making power in the case of marketing authorisations lies with the Commission, and not the agency. Upon receipt of the EMA opinion, the Commission drafts a decision.[110] If the draft decision departs from the EMA opinion, this has to be substantiated by the Commission.[111] In practice, the Commission usually follows the CHMP opinion.[112]

The Commission's draft decision is forwarded to Member States and the applicant.[113] The Member States are then entitled to submit written observations to the Commission.[114] Where these written observations raise important scientific issues that have been neglected in the evaluation thus far, the application will be referred back to the agency.[115] This is, however, rather unlikely since the Member State would have to show that the issue is very important and has been neglected by the applicant, the CHMP, the EMA itself and the Commission.[116] In the applicable examination procedure laid down in Article 5 of Regulation (EU) 182/2011,[117] the Commission also forwards the draft decision to the Standing Committee on Medicinal Products for Human Use, composed of Member State representatives, which votes on the adoption of this draft decision by qualified majority. A positive Commission Implementing Decision grants a marketing authorisation valid within the whole Union for five years, meaning that the decision is binding upon the Member States.[118] After these five years, the marketing authorisation can be renewed when the agency carries out a renewed positive risk-benefit evaluation.[119] The renewed marketing authorisation then has unlimited validity, unless specified otherwise.[120]

Thus, the procedure is centralised at the EU level: the decision-making power lies with the European Commission, and the main scientific foundation for the

[108] Regulation (EC) No 726/2004, art 9(2).
[109] Ibid, arts 6, to 9.
[110] Ibid, art 10.
[111] Ibid, art 10.
[112] T Gehring and Krapohl, 'Supranational Regulatory Agencies between Independence and Control. The EMEA and the Authorisation of Pharmaceuticals in the European Single Market' (2007) 14 *Journal of European Public Policy* 208, 216; Feick (2005) 14. A notable exception was the disagreement between the EMA and the Commission over the drug Orphacol.
[113] Regulation (EC) No 726/2004, OJ L136/1, art 10(1).
[114] Ibid, art 10(3)(b).
[115] Ibid, art 10(4).
[116] S Borrás, C Koutalakis and F Wendler, 'European Agencies and Input Legitimacy: EFSA, EMEA and EPO in the Post-Delegation Phase' (2007) 29 *Journal of European Integration* 583, 592f.
[117] Regulation (EU) No 182/2011 of the European Parliament and of the Council of 16 February 2011 laying down the rules and general principles concerning mechanisms for control by Member States of the Commission's exercise of implementing powers, [2011] OJ L55/13.
[118] Regulation (EC) No 726/2004, arts 13–14.
[119] Ibid, art 14(2).
[120] Ibid, art 14(3).

decision lies with the EMA. However, as was shown, Member States also have a significant role in this process: first through the CHMP whose members in the majority are representatives of competent authorities, and also through the involvement of Member States in the Standing Committee on Medicinal Products for Human Use.[121]

B. The Mutual and Decentralised Recognition Procedure

The Decentralised and Mutual Recognition Procedures provide for a marketing authorisation route where a medicinal product is supposed to be marketed in more than one Member State.[122] They are laid down in the Community code relating to medicinal products (Directive 2001/83/EC).[123] Both procedures are of a hybrid nature, since the actual decision to authorise lies within the national system and the European level is only turned to as an arbitration mechanism.

While the two procedures follow the same scheme, the starting point of the procedures differs. The Mutual Recognition procedure foresees authorisation in other Member States based on a marketing authorisation already granted in one Member State.[124] This procedure is compulsory if a product has a marketing authorisation in one Member State and an application is made to market it in another Member State.[125] The Decentralised Procedure is used where the product has not yet obtained a marketing authorisation in a Member State. The company has to request a draft assessment report, a draft summary of product characteristics, and a draft of the labelling and package leaflet from the regulatory authority of Member State of its choice.[126]

The Mutual Recognition and Decentralised Procedures are characterised by three phases: (i) a national phase with reference and concerned Member States involved in a process of mutual recognition; (ii) an inter-administrative phase in the coordination group; and (iii) binding supranational arbitration in the EMA and the Commission.[127] The reference Member State forwards its assessment to the other Member States where authorisation is sought (the concerned Member States). These concerned Member States have 90 days to recognise the marketing

[121] Vos (1999) 223; Feick (2005) 13.

[122] For more information on the mutual recognition and decentralised procedure see: Manley and Vickers (2015) 81 ff; Shorthose (2013) 127 ff; Jackson (2012) 74ff; Pilgerstorfer (2017) 163ff; Röttger-Wirtz and Eliantonio (2019); Röttger-Wirtz (2020a).

[123] Directive 2001/83/EC, arts 28–39.

[124] The mutual recognition procedure fosters competition between the European regulatory authorities, as the industry has an incentive to choose Member States with fast approval procedures as reference Member States. While beneficial for the industry as well as patients in urgent need of treatment, this could lead to less thorough assessment, raising safety concerns. See: Hervey and McHale (2004) 296ff; Hervey and McHale (2015) 330f; Jackson (2012) 75; Pilgerstorfer (2017) 164.

[125] Directive 2001/83/EC, arts 28(2).

[126] Ibid, arts 28(1), 28(3).

[127] Feick (2005) 15f.

approval decision of the reference Member State, including the summary of product characteristics, the labelling and the package leaflet.[128] They have 30 days to grant the national marketing authorisation.[129] If a concerned Member State refuses to accept the assessment of the reference Member State for reasons of potential serious risk to public health,[130] the matter will be referred to the Coordination Group for Mutual Recognition and Decentralised Procedures (CMDh),[131] where the Member States try to reach consensus and resolve differences in assessment.[132] If consensus is not found within 60 days, the matter will be referred to the EMA for arbitration.[133] Within the EMA, the CHMP will provide a scientific opinion on the matter. This scientific opinion is then forwarded to the Commission, which will adopt a decision that is binding upon the Member States, after consulting the Standing Committee on Pharmaceuticals under the examination procedure.[134]

Thus, while in the Mutual Recognition Procedure a finalised decision by one Member State is to be accepted by the others, the Decentralised Procedure is based in co-decision and exchange of information.[135] According to AG Bobek: '[I]n a Decentralised Procedure, all of the Member States participate in the elaboration of their decision at the same time. To put it metaphorically, cooking with friends is not the same as sharing meals that have already been prepared'.[136] The Mutual Recognition Procedure, as the name suggests, is a proceduralised coordination of the mutual recognition principle introduced in the *Cassis de Dijon* case.[137] However, although both procedures are mutual recognition principle based, in the Decentralised Procedure the emphasis is on 'mutual', thus on the collaboration, whereas in the Mutual Recognition Procedure it is on the 'recognition' of existing authorisations.[138]

128 Directive 2001/83/EC, art 28(4).

129 Ibid, art 28(5).

130 For a definition of 'potential serious risks to human health' see: European Commission, 'Guideline on the definition of a potential serious risk to public health in the context of article 29(1) and (2) of Directive 2001/83/ EC' [2006] OJ C133/5. Mutual recognition may not be refused on other grounds: see Case 452/06 *Synthon*, ECLI: EU:C:2008:565.

131 The CMDh is established according to art 27 of Directive 2001/83/EC and composed of one representative per Member State, with the Commission as observer. The CMDh does not form part of the EMA; however, its Secretariat is provided by the EMA.

132 Directive 2001/83/EC, art 29.

133 Ibid, art 29(4).

134 Ibid, arts 32–34. In the context of the Lisbon Treaty the comitology procedure referred to in Directive 2001/83/EC, which was the management procedure according to art 4 of the Comitology Decision (Council Decision 1999/468/EC laying down the procedures for the exercise of implementing powers conferred on the Commission, OJ L184/23) has been replaced by the examination procedure as established in art 5 of the new Comitology Regulation No 182/2011.

135 Opinion of AG Bobek in Case C-557/16 *Astellas Pharma GmbH*, ECLI:EU:C:2017:957, para 70. For a discussion of this difference see: Röttger-Wirtz (2020a). For a discussion of its impact on judicial review see: Röttger-Wirtz and Eliantonio (2019).

136 Opinion of AG Bobek in *Astellas Pharma Gmbh*, para 49.

137 C-120/78 *Rewe-Zentral AG v Bundesmonopolverwaltung für Branntwein*, ECLI:EU:C:1979:42 (*Cassis de Dijon* case).

138 Röttger-Wirtz (2020a) 75.

III. THE ROLE OF ADMINISTRATIVE RULE-MAKING IN EU PHARMACEUTICAL REGULATION

The previous sections explained that pharmaceutical law on EU level is mainly a market driven phenomenon that aims to regulate risks while facilitating the free movement of goods. It is therefore not surprising that 'expert executive power'[139] plays a big role in the EU's regulatory framework for pharmaceuticals. Post-legislative guidance has become increasingly important in the regulation of complex risks and problems in the Union.[140] As explained by Hervey and de Ruijter in their discussion of what they call the 'dynamic potential' of EU health law,[141] the regulatory details of health policies with regard to pharmaceuticals, but also the regulation of the safety of medical devices, food or chemicals, are subject to technocratic decision-making in agencies, expert committees or private standard-setting bodies.[142] Thus, it is not the 'broad-brush legislation'[143] but the various non-legislative, regulatory measures which contain 'the specifics about the European ways of thinking about health – and especially public health'.[144]

The assessment of the pharmaceutical regulatory framework in this chapter would therefore not be complete if it ignored the widespread use of non-binding measures adopted by the European Commission and the EMA to govern pharmaceuticals. The overarching lines of certain regulatory policies and often also the procedures necessary to execute them will be laid down in legislation, and supplemented by an array of non-legislative measures in the form of Commission Regulations and Directives, and (since the Lisbon Treaty) Commission Delegated or Implementing Regulations and Decisions.[145] However, the detailed regulatory and scientific requirements are increasingly provided for and elaborated on in guidance documents. The aim of this section is to shed light on the often-neglected extent and impact of these guidance documents in the regulatory framework for pharmaceuticals.

[139] E Fisher, 'Expert Executive Power, Administrative Constitutionalism and Co-production: Why They Matter', in M Weimer and A de Ruijter, *Regulating Risks in the European Union – The Co-production of Expert and Executive Power* (Oxford: Hart, 2017).

[140] The literature on post-legislative guidance is particularly well-developed in the field of environmental law, see eg: J Scott, 'In Legal Limbo: Post-Legislative Guidance as Challenge for Administrative Law' (2011) 48 *Common Market Law Review* 329; E Korkea-aho, 'Legal Interpretation of EU Framework Directives: A Soft Law Approach' (2015) 40 *European Law Review* 70. See also: L Senden, 'Soft Post-Legislative Rulemaking: A Time for More Stringent Control' (2013) 19 *European Law Journal* 57.

[141] Hervey and de Ruijter (2020) 9.

[142] Ibid.

[143] Ibid.

[144] Ibid.

[145] For a discussion of these non-legislative measures see: S Röttger-Wirtz, 'Delegated and implementing acts in the regulation of pharmaceuticals – an analysis through the lens of subsidiarity', in E Tauschinsky and W Weiß (eds), *The Legislative Choice Between Delegated and Implementing Acts: Walking a Labyrinth* (Cheltenham: Edward Elgar, 2018b).

A. Governing Pharmaceuticals through Post-Legislative Administrative Guidance

Non-binding measures have regulated pharmaceuticals in the EU since the early days of EU pharmaceutical law and significantly contributed to the harmonisation of regulatory requirements which lie at the core of the regulatory framework. The Committee for Proprietary Medicinal Products, established by Council Directive 75/319/EEC,[146] formed working groups which advised the European Commission in the drafting of scientific guidelines.[147] These 'notes for guidance' clarified the required information and documentation to be compiled in a dossier for marketing authorisations, harmonising the national rules on these matters.[148]

In order to respect the competence of the Member States, which were still responsible for the final marketing authorisation decisions, the guidance was published in the form of a non-binding Council Recommendation[149] and since 1986 by the Commission as so-called 'Notice to Applicants' (NTA).[150] The choice for a non-binding measure also responded to fears in the industry that binding provisions would result in a 'race-to-the-top', compiling the strictest national practices in a document, that would not allow for deviation.[151] The adoption of non-binding measures has augmented over time, leading to increasing detail in the harmonisation of regulatory requirements.[152]

The Commission and the EMA share responsibility for publishing guidelines. While the Commission guidance usually addresses regulatory aspects (such as the renewal of marketing authorisations, variations to marketing authorisations or package leaflet requirements),[153] the EMA guidelines are scientific and concerned with filling in the details of the legislative requirements of quality, safety and efficacy.[154] In contrast to the EMA scientific guidelines, the aim of the Commission guidelines is not to provide scientific details, but rather to describe and clarify applicable procedures in detail and define terminology used in the legislation. The EMA defines a guideline as:

> a Community document with explicit legal basis referred to in the legislative framework as intended to fulfil a legal obligation laid down in the Community

[146] Second Council Directive 75/319/EEC, art 8.

[147] F Sauer, 'Preface', in J van de Laan and J DeGeorge (eds), *Global Approach in Safety Testing – ICH Guidelines Explained* (New York: Springer, 2013) v–viii, at vi.

[148] Lisman and Lekkerkerker (2005) 75; RVIM (2014) 16.

[149] Council Recommendation 83/571/EEC of 26 October 1983 concerning tests relating to the placing on the market of proprietary medicinal products, [1983] OJ L332/11. See: Hancher (1989) 108.

[150] European Commission, Volume 2B – Notice to Applicants – Medicinal Products for Human Use (Update May 2008), 2.

[151] Hancher (1989) 108.

[152] Feick (2005) 21.

[153] European Medicines Agency, Procedure for European Union Guidelines and Related Documents within the Pharmaceutical Legislative Framework, EMEA/P/24143/2004 Rev 1 corr, 18 March 2009, 6.

[154] Ibid.

> pharmaceutical legislation. It provides advice to applicants or marketing authorisation holders, competent authorities and/or other interested parties on the best and most appropriate way to fulfil an obligation laid down in the community pharmaceutical legislation.[155]

As shown by this quote, guidelines are addressed either to companies searching marketing authorisation or the national competent authorities having to assess the data submitted for marketing authorisation. In this respect, guidelines serve as tools for the clarification and substantiation of legislative requirements, working in favour of the regulated industry as well as of the public administration.[156] The use of non-binding guidance allows for these documents to be updated according to scientific process or changing administrative requirements, without going through a laborious and time-consuming legislative amendment.

The pharmaceutical guidance adopted by the Commission and EMA forms part of the Union's soft law. Emerging in public international law scholarship, the concept of 'soft law' was introduced to conceptualise the evolution of international cooperation beyond traditional international law in the form of treaties.[157] Although the academic debate surrounding the concept of soft law has existed since the 1970s,[158] its definition, effects and even the recognition of its existence is far from well-established.[159] Soft law has also attracted attention in the EU law scholarship.[160] In this context, Senden defined soft law as meas-

[155] Ibid, 4.

[156] Cuvillier (2001) 139; I Schneider, *Das Kooperationsprinzip im Vorfeld der Arzneimittelzulassung – Zum national und Europarechtlichen Rahmen des Zusammenwirken von Potentiellen Antragsstellern und Zulassungsbehörden* (Frankfurt am Main: Peter Lang Europäischer Verlag der Wissenschaften, 2003) 94–100. See also: J Schwarze, 'Soft Law im Recht der Europäischen Union' (2011) 1 *Europarecht* (2011) 3; H Hofmann, G Rowe and A Türk, Administrative Law and Policy of the European Union (Oxford: Oxford University Press, 2011) 536ff.

[157] For more detail on the concept of soft law in international law see Chapter 2.

[158] M Knauff, *Der Regelungsverbund: Recht und Soft Law im Mehrebenensystem* (Tübingen: Mohr Siebeck, 2010) 211.

[159] See especially: P Weil, 'Towards Relative Normativity in International Law?' (1983) 77 *American Journal of International Law* 413; A Aust, *Handbook of International Law*, 2nd edn (Cambridge: Cambridge University Press, 2010) 11; A Peters and I Pagotto, 'Soft Law as a New Mode of Governance: A Legal Perspective', New Modes of Governance Project Paper 04/D11 (2006); G Shaffer and M Pollack, 'Hard and Soft Law', in J Dunoff and M Pollack (eds), *Interdisciplinary Perspectives on International Law and International Relations – The State of the Art* (Cambridge: Cambridge University Press, 2013). For a detailed discussion of soft law and an account of the different scholarly approaches to the topic see: M Goldmann, 'Inside Relative Normativity: From Sources to Standard Instruments for the Exercise of International Public Authority', in A von Bogdandy, R Wolfrum, J von Bernstorff, P Dann and M Goldmann (eds), *The Exercise of Public Authority by International Institutions: Advancing International Institutional Law* (Heidelberg: Springer, 2010). For a critical perspective on the existence and usefulness of soft law as concept see: J Klabbers, 'The Redundancy of Soft Law' (1996) 65 *Nordic Journal of International Law* 167; J Klabbers, 'The Undesirability of Soft Law' (1998) 67 *Nordic Journal of International Law* 381; M Bothe, 'Legal and Non-Legal Norms – A Meaningful Distinction in International Relations?' (1980) 11 *Netherlands Yearbook of International Law* 65.

[160] See eg: F Snyder, 'Soft Law and the Institutional Practice in the European Community', in S Martin (ed), *The Construction of Europe – Essays in Order of Emile Noel* (Dordrecht: Kluwer, 1994); L Senden, *Soft Law in European Community Law: Its Relationship to Legislation*

ures which are not legally binding but nonetheless determine rules of conduct or policy directions in a measure that, although devoid of legally binding power, does have practical and either direct or indirect legal effects.[161]

The pharmaceutical guidelines do not constitute legal measures in EU law as enshrined in Article 288 to 291 TFEU, nor are they recommendations or opinions, which are the only acts without legally binding force acknowledged in the Treaties. However, these Treaty provisions by no means reflect or account for the multitude of types non-binding measures acts adopted by EU institutions or bodies.[162] As early as 1993, Francis Snyder pointed to the fact that soft law, and specifically 'Commission soft law', formed an important part of the Community's rules, and that this importance was likely to grow due to the Commission's ever-increasing administrative responsibility.[163] Today, this assumption can only be confirmed. Together with the Commission as the main source of European soft law,[164] European agencies like the EMA are increasingly becoming sources of administrative soft law.[165] In the case of EMA, this role is by no means self-evident, as the founding Regulation does not refer to the adoption of guidance as one of the tasks of the agency.[166]

In Article 6(4) of Regulation (EC) 726/2004, the Commission was mandated with 'drawing up a detailed guide regarding the form in which applications are to be presented' together with the EMA, the Member States and other interested parties. The Commission made use of this power by drafting an extensive collection of guidance documents.[167] The guidelines drafted by the Commission are published on its Eudralex website.[168] This website comprises the so-called 'rules governing medicinal products in the European Union' that, along with the basic pharmaceutical legislation, also include guidelines for both human and veterinary medicinal products.

The most important post-legislative guidance in the EU's pharmaceutical regulation is the so-called 'Notice to Applicants' in Volume 2 of the rules

(Nijmegen: Wolf Legal Publishers, 2003); F Terpan, 'Soft Law in the European Union – The Changing Nature of EU Law' (2015) 21 *European Law Journal* 68; M Eliantonio and O Stefan (eds), 'Soft Law in the EU Legal Order: Reflections and Contemporary Trends' [Special Issue] (2017) 37 *Yearbook of European Law* 457.

[161] Senden (2003) 104.

[162] See especially: Senden (2003).

[163] Snyder (1994) 200.

[164] Knauff (2010) 299.

[165] See eg: L Senden and A van den Brink, 'Checks and Balances of Soft EU Rule-Making', European Parliament – Directorate General for Internal Policies Study (2012) PE 462.433, 8; S Vaughan, 'Differentiation and Dysfunction: An Exploration of Post-Legislative Guidance Practices in 14 EU Agencies' (2015) 17 *Cambridge Yearbook of European Legal Studies* 66; H Hofmann, 'European Regulatory Union? The Role of Agencies and Standards', in P Koutrakos and J Snell, *Research Handbook on the Law of the EU's Internal Market* (Cheltenham: Edward Elgar, 2017).

[166] The mandate of EMA is laid down in art 57 of Regulation (EC) No 726/2004. See also: Vaughan (2015) 76; E Chiti, 'European Agencies' Rulemaking: Powers, Procedures and Assessment' (2013) 19 *European Law Journal* 93, 97f.

[167] ec.europa.eu/health/documents/eudralex/vol-2/index_en.htm.

[168] ec.europa.eu/health/documents/eudralex/index_en.htm.

governing medicinal products in the European Union. The Notice to Applicants is divided in three parts: one dealing with the procedures for marketing authorisation (Volume 2A); the second with the presentation and content of the dossier (Volume 2B); and the third containing so-called 'regulatory guidelines' (Volume 2C). The Notice to Applicants Volume 2A provides detailed guidance on marketing authorisation procedures in the Union and the institutional practices concerning this procedure, including clarification in the form of timelines. Volume 2B is concerned with the format of the marketing authorisation dossier, ie the Common Technical Document (CTD).[169] The Commission's regulatory guidelines compiled in Volume 2C address variations and renewals of marketing authorisations, changing the classification for the supply, and the readability of the labelling and package leaflet. They supplement the legislation where it does not provide for the definition of certain terms,[170] or entail specifications of legislative requirements.[171] In addition to Volume 2, further Notice to Applicants Volumes contain guidelines drafted by the Commission for good manufacturing practice (Volume 4) and clinical trials (Volume 10).

EMA guidelines are drafted with the intention of harmonising the interpretation and application of the legislative requirements of quality, safety and efficacy, providing detailed guidance on these matters.[172] Moreover, they give guidance to marketing authorisation applicants on how the pharmaceutical product has to be tested during its development, and how an application needs to be substantiated by documentation.[173] Due to the rapidly changing scientific background of the criteria for marketing authorisation and the sheer amount of technical details necessary to define them for different products, these scientific requirements are not laid down in legislative measures, for which there is a long and cumbersome process for amendments, but in the form of guidelines.[174] The scientific guidelines drafted by the EMA constituted Volume 3 of the Notice to Applicants but are now found on the website of the EMA.[175] The guidelines are adopted by the EMA's scientific committees and most of them originate in

[169] For further details on the CTD see Chapter 4.

[170] For example, the guidance on a new therapeutic indication for a well-established substance clarifies what is a 'new indication' in the sense of art 10(5) Directive 2201/83/EC (European Commission, Guidance on a New Therapeutic Indication for a Well Established Substance, Brussels, November 2007).

[171] For example, the guideline on the readability of the labelling and package leaflet of medicinal products for human use provides *inter alia* the font size that should be used for the package leaflet (European Commission, Guideline on the Readability of the Labelling and Package Leaflet of Medicinal Products for Human Use, ENTR/F/2/SF/jr (2009)D/869, 12 January 2009).

[172] European Medicines Agency, EMEA/P/24143/2004 Rev 1 corr, 6. See also: S Vamvakas, 'EU Perspectives on ICH', in J van de Laan and J DeGeorge (eds), *Global Approach in Safety Testing – ICH Guidelines Explained* (New York: Springer, 2013) 16.

[173] EMA, EMEA/P/24143/2004 Rev 1 corr, 6.

[174] See also: Knauff (2010) 251f.

[175] www.ema.europa.eu.

the main scientific committee for human medicinal products, the CHMP. The preparation of the guidelines might take place in standing or temporary working groups established by these committees.[176]

The EMA, also in comparison to other agencies,[177] publishes a large number of guidelines. It is not easy to determine the precise number as the guidelines are published on the website in different sections and multiple languages. An examination of the EMA website in March 2015 revealed that with 337 scientific guidelines for human medicinal products in force in various regulatory areas, the EMA has made extensive use of non-legally binding guidance documents.[178] Table 1 shows the number of guidelines identified in each regulatory area.

Table 1 EMA guidelines governing pharmaceuticals

Scientific guidelines for human medicinal products adopted by the EMA and its committees (as at 19 March 2015).

Regulatory area	**Number of guidelines**
Quality	57
Biologicals	56
Non-clinical	43
Clinical efficacy and safety	125
Multidisciplinary	49
Other	7
Total	**337**

Source: www.ema.europa.eu.

These scientific guidelines represent 'a harmonised EU approach … based on the most up-to-date scientific knowledge'.[179] For example, the EMA has established a guideline on testing the carcinogenic potential – the potential to cause cancer – of medicinal products for human use.[180] This guideline defines how to conduct carcinogenicity studies in animals, providing specific details on the duration of the studies, the number of animals, and the monitoring of the study, as well as the reporting of the study results. Other guidelines govern a specific category of medicinal products. For example, the guideline on medicinal

[176] Regulation (EC) No 726/2004, art 56(2).

[177] Vaughan (2015) 73.

[178] The research reflects the status of guidelines on 19 March 2015 as published on the website of the EMA (www.ema.europa.eu). The guidelines only were counted, excluding other documents like reflections papers, Q&As or Addenda. An effort was made to count every guideline only once, even if it was presented in more than one section of the website.

[179] EMA, EMEA/P/24143/2004 Rev 1 corr, 4.

[180] Committee for Proprietary Medicinal Products (CPMP), Note for guidance on carcinogenic potential, CPMP/SWP/2877/00.

products for the treatment of insomnia defines diagnostic criteria for insomnia and provides details on the assessment of the therapeutic efficacy of the medicinal product.[181]

B. Pharmaceutical Guidelines as Soft Law: Examining Direct and Indirect Legal Effects

The pharmaceutical guidelines discussed above do not constitute legally binding measures and are soft law. In this regard, the guidelines of the European Commission are published with a disclaimer. The website providing the Notice to Applicants explicitly states that the notice 'has no legal force' and that '(i)n case of doubt, therefore, reference should be made to the appropriate Union Directives and Regulations'.[182] This is also underlined by the EMA's guideline adoption procedure: '(w)ithin the framework of pharmaceutical legislation, guidelines do not have legal force and the definite legal requirements are those outlined in the relevant Community legislative framework ... as well as appropriate national rules'.[183] Thus, the non-binding status of the guidelines is emphasised and communicated. Legislation will take priority over any guidelines and the content of the guidelines cannot contravene legislation, as was also emphasised in an interview with officials of the Legal Department of the EMA.[184]

However, in order to truly understand the legal nature of pharmaceutical guidelines, it is necessary to look beyond their formal status and the disclaimers towards the potential legal effects – direct or indirect – and practical effects these instruments are prompting. Such effects might for example be caused by their interaction with legally binding measures applicable to pharmaceuticals.[185] For those guidelines which have a basis in secondary law, the EMA's procedure for guideline adoption is very instructive as the document qualifies the guidelines as soft law and emphasises that in cases where a guideline adopted by the Commission or the EMA serves as clarification of a legal obligation, it can become 'quasi-binding' through this legal basis.[186]

In general, the guidelines drafted by the EMA and the Commission are reinforced through legislation. According to Article 8(3) of Directive 2001/83/EC, a marketing authorisation application needs to be submitted in the specific format

[181] Committee for Medicinal Products for Human Use (CHMP), Guideline on medicinal products for the treatment of insomnia, EMA/CHMP/16274/2009 Rev 1.

[182] ec.europa.eu/health/documents/eudralex/vol-2/index_en.htm. A similar disclaimer is also found in Chapter 1 of the Notice to Applicants.

[183] EMA, EMEA/P/24143/2004 Rev 1 corr, 4.

[184] Interview with two officials of the Legal Department of the European Medicines Agency, conducted in London on 23 March 2015, notes on file with the author.

[185] Hofmann, Rowe and Türk (2011) 552.

[186] EMA, EMEA/P/24143/2004 Rev 1 corr, 4.

and containing the documents that are listed in Annex 1 of the Directive. Annex 1 to Directive 2001/83/EC under (1) sets out that the application shall follow the format set out in the Notice to Applicants, in Volume 2B. It also sets out under (4) in the Annex that in assembling the dossier, the applicant shall take the guidelines published by the EMA and the Commission into account. In order to harmonise the requirements of the marketing authorisation, this Annex is referred to not only in the Directive which governs decentralised and national procedures, but also in Article 6(1) of Regulation (EC) 726/2004, which regulates the Centralised Procedures and requires the application of Annex 1 of the Directive. Thus, although not legally binding, through reinforcement by the Regulation and the Directive, the guidelines have to be taken into account both in the Centralised and also the Decentralised and Mutual Recognition marketing authorisation procedures, as well as in national procedures. The guidelines do not become binding, but the reference in the legislation certainly fortifies their significance in marketing authorisation applications.

How this interaction between hard and soft law works in practice can be illustrated by an examination of the rules and principles forming 'Good Manufacturing Practice' (GMP), which regulates the manufacturing process of medicinal products, addressing issues such as hygiene or documentation of the production. Along with the obligation to obtain marketing authorisation prior to the marketing of a medicinal product, the manufacturing of medicinal products is also subject to an authorisation requirement.[187] According to Article 46(f) of Directive 2001/83/EC, manufacturers are obliged to comply with GMP. However, the Directive does not specify what GMP entails. Therefore, Article 47 mandates the adoption of a directive to amend non-essential elements of Directive 2001/83/EC by supplementing it. This led to the adoption of Commission Directive 2003/94/EC providing the general rules of GMP.[188] Moreover, Article 47 of Directive 2001/83/EC mandates the adoption of delegated acts to establish principles and guidelines of GMP for active substances.[189] Furthermore, it allows for the drafting of detailed guidelines by the Commission. These Commission guidelines are contained in Volume 4 of the Eudralex website, defining GMP in accordance with the legislative requirements in detail.[190]

The interaction of these measures can be imagined like a cascade, where the general requirements are laid down in the legislative measure. These principles

[187] Directive 2001/83/EC, art 40.

[188] Commission Directive 2003/94/EC of 8 October 2003 laying down the principles and guidelines of good manufacturing practice in respect of medicinal products for human use and investigational medicinal products for human use, [2003] OJ L262/22.

[189] On the basis of this provision, the Commission has adopted: Commission Delegated Regulation (EU) No 1252/2014 of 28 May 2014 supplementing Directive 2001/83/EC of the European Parliament and of the Council with regard to principles and guidelines of good manufacturing practice for active substances for medicinal products for human use, [2014] OJ L337/1.

[190] European Commission, Eudralex – The Rules Governing Medicinal Products in the European Union – Volume 4 EU Guidelines for Good Manufacturing Practice for Medicinal Products for Human and Veterinary Use – Introduction, SANCO/C8/AM/sl/ares(2010)1064597.

are then further established in a legally binding Commission measure, and the regulatory details are laid down in non-binding guidelines. For example, Directive 2001/83/EC prescribes adherence to GMP. The core principles of this practice are laid down in Commission Directive 2003/94/EC, which *inter alia* establishes that 'manufacturers shall establish and implement an effective pharmaceutical quality assurance system'.[191] The requirements of such a pharmaceutical quality system are further specified in a Commission guideline.[192] In the following paragraphs it will be further examined what direct and indirect legal effects Commission and EMA guidelines can have on three types of actors: (i) the Commission and the EMA themselves; (ii) marketing authorisation applicants; and (iii) the Member States.

The direct or indirect legal effects on the Commission and the EMA are to be assessed, as administrative rules can be 'self-binding' upon the body that publishes them.[193] In general, the Court of Justice of the European Union (CJEU) has followed the principle that, provided the soft law instruments are compatible with the Treaties, an institution is bound by the guidelines it has adopted.[194] Thus, guidelines considerably limit the discretion of the authoring institution and impose a duty of compliance.[195] The Court based the self-binding effect of soft law measures on the basis of general principles of law such as equal treatment, legitimate expectations and legal certainty.[196] Thus, these administrative rules might generate legal effects.[197] Especially in staff cases and competition law cases, the self-binding power of soft law, allowing for deviation only where this is duly reasoned, has been established.[198] Although these rules

[191] Commission Directive 2003/94/EC, art 6.

[192] European Commission, Eudralex – The Rules Governing Medicinal Products in the European Union – Volume 4 EU Guidelines for Good Manufacturing Practice for Medicinal Products for Human and Veterinary Use – Chapter 1 Pharmaceutical Quality System, SANCO/AM/sl/ddg1.d.6(2012)860362.

[193] Schwarze (2011) 8.

[194] See: Case C-382/99 *Netherlands v Commission*, ECLI:EU:C:2002:363, para 24; Case C-313/90 *Comité International de la Rayonne et des Fibres Synthétique (CIRFS) and Others v Commission*, ECLI:EU:C:1993:111, paras 34 and 36; Case C-311/94 *IJssel-Vliet Combinatie v Minister van Economische Zaken*, ECLI:EU:C:1996:383, para 42; Case T-214/95 *Vlaamse Gewest v Commission*, ECLI:EU:T:1998:77, para 79.

[195] Joined cases C-189, 202, 205, 208 and 213/02P *Dansk Rørindustri and others v Commission*, ECLI:EU:C:2005:408, para 211. See also: A Simonati, 'The Principles of Administrative Procedure and the EU Courts: An Evolution in Progress?' (2011) 4 *Review of European Administrative Law* 45, 58; O Stefan, 'European Union Soft Law: New Developments Concerning the Divide Between Legally Binding Force and Legal Effects' (2012) 75 *The Modern Law Review* 865, 882.

[196] Joined cases C-189, 202, 205, 208 and 213/02P *Dansk Rørindustri and others v Commission*, ECLI:EU:C:2005:408, para 211; Case T-73/04 *Carbone-Lorraine v Commission*, ECLI:EU:T:2008:416, para 71. See also: Hofmann, Rowe and Türk (2011) 567; O Stefan, 'Helping Loose Ends Meet? The Judicial Acknowledgement of Soft Law as a Tool of Multi-Level Governance' (2014) 21 *Maastricht Journal of European and Comparative Law* 359, 367f.

[197] Joined cases C-189, 202, 205, 208 and 213/02P *Dansk Rørindustri and others v Commission*, ECLI:EU:C:2005:408, para 211.

[198] Senden (2003) 415–58; Stefan (2014).

are developed in specific regulatory areas and their application in other areas of regulation is not clear,[199] it is difficult to argue that the same principles of equal treatment, legitimate expectations and legal certainty would not apply in the field of pharmaceuticals.

As previously explained, a marketing authorisation applicant needs to take the guidelines of both the Commission and the EMA into account when submitting an application. The Commission guidelines usually address regulatory aspects which clarify legislative requirements.[200] For example, Commission guidelines address in detail product labelling and packaging requirements according to Articles 8(3)(j), 57, 60, 62 and 65(f) of Directive 2001/83/EC.[201] As these regulatory matters are presented as further clarification of legislative requirements, it is questionable whether there is indeed room for the applicant to deviate from the guidelines. With regard to the EMA's scientific guidelines, the EMA's clarification of the legal status of these guidelines provides that if regulators and marketing authorisation applicants adhere to these guidelines this 'will facilitate assessment, approval and control of medicinal products in the European Union'.[202]

Adherence to the guidelines is thus presented as the route to enable the assessment of the application. In essence, the guidelines regulate which scientific evidence required in the application dossier and, thereby, establish the basis for the assessment by the scientific committee. Moreover, the EMA states that where guidelines are adopted but have not yet entered into effect, applicants can follow such guidelines, while 'competent authorities should wait until this period has expired before requiring the guideline to be taken into account'.[203] Given the non-binding character of the guidelines, the choice of the word 'requiring' is interesting, as it indicates that the leeway given to decide not to apply the guidelines might be smaller than their non-binding character might suggest. Indeed, on the agency's website, the message regarding the status of guidelines is firm: '(t)he Agency strongly *encourages* applicants and marketing-authorisation holders to follow these guidelines. Applicants need to justify **deviations from guidelines** fully in their applications at the time of submission'.[204]

Undoubtedly, not all scientific questions for every product can be regulated in these guidelines. The science in the guidelines is certainly not set in stone and deviation is possible if justified.[205] However, compliance with the

[199] Hofmann, Rowe and Türk (2011), 568.

[200] EMA, EMEA/P/24143/2004 Rev 1 corr, 6.

[201] European Commission, Guideline on the Packaging Information of Medicinal Products for Human Use Authorised by the Union, July 2015, Revision 14.3.

[202] European Medicines Agency, Status of EMEA Scientific Guidelines and European Pharmacopoeia Monographs and chapters in the regulatory framework applicable to medicinal products, 11 September 2008, EMEA/42371/2008 – corr, p 2.

[203] EMA, EMEA/P/24143/2004 Rev 1 corr, 13.

[204] www.ema.europa.eu/en/human-regulatory/research-development/scientific-guidelines, (emphasis in original).

[205] Interview with two officials of the Legal Department of the European Medicines Agency, conducted in London on 23 March 2015, notes on file with the author.

guidelines – provided that the result of the prescribed tests confirm what is sought to be proven – creates a presumption of conformity with the legislative requirements of quality, safety and efficacy, whereas deviations from guidelines have to be duly justified,[206] and this can be a deterrent. Where applicants deviate from the scientific guidelines the burden of proof faced with regard to compliance with legislative requirements is shifted: a presumption of conformity lies in the adherence to standards, while deviation requires the extra step of justification by the applicant.[207] Given that some of the guidelines would already have to be taken into account in the research and development process of the product, there would be a risk of not being able to justify a deviation from the guidelines when at the end of a long and highly expensive process.

It is possible for companies to request scientific advice from the EMA on the appropriate test to demonstrate the quality, safety and efficacy of medicinal products.[208] However, this advice is not legally binding on the agency in an ensuing authorisation procedure and a fee must be paid.[209] In an interview with an official of the European Federation of Pharmaceutical Industries and Associations (EFPIA), it was confirmed that companies in practice usually follow the guidelines, rather than trying to justify a deviation from the guidelines.[210] Overall, although both the Commission and EMA guidelines are non-binding measures, it has to be concluded that their application to marketing authorisation requests is compelling, and they indirectly become binding where deviation cannot be justified. As noted by Chiti: 'Their legal status is that of soft law measures, inherently in tension between the form of non-binding provisions and the substance of rules *de facto* affecting and conditioning private parties' behaviours.'[211]

Another dimension of the 'quasi-binding' nature of these guidelines is their effect on the Member States. The national procedures underlie the European harmonisation through Directive 2001/83/EC, as Articles 6 and 8 require the application of Annex 1. Therefore, the guidelines formed on the European level, both by the Commission and the EMA, also work through to purely national authorisation procedures.[212] However, some of the guidelines will not apply to

[206] EMA, EMEA/P/24143/2004 Rev 1 corr, 5.

[207] See also: J Scott, 'International Trade and Environmental Governance: Relating Rules (and Standards) in the EU and WTO' (2004) 15 *European Journal of International Law* 307, 314.

[208] Regulation (EC) No 726/2004, art 57(1)(n).

[209] European Medicines Agency, Guidance for applicants seeking scientific advice and protocol assistance, EMA/691788/2010 Rev 10, 19 October 2020; European Medicines Agency, Explanatory Note on the fees payable to the European Medicines Agency, EMA/336497/2020.

[210] Interview with an official of the European Federation of Pharmaceutical Industries and Associations (EFPIA), conducted in Brussels on 17 February 2015, notes on file with the author.

[211] Chiti (2013) 98.

[212] In an interview with an official of the Bundesinstitut für Arzneimittel und Medizinprodukte (BfArM) it was confirmed that European soft law rules form an important part of national pharmaceutical regulation. Interview with an official of the BfArM, conducted in Bonn on 26 February 2015, notes on file with the author.

the Member States, where the products covered in the guidelines by their very nature are subject to the centralised procedure under Regulation (EC) 726/2004 and therefore are not covered by the national procedures.[213]

As far as the national courts are concerned, in the *Grimaldi* case the Court of Justice obliged national courts to take a non-binding recommendation into account, where they rule on a dispute which requires an interpretation of EU law.[214] Korkea-aho in her analysis of the ruling and its subsequent development in the CJEU jurisprudence argues that in this regard one has to differentiate between soft law measures adopted by EU bodies on the basis of a mandate in primary or secondary law and soft law that lacks such a legal basis.[215] Where soft law is adopted with a legal basis the nation courts will have to take the guidance into account and will only be able to 'depart from the interpretation offered in such documents only where they can provide specific, detailed, and substantively grounded reasons as to why the soft law act does not apply'.[216] Thus, pharmaceutical guidelines which have a basis in legislation will have to be used by national courts as interpretative aids and are thus reinforced by those rulings.

In general, European administrative guidelines are very influential on the Member States. A study by Senden and van den Brink shows that guidelines serving as a soft law guidance measure will have an effect on the national legislator transposing European law, and also on the national administration applying the respective legislation, as well as on the judiciary in the Member States.[217] All of these national actors will look for guidance on the interpretation of EU legislation in non-binding guidelines. Therefore, although not legally binding, guidelines do establish practical guidance for various actors in the Member States to comply with EU law.[218]

IV. CONCLUSION: INCREMENTAL INTEGRATION, EXTENSIVE (RISK) REGULATION AND THE SIGNIFICANCE OF ADMINISTRATIVE GUIDANCE

This chapter has shown that the history of harmonisation in the pharmaceuticals field in the EU is a history of incremental integration, from the introduction of marketing authorisation requirement; to harmonisation of the regulatory requirements concerning quality, safety and efficacy; culminating in the creation

[213] Interview with two officials of the Legal Department of the European Medicines Agency, conducted in London on 23 March 2015, notes on file with the author.

[214] Case C-322/88 *Salvatore Grimaldi v Fonds des Maladies Professionnelles*, ECLI:EU:C:1989:646, para 18.

[215] E Korkea-aho, 'National Courts and European Soft Law: Is Grimaldi Still Good Law?' (2018) *Yearbook of European Law* 470.

[216] Ibid, 494.

[217] Senden and van den Brink (2012) 8.

[218] Hofmann, Rowe and Türk (2011) 569.

of mutual recognition procedures allowing for discussion and collaboration between the Member States, and a centralised, EU-level procedure for innovative products. Various marketing authorisation procedures co-exist: applicants can either apply for purely national authorisation, or take the route of a Decentralised or Mutual Recognition Procedure, or apply for a centralised marketing authorisation.

Thus, different types of pharmaceuticals are subject to diverging degrees of harmonisation and 'institutional layering'[219] of authorisation procedures relying on different actors. After more than 50 years of European pharmaceutical regulation, the legislative framework covering pharmaceuticals extensively regulates the market access of medicinal products and risks related to medicinal products. This has been complemented not only by other EU legislative measures concerning labelling, advertising and the wholesale of pharmaceuticals, but also instruments that aim to steer innovation in the direction of otherwise neglected patients such as children or persons suffering from rare diseases. This legislative framework has been supported by an institutional structure consisting of the European Commission and the EMA as key actors.

What this chapter has shown is that this legislative framework is supplemented by extensive administrative rule-making. The Commission has adopted a large variety of regulatory guidelines including the extensive 'Notice to Applicants'. Furthermore, the EMA has adopted a considerable number of guidelines, which fill the legislative requirements of quality, safety and efficacy with life through the establishment of scientific and technical norms. Although the guidelines adopted by the Commission and EMA are labelled as non-binding instruments, they are powerful regulatory tools with considerable practical effects, and at times indirect legal effects, on individuals and Member States, and also on the Commission and EMA themselves. The freedom to deviate from the guidelines for all these actors is heavily restricted and their non-binding nature only superficially disguises this. These guidelines, therefore, form an important part of the EU pharmaceutical regulatory framework.

[219] Feick (2005) 19.

2

EU Risk Regulation in a Globalised World: Global Standards

THE REGULATION OF the EU's internal market, and specifically the regulation of risks related to goods that move within this market, such as pharmaceuticals, is changing. It has evolved from being largely enshrined in legislation to a regulatory system with diverse forms of measures adopted by miscellaneous actors, where not only the legislator but also executive and administrative bodies, as well as private actors as co-regulators shape the regulatory framework.[1] This has become evident with regard to the EU's pharmaceutical regulation, discussed in the previous chapter.

Part of this transformation is the increasing reliance on standards, to complement or even partially substitute legislative regulation. The reliance on standards as regulatory tools in the EU has already received academic attention. However, a specific type of standards, the so-called 'European Standards', have so far formed the focus of scholarly debate with regard to standards in the EU.[2] This standard-setting practice under the New Approach entails that the setting of technical standards has been outsourced through the delegation of standard-setting power from the Commission to three private standard-setting bodies: the European Committee for Standardisation (CEN), the European Committee for

[1] For a comprehensive account see: H Hofmann, 'European regulatory union? The role of agencies and standards', in P Koutrakos and J Snell, *Research Handbook on the Law of the EU's Internal Market* (Cheltenham: Edward Elgar, 2017). See further: G Majone, 'The Rise of the Regulatory State in Europe' (1994) 17 *West European Politics* 77; D Curtin, *Executive Power of the European Union – Law, Practice and the Living Constitution* (Oxford: Oxford University Press, 2009).

[2] In the EU standards became a popular tool of regulation with the introduction of the 'New Approach' in 1985. Whereas before, different categories of products and hazards had been dealt with within individual Directives, now Directives covered a whole sector and only contained 'essential requirements', the details of which would be clarified through voluntary standards. Selected publications in the area are: H Schepel, *The Constitution of Private Governance – Product Standards in the Regulation of Integrating Markets* (Oxford: Hart, 2005); J Pelkmans, 'The New Approach to Technical Harmonization and Standardisation' (1987) 25 *Journal of Common Market Studies* 249; R van Gestel and H Micklitz, 'European Integration through Standardization: How Judicial Review is Breaking Down the Club House of Private Standardization Bodies' (2013) 50 *Common Market Law Review* 145; H Schepel, 'The New Approach to the New Approach: The Juridification of Harmonized Standards in EU Law' (2013) 20 *Maastricht Journal of European and Comparative Law* 521; M Eliantonio and C Cauffman (eds), *The Legitimacy of Standardisation as a Regulatory Technique: A Cross-Disciplinary and Multi-Level Analysis* (Cheltenham: Edward Elgar, 2020).

Electrotechnical Standardisation (Cenelec), and the European Telecommunications Standards Institute (ETSI).[3]

However, in the process of globalisation the EU has experienced a 'progressive externalization (and internationalization) of many EU policies and programmes',[4] which ultimately also leads to the absorption of global standards in various areas of European risk regulation. Thus, next to the technical and scientific norms that are developed by EU agencies in the form of post-legislative guidance, such as the adoption of guidelines by the EMA concerning the quality, safety and efficacy of medicines,[5] such norms are also adopted on international level and subsequently received in the EU. Thus, the regulation of the EU's internal market in the globalised world is characterised by substantial interaction between regulatory measures adopted on the global level and the EU's regulatory frameworks. This chapter will scrutinise the phenomenon of global standard-setting, introducing the complex regulatory structures that have developed on global level, and elaborate on the interaction of global standards with EU law, as well as the participation of EU actors in global standard-setting.

I. THE PHENOMENON OF GLOBAL STANDARD-SETTING

Although standards are often colloquially only associated with the compatibility of technical components, standards appear in a large variety, their form and content being shaped by their field of application.[6] Standards are concerned with technological interconnectivity or ensure the smooth functioning of commercial transactions by harmonising measurements; however, they are also common tools in the regulation of physical externalities such as pollution or arise where the safety of products is regulated.[7] Next to the regulation of products, they are

[3] Regulation (EU) No 1025/2012 of the European Parliament and of the Council of 25 October 2012 on European standardisation, [2012] OJ L316/12.

[4] M Groenleer and S Gabbi, 'Regulatory Agencies of the European Union as International Actors: Legal Framework, Development over Time and Strategic Motives in the Case of the European Food Safety Authority' (2013) 4 *European Journal of Risk Regulation* 479, 481.

[5] See Chapter 1 section III.

[6] For examples of standards as regulatory tools in various policy fields see for example: K Abbott and D Snidal, 'International "Standards" and International Governance' (2001) 8 *Journal of European Public Policy* 345; D Kerwer, 'Rules that Many Use: Standards and Global Regulation' (2005) 18 *Governance* 61; E Fisher, 'Drowning by Numbers: Standard-Setting in Risk Regulation and the Pursuit of Accountable Public Administration' (2000) 20 *Oxford Journal of Legal Studies* 109; H Morais, 'The Quest for International Standards: Global Governance vs. Sovereignty' (2001–2002) 50 *University of Kansas Law Review* 779; T Büthe and W Mattli (eds), *The New Global Rulers: The Privatization of Regulation in the World Economy* (Princeton: Princeton University Press, 2011); P Delimatsis (ed), *The Law, Economics and Politics of International Standardization* (Cambridge University Press, 2015a); M Cantero Gamito and H Micklitz (eds), *The Role of the EU in Transnational Legal Ordering – Standards, Contracts and Codes* (Cheltenham: Edward Elgar, 2020).

[7] Abbott and Snidal (2001).

also well known in the regulation of other areas such as finance or labour.[8] Thus, today standards extend far beyond technical compatibility and have evolved into important regulatory tools for organising markets and regulating risks.[9]

A. Risk Regulation through Voluntary, Expertise-Based Rules

In the context of risk regulation, standards regulate the safety and quality of products and production processes.[10] While product standards regulate details of a product, as well as its health or safety effect, production standards regulate aspects of a production process.[11] In this regulatory context a standard is defined as a voluntary expertise based rule,[12] constituting measurable criteria by which a product or a production process or service can be evaluated on the basis of technical or physical conditions.[13]

The risks for human health and the environment that society faces are increasingly complex in terms of their causes, and interconnected factors or interactions influencing their materialisation.[14] The effort to regulate such complex risks is complicated since some risks are 'uncertain' or unpredictable due to a lack of scientific knowledge.[15] Through the globalisation of markets and mobility of products and people, regulation on a purely national level ceases to address such risks efficiently.[16] As the complexity of risks and interconnection

[8] For example, standards in the area of finance are developed through the Basel Committee: M de Bellis, 'The Legitimacy of Banking and Financial Standards: Representation, Due Process and Regulatory Capture', in M Eliantonio and C Cauffman (eds), *The Legitimacy of Standardisation as a Regulatory Technique: A Cross-Disciplinary and Multi-Level Analysis* (Cheltenham: Edward Elgar, 2020). The International Labour Association (ILO) is well-known in the area of labour standards: T Börzel and T Risse, 'Public-Private Partnerships: Effective and Legitimate Tools of International Governance?', in E Grande and L Pauly (eds), *Complex Sovereignty: On the Reconstruction of Political Authority in the 21st Century* (Toronto: University of Toronto Press, 2007).

[9] S Jasanoff, 'Constitutions of Modernity: Science, Risk and Governable Subjects', in M Weimer and A de Ruijter, *Regulating Risks in the European Union – The Co-production of Expert and Executive Power* (Oxford: Hart, 2017) 19–36.

[10] E Fisher, Risk Regulation and Administrative Constitutionalism (Oxford: Hart, 2010) 3.

[11] K Nadvi and F Wältring, 'Making Sense of Global Standards', INEF Report Heft 58/2002 (2002) 6; W Mattli and T Büthe, 'Setting International Standards: Technological Rationality or Primacy of Power?' (2003) 56 *World Politics* 3.

[12] D Kerwer, 'Standardising as Governance: The case of credit rating agencies', MPI Collective Goods Preprint, No 2001/3, (2001) 8.

[13] Nadvi and Wältring (2002) 6.

[14] J Black, 'Critical Reflections on Regulation', Centre for Analysis of Risk and Regulation, CARR Discussion Papers DP 4, London School of Economics and Political Science (London, 2002) 3.

[15] Fisher (2010) 7; M Everson and E Vos, 'The Scientification of Politics and the Politicization of Science', in M Everson and E Vos (eds), *Uncertain Risks Regulated* (Oxon: Routledge/Cavendish, 2009) 3.

[16] For a similar observation in terms of broader policy issues such as pollution or organised crime see: A Peters, L Koechlin and G Fenner Zinkernagel, 'Non-state Actors as Standard Setters: Framing the Issue in an Interdisciplinary Fashion' in A Peters, L Koechlin, T Förster and G Fenner Zinkernagel (eds), *Non-State Actors as Standard-Setters* (Cambridge: Cambridge University Press, 2009) 1–32.

of markets is creating a breeding ground for increased regulatory cooperation, it augments the importance of global standards as regulatory tools. Global standards, rather than being established within national or regional jurisdictions in isolation, are the product of cooperation beyond the confines of a single jurisdiction. 'Global' thus refers to standard-setting beyond the nation state, on what is often termed the 'international' level. However, using the term 'global' also accounts for the increasing importance of other actors than nation states in the setting of these norms and also more appropriately reflects the interconnection of different levels of regulation – regional, national and international.[17] It should, however, also be acknowledged that global standards are not necessarily open to input from all countries and actors, or that they would always be universally applicable. Global standards can originate in bodies with limited membership, such as for example the Organisation for Economic Co-operation and Development (OECD),[18] which are confined to selected states, for example on geographical or economic criteria.[19]

Global standard-setting is based on the rationale that harmonisation of regulatory requirements through global standards is beneficial for regulators as well as the regulated industries. These global standards harmonise regulatory systems to create a level playing field in international trade.[20] From an economic perspective, setting standards at global level as opposed to diverging national or regional norms is decreasing the compliance costs for companies, as well as 'addressing network externalities, interoperability issues and information asymmetries'.[21] The adoption of harmonised standards facilitates barrier-free worldwide trade in products, relieving producers from the duty of having to repeatedly adapt their products to differing national standards, and considerably decreasing production costs.[22] Participating regulatory authorities benefit from global standard-setting as it responds to the increased need for very specific expertise in the regulation of highly technical areas. Bundling regulatory competences on a global level allows for cost-sharing and prevents the duplication of

[17] A von Bogdandy, P Dann and M Goldmann, 'Developing the Publicness of Public International Law', in A von Bogdandy, R Wolfrum, J von Bernstorff, P Dann and M Goldmann (eds), *The Exercise of Public Authority by International Institutions: Advancing International Institutional Law* (Heidelberg: Springer, 2010) 7.

[18] J Wouters and S van Kerckhoven, 'The OECD and the G20: An Ever Closer Relationship?' (2011) Leuven Centre for Global Governance Studies Working Paper No 71.

[19] H Röhl, 'Internationale Standardsetzung', in C Möllers, A Vosskuhle and C Walter (eds), *Internationales Verwaltungsrecht – Eine Analyse Anhand von Referenzgebieten* (Tübingen: Mohr Siebeck, 2007) 322.

[20] Morais (2001–2002) 790.

[21] P Delimatsis, 'Introduction: Continuity and Change in International Standardization', in P Delimatsis (eds), *The Law, Economics and Politics of International Standardization* (Cambridge: Cambridge University Press, 2015b) 3.

[22] J Wouters and S Verhoeven, 'Regulation and Globalization: Interaction between International Standard-Setting Agencies and the European Union', in D Geradin, R Muñoz, and N Petit (eds), *Regulation Through Agencies in the EU: A New Paradigm of European Governance* (Cheltenham: Edward Elgar, 2006).

efforts. Additionally, it allows for the assessment of data collected in various geographic areas, which can be an important contribution to assessing the factors leading to a risk emerging. Another factor making global standards attractive, at least for governments with important markets, is the potential to achieve a strong influence on the standards agreed upon, and make those standards applicable worldwide.[23]

Compliance with standards is by definition voluntary, and thus standards constitute a 'guide for behaviour and for judging behaviour' in very broad terms.[24] By prescribing certain features, actions, processes or properties, standards harmonise their area of application. In contrast to mutual recognition agreements they presuppose convergence to one point of reference establishing a specific requirement and the harmonisation of this requirement.[25] Generally, depending on the type of standard-setting body, these standards are addressed to governments and/or regulators, economic actors such as companies producing the regulated products, and/or other national and international standard-setting institutions.[26] Global standards are often addressed to regulators, which are expected to implement these standards in their regulatory system to harmonise regulatory requirements. However, global standards ultimately have to be taken into account by the regulated industry in the development, testing and production of their products. Thus, such standards, although often addressed to regulators, strongly affect private actors in the end.[27]

B. The Legal Nature of Global Standards: Soft Law in International Law

Standards are voluntary measures and represent the agreement of standard-setting body members on technical and scientific requirements without being legally binding. Accordingly, they 'seek to convince rather than to coerce'.[28]

[23] In the pharmaceuticals sector this is a declared goal of the Commission, which has announced: 'Establishing and enforcing international public health standards is essential to minimise the risk that unsafe products enter the EU market. The work carried out with the US and Japan at the International Conference on Harmonisation (ICH) is essential in this context and must be expanded. ICH standards should be promoted so that they can become worldwide standards.' See: European Commission, Communication from the Commission to the Parliament, the Council, the European Economic and Social Committee and the Committee of the Regions – Safe, Innovative and Accessible Medicines: a Renewed Vision for the Pharmaceutical Sector, COM(2008) 666 final, 13.

[24] Abbott and Snidal (2001) 345.

[25] Wouters and Verhoeven (2006) 261.

[26] S Charnovitz, 'International Standards and the WTO', GW Law Faculty Publications & Other Works, Paper 394, (2005) 6.

[27] In this regard Goldmann argues that besides the explicit recipients of a measure ('first level addressees') the measure may affect other groups ('second level addressees') indirectly, by obliging the first level addressees to impose obligations or affect the legal situation of individuals. See: M Goldmann, 'Inside Relative Normativity: From Sources to Standard Instruments for the Exercise of International Public Authority', in A von Bogdandy, R Wolfrum, J von Bernstorff, P Dann and M Goldmann (eds), *The Exercise of Public Authority by International Institutions: Advancing International Institutional Law* (Heidelberg: Springer, 2010) 661–711.

[28] Kerwer (2005) 611.

These norms are not adopted in a legally binding form and are not enforceable against addressees that fail to implement the agreed standards. Still, these standards – at least the ones set by or with the involvement of public authorities – are set in order to harmonise the regulatory frameworks of the respective areas they govern.[29] Therefore, similar to the Commission and EMA post-legislative guidance discussed in Chapter 1, an assessment of the legal nature of global standards as regulatory measures is imperative.

Standards do not gain their influence from hierarchical power but rather gain force through being the result of the horizontal cooperation of the concerned parties.[30] Since the standards represent a common agreement of the participating parties on very specific details, the fact that they are the product of regulatory cooperation gives them authority. Moreover, they certainly entail commitments in accordance with good faith.[31] Thus, although no legal consequences would be attached to a non-implementation of a global standard in the regulatory practice of a party, this does not mean that the standards are not followed in practice, or that members were completely free to ignore them.[32] Indeed, for all international law – hard or soft – diplomatic and moral pressure is evaluated as an important enforcement mechanism.[33]

Global standards are certainly atypical acts when they are assessed from an international law perspective. In international law, agreements only acquire legally binding force where the parties intentionally determine the agreement to be binding, and to confer rights and obligations on the parties governed by international law.[34] The traditional sources of law used at the international level are reflected in Article 38(1) of the Statute of the International Court of Justice, encompassing international conventions, international custom, the general principles of law, as well as – to a limited extent, serving interpretative purposes – case law and scholarly writings.[35] Nevertheless, this binary or absolute perspective on international law has not prevented the rise of a variety of measures used by actors on the international plane. Although not conforming to the definition of traditional international law, these measures do have (indirect) legal effects.[36] In the practice of international relations and the scholarly account thereof, the boundaries between law and non-law are not as clear as Article 38(1) of the ICJ Statute implies. This growing tendency to depart from

[29] Röhl (2007) 319.

[30] Röhl (2007) 321.

[31] A Boyle, 'Some Reflections on the Relationship of Treaties and Soft Law' (1999) 48 *International and Comparative Law Quarterly* 901, 902.

[32] O Schachter, 'The Twilight Existence of Nonbinding International Agreements' (1977) 71 *The American Journal of International Law* 296, 300.

[33] C Chinkin, 'The Challenge of Soft Law: Development and Change in International Law' (1989) 38 *International and Comparative Law Quarterly* 850, 866.

[34] Schachter (1977) 296.

[35] Statute of the International Court of Justice, 18 April 1946, art 38(1).

[36] A Peters and I Pagotto, 'Soft Law as a New Mode of Governance: A Legal Perspective', New Modes of Governance Project Paper 04/D11 (2006) 7.

traditional legal measures goes hand in hand with the diversification of actors and forms of interaction on a global level.[37]

From a relativist view on international law it is acknowledged that there is a whole range of instruments, spanning from binding law in the strict sense, to measures having legal effects although they are not legally binding.[38] According to this argumentation there is a scale of legal normativity. 'Soft law' begins where measures convey fewer obligations on its drafters than traditional 'hard' law, either through a diminished binding power, less precision and/or the lack of delegation of authority for its interpretation and implementation.[39] However, in order for a non-legally binding norm to qualify as soft law, it needs to introduce a certain obligation or be subject to an enforcement mechanism,[40] beyond mere political agreement.[41] A large variety of instruments such as guidelines, principles, codes of practice, recommendations or declarations can fall within this remit.[42] In this regard Shelton defines soft law broadly as 'any written international instrument, other than a treaty, containing principles, norms, standards, or other statements of expected behavior'.[43] Diverging from regulation through 'hard law' means less sovereignty costs,[44] more flexibility in terms of amendment,[45] and a larger likelihood of compromise.[46] Moreover, where standards are established in informal regulatory cooperation, soft law is often the only available regulatory tool, as the actors lack the capacity to enter into binding commitments under international law.[47] The fact that soft law generally escapes the formal internal ratification processes means that the use of soft law in contrast to hard law allows for speedy reactions to developments in science, technology or the environment, which is highly advantageous in risk regulation.[48] Yet the downside to using international soft law as a faster and more flexible regulatory tool is precisely the evasion of democratic control and accountability functions, as exercised through the ratification procedure.[49]

[37] See: Section II A.

[38] Goldmann (2010) 671. This relativist view on law and the existence of soft law is contested. See Chapter 1.

[39] K Abbott, R Keohane, A Moravcsik, A Slaughter and D Snidal, 'The Concept of Legalization' (2000) 54 *International Organization* 401.

[40] F Terpan, 'Soft Law in the European Union – The Changing Nature of EU Law' (2015) 21 *European Law Journal* 68.

[41] K Abbott and D Snidal, 'Hard and Soft Law in International Governance' (2000) 54 *International Organization* 421, 422.

[42] A Aust, *Handbook of International Law*, 2nd edn (Cambridge: Cambridge University Press, 2010) 11.

[43] D Shelton, 'Soft Law', in D Armstrong (ed), *Routledge Handbook of International Law* (Oxon: Routledge, 2009) 69.

[44] Abbott and Snidal (2000) 436ff.

[45] Boyle (1999) 903.

[46] Kerwer (2005) 616.

[47] M Knauff, Der Regelungsverbund: Recht und Soft Law im Mehrebenensystem (Tübingen: Mohr Siebeck, 2010) 286.

[48] G Majone, 'Science and Trans-Science in Standard Setting' (1984) 9 *Science, Technology, & Human Values* 15, 19; Abbott and Snidal (2000) 442.

[49] Boyle (1999) 903; Goldmann (2010) 668.

Additionally, although global standards might be 'soft law' measures in international law, this qualification may change again with the implementation of these standards in the regulatory framework of a state or region, where the standards are implemented in legislation or used to further define legislative requirements.[50] In such cases, standards 'would be closer to "hard law" than to "soft law"'.[51] Even without legislative enforcement, in some regulated areas it is also common for private companies to certify and audit the compliance of certain standards. NGOs can function as watchdogs, contributing to the fact that standards that were originally non-mandatory may become subject to complex control structures, making them less voluntary and subject to private enforcement.[52]

II. THE INSTITUTIONAL LANDSCAPE OF GLOBAL STANDARD-SETTING

Global standard-setting is a multifaceted phenomenon: where public administrative regulators and private interest bodies can be identified as main actors in the setting of regulatory standards, the institutional structures in the context of which these actors interact demonstrate a large degree of diversity. New forms of regulatory mechanisms such as non-hierarchical cooperations of a variety of actors replace state-centred forms of regulation by binding law.[53] Shifts to standard-setting at a global level leads to the regulation of risk in a 'polycentric regime',[54] where power is not concentrated in one state but where 'state and non-state actors are both regulators and regulated'[55] in complex interactions on multiple levels of government and with a variety of actors.

A. The Actors Engaged in Global Standard-Setting

Global standard-setting not only deviates from traditional international law in the sense that standards are soft law, but also the actors involved in standard-setting are atypical when compared to traditional state-centred international law. National regulators and private parties are the main actors in the global standard-setting arena. The increasing influence of global standards can thus be seen as epitomising the shift from 'government' to 'governance'.[56] Regulation

[50] Knauff (2010) 287.
[51] Morais (2001–2002) 781.
[52] Kerwer (2005) 618.
[53] M Ruffert, Die Globalisierung als Herausforderung an das Öffentliche Recht (Stuttgart: Boorberg, 2004) 27 and 29.
[54] J Black, 'Constructing and Contesting Legitimacy and Accountability in Polycentric Regulatory Regimes' (2008) 2 *Regulation & Governance* 137.
[55] Ibid, 137.
[56] See generally: J Rosenau and E Czempiel (eds), *Governance without Government: Order and Change in World Politics* (Cambridge: Cambridge University Press, 1992); K van Kersbergen and

takes place beyond the formal legal authority of a nation state or a regional organisation like the EU,[57] where the regulatory processes may be permeable to the participation of actors other than governments and their administrative counterparts, moving towards increasing participation by private stakeholders.[58] This changing approach to regulation has been observed internationally,[59] within the EU,[60] and also in national contexts.[61]

Within the jurisdiction of a state (or regional organisation like the EU), it is generally the competence of the executive to establish the standards in question, due to its power to 'control, from day-to-day, the instruments of coercion, wealth and information'.[62] As became visible with regard to pharmaceutical regulation in the EU discussed in Chapter 1, the legislator will determine the policy framework and often also the procedures to come to regulatory decision, but it will be the task of the administration, often in the form of unelected expert bodies, to decide on the acceptable risk in setting a specific standard.[63] The setting of regulatory standards can thus be qualified as a form of 'executive rule making'.[64] However, administrative power only comprises activities within the legal order of this jurisdiction.[65] In this regard, a trend away from regulation in nation states towards the evolution of international governance structures can be observed.[66]

F van Waarden, '"Governance" as a Bridge between Disciplines: Cross-Disciplinary Inspiration Regarding Shifts in Governance and Problems of Governability, Accountability and Legitimacy' (2004) 43 *European Journal of Political Research* 143.

[57] J Rosenau, 'Governance, Order and Change in World Politics', in J Rosenau and E Czempiel (eds), *Governance without Government: Order and Change in World Politics* (Cambridge: Cambridge University Press, 1992) 5.

[58] M Shapiro, 'Administrative Law Unbounded: Reflections on Government and Governance' (2001) 8 *Indiana Journal of Legal Studies* 369.

[59] Shapiro (2001); Rosenau (1992).

[60] See eg: B Kohler-Koch and R Eising (eds), *The Transformation of Governance in the European Union* (London: Routledge, 1999). In European scholarship the debate has largely taken place in terms of 'New Governance': G de Búrca and J Scott (eds), *Law and New Governance in the EU and the US* (Oxford: Hart Publishing, 2006); M Dawson, *New Governance and the Transformation of European Law: Coordinating EU Social Law and Policy* (Cambridge: Cambridge University Press, 2011); J Scott and D Trubek, 'Mind the Gap: Law and New Approaches to Governance in the European Union' (2003) 8 *European Law Journal* 1.

[61] See eg: J Kooiman (ed), *Modern Governance: New Government – Society Interactions* (London: Sage, 1993); R Rhodes, *Understanding Governance: Policy Networks, Reflexivity and Accountability* (Buckingham: Open University Press, 1997).

[62] Curtin (2009) 20.

[63] Fisher (2010) 19.

[64] H Hofmann, 'Dealing with Trans-Territorial Executive Rule-Making' (2013) 78 *Missouri Law Review* 423.

[65] C Tietje, *Internationalisiertes Verwaltungshandeln* (Berlin: Duncker & Humblot GmbH, 2001) 174ff.

[66] See eg: C Möllers, 'Transnationale Behördenkooperation – Verfassungs- und Völkerrechtliche Probleme Transnationaler Administrativer Standardsetzung' (2005) 65 *Zeitschrift für ausländisches öffentliches Recht und Völkerrecht* 351; J Tallberg, 'Delegation to Supranational Institutions: Why, How, and With What Consequence' (2002) 25 *West European Politics* 23; Hofmann (2013); Tietje (2001); van Kersbergen and van Waarden (2004).

Administrative regulators such as national civil servants increasingly cooperate with their counterparts on the global level.[67] The cooperation of administrative bodies at the global level is a phenomenon that was theorised as 'transgovernmental relations' in 1974 by Keohane and Nye, defined as 'sets of direct interactions among sub-units of different governments that are not controlled or closely guided by the policies of the cabinets or chief executives of those governments'.[68] This stands in contrast to the traditional approach to external relations of states, which used to be centred around 'one central authority, the foreign office and its diplomatic service',[69] where the actors usually were Heads of States, government officials or embassy staff.[70] An additional 'regulatory layer' is added to the traditional bilateral, multilateral and constitutional layers of international law.[71] This can occur in various degrees of formalisation: from cooperation in the form of existing international organisations, through the establishing of new international organisations with an explicit regulatory mandate, to interaction in fora that are not formally established under international law. In this setting, risk regulation standards developed through the cooperation of national regulators challenge the conventional structures of international law. States are 'disaggregating'[72] from unitary actors to actions taken by legislative, judicial and executive actors separately, as they cooperate with their corresponding partners in other states. The shift of regulatory power to the global level has thus led to a 'global administrative space',[73] characterised by the complex interaction between different institutions on different levels (local, national, regional and global), often resorting to non-binding forms of organisation and decision-making.

Next to the increase of cooperation of regulatory bodies, private parties are also increasingly involved in regulatory decision-making and can act as (self-) regulators.[74] In this regard, German scholars speak of 'korporative Staatsgewalt',

[67] S Cassese, 'Administrative Law without the State? The Challenge of Global Regulation' (2005) 37 *International Law and Politics* 663, 681; M Ruffert, '§17 Rechtsquellen und Rechtsschichten des Verwaltungsrechts', in W Hoffmann-Riem, E Schmidt-Aßmann and A Voßkuhle (eds), *Grundlagen des Verwaltungsrechts Band I* (München: Beck, 2012).

[68] R Keohane and J Nye, 'Transgovernmental Relations and International Organizations' (1974) 27 *World Politics* 39, 43.

[69] C Möllers, 'European Governance: Meaning and Value of a Concept' (2006) 43 *Common Market Law Review* 313. See also: Möllers (2005), 352ff.

[70] J Pauwelyn, 'Informal International Lawmaking: Framing the Concept and Research Questions', in J Pauwelyn, R Wessel and J Wouters (eds), *Informal International Lawmaking* (Oxford: Oxford University Press, 2012) 19. In the Informal International Lawmaking project, this deviation from the traditional actors in international law is termed 'actor informality'.

[71] J Weiler, 'The Geology of International Law – Governance, Democracy and Legitimacy' (2004) 64 *Zeitschrift für ausländisches öffentliches Recht und Völkerrecht* 547, 549.

[72] A Slaughter, 'The Real New World Order' (1997) 76 *Foreign Affairs* 183, 184.

[73] N Krisch and B Kingsbury, 'Introduction: Global Governance and Global Administrative Law in the International Legal Order' (2006) 17 *The European Journal of International Law* 1, 1.

[74] F Cafaggi, 'Rethinking Private Regulation in the European Regulatory Space', European University Institute Department of Law, EUI Working Papers Law No 2006/13, (2006) 2.

which can be translated as 'corporative state authority', alluding to organised private interest as a new weight in the balance of power of exercising state functions.[75] The rise of private actors, be they commercial or non-commercial, has also been discussed in several policy areas at the international level.[76] Fisher for example argues that the involvement of private actors in EU environmental law has evolved from occasional cases to 'a non-negotiable requirement of regulatory action'.[77] This also holds true with regard to standard-setting. In the EU and on the global level, private bodies like public interest non-governmental organisations (NGOs), businesses and organisations in various forms either participate in public standard-setting processes, or have arisen as a source of standards.[78]

Regulation (co-)developed by the respective experts is suggested to be efficient and effective. Private actors have increasingly established themselves as important participants in standard-setting as they provide the required expertise and their participation brings the decision-making closer to the subjects of the standards.[79] Often expertise is located at the level of the regulatee, such as a specific industry sector.[80] Since standards are voluntary measures, in principle their impact is dependent on whether they represent the current technical and scientific state of the art.[81] Thus, the aim of enhancing compliance with the standards can also lead to the involvement of private actors.[82] Overall, in the regulation of science and technology, purely hierarchical regulation through public bodies is decreasing.[83] Rather, '... the very distinction between governmental and non-governmental has become blurred, since the real decision-making process now continually involves, and combines, public and private actors'.[84]

[75] H Derderer, *Korporative Staatsgewalt – Integration Privat Organisierter Interessen in die Ausübung von Staatsfunktionen. Zugleich eine Rekonstruktion der Legitimationsdogmatik* (Tübingen: Mohr Siebeck, 2004).

[76] See: C Cutler, V Haufler and T Porter (eds), *Private Authority and International Affairs* (Albany: State University of New York Press, 1995).

[77] E Fisher, 'Unpacking the Toolbox: Or Why the Public/Private Divide is Important in EC Environmental Law', Florida State University College of Law – Public Law and Legal Theory Working Paper No 35 (August 2001), 18.

[78] Schepel (2005); Peters, Koechlin and Fenner Zinkernagel (2009).

[79] Peters, Koechlin and Fenner Zinkernagel (2009) 3; F Cafaggi and A Renda, 'Public and Private Regulation – Mapping the Labyrinth', Centre for European Policy Studies, CEPS Working Document No 370 (October 2012).

[80] Cafaggi (2006) 5; Cafaggi and Renda (2012) 5.

[81] Kerwer (2005) 618.

[82] Cafaggi (2006) 7.

[83] S Borrás, 'Three Tensions in the Governance of Science and Technology', in D Levi-Faur (ed), *The Oxford Handbook of Governance* (Oxford: Oxford University Press, 2012) 433.

[84] Shapiro (2001) 370.

B. A Typology of Global Standard-Setting Bodies

In the risk regulation context, four types of global standard-setting bodies can be distinguished:

I) international organisations,
II) transnational regulatory networks,
III) private standard-setting bodies, and
IV) public-private partnerships.[85]

The first two types of bodies are of a public nature, as their members are state representatives or representatives of public regulatory authorities: in the case of international organisations the actors are usually government officials, and in transnational regulatory networks, representatives of regulatory bodies cooperate in informal structures. On the other end of the public-private spectrum, purely private bodies (type III) set up by non-governmental actors such as companies, associations or NGOs also engage in global standard-setting. Finally, standard-setting bodies may be characterised by a collaboration of public and private actors in public-private partnerships (type IV). Such bodies transcend the traditional classification in public or private terms and are established in various forms.

i. International Organisations

Standard-setting can take place under the auspices of traditional international organisations which progressively take over administrative tasks, as well as their more traditional mandate of 'high politics'. International organisations find their legal basis in a treaty agreed upon by subjects of international law, namely authorised representatives of a sovereign state or international organisations. This treaty basis forms their pivotal defining element as international organisations. It can provide them with international legal personality, which enables the retention of rights and duties subject to international law, such as the right to bring claims or to enter into treaties.[86]

[85] See also: Kerwer (2005) 624ff; Röhl (2007) 321f; S Wheatley, 'Democratic Governance beyond the State: The Legitimacy of Non-State Actors as Standard-Setters', in A Peters, L Koechlin, T Förster and G Fenner Zinkernagel (eds), *Non-State Actors as Standard-Setters* (Cambridge: Cambridge University Press, 2009) 219. For a similar categorisation, however, with regard to global regulatory bodies in general: B Kingsbury and R Stewart, 'Legitimacy and Accountability in Global Regulatory Governance: The Emerging Global Administrative Law and the Design and Operation of Administrative Tribunals of International Organizations', in K Papanikolaou and M Hiskaki (eds), *International Administrative Tribunals in a Changing World* (London: Esperia, 2008).

[86] International Court of Justice, *Reparations for Injuries Suffered in the Service of the United Nations Case* (1949) ICJ Reports 174, 179. See eg: J Klabbers, *An Introduction to International Institutional Law*, 3rd Edn (Cambridge: Cambridge University Press, 2015).

An example of an international organisation that sets risk regulation standards is the Organisation for Economic Co-operation and Development (OECD), which currently comprises 37 member countries.[87] Since the late 1970s the OECD has developed guidelines for the testing of chemicals through the cooperation of experts from specialised authorities of the member countries.[88] Moreover, through its Environmental Directorate the OECD has developed the Principles of Good Laboratory Practice (GLP),[89] aiming to ensure the quality and validity of chemical safety testing data. According to the OECD the GLP is 'a managerial concept covering the organisational process and the conditions under which laboratory studies are planned, performed, monitored, recorded and reported'.[90] These non-binding principles become highly relevant in risk regulation as many jurisdictions, including the EU,[91] require chemical testing facilities to comply with these standards where they carry out studies required in the context of assessment and authorisation procedures for products such as pharmaceuticals, food additives or pesticides.[92]

While the OECD is formed by a treaty amongst states,[93] international organisations are also capable of forming separate standard-setting bodies, as exemplified by the Codex Alimentarius, a subsidiary organ of the Food and Agriculture Organization (FAO) and the World Health Organization (WHO).[94] It was established through resolutions of the FAO Conference in 1961 and of the

[87] For a list of members see: www.oecd.org/about/membersandpartners/.

[88] OECD, OECD Series on Testing and Assessment Number 1 – Guidance Document for the Development of OECD Guidelines for the Testing of Chemicals, ENV/JM/MONO(2006)20/REV1. For a detailed account of the process of developing the OECD Chemicals Testing Guidelines see: M Herberg, 'Global Governance Networks in Action: The Development of Toxicological Test Methods at the OECD', in O Dilling, M Herberg and G Winter (eds), *Transnational Administrative Rule-Making – Performance, Legal Effects and Legitimacy* (Oxford: Hart Publishing, 2011).

[89] OECD, OECD Series on Principles of Good Laboratory Practice and Compliance Monitoring Number 1 – OECD Principles on Good Laboratory Practice ENV/MC/CHEM(98)17.

[90] Ibid, 7.

[91] See: European Commission, EU Legislation with Good Laboratory Practice (GLP) Provision, March 2016, Ref Ares(2016)2466364 – 27/05/2016.

[92] For a discussion of how the costs of compliance affect the research process: G Bache, M Flear and T Hervey, 'The Defining Features of the European Union's Approach to Regulating New Health Technologies', in M Flear, A Farrell, T Hervey and T Murphy (eds), *European Law and New Health Technologies* (Oxford: Oxford University Press, 2013) 27.

[93] OECD, Convention on the Organisation for Economic Co-operation and Development of 14 December 1960.

[94] For more detail on the Codex Alimentarius Commission and its standard-setting activities see: M Masson-Matthee, *The Codex Alimentarius Commission and Its Standards* (The Hague: TMC Asser Press, 2007); A Herwig, 'The Contribution of Global Administrative Law to Enhancing the Legitimacy of the Codex Alimentarius Commission', in O Dilling, M Herberg and G Winter (eds), *Transnational Administrative Rule-Making – Performance, Legal Effects and Legitimacy* (Oxford: Hart Publishing, 2011); R Pereira, 'Why Would International Administrative Activity Be Any Less Legitimate? – A Study of the Codex Alimentarius Commission', in A von Bogdandy, R Wolfrum, J von Bernstorff, P Dann and M Goldmann (eds), *The Exercise of Public Authority by International Institutions: Advancing International Institutional Law* (Heidelberg: Springer, 2010); D Bevilaqua, 'The Codex Alimentarius Commission and its Influence on European and National Food Policy' (2006) 1 *European Food and Feed Law Review* 3.

WHO in 1963.[95] Today, the Codex Alimentarius Commission has 188 member countries and, additionally, the EU as a member organisation.[96] Through its Joint Food Standards Programme it develops the Codex Alimentarius, which is a compilation of food standards related to issues like food safety and quality, labelling and the classification of food.[97]

Although an international organisation by definition can only have subjects of international law – states and (other) international organisations – as members, this does not prevent private interest representatives from taking part in the standard-setting process. For example, the OECD leaves room in its standard-setting process for non-state experts to participate in meetings. The OECD has established a broad network of experts, consisting of participants from industry, trade unions as well as environmental and animal welfare NGOs, that provide input for the proposed new Test Guidelines.[98] The Codex Alimentarius Commission has opened its operation to private interests, as it was one of the first organisations to invite international NGOs as observers to sessions of the Commission and its organs, providing them with the right to speak and to obtain documents.[99] Thus, although international organisations do not facilitate the participation of those with private interests as full members, they increasingly open up the participation of private parties through different channels, and hence leave room for influence by private parties.

ii. Transnational Regulatory Networks

Whereas international organisations have been introduced as the classic format of institutionalisation at a global level, less formalised bodies are gaining increasing importance as fora for international regulatory cooperation. In these cases cooperation is not framed through the founding of traditional international organisations, but rather in the form of an informal network. Regulatory actors take part in their administrative function rather than as representatives of the state.

The network as an organisational format has attracted plenty of scholarly attention in political science and especially in the field of international

[95] WHO/FAO, Statutes of the Codex Alimentarius Commission (Adopted in 1961 by the 11th Session of the FAO Conference and in 1963 by the 16th Session of the World Health Assembly, Revised in 1966 and 2006), in Codex Alimentarius Commission, Procedural Manual – Twenty-third edition, Rome, 2015, 4–6.

[96] See: http://www.fao.org/fao-who-codexalimentarius/about-codex/members/pt/.

[97] A full list of the Codex Standards can be found at: http://www.fao.org/fao-who-codexalimentarius/codex-texts/list-standards/en/.

[98] OECD, OECD Series on Testing and Assessment Number 1 – Guidance Document for the Development of OECD Guidelines for the Testing of Chemicals (as revised in 2009), ENV/JM/MONO(2006)20/REV1, 24.

[99] Masson-Matthee (2007) 27ff; M Livermore, 'Authority and Legitimacy of Global Governance: Deliberation, Institutional Differentiation, and the Codex Alimentarius' (2006) 81 *New York University Law Review* 766.

relations,[100] but also increasingly in legal literature.[101] However, what exactly constitutes a network is not uniformly defined. Börzel, establishing a common denominator, defined a network as 'a set of relatively stable relationships which are of non-hierarchical and interdependent nature linking a variety of actors, who share common interests with regard to a policy, and who exchange resources to pursue these shared interest acknowledging that co-operation is the best way to achieve common goals'.[102]

Networks thus are understood to constitute a way in which global interactions can be structured without legal formalisation. Transnational regulatory networks can be characterised by the following criteria:

(i) in contrast to traditional international organisations, participating representatives are officials of regulatory bodies working in the area concerned, as opposed to diplomats or high level government representatives;[103] and
(ii) the relationships between actors are not legally formalised but adhere to a loose, yet frequently reoccurring interactional format with different degrees of formalisation;[104]
(iii) the members are equal partners and no formal hierarchy applies;[105]
(iv) the members share resources to reach a common goal;[106]
(v) the network does not follow a strict organisational plan, predetermining the institutional structure, but is free to evolve over time, adapting to the needs of the parties.[107]

One example of a transnational regulatory network engaged in the setting of global standards in the area of pharmaceutical regulation is the Pharmaceutical Inspection Co-operation Scheme (PIC/S).[108] PIC/S is a network of national regulatory authorities which develops Good Manufacturing Practice (GMP) standards, and aims at harmonising standards and improving cooperation in GMP inspections. The founding agreement of the network makes clear that

[100] Networks have been subject to scholarly debate since the 1990s with a large amount of literature discussing their prospects. For an introduction see eg: A Slaughter, *A New World Order* (Princeton: Princeton University Press, 2004); A Slaughter and D Zaring, 'Networking Goes International: An Update' (2006) 2 *Annual Review of Law and Social Science* 211; F van Waarden, 'Dimensions and Types of Policy Networks' (1992) 21 *European Journal of Political Research* 29.

[101] For example: K Ladeur, 'Towards a Legal Theory of Supranationality – The Viability of the Network Concept' (1997) 3 *European Law Journal* 3; K Raustiala, 'The Architecture of International Cooperation: Transgovernmental Networks and the Future of International Law' (2002-2003) 43 *Virginia Journal of International Law* 1.

[102] T Börzel, 'Organizing Babylon – On the Different Conceptions of Policy Networks' (1998) 76 *Public Administration* 253, 254.

[103] Slaughter and Zaring (2006) 215; Raustiala (2002–2003) 4–5.

[104] Raustiala (2002–2003) 5; Börzel (1998) 254.

[105] Börzel (1998) 254.

[106] Börzel (1998) 254; Slaughter (2004) 186.

[107] Ladeur (1997) 48.

[108] Information is available via picscheme.org or www.ema.europa.eu/en/partners-networks/international-activities/multilateral-organisations-initiatives/pharmaceutical-inspection-co-operation-scheme.

although PIC/S is established as an association under the Swiss Civil Code, it is not an international organisation, but a legally non-binding agreement between national authorities with equal rights and obligations for all members.[109]

iii. Private Standard-Setting Bodies

Private self-regulation of certain industry sectors by means of standardisation can be noticed in sectors of high technical complexity, and might substitute, complement or even precede regulation through law.[110] More and more private bodies exercise tasks on an international level than traditionally would have been attributed to the public sphere.[111] Global private standard-setting bodies can be set up by associations of companies, such as the Global Good Agricultural Practices (Global GAP) which is an initiative set up by retailers establishing food safety and production standards.[112] NGOs are also active in standard-setting as exemplified in the area of environmental protection by the Forest Stewardship Council (FSC), a non-governmental organisation encompassing stakeholders such as the World Wildlife Fund (WWF) and businesses like Tetra Pak, enacting standards for forest management.[113]

The most well-known private source of global standards is the International Organization for Standardization (ISO), which is composed of over 160 national standard-setting organisations,[114] working in a wide variety of economic, technical and scientific fields.[115] One area of ISO activity is standardisation in the area of medical device quality management systems (ISO 13485).[116] The ISO has civil personality as an association under the Swiss Civil Code.[117] It is a private standard-setting body, consisting of various – mostly private – national standards organisations.[118]

[109] Pharmaceutical Inspection Co-operation scheme (PIC/S), PIC/S 1/95 (Rev. 6) 12 November 2019, available via: picscheme.org/docview/2147.

[110] Delimatsis (2015a); M Cantero Gamito and H Micklitz (eds), *The Role of the EU in Transnational Legal Ordering – Standards, Contracts and Codes* (Cheltenham: Edward Elgar, 2020).

[111] For more detail on private standard-setting bodies see: A Marx, M Maertens, J Swinnen and J Wouters, *Private Standards And Global Governance – Economic, Legal and Political Perspectives* (Cheltenham: Edward Elgar Publishing Ltd, 2012); Peters, Koechlin, Förster and Fenner Zinkernagel (2009); Schepel (2005).

[112] N Hachez and J Wouters, 'A Glimpse at the Democratic Legitimacy of Private Standards: Assessing the Public Accountability of Global G.A.P.' (2011) 14 *Journal of International Economic Law* 677; C Lin, 'Public-Private Regime Interactions in Global Food Safety Governance' (2014a) 69 *Food and Drug Law Journal* 143.

[113] E Meidinger, 'The Administrative Law of Global Private-Public Regulation: the Case of Forestry' (2006) 17 *European Journal of International Law* 47.

[114] www.iso.org/about-us.html.

[115] See: Röhl (2007) 322ff. For a closer analysis of the legitimacy of ISO standards in the field of nanotechnology see: E Kica and D Bowman, 'Transnational Governance Arrangements: Legitimate Alternatives to Regulating Nanotechnologie?' (2013) 7 *NanoEthics* 69.

[116] International Organisation for Standardization, ISO 13485:2016 Medical devices – Quality management systems – Requirements for regulatory purposes.

[117] International Organisation for Standardization, ISO Statutes, 19th Edition, 2018, art 22(1).

[118] A detailed description of the particular organizational character of ISO can be found here: E Shamir-Borer, 'Legitimacy without Authority in Global Standardization Governance: The Case

iv. Public-Private Partnerships

Whereas the types of standard-setting bodies introduced so far can be clearly characterised as either public or private standard-setting bodies, this separation is blurred where standards arise from the cooperation of public and private actors. Such forms of cooperation between state and non-state actors are subsumed under the term 'public-private partnership' (PPP).[119] Their characteristic trait is the joint decision-making of public actors and private actors, which entails the sharing of rights and responsibilities between these actors.[120] PPPs do not correspond to one specific form of legal establishment and occur in various organisational forms, complicating the positioning of the term in traditional legal categories.[121] With regard to membership, public parties can be either regulatory bodies or representatives of governments. Private members may be for-profit organisations or non-profit private interest groups like NGOs.

On the global level, PPPs are often used in the context of development aid or the promotion of health policy. Partnerships like the Global Fund to Fight AIDS, Malaria and Tuberculosis, or the Global Alliance for Vaccine Immunization (GAVI Alliance), which promotes global health through supporting the research and development of pharmaceutical products for neglected diseases, or improving access to vaccines, recently also attracted the attention of legal scholars.[122] Going beyond policy promotion tasks, or the distribution of funds, public-private partnerships also increasingly engage in regulatory tasks and specifically in standard-setting.[123] An example in the area of sports law is the World Anti-Doping Agency (WADA), set up as a foundation under Swiss law, which encompasses governments and private representatives of the Olympic Movement.

of the International Organization for Standardization (ISO)', in S Cassese, B Carotti, L Casini, E Cavalieri and E MacDonald (eds), *Global Administrative Law: The Casebook*, 3rd ednn (2012, IRPA-IILJ, ebook).

[119] For a general overview on public-private partnerships: Börzel and Risse (2007); P Vaillancourt Rosenau (ed), *Public-Private Policy Partnerships* (Cambridge: MIT Press, 2000); M Schäferhoff, S Campe and C Kaan, 'Transnational Public-Private Partnerships in International Relations: Making Sense of Concepts, Research Frameworks, and Results' (2009) 11 *International Studies Review* 451.

[120] I Kaul, 'Exploring the Space between Markets and States: Global Public-Private Partnerships', in I Kaul and P Conceicao (eds), *The New Public Finance: Responding to Global Challenges* (Oxford: Oxford University Press, 2006) 222.

[121] K Abbott, 'Public Private Partnership', in R. Wolfrum (ed), *The Max Planck Encyclopedia of Public International Law* (Oxford: University Press Oxford, 2016), article last updated February 2008, available via: opil.ouplaw.com/home/EPIL.

[122] L Clarke, 'The Exercise of Public Power over Global Health through Public-Private Partnerships and the Question of Responsibility Under International Law' (2011) 105 *Proceedings of the Annual Meeting of the American Society of International Law* 96; G Burci, 'Public/Private Partnerships in the Public Health Sector' (2009) 6 *International Organizations Law Review* 359; D Aziz, 'Global Public-Private Partnerships in International Law' (2012) 2 *Asian Journal of International Law* 339.

[123] Peters, Koechlin and Fenner Zinkernagel (2009) 2; L Koechlin and R Calland, 'Standard Setting at the Cutting Edge: An Evidence-Based Typology for Multi-stakeholder Initiatives', in A Peters, L Koechlin, T Förster and G Fenner Zinkernagel (eds), *Non-State Actors as Standard-Setters* (Cambridge: Cambridge University Press, 2009) 84–112; Kaul (2006) 233.

It sets standards with regard to prohibited substances and their detection, which in turn influences the laws of its member countries.[124] Another example is the International Labour Organisation (ILO), a UN agency where governments, workers and employers agree on labour standards.[125] The International Council for Harmonisation of Technical Requirements for Pharmaceuticals for Human Use (International Council for Harmonisation, ICH), the most important standard-setting initiative in the area of pharmaceutical regulation, which will be examined in this book, is also a public-private partnership.[126]

Generally, a public-private partnership can either occur in an organisation legally established in national or international law, or through a cooperative process where public and private actors collaborate but do not form a legally established organisation. This means that in order to identify a public-private partnership, one has to look beyond the question of legal establishment of a body and identify whether it is characterised by the cooperation of public and private actors. Thus, even where a body is established as a private foundation under national law, it can be a public-private partnership depending on its membership, institutional structure and decision-making process. This is exemplified by WADA, which is established as a foundation under Swiss law.[127] Public-private partnerships organised as networks have to be distinguished from the transnational regulatory networks (like the PIC/S) on the basis of their membership.[128] Whereas the actors in transnational regulatory networks are exclusively public officials, the PPPs that are organised as networks are characterised by the collaboration between public officials and private interest representatives.

III. THE INTERPLAY BETWEEN GLOBAL STANDARDS AND EU RISK REGULATION

Standards developed in global standard-setting bodies are integrated into EU policies concerning the internal market especially in the context of risk regulation.[129] Wouters and Verhoeven for example identify influences on EU law of standards set by the Codex Alimentarius Commission, the International Office of Epizootics, and the Secretariat of the International Plant Protection Convention, but also in the regulation of financial as opposed to product risk, for example by the Basel Committee on Banking Supervision, the Financial

[124] L Casini, 'Global Hybrid Public-Private Bodies: The World Anti-Doping Agency (WADA)' (2009) 6 *International Organizations Law Review* 421.

[125] International Labour Organization (ILO), Constitution of the International Labour Organisation (ILO), 1 April 1919. See further: Börzel and Risse (2007).

[126] See: Chapter 3.

[127] Casini (2009) 430.

[128] See: Section II B ii.

[129] Hofmann (2017).

Action Task Force, as well as the United Nations Economic Commission for Europe.[130] Moreover, global standards are not merely implemented in the EU, with the EU as a passive recipient, but European administrative bodies also actively participate in forming regulatory measures on the global level.

A. The European Union's Reliance on Global Standards

Although the implementation of global standards in the EU has certainly increased in the era of globalisation, it is not a new phenomenon. In the *Beer Purity* case of 1984 the Court of Justice of the European Union obliged Member States to take into account 'the findings of international scientific research, and, in particular the work of the Community's Scientific Committee for Food, the Codex Alimentarius Committee of the FAO and the World Health Organisation'.[131] The obligation to integrate the standards set by a global body concerned with foodstuffs, the Codex Alimentarius Commission, into the risk regulation within the Member States shows that the Court realised early on that regulatory systems – global, European and national – do not function in isolation.

Nowadays the obligation to take account of global standards is deeply rooted in various legal measures of the EU. For example, Article 5(3) of the EU's General Food Law sets out that international standards need to be taken into consideration when passing or amending EU legislation in this field.[132] The preamble of the REACH Regulation for chemicals also states that the European Chemicals Agency should, on the one hand, contribute to global harmonisation initiatives and, on the other hand, take international standards into account.[133] With regard to pharmaceuticals, the preamble of Regulation 726/2004 establishing the EMA envisages a role for 'the Agency to participate actively in international scientific dialogue and to develop certain activities that will be necessary, in particular regarding international scientific harmonisation and technical cooperation …'.[134]

[130] Wouters and Verhoeven (2006).

[131] Case 178/84 *Commission v Germany*, ECLI:EU:C:1987:126, para 52. See also: E Vos and C Joerges, 'Structures of Transnational Governance and their Legitimacy', in J Vervaele (ed), *Compliance and Enforcement of European Union Law* (London: Kluwer, 1999) 90.

[132] Regulation (EC) No 178/2002 of the European Parliament and of the Council of 28 January 2002 laying down the general principles and requirements of food law, establishing the European Food Safety Authority, and laying down procedures in matters of food safety, [2002] OJ L31/1, art 5(3).

[133] Regulation (EC) No 1907/2006 of the European Parliament and of the Council of 18 December 2006 concerning the Registration, Evaluation, Authorisation and Restriction of Chemicals (REACH), establishing a European Chemicals Agency, [2006] OJ L396/1, Preamble para 109.

[134] Regulation (EC) No 726/2004 laying down Community procedures for the authorisation and supervision of medicinal products for human and veterinary use, and establishing a European Medicines Agency, and Regulation (EC) No 1394/2007 on advanced therapy medicinal products, [2004] OJ L136/1, preamble (27).

The important role of global standards in EU risk regulation is thus not only a momentary observation of a factual development, but also a longstanding policy promoted by the Court and incorporated into legislation. Instead of being a process that only materialises in the back-chambers of regulatory authorities, the incorporation of global standards is openly promoted in the EU. As the Commission stated: 'enhanced regulatory cooperation – both in order to promote equivalence or convergence (of rules, standards, testing and certification practices) internationally and to minimize unnecessary costs in regulation worldwide – is an important aspect of our trade relationships'.[135]

In this regard, the reference to international standards by the Sanitary and Phytosanitary (SPS) Agreement and the Technical Barriers to Trade (TBT) Agreement of the World Trade Organisation (WTO) has given international standards increased importance and influence.[136]

Article 3.1 of the SPS Agreement and Article 2.4 of the TBT Agreement promote these international standards through an obligation for WTO members to use them as a basis for measures they adopt.[137] Moreover under Article 3.2 of the SPS Agreement and Article 2.5 TBT Agreement, measures of the WTO members in conformity with international standards are presumed to be in accordance with WTO law.[138] Article 3.3 of the SPS Agreement allows the possibility of introducing or maintaining a high level of protection through a national measure in deviation from international standards to situations where this can either be scientifically justified or through a risk assessment and redetermination of the standard of protection in accordance with Article 5 of the SPS Agreement. It is argued that Article 3 of the SPS Agreement in essence makes standards set by the Codex Alimentarius obligatory, or at least *de facto* binding, due to the fact that diversion from these standards is extremely difficult or even impossible to scientifically substantiate.[139] This fosters adherence to international standards in the EU. Indeed, Masson-Matthee observed in her study

[135] European Commission, 'Trade, Growth and World Affairs – Trade Policy as a Core Component of the EU's 2020 Strategy', COM(2010) 612, 9 November 2010, 7.

[136] WTO, Agreement on the Application of Sanitary and Phytosanitary Measures, 15 April 1994, 1867 U.N.T.S. 493 (1994); WTO, Agreement on Technical Barriers to Trade, 15. April 15, 1994, 1868 U.N.T.S. 120 (1994). See: L Wallach, 'Accountable Governance in the Era of Globalization – The WTO, NAFTA and International Harmonization of Standards' (2001–2002) 50 *Kansas Law Review* 823; J Scott, 'International Trade and Environmental Governance: Relating Rules (and Standards) in the EU and WTO' (2004) 15 *European Journal of International Law* 307; M Mataija, 'Private standard setting in the TBT Agreement: control and recognition', in M Cantero Gamito and H Micklitz (eds), *The Role of the EU in Transnational Legal Ordering – Standards, Contracts and Codes* (Cheltenham: Edward Elgar, 2020) 135–54; Herwig (2011); Livermore (2006).

[137] See: Masson-Matthee (2007) 140ff.

[138] Scott (2004) 324; Masson-Matthee (2007) 153.

[139] D Bevilaqua, 'Global Food Safety Regulation and the Interplay between Global Standards and WTO Law: How to Close the Legitimacy Gap?', in M Eliantonio and C Cauffman (eds), *The Legitimacy of Standardisation as a Regulatory Technique: A Cross-Disciplinary and Multi-Level Analysis* (Cheltenham: Edward Elgar, 2020); Wouters and Verhoeven (2006) 250; Masson-Matthee (2007) 159ff.

of the Codex Alimentarius that EU secondary legislation, especially since the coming into force of the General Food Law, and the full membership of the EU in the Codex, 'frequently take Codex measures or their scientific basis into consideration, which has led to the adjustment of several EC measures'.[140]

Finally, the EU's resort to global standard-setting should also be seen in the context of efforts to address the decrease in consumer confidence faced by regulators, caused by several incidents of regulatory failure. In the EU, the BSE (bovine spongiform encephalopathy) crisis in particular has left consumers with distrust in the ability of public authorities to prevent the manifestation of risks.[141] Setting standards on the global level in this context can thus be viewed as an attempt to reassure the consumer that the standards set represent world-wide expertise as a sign of inclusiveness and quality.[142]

B. EU Bodies as Participants in Global Standard-Setting

Increasing scholarly attention is being paid to the role of the EU as 'global actor',[143] examining the EU as a power in global politics,[144] as well as the participation of the EU in international organisations.[145] Also the EU's influence on the forming of regulatory norms and governance in different policy areas is being analysed.[146] However, assessment from the perspective of regulatory

[140] Masson-Matthee (2007) 133. See also: E Vos and S Röttger-Wirtz, 'EU Food Law and the WTO: Trade, Science and Politics', in D Prévost, I Alexovičová and J Hillebrand Pohl (eds), *Restoring Trust in Trade: Liber Amicorum in Honour of Peter Van den Bossche* (Oxford: Hart Publishers, 2018).

[141] M Everson and E Vos, 'European Risk Governance in a Global Context', in E Vos (ed), *European Risk Governance – Its Science, its Inclusiveness and its Effectiveness*, Connex Report Series No 6 (2008) 7–36; Everson and Vos (2009).

[142] Specifically for the case of pharmaceuticals see: P Lezotre, *International Cooperation, Convergence and Harmonization of Pharmaceutical Regulations – A Global Perspective* (Oxford: Academic Press Elsevier, 2014) 173.

[143] M Cremona, 'The Union as Global Actor: Roles, Models and Identity' (2004) 4 *Common Market Law Review* 553; J Howorth, 'The EU as a Global Actor: Grand Strategy for a Global Grand Bargain?' (2010) 48 *Journal of Common Market Studies* 455; B van Vooren and R Wessel, 'The EU as Global Legal Actor', in B van Vooren and R Wessel (eds), *EU External Relations Law – Text, Cases and Materials* (Cambridge: Cambridge University Press, 2014).

[144] C Bretherton and J Vogler, *The European Union as Global Actor*, 2nd edn (Oxon: Routledge, 2006).

[145] P Eeckhout, *EU External Relations Law*, 2nd edn (Oxford: Oxford University Press, 2011) 222–31; J Wouters, J Odermatt and T Ramopoulos, 'The EU in the World of International Organizations: Diplomatic Aspirations, Legal Hurdles and Political Realities', Leuven Centre for Global Governance Studies, Working Paper 121, September 2013.

[146] D Bach and A Newman, 'The European Regulatory State and Global Public Policy: Micro-institutions, Macro-influence' (2007) 14 *Journal of European Public Policy* 827; B van Vooren, S Blockmans and J Wouters (eds), *The EU's Role in Global Governance – The Legal Dimension* (Oxford: Oxford University Press, 2013). The work of Joanne Scott on the extraterritorial application of European law is also relevant: J Scott, 'The New EU "Extraterritoriality"' (2014a) 51 *Common Market Law Review* 1343; J Scott, 'Extraterritoriality and Territorial Extension in EU Law' (2014) 62 *American Journal of Comparative Law* 87. For the EU's influence in standard-setting: Cantero Gamito and Micklitz (2020).

cooperation is largely under-theorised, and specifically an analysis of the EU bodies as global actors in regulatory cooperation, such as the setting of global standards is not well explored.[147]

Generally, the EU is able to establish external relations as Article 47 TEU confers international legal personality upon the Union. Several Treaty articles envisage international cooperation with third countries and international organisations.[148] For example, 168(3) TFEU provides: 'The Union and the Member States shall foster cooperation with third countries and the competent international organisations in the sphere of public health.' However, the competence for external relations is divided from a vertical perspective, between the EU and its Member States,[149] subject to the limitations set by the principle of conferral.[150] The competence for external action can be exclusive or shared and can follow explicitly or implicitly from the Treaty provision or from secondary legislation.[151] No Treaty provision deals explicitly with international standard-setting, which means that with regard to every specific standard-setting body, it will have to be established if the EU is competent to engage in external action and participate in the standard-setting process in the relevant policy field. Where the EU is competent to regulate certain products or processes in the internal market, the internal competences to set risk regulation standards following from the Treaty or secondary legislation can serve as a basis for the implied competence of the EU to participate in international organisations, acting as global standard-setters.[152]

Aside from the European Commission, European agencies also play an increasingly important role in global standard-setting. Established as independent expert bodies in order to provide scientific and technical advice to the Commission,[153] these bodies also act as a support for the European Commission in global standard-setting initiatives. The external dimension of the agencies' work is often induced by their role as sources of scientific expertise in the Union, which creates an incentive for these bodies to cooperate with their counterparts and other experts all over the world in order to make use of the most up-to-date

[147] This gap has also been identified by other authors. See: H Hofmann, 'Seven Challenges for EU Administrative Law' (2009) 2 *Review of European Administrative Law* 37, 55; C Möllers and J Terhechte, '§40 Europäisches Verwaltungsrecht und Internationales Verwaltungsrecht', in J Terhechte (ed), *Verwaltungsrecht der Europäischen Union* (Baden-Baden: Nomos, 2011), 1445.

[148] Specifically, Arts 3(5) TEU, 21(1) TEU and 220 TFEU.

[149] In general, besides cases where the European Union has explicit competences to establish external relations – such as the Common Commercial Policy in Art 207 TFEU or development policy in Art 211 TFEU – the Union will also be competent to establish relations with international organisations and third states where this follows implicitly from a treaty provision or from secondary legislation.

[150] Art 5 TEU.

[151] Case 22/70 *Commission v Council*, ECLI:EU:C:1971:32, concerning a European Road Transport Agreement (ERTA). The *ERTA* doctrine is now codified in Art 216(1) TFEU and Art 3(2) TFEU.

[152] See also: Eeckhout (2011) 122.

[153] See: Chapter 1 Section I C.

knowledge and to share resources.[154] The close cooperation with international partners provides them with the opportunity to establish themselves as a 'hub of regulatory science by providing leadership and catalysing improvements and developments'.[155] Thus, regulatory cooperation not only provides agencies with the benefits of resource sharing, but also forms a route to the consolidation of their expert status vis-à-vis their international counterparts, and within the EU internally.[156]

However, the participation of the Commission and European agencies in global standard-setting or other forms of regulatory cooperation raises questions on the legal basis and constitutional limits for these activities. For global standard-setting within international organisations, once it is established that the EU is competent to be a member of an international organisation, it can conclude an accession agreement,[157] pursuant to the procedure established in Article 218 TFEU. As far as representation in international organisations is concerned, based on Article 218 TFEU the Council has the mandate to externally represent the Union where binding international agreements are adopted. However, standards are not legally binding and, therefore, fall outside of the scope of Article 218 TFEU, except where these standards are 'capable of decisively influencing the content of the legislation adopted by the EU legislature', as decided by the Court in the *OIV* case.[158] In such cases, the Court in the *OIV* case indicated that the procedure of Article 218(9) TFEU can also apply to standards. Where standards fall short of producing 'legal effects', the specific procedure for international agreements under this article does not apply and the general norm of external representation of the EU has to be relied upon. The same holds true for standard-setting that takes place in transnational regulatory networks or public-private partnerships, thus in fora that are not formally established under international law, where the procedure established by Article 218 TFEU also does not apply.[159]

[154] Hofmann (2017).

[155] ECHA, Multi-Annual Work Programme 2014–2018, ECHA-13-A-06.01-EN, September 2013, 35.

[156] See: M Groenleer, 'Linking Up Levels of Governance: Agencies of the European Union and International Institutions', in O Costa and K Joergensen (eds), *The Influence of International Institutions on the European Union: When Multilateralism Hits Brussels* (Basingstoke: Palgrave Macmillan, 2012); Groenleer and Gabbi (2013).

[157] Opinion 1/76 of the Court of 26 April 1977, Opinion given pursuant to article 228(1) of the EEC Treaty – 'Draft Agreement establishing a European Laying-up Fund for Inland Waterway Vessels', ECLI:EU:C:1977:63, para 5. See also: Eeckhout (2011); R Wessel, 'The Legal Framework for the Participation of the European Union in International Institutions' (2011) 33 *European Integration* 621.

[158] Case C-399/12 *Federal Republic of Germany v. Council of the European Union*, ECLI:EU:C:2014:2258, para 63. Although the recommendations by the International Organisation of Vine and Wine (OIV) are not binding under international law, the EU Regulations applicable to wine in the internal market compared the OIV recommendations to EU law and obliged the Commission to base its decisions on the authorisation of oenological practices on these recommendations, as explained in paras 61–64 of the judgment.

[159] Case C-233/02 *French Republic v. Commission*, ECLI:EU:C:2004:173, para 45.

In this regard, the role that the European Commission can play in the external relations of the Union and in how far, therefore, it can take part in global standard-setting bodies is disputed in court,[160] and subject to academic debate.[161] Article 17(1) TEU stipulates that the Commission, '... shall ensure the Union's external representation' and Article 220(2) TFEU provides that the Commission, together with the High Representative, implements the EU's relationships with international organisations. However, the Council is granted policy-making power in Article 16(1) TEU, which also has to be respected on external representation. According to the Commission, the established practice for international non-binding measures which are not politically important – which will presumably be the case for standards due to their technical and scientific nature – is that the Commission will establish the EU position.[162] It will inform the responsible Council working party in advance and, if required, will conduct a discussion on the topic with the working party.[163] Thus, the EU can be represented by the Commission, as long as this does not infringe on the policy-making power of the Council.[164]

For European agencies, such as the EMA, the legal framework for their external relations activities and especially participation in global standard-setting bodies is even less clear. There is no Treaty provision establishing a legal basis for the creation of EU agencies, let alone addressing their role in external relations. Also, there is a lack of case law from the Court of Justice.[165] However, the role of European agencies as actors on the global level is gradually receiving

[160] Chamon lists 14 CJEU cases since 2012 on disputes regarding the institutional balance in external relations. In these cases the Commission, the Council as well as the Parliament in various applicant/defendant combinations claim the infringement of their respective prerogatives. See: M Chamon, 'A Constitutional Twilight Zone: EU Decentralized Agencies' External Relations' (2019) 56 *Common Market Law Review* 1509, 1511.

[161] A Ott and S Bartelt, 'The Administrative Cooperation of the European Commission with Third Countries and International Organisations' (2016) 29 *Europarecht* 143; A Ott, 'Informalization of EU Bilateral Instruments: Categorization, Contestation, and Challenges' (2020) 28 *Yearbook of European Law*; M Chamon and V Demedts, 'Constitutional Limits to EU agencies' external relations', in H Hofmann, E Vos and M Chamon (eds), *The External Dimension of EU Agencies and Bodies – Law and Policy* (Cheltenham: Edward Elgar, 2019); Chamon (2019).

[162] European Commission, Vademecum on the External Action of the European Union, SEC(2011)881/3, p 24.

[163] Ibid.

[164] However, the power of the Commission to represent the EU externally is subject to strict limitations. In *France v Commission I* (Case C-327/91 *French Republic v Commission*, ECLI:EU:C:1994:305), it was determined that the Commission lacks the power to conclude legally binding agreements on behalf of the European Union. Moreover, the case *France v Commission II* (Case C-233/02 *French Republic v Commission*, ECLI:EU:C:2004:173, para 40) clarified that where the Commission concludes guidelines on behalf of the Union, it also has to respect the division of powers and the principle of institutional balance – in this case between the Commission and the Council – in the case of such non-binding measures. According to the principle of institutional balance enshrined in Art 13(2) TEU, the Commission needs to respect the policy-making power granted to the Council under Art 16(1) TEU. (See also: Case C-660/13 *Council v Commission*, ECLI:EU:C:2016:616.) See in more detail: Chamon (2019); Chamon and Demedts (2019).

[165] Chamon and Demedts (2019) 13.

more academic attention.[166] While the agencies generally are not competent to act externally as official EU representatives or to enter into binding commitments in the name of the EU,[167] they often take part in the Union's delegations to international fora as experts. The external regulatory cooperation activities of agencies can take the form of cooperation activities with agencies of third countries or the participation of agencies in specialised international organisations and bodies, and have to be based on a specific mandate. Such mandates are included in the majority of the founding regulations of the European agencies.[168]

For example, the mandate for the participation of the EMA in global standard-setting can be deducted from Article 57(1)(j) Regulation 726/2004 describing one of the tasks of the agency as: '[U]pon request, providing technical and scientific support in order to improve cooperation between the Union, its Member States, international organisations and third countries on scientific and technical issues relating to the evaluation of medicinal products, in particular in the context of discussions organised in the framework of international conferences on harmonisation.'[169] Other European agencies take part in global standard-setting initiatives as well. One example is the European Chemicals Agency (ECHA), which in accordance with Article 77 of the REACH Regulation participates in the setting of global chemicals standards and takes part in working groups and task forces of the OECD in support of the Commission.[170] The work of the European Food Safety Authority (EFSA) also has an external dimension in supporting the Commission in the Codex Alimentarius Commission and other international organisations.[171] Article 23(i) of the General Food Law, which set up the EFSA, provides that one of the tasks of the Authority is: '(i) to provide scientific and technical assistance, when requested to do so by the

[166] See: F Coman-Kund, European Union Agencies as Global Actors – A Legal Study of the European Aviation Safety Agency, Frontex and Europol (London: Routledge, 2018); H Hofmann, E Vos and M Chamon (eds), The External Dimension of EU Agencies and Bodies – Law and Policy (Cheltenham: Edward Elgar, 2019); A Ott, E Vos and F Coman-Kund, 'European Agencies on the Global Scene: EU and International Law Perspectives', in M Everson, C Monda and E Vos (eds), European Agencies in between Institutions and Member States (Alphen aan den Rijn: Kluwer Law International, 2014); A Ott, 'EU Regulatory Agencies in EU External Relations: trapped in a Legal Minefield Between European and International Law' (2008) 13 European Foreign Affairs Review 515; Groenleer (2012); Groenleer and Gabbi (2013); Chamon (2019).

[167] European Commission, Vademecum on the External Action of the European Union, SEC(2011)881/3, 18f.

[168] Ott, Vos and Coman-Kund (2014). See also: Ott (2008) 528; Groenleer and Gabbi (2013) 481; Chamon and Demedts (2019) 18.

[169] Regulation (EC) No 726/2004, art 57(1)(j).

[170] Regulation (EC) No 1907/2006, art 77.

[171] Groenleer and Gabbi (2013). Alongside the Codex, Groenleer and Gabbi point out that the EFSA also supports the Commission in the World Organisation for Animal Health (OIE), the International Plant Protection Convention (IPPC), the European and Mediterranean Plant Protection Organisation (EPPO), the Joint FAO/WHO Expert Committee on Food Additives (JECFA), the World Health Organisation (WHO) and the Food and Agriculture Organisation (FAO).

Commission, with a view to improving cooperation between the Community, applicant countries, international organisations and third countries, in the fields within its mission'.[172]

However, agencies need to act within the limits of their mandate and 'are not seen as representing the EU position to an outside audience or as committing the EU to international obligations'.[173] Moreover, the agencies do not act autonomously in their external cooperation in global standard-setting bodies, but under the control of and in cooperation with the Commission in order to preserve the unity of the EU position.[174] Nonetheless, the mandates in secondary legislation are remarkably empty in terms of delimiting the freedom of agency participation in international regulatory cooperation.[175] They neither impose procedural requirements on the agency nor a limit on the subject of cooperation. Thus, although European agencies play a significant role in global regulatory cooperation, this is not extensively regulated in the EU's institutional law.[176]

IV. CONCLUSION: INSTITUTIONAL DIVERSITY IN THE FACE OF REGULATORY COMPLEXITY

EU risk regulation in a globalised world is inherently interconnected with norms developed in global regulatory cooperation and through global standard-setting. The complex institutional landscape of global standard-setting as described in this chapter shows how the phenomenon of global standard-setting deviates from traditional international law with regard to the bodies undertaking the standard-setting and the actors involved in them.

With the increase of standards originating in regulatory cooperation, administrators have entered the remit of transnational relations. Where the risks transcend national borders, the regulatory response has to follow suit. Therefore, one can witness the development of a 'global administrative space'[177] in which domestic regulators harmonise their activities with counterparts around the world. In addition, private actors are increasingly gaining importance as actors on the global level, often due to the specific expertise they can contribute to the standard-setting processes.

[172] Regulation (EC) No 178/2002, art 23(i).

[173] European Parliament, Council of the European Union and European Commission, 'Joint Statement of the European Parliament, Council of the EU and European Commission on decentralised agencies', 19 July 2012, 8.

[174] Groenleer and Gabbi (2013) 481.

[175] See also: Ott (2008) 531; J Mendes, 'EU Law and Global Regulatory Regimes: Hollowing Out Procedural Standards?' (2012) 10 *International Journal of Constitutional Law* 988, 1014.

[176] Chamon (2019).

[177] Krisch and Kingsbury (2006) 1.

The standards that arise from these global standard-setting bodies are frequently implemented into the risk regulation framework of the EU and shape the regulatory system in the EU. At the same time the EU, and especially the Commission and European agencies, actively take part in global standard-setting processes. In this regard, EU institutional law still has not established a clear approach to the growing externalisation of EU risk regulation. This is especially noticeable with regard to European agencies which increasingly participate in standard-setting bodies.

3

The International Council for Harmonisation: Pharmaceutical Standard-Setting on the Global Level

WHILE THE FIRST chapter of this book introduced the elaborate regulatory framework for pharmaceuticals in the EU, the previous chapter introduced the phenomenon of global standard-setting and pointed towards the fact that global standards are also set for pharmaceuticals. Indeed, while the regulation of access to pharmaceutical markets used to be 'virtually synonymous with national sovereignty',[1] as it is closely linked to the administrative and socio-economic culture of a state,[2] the pharmaceutical sector has witnessed growing cooperation and harmonisation of regulatory requirements on the international level due to globalisation of trade.[3]

An impressive number of bilateral and also regional regulatory cooperation initiatives have been established; however, multilateral initiatives are less widespread.[4] An EMA mapping exercise highlighted the World Health Organisation (WHO), the International Council for Harmonisation of Technical Requirements for the Registration of Pharmaceuticals for Human (International Council of Harmonisation, ICH),[5] the Pharmaceutical Inspection Co-operation Scheme (PIC/S), the International Pharmaceutical Regulatory Forum (IRPF), the International Coordination of Medicines Regulatory Authorities (ICMRA),

[1] D Vogel, 'The Globalization of Pharmaceutical Regulation' (1998) 11 *Governance* 1, 1. See also: D Kidd, 'The International Conference on Harmonization of Pharmaceutical Regulations, the European Medicines Evaluation Agency, and the FDA: Who's Zooming Who?' (1996) 4 *Indiana Journal of Global Legal Studies* 183, 203.

[2] A Spina, 'The Regulation of Pharmaceuticals Beyond the State: EU and Global Administrative Systems', in E Chiti and B Mattarella (eds), *Global Administrative Law and EU Administrative Law* (Heidelberg: Springer, 2011) 250.

[3] J Valverde, 'The Globalization of Medicines as a Challenge for Governments' (2016) 18 *Pharmaceuticals Policy and Law* 19; X Seuba, 'International Harmonization of Pharmaceutical Standards: Trade, Ethics and Power', in G Burci and B Toebes, *Research Handbook in Global Health Law* (Cheltenham: Edward Elgar, 2018).

[4] EMA, 'Connecting the dots – Towards global knowledge of the international medicine regulatory landscape: mapping of international initiatives' (2016), EMA/546107/2016.

[5] The ICH used to be called International Conference on Harmonisation of Pharmaceuticals for Human Use and was renamed in 2015 in line with its institutional reform, which will be discussed in detail in this chapter.

the International Generic Drug Regulator's Programme (IGDPR), the Council for International Organizations of Medical Sciences (CIOMS), and the health division of the Organisation for Economic Co-operation and Development (OECD).[6] Most of these initiatives serve to improve the exchange of information or facilitate cooperation amongst regulatory authorities.

Amongst these initiatives only the ICH has standard-setting as its core mandate and objective, although standard-setting is also carried out to some extent by the PIC/S (limited to Good Manufacturing Practice), the WHO,[7] and the OECD. Having standard-setting as its main task and with the aim of harmonising the full spectrum of regulatory standards for pharmaceuticals, the ICH forms the most pronounced and also prolific source of global pharmaceuticals standards.[8] This chapter will introduce the history, examine its mandate and institutional structure and discuss the process through which the ICH standards are adopted. A focus will be placed on the reform process the ICH has undergone in recent years, introducing changes to its organisational format and membership structure.

I. PHARMACEUTICAL REGULATION IN A GLOBALISED WORLD: THE HISTORY OF THE ICH

The creation of harmonised pharmaceutical regulatory standards on a global level was a response to the increasing globalisation of pharmaceutical trade, leading to a market structure where production, manufacturing and marketing of medicines takes place in separate countries.[9] This internationalisation of the pharmaceutical business meant that effective regulation of pharmaceuticals could not remain a purely national task, as observed by Hancher as early as 1989, shortly before the inception of the ICH.[10] Moreover, the move towards global standard-setting was based on both economic factors, including the lowering of costs for manufacturers to comply with diverging regulatory schemes, and regulatory factors, such as increasing the speed of marketing authorisations and prevention of unnecessary duplicate trials.[11] For example, some countries

[6] EMA, EMA/546107/2016.

[7] Seuba (2018).

[8] See eg Flear's elaboration especially with regard to clinical trials standards: M Flear, 'Charting a roadmap towards membership and formal voice in global bioethics standard-setting: Health research and the case of the International Council on Harmonisation' (2018) *Medical Law International* 157.

[9] R Kanusky, 'Pharmaceutical Harmonization: Standardizing Regulations among the United States, the European Economic Community, and Japan' (1994) 16 *Houston Journal of International Law* 665, 667.

[10] L Hancher, *Regulating for Competition – Government, Law and the Pharmaceutical Industry in the United Kingdom and France* (Alblasserdam: Haveka, 1989) 22.

[11] In this regard, the ICH has published two information brochures available via ww.ich.org: ICH, 'The Value and Benefits of ICH for Industry', January 2000; ICH, 'The Value and Benefits of ICH to Drug Regulatory Authorities', November 2010. See also: A Berman, 'The Public-Private Nature of Harmonisation Networks', (2011) CTEI Working Paper, CTEI-2011-06, 13.

like the US required clinical trials delivering the obligatory data for a marketing authorisation to be carried out in their own country.[12] Thus, clinical trials for the same medicine had to be duplicated whenever a product was to be marketed in multiple countries. Moreover, the production of the marketing authorisation applications was costly, encompassing thousands of pages, which had to be adjusted laboriously to diverging national requirements.[13]

Also the rise of the EU as a regulatory power and the problems concerning excessive time loss in the authorisation process by the US Food and Drug Administration (FDA) in the 1980s paved the way for harmonised regulatory standards for quality, safety and efficacy of medicinal products.[14] Until the 1990s, the US FDA dominated the regulation of medicinal products, determining the standards applicable to quality, safety and efficacy, not only for the US but also globally due to its large regulatory impact.[15] Nonetheless, the US faced a severe crisis in medication approval in the 1980s, with products taking over 10 years to be authorised for use on the US market. The FDA regulatory process had slowed down, while the European process had sped up, leading to shorter approval times in the EU.[16] Through the progress of European harmonisation as described in Chapter 1 – with centralisation, institutional reforms and coordination of regulation amongst the Member States – the EU had strongly gained in regulatory capacity.[17]

These developments paved the way for the start of an unprecedented harmonisation initiative in the field of pharmaceuticals: the ICH. The ICH is of exemplary importance in the area of global risk regulation standards, not only because of the impact of its standards in the European and global context, but also because in the politically sensitive field of pharmaceuticals, it was the first initiative to bring a group of national regulators together in one harmonisation forum. The involvement of industry in such a body was a novelty in terms of pharmaceutical regulation.[18] It is noteworthy that with the creation of the ICH, the regulatory parties choose to deviate from fostering a harmonisation initiative within the framework of the WHO,[19] which as international organisation

[12] Vogel (1998) 9.

[13] B Kuhnert, 'ICH at 20: An overview' (2011) 3 *Drug Information Association Global Forum* 17, 18.

[14] D Vogel, *The Politics of Precaution – Regulating Health, Safety and Environmental Risks in Europe and the United States* (Princeton: Princeton University Press, 2012); Berman (2011) 13.

[15] D Bach and A Newman, 'Governing Lipitor and Listerine: The Domestic Roots of International Pharmaceutical and Cosmetics Regulation', IE Business School Working Paper, WP08-17, (11 March 2008), 4.

[16] F Rockhold, 'Industry Perspectives on ICH Guidelines' (2002) 21 *Statistics in Medicine* 2949, 2950.

[17] Bach and Newman (2008) 4.

[18] Berman (2011) 3.

[19] Notably, however, the WHO has attended the ICH Steering Committee meetings as observer since the establishment of the ICH, ensuring an institutional link between the WHO and the ICH.

of the United Nations presumably enjoys high legitimacy.[20] This could have been based on a need for more efficiency, as processes in the WHO were regarded as too slow and bureaucratic,[21] and reaching consensus in truly global harmonisation processes would be too cumbersome.[22]

A. The Creation of the ICH: The International Conference on Harmonisation

The catalyst to forming the ICH was a sequence of bilateral and trilateral negotiations between EU, US and Japanese regulators which formed the largest markets for the development of research-based medicines.[23] The US and Japan had been working together since the mid-1980s on the opening up of the Japanese markets, also leading to some degree of harmonisation within their pharmaceutical regulation.[24] In 1988, the EU and Japan also addressed problems arising from diverging pharmaceutical regulations, such as unnecessary double-testing, and for a longer period between the development of a drug and its actual marketing.[25] During the same period, a subcommittee of the European Commission organised a conference with representatives from the US Food and Drug Administration (FDA), and the Ministry of Health and Welfare in Japan (MHW, today MHLW for Ministry of Health, Labour and Welfare).[26] The regulatory authorities had a strong interest in cooperation in order to benefit from each other's experience. In this regard, the EU served as an example of the harmonisation of diverging regulatory requirements.[27] Moreover, the

[20] S Dagron, 'Global Harmonization through Public-Private Partnership: The Case of Pharmaceuticals', Instituto di Ricerche sulla Pubblica Amministrazione, Global Administrative Law Working Papers (2012), IRPA GAL Working Paper 2012/2, 16.

[21] Berman (2011) 16.

[22] R Arnold, 'Objectives and Preparation of the Conference and the Role of the Workshops', in P D'Arcy and D Harron (eds), *Proceedings of the First International Conference on Harmonisation – Brussels 1991* (Belfast: The Queen's University Belfast, 1992) 8.

[23] D Jordan, 'International Regulatory Harmonization: A New Era in Prescription Drug Approval' (1992) 25 *Vanderbilt Journal of Transnational Law* 471, 492. For an account of the ICH history see: www.ich.org/page/history.

[24] Arnold (1992) 8.

[25] P Bahri and P Tsintis, 'Pharmacovigilance-related topics at the level of the International Conference on Harmonisation (ICH)' (2005) 14 *Pharmacoepidemiology and Drug Safety* 377, 378.

[26] J Contrera, 'The Food and Drug Administration and the International Conference on Harmonisation: How Harmonious Will International Pharmaceutical Regulations Become?' (1994–1995) 8 *The Administrative Law Journal* 927, 939.

[27] L Lindström-Gommers and T Mullin, 'International Conference on Harmonization: Recent Reforms as a Driver of Global Regulatory Harmonization and Innovation in Medical Products' (2019) 105 *Clinical Pharmacology & Therapeutics* 926, 926; C Lourenco, N Orphanos and C Parker, 'The International Council for Harmonisation: Positioning for the future with its recent reform and over 25 years of harmonisation work' (2016) *Pharmaceuticals Policy and Law* 79, 78.

pharmaceutical industry at the time also strongly advocated harmonising the technical and scientific requirements for marketing authorisations.[28]

In April 1990, the European Federation of Pharmaceutical Industries and Associations (EFPIA) in Brussels hosted a meeting with representatives from the three regulatory authorities and industry associations of the research-based pharmaceutical industry, where the participant started outlining concrete plans for the ICH.[29] The first meeting of the ICH Steering Committee, which became the main governing body of the ICH, took place in April 1990,[30] leading to agreement about the 'Terms of Reference' setting out the ICH mandate. In addition to that, it was agreed that the harmonisation would be conducted through large-scale conferences, where an extensive range of experts could discuss future guidelines.[31] The initial ICH Conference took place 1991 in Brussels, harmonising the first aspects of drug regulation, especially with regard to testing requirements.[32] The Conference was attended by 1,000 participants from the regulatory authorities and industry associations of the EU, US and Japan but also other regulatory authorities from all over the world, paving the way for regulatory and industry cooperation to form common standards.[33]

Thus, the ICH was set up as a regionally limited initiative between the regulators and industry associations representing the research-based pharmaceutical industry of the US, EU and Japan, independent from existing international initiatives. At the time of the ICH establishment, these three regions represented the largest pharmaceutical markets of the world, with 75% of pharmaceuticals produced in these regions and 90% of research and development taking place there,[34] and are still the most important markets today. Hence, from the outset ICH membership was subject to regional limitations according to market size in terms of pharmaceuticals.

Moreover, the ICH was established not as an international organisation but as an informal, meeting-based process, without a founding treaty. The fact that the ICH founders deviated from establishment as an international organisation needs to be seen in the wider context of developments, with regard to a broad-

[28] O Doi, 'Role and Public Health Responsibilities of the Authorities', in P D'Arcy and D Harron (eds), *Proceedings of the First International Conference on Harmonisation – Brussels 1991* (Belfast: The Queen's University Belfast, 1992) 20.

[29] F Sauer, 'Preface', in J van de Laan and J DeGeorge (eds), *Global Approach in Safety Testing – ICH Guidelines Explained* (New York: Springer, 2013) vii.

[30] Ibid.

[31] Ibid.

[32] J Abraham and T Reed, 'Trading Risks for Markets: The International Harmonization of Pharmaceuticals Regulation' (2001) 1 *Health, Risk and Society* 113; D Katsikas, 'International Conference on Harmonization of Technical Requirements for the Registration of Pharmaceutical Products', in T Hale and D Held (eds), *Handbook of Transnational Governance – Institutions & Innovations* (Cambridge: Polity Press, 2011) 89.

[33] M Bangemann, 'Welcome Address by Mr Martin Bangemann', in P D'Arcy and D Harron (eds), *Proceedings of the First International Conference on Harmonisation – Brussels 1991* (Belfast: The Queen's University Belfast, 1992) 1.

[34] Jordan (1992) 492.

ening of the spectrum of bodies taking on regulatory tasks at the global level, as described in Chapter 2. One factor that probably deterred the founders from establishing an international organisation was that the ICH was intended to be a temporarily limited initiative, to be terminated once the harmonisation was carried out, which was estimated to need six years.[35] Moreover, international organisations traditionally do not provide the possibility of having private parties as full members on a par with states, due to the debated international legal personality of international non-governmental organisations (INGOs).

From 1991 until 2003 the Steering Committee, forming the ICH's main decision-making body, and the Expert Working Groups, which are the scientific expert bodies for the respective harmonisation topics, met at six-monthly intervals. Moreover, the parties conducted international conferences every two to three years where representatives of the six sponsors gathered, as a distinguishable characteristic of the ICH harmonisation process.[36] The ICH Conferences were conducted on a large scale with over a thousand participants invited for the first Conference, to discuss the topics prepared by the Steering Committee together with the working groups.[37] Since its inception the ICH has convened in a large-scale international conference format six times: 1991 in Brussels (Belgium), 1993 in Orlando (USA), 1995 in Yokohama (Japan), 1997 in Brussels (Belgium) again, in 2000 in San Diego (USA), and the last time being the ICH6 in November 2003, taking place in Osaka (Japan).[38]

The large-scale conference format was abolished in the Steering Committee meeting of May 2007 taking place in Brussels.[39] It was replaced with Steering Committee and Expert Working Group meetings twice a year during the so-called 'ICH week'. Furthermore, the ICH decided to conduct so-called ICH Public Events at the end of the Steering Committee meetings, or as specifically organised regional meetings.[40] These Public Events were intended for the communication of ICH activities and also took the form of preparatory meetings, where the participants commented on topics that would be discussed in the next Steering Committee and Expert Working Group Meetings.

Thus, the ICH was organised as an informal network.[41] The ICH operated on the basis of recurring meetings, with the six founding members interacting

[35] Katsikas (2011) 89. See also: Berman (2011) 18.

[36] J Lee, 'What is Past is Prologue: The International Conference on Harmonization and Lessons Learned from European Drug Regulations Harmonization' (2005) 26 *University of Pennsylvania Journal of International Economic Law* 151, 179.

[37] Sauer (2013) vii.

[38] Katsikas (2011) 89.

[39] Ibid, 90.

[40] For an overview see: https://www.ich.org/page/ich-public-events.

[41] For other discussions on the ICH network character see: Spina (2011); A Berman, 'Public-Private Harmonization Networks: The Case of the International Conference on Harmonization (ICH)', in S Cassese, B Carotti, L Casini, E Cavalieri and E MacDonald (eds), *Global Administrative Law: The Casebook*, 3rd edn (2012a, IRPA-IILJ, ebook).

as equals and sharing resources, while lacking a strict organisational plan. As the ICH integrated the regulated industry as members, in the literature the ICH was described as a 'public/private platform'[42] or 'public-private collaboration',[43] and 'public-private network'.[44] Referring back to the discussion of the institutional landscape of global standard setting in Chapter 2, it is to be defined as a public-private partnership in the organisational format of a network. Although the ICH operated in a rather informal meeting format, it should not be underestimated with regard to its actual influence on global pharmaceutical regulation. The pharmaceutical industry used these guidelines immediately and by 1996, 90% of pharmaceutical companies were using existing ICH quality guidelines, with the largest companies almost entirely following the ICH guidance.[45]

B. The ICH as a Global Standard-Setter and the Reform of the ICH

The ICH work was at first mostly devoted to harmonising the quality, safety and efficacy requirements of the three founding regions, and it entered gradually into communicating its activities to non-ICH regulators.[46] The impact of ICH guidelines on non-ICH countries was well recognised and they were used as references or educational materials, for example for seminars conducted in the regional harmonisation efforts of the Association of Southeast Asian Nations (ASEAN).[47] Although the ICH guidelines were also implemented in non-ICH countries, regulatory authorities of other countries were not granted membership in the ICH at first.

In response to the increasing influence of ICH standards beyond the founding regions, the ICH created the Global Cooperation Group (GCP) in 1999 as a subcommittee of the Steering Committee.[48] It was composed of one representative

[42] Spina (2011) 258.
[43] Berman (2011) 3.
[44] Berman (2012a).
[45] Vogel (1998) 13.
[46] This statement can be found on the ICH website (https://www.ich.org/page/history): 'Since ICH's inception in 1990, the ICH process has gradually evolved. ICH's first decade saw significant progress in the development of ICH Guidelines on Safety, Quality and Efficacy topics. Work was also undertaken on a number of important multidisciplinary topics, which included MedDRA (Medical Dictionary for Regulatory Activities) and the CTD (Common Technical Document). As ICH started into a new millennium, the need to expand communication and dissemination of information on ICH Guidelines with non-ICH regions became a key focus. Attention was also directed throughout the second decade towards facilitating the implementation of ICH Guidelines in ICH's own regions and maintaining already existing ICH Guidelines as science and technology continued to evolve. Now in its third decade of activity, ICH's attention is directed towards extending the benefits of harmonisation beyond the founding ICH regions.').
[47] WHO, 'The Impact of Implementation of ICH Guidelines in Non-ICH Countries', Regulatory Support Series No 009, 2002, 15.
[48] ICH, 'The Value and Benefits of ICH to Drug Regulatory Authorities', November 2010, 18–19. See further: Dagron (2012); S Dagron, 'Die International Conference on Harmonization of Technical Requirements for Registration of Pharmaceuticals for Human Use (ICH)' in C Lenk, G Duttge

of each ICH Steering Committee member as well as one representative per observer and one representative of the ICH Secretariat. The group published information materials and held presentations on the ICH. The Group was subsequently opened up to participation by non-ICH Regional Harmonisation Initiatives (RHIs) and members of Drug Regulatory Authorities (DRAs) or Departments of Health (DoHs) of countries such as Australia, Chinese Taipei, Singapore and South Korea. As of June 2013, the Global Cooperation Group was abolished and the topics formerly covered by this group were integrated in the Steering Committee Meeting Agenda to facilitate better involvement of the global regulators.[49]

Besides the Global Cooperation Group, the so-called Regulators Forum met for the first time in Portland in June 2008. This included the regulatory ICH parties as well as regulators of other countries which had implemented ICH guidelines, such as Australia, Chinese Taipei, Singapore and South Korea. Regulators of countries vital to the production of pharmaceuticals and the carrying out of clinical trials, such as Brazil, China, India and Russia, were also involved.[50] The purpose of the Regulators Forum was declared to be the exchange of best practices regarding the implementation of ICH guidelines. It was also to create a forum for discussion amongst regulators of the impact of ICH guidelines on the regulatory system of non-ICH countries.[51] Although the forum still meets in conjunction with the ICH week and continues to discuss the implementation of ICH guidelines, the forum obtained a more formal status – removed from the ICH's institutional structure – as the International Pharmaceutical Regulators Forum (IPRF) in 2013.[52]

Thus, the ICH's institutional structure was progressively modified to open up to the increasing involvement of non-ICH member industrial organisations, regional harmonisation initiatives and regulatory authorities. However, as much as the non-ICH countries and regions were supported in the implementation of ICH guidelines, they remained merely recipients of the guidelines. Other countries were not represented as full members within the ICH, lacking voting rights in the adoption of the guidelines. Questions were raised with regard to the ICH's role as a globally dominant reference point for pharmaceutical standards, due to the lack of inclusiveness.[53] In particular, this was criticised because ICH members

and H Gangerau, *Handbuch Ethik und Recht der Forschung am Menschen* (Heidelberg: Springer, 2014), A Berman, 'The Distributional Effects of Transnational Pharmaceutical Regulation' (2012) CTEI Working Paper, CTEI-2012-01.

[49] ICH, ICH Steering Committee, La Hulpe, Belgium, June 2013, Press Release, available via: https://www.ich.org/pressrelease/ich-steering-committee-la-hulpe-belgium-june-2013.

[50] ICH, 'The Value and Benefits of ICH to Drug Regulatory Authorities', November 2010, 20.

[51] Ibid.

[52] In 2018 the IRPF merged with the International Generic Drug Regulators Programme (IGDRP) to form the International Pharmaceutical Regulators Programme (IPRP), information is now available via: www.iprp.global.

[53] Dagron (2012).

were leading in the advancement of technology within the pharmaceutical field. Developing countries faced difficulties in enforcing these high standards without endangering their own industrial or public health policies.[54]

In 2012, the ICH started working on new principles of governance, aiming for a redefinition of the roles of regulators and industry parties, as well increasing the transparency of ICH processes.[55] These procedural changes soon extended into an in-depth reform that concerned the institutional structure of the ICH, with special attention to an improved exchange with global regulators.[56] The reform process was triggered by changes in the pharmaceutical market and also the regulatory environment. Central points of the reform were declared to be the broadening of membership (with regard to regulators and industry organisations[57]), the clarification of the distinct roles of industry and regulators, the establishment of a new legal entity and a change in the funding of the ICH.[58] Another factor was the lack of legal personality of the ICH.[59]

Through this reform the ICH sought to establish itself as the focal point for global pharmaceutical regulatory harmonisation, involving the key global and regulatory actors, while keeping the harmonisation process efficient. It aimed at broadening ICH membership in order to reflect the national regulators and international industry associations actually affected by the guidelines. As stated by Lindström-Gommers and Mullin: 'There was also a shared interest among all ICH parties in global outreach by opening up membership in ICH … In addition, other considerations (e.g., the need for increased transparency appropriate to a modern organization operating in the public sphere) were recognized.'[60]

One of the core ideas behind the reform process was to make the ICH more regulator driven, especially in terms of the standard-setting process.[61] In addition, the funding of the ICH needed to be revised, as prior to the reform the industry parties had covered most of the expenses of the ICH and they had usually paid the costs for the organisation of the bi-annual meetings, including the travel expenses of some of the participants of the Global Cooperation

[54] WHO, 'The Impact of Implementation of ICH Guidelines in Non-ICH Countries', Regulatory Support Series No. 009, 2002, p. 19ff; Berman (2012b).

[55] ICH, Press Release – ICH Steering Committee, Fukuoka, Japan, 6–7 June 2012, available via: www.ich.org/page/press-releases.

[56] ICH, Press Release – ICH Steering Committee, San Diego, USA, 14–15 November 2012, available via: www.ich.org/page/press-releases. For a critical discussion of the opening up of several international governance bodies including the ICH to include also developing countries: A Berman, 'Accordion Governance' (2019) 13 *Vienna Journal on International* Constitutional Law 203.

[57] ICH, Press Release – ICH Steering Committee, Osaka, Japan November 2013, available via: www.ich.org/page/press-releases.

[58] ICH, Press Release – ICH Steering Committee, Minneapolis, MN, USA, June 2014, available via: www.ich.org/page/press-releases.

[59] Lindström-Gommers and Mullin (2019) 929.

[60] Ibid, 927.

[61] Ibid, 928; Also confirmed via: Interview with two officials of the European Commission, conducted in Brussels on 17 February 2015, notes on file with the author.

session. The industry associations covered the costs of the ICH Secretariat.[62] For the European regulators, the Commission compensated the travel costs of its own staff and the national experts from the EMA Committees participating in the ICH working groups, while the EMA covered the travel costs of its own staff.[63] This has to be viewed critically, as it led to a dependence of the regulators on industry. In an organisation like the ICH, which has a public health mandate and sets standards that are aimed at protecting patients and ensuring the quality, safety and efficacy of medicinal products, such dependence on the regulated industry is indeed problematic.

The organisational reform started taking shape in December 2014.[64] At the ICH Inaugural Assembly on 23 October 2015 the ICH Founding Members adopted the Articles of Association, which established the ICH as an association under Article 60 et seq of the Swiss Civil Code, and introduced 'International Council for Harmonisation of Technical Requirements for Pharmaceuticals for Human Use' as the official name of the association.[65] With regard to its legal establishment, a Swiss association was chosen, as this form of legal personality is highly flexible in terms of membership criteria, the process for adding members and leaving the association, as well as adopting a funding framework.[66]

Whereas the ICH used to be a meeting-based body, lacking any formal legal establishment, with the reform the legal nature of the ICH has been clarified. It is now an association under the Swiss Civil Code, a body established under private law. Moreover, according to its Articles of Association, the ICH is an international non-profit association,[67] funded through annual membership fees.[68] These fees are reflective of the membership category, with founding members paying higher fees than other members, while standing members pay more than new members.[69] The amount of the membership fee is determined by the Assembly and should be 'fair, proportionate, and transparent'.[70] This is now enshrined in article 58 of the Articles of Association, which states that the ICH is to be financed through membership fees to be paid annually, as well as grants or other mechanisms, which the regulatory members can provide in accordance with their laws.[71] Moreover, additional funds may be generated

[62] Ibid, 929; Also confirmed via: Interview with an official of the EFPIA, conducted in Brussels on 17 February 2015, notes on file with the author.

[63] Interview with two officials of the European Commission, conducted in Brussels on 17 February 2015, notes on file with the author.

[64] ICH, Press Release – ICH Steering Committee, Lisbon, Portugal, December 2014, available via: www.ich.org/page/press-releases.

[65] ICH, International Council for Harmonisation of Technical Requirements for Pharmaceuticals for Human Use – Articles of Association, Adopted by the ICH Founding Members at ICH Inaugural Assembly on 23 October 2015, Approved by the Assembly on 19 November 2019, art 1.

[66] Lindström-Gommers and Mullin (2019) 929; Also confirmed via: Interview with two officials of the European Commission, conducted in Brussels on 17 February 2015, notes on file with the author.

[67] ICH, Articles of Association, art 2(2).

[68] Lindström-Gommers and Mullin (2019) 929.

[69] Ibid, 929–30.

[70] ICH, Articles of Association, art 59.

[71] Ibid, art 58(2).

through participation fees, financial contributions and through the organisation of events and meetings.[72]

II. THE ICH: MANDATE AND MEMBERSHIP

Since its inception the ICH has established itself as the key source of regulatory pharmaceutical standards. By means of the reform process carried out over the last decade, its membership structure was revised in order to better reflect its mandate and role as global standard setter. However, as will be shown in this section, to a certain extent the newly established association carries over a legacy from the pre-reform ICH, as membership and observer categories differentiate between 'old' and 'new' actors in the ICH.

A. Mandate

With the establishment of the ICH, the founding parties agreed to a mandate of harmonising the technical requirements for the authorisation of pharmaceutical products throughout the three regions. These requirements concern the quality, safety and efficacy of a medicinal product. It is important to note, however, that the idea underlying the ICH and also its current mandate is not the harmonisation of the marketing authorisation procedure in the sense of a mutual recognition of regulatory assessments, nor through a 'central' ICH decision that would grant a marketing authorisation for the member markets. Every authority in the ICH regions continues to carry out its own scientific assessment and grants marketing authorisations independently.

The purpose of the ICH, according to its Articles of Association is 'to promote public health through international harmonisation of technical requirements',[73] which:

> contributes to the timely introduction of new medicines and continued availability of the approved medicines to patients, to the prevention of unnecessary duplication of clinical trials in humans, to the development, registration and manufacturing of safe, effective, and high quality medicines in an efficient and cost-effective manner, and to the minimisation of the use of animal testing without compromising safety and effectiveness.[74]

Its tasks and aims are:

a) to make recommendations towards achieving greater harmonisation in the interpretation and application of technical guidelines and requirements for pharmaceutical product registration and the maintenance of such registrations;

[72] Ibid, art 58(3).
[73] Ibid, art 2(1).
[74] Ibid.

b) to maintain a forum for a constructive dialogue on scientific issues between regulatory authorities and the pharmaceutical industry on the harmonisation of the technical requirements for pharmaceutical products;
c) to contribute to the protection of public health in the interest of patients from an international perspective;
d) to monitor and update harmonised technical requirements leading to a greater mutual acceptance of research and development data;
e) to avoid divergent future requirements through harmonisation of selected topics needed as a result of therapeutic advances and the development of new technologies for the production of medicinal products;
f) to facilitate the adoption of new or improved technical research and development approaches which update or replace current practices;
g) to encourage the implementation and integration of common standards through the dissemination of, the communication of information about and provision of training on, harmonised guidelines and their use; and
h) to develop policy for the ICH Medical Dictionary for Regulatory Activities Terminology (MedDRA) whilst ensuring the scientific and technical maintenance, development and dissemination of MedDRA as a standardised dictionary which facilitates the sharing of regulatory information internationally for medicinal products used by humans.[75]

The ICH thus envisages itself as a platform for exchange ultimately leading to harmonisation, for the benefit of industry and regulators alike, while contributing to public health. Moreover, this mandate stresses the ongoing harmonisation mandate with regard to scientific and technical progress, which can be seen as recognition that the harmonisation of technical requirements is a perpetual exercise, as its scientific basis is in constant change.

B. ICH Membership

The parties founding the ICH were representatives from regulatory authorities and research-based pharmaceutical industry associations of the three largest drug markets at the time:

- the European Commission together with the European Medicines Agency (EMA), after the EMA was established in 1993;
- the Ministry of Health, Labour and Welfare (MHLW) from Japan, supported by the Pharmaceuticals and Medical Devices Agency (PMDA);
- the US Food and Drug Administration (FDA);
- European Federation of Pharmaceutical Industries and Associations (EFPIA);
- the Japan Pharmaceutical Manufacturers Association (JPMA); and
- the Pharmaceutical Research and Manufacturers of America (PhRMA).

[75] Ibid, art 3.

ICH membership remained limited to these regions for most of its operational history. However, in June 2014, the regulatory authority of Switzerland (Swissmedic) and the Health Products and Food Branch (HPFB) of the Canadian authority Health Canada became members of the Steering Committee.[76] Before that, they had observer status, giving them the right to attend meetings but not to take part in the decision-making. The change in status was recognition of the long-term active contribution of these two parties to the ICH process and their commitment to implementing the ICH guidelines.[77] This formed the first step in the institutional reform process of the ICH.[78]

Through the reform, the membership structure of the ICH has been fundamentally changed. The Articles of Association, which were adopted at the ICH Inaugural Assembly on 23 October, introduced five different categories of membership:

- Founding Regulatory Members;
- Founding Industry Members;
- Standing Regulatory Members;
- Regulatory Members; and
- Industry Members.[79]

Attached to the different categories of membership are specific rights and duties, and distinctive influence on the decision-making process in the ICH.[80] In principle, the six original ICH members still maintain a special status, as they are now Founding Regulatory Members or Founding Industry Members. Thus, Founding Regulatory Member status is confined to the European Commission, the Ministry of Health, Labour and Welfare of Japan (MHLW) (also represented by the Pharmaceuticals and Medical Devices Agency (PMDA)), and the US Food and Drug Administration (FDA).[81] Founding Industry Member status is limited to the European Federation of Pharmaceutical Industries and Associations (EFPIA), the Japan Pharmaceuticals Manufacturers Association (JPMA), and the Pharmaceutical Research and Manufacturers of America (PhRMA).[82] Besides the Founding Regulatory and Industry Members, the ICH reform also introduced the category of Standing Regulatory Members. This category covers legislative or administrative authorities, which are responsible for regulating pharmaceutical products for human use and were members of the Steering Committee of the ICH before its establishment as an association.[83] This type of

[76] ICH, Press Release – ICH Steering Committee, Minneapolis, MN, USA, June 2014, available via: www.ich.org/page/press-releases.
[77] Ibid.
[78] Ibid.
[79] ICH, Articles of Association, art 7.
[80] See also: Section III.
[81] ICH, Articles of Association, art 8.
[82] Ibid, art 9.
[83] Ibid, art 10.

membership is restricted in fact to Swissmedic and Health Canada only, which became members of the Steering Committee in 2014 and were not ICH founding members.[84]

Consequently, two categories of membership are left for those bodies and organisations joining the ICH after the reform process: Regulatory Members and Industry Members. Regulatory Members can be either legislative and administrative authorities or Regional Harmonisation Initiatives (RHIs).[85] To become a Regulatory Member, a legislative or administrative authority needs to have legal personality and be responsible for the regulation of pharmaceutical products for human use.[86] Moreover, it may not already be represented in the ICH via being part of a RHI that is an ICH member.[87] A RHI can become a Regulatory Member if it has legal personality and encompasses legislative and/or administrative authorities responsible for the regulation of pharmaceutical products for human use.[88] Furthermore, it must be able to be represented by either a member authority or a secretariat, and it must also be capable of speaking and committing on behalf of its members.[89] Moreover, the RHI should be the sole Regulatory Member of its region, so the RHI members should not be ICH members or observers in their own right.[90]

For both Regional Harmonisation Initiatives as well as individual legislative or administrative authorities, a certain legacy of ICH participation is required: in the last two consecutive years before the application, it must have participated in three meetings of the ICH Assembly or three meetings held by the prior form of establishment, the International Conference of Harmonisation, immediately before the reform.[91] Additionally, to be eligible to make an application the body has to have appointed experts to two Working Groups of either the Association or the ICH pre-reform, immediately prior to the reform.[92] As a final membership requirement, the Articles of Association require the implementation of the ICH Q1, ICH Q7 and ICH E6 Guidelines for individual authorities as well as all members of a Regional Harmonisation Initiative.[93] Thus, in order to become a Regulatory Member, active participation in the ICH process prior to the application, as well as the implementation of a basic set of ICH guidelines, is required.

With regard to Industry Members, international organisations, which represent the pharmaceutical industry producing products for human use and which have legal personality are eligible for membership application.[94] This option was

[84] See Section II B.
[85] ICH, Articles of Association, arts 11(1) and 11(2).
[86] Ibid, art 11(1).
[87] Ibid, art 11(1)(e).
[88] Ibid, art 11(2).
[89] Ibid.
[90] Ibid, art 11(2)(g).
[91] Ibid, art 11(1)(c) and 11(2)(d).
[92] Ibid, art 11(1)(d) and 11(2)(e).
[93] Ibid, art 11(1) and 11(2).
[94] Ibid, art 12.

created in order to ensure access to the ICH for industry organisations beyond the research-based industry members which had been participating since the beginning, such as representatives of the generic pharmaceutical industry.[95] Moreover, a certain degree of international character is required, as only organisations with members from 'several countries in at least three continents' are eligible.[96] In addition to this requirement, it must be demonstrated that the organisation itself or its members are affected by at least some ICH Guidelines.[97] However, application is only possible where the organisation has been an observer to the Association or was an Interested Party in the pre-reform ICH, and it must have participated in three meetings of the ICH Assembly or three meetings held by the prior form of establishment, the International Conference of Harmonisation, immediately before the reform.[98] Moreover, it needs to have appointed experts in at least two Working Groups either in the Association or the pre-reform ICH immediately before the reform.[99]

Aspiring Regulatory Members and Industry Members can submit their application to the ICH Secretariat in writing. Membership is then subject to a decision on admission by the Assembly, which will receive a recommendation from the Management Committee on approval or rejection beforehand.[100] In December 2020, the ICH has admitted six Regulatory Members, from Brazil, Singapore, the Republic of Korea, China, Turkey and Taiwan.[101] The ICH also admitted three Industry Members, the International Generic and Biosimilar Medicines Association (IGBA), the Global Self-Care Federation, and the Biotechnology Innovation Organisation (BIO).[102]

Each of the members should appoint an ICH Coordinator to function as a contact point within the respective member's organisation for the ICH Secretariat.[103] They are specifically responsible for the facilitation of information exchange between the experts of the members and the ICH Secretariat, ensuring ICH documents to reach the appropriate persons and supporting the Working Groups. Members may also designate an ICH Technical Coordinator, with the task of supporting their respective Assembly and/or Management Committee representative with their scientific knowledge.[104]

[95] Lindström-Gommers and Mullin (2019) 930

[96] ICH, Articles of Association, art 12(b).

[97] Ibid, art 12(c).

[98] Ibid, art 12(d).

[99] Ibid, art 12(e).

[100] Ibid, art 13.

[101] A list is available on the ICH website: https://www.ich.org/page/members-observers.

[102] Ibid.

[103] ICH, International Council for Harmonisation of Technical Requirements for Pharmaceuticals for Human Use – Standard Operating Procedure of the ICH Working Groups, Version 9.0, Approval by the ICH Management Committee on 19 November 2019, p 6.

[104] ICH, International Council for Harmonisation of Technical Requirements for Pharmaceuticals for Human Use – Standard Operating Procedure of the ICH Working Groups, 8.

C. The EU in the ICH

From an EU perspective it is remarkable that after the reform the European Commission is mentioned as a Founding Regulatory Member, while the EMA is no longer listed among the members. In the past, the website of the ICH stated:

> The ICH Parties are comprised of representatives from the following Regulatory Parties:
>
> – European Union, the Regulatory Party is represented by the European Commission (EC) and the European Medicines Agency (EMA) ...[105]

Thus, the focus has shifted from the EU being a member, to the European Commission being a member. This seems to be due to a shift in emphasis in the structure of the ICH from membership of countries or regions, to granting membership to regulatory authorities responsible for the regulation of pharmaceutical products for human use. Thus, in the case of the EU, it is logical that the membership is assigned to the Commission, as the authority taking final decision in pharmaceutical authorisations, while the scientific opinion of the EMA is not binding.[106]

As far as the Commission is concerned, the previous chapter has already alluded to the complicated competence allocation in EU external relations.[107] In cases of standard-setting bodies that are not international organisations, the Commission takes part in the setting of standards on the basis of its EU internal regulatory competences, while it has to respect the policy-making power of the Council. This is relevant for the question of whether the Commission is competent to be a member of the ICH as a Swiss Association. In principle, the Swiss Association is founded by the adoption of Articles of Association in accordance with Article 60 of the Swiss Civil Code. There is no binding international agreement between the respective members that would create the ICH. However, in the context of the ICH reform process, the Commission adopted a decision establishing its participation as Founding Regulatory Member in the ICH and approving the ICH Articles of Association.[108] The preamble of the Commission Decision on the participation of the Commission in the ICH is quite instructive regarding the competence question:

> (6) The Commission's primary responsibility in the pharmaceutical sector is to propose legislation, ensure compliance with existing legislation, and to develop policy. The work of the ICH assists in the development of Union policy in this field.

[105] Source: www.ich.org/about/faqs.html. (This website was last accessed on 24 February 2016. The information has now been removed from the website. A copy is on file with the author.)

[106] Chapter 1 Section III.

[107] Chapter 2 Section III B.

[108] European Commission, Commission Decision C(2015) 7256 final of 23 October 2015 on the participation of the Commission as Founding Regulatory Member in the 'International Council for Harmonisation of Technical Requirements for Pharmaceuticals for Human Use'. This decision is not in the public domain but has been obtained through an access to documents request. A copy is on file with the author.

> The activities of ICH are purely technical and scientific as the purpose is to agree on common scientific and technical standards relating to medicinal products for human use in the form of non-binding ICH guidelines. The technical and scientific collaboration in the ICH Association thus complements Union policy and legislation in this field.[109]

The membership of the Commission in the ICH is thus presented as a natural extension of its internal regulatory function which does not distort the institutional balance, as the ICH guidelines do not legally bind the EU.

As far as the EMA is concerned, it is remarkable that the Japanese Pharmaceuticals and Medical Devices Agency is listed as being able to represent the Japanese Ministry of Health, Labour and Welfare of Japan, whereas the EMA is not even mentioned.[110] This might, however be due to the fact that the EMA cannot represent the Commission in the ICH because of the allocation of competences in European institutional law.[111] The EMA will, however, continue to support the Commission: the Rules of Procedure of the ICH Assembly also mention that the delegation of the European Commission will include EMA representatives.[112] Also the Commission's Decision on the Commission participation in the ICH states that the 'EMA should continue to support the Commission by having ongoing involvement in the ICH Association, if requested by the Commission, and this support is fully in line with Regulation (EC) No 726/2004 on the establishment of the EMA'.[113] Thus, although the EMA is not formally acknowledged within the ICH, it carries out important supporting functions upon request of the Commission, based on the mandate contained in Article 57(1)(j) of its founding regulation.[114]

D. ICH Observers

In addition to membership it is also possible to obtain observer status within the ICH. The Articles of Association, therefore, now distinguish three different categories of observers, according special status to organisations which were observers before, and paying its dues to its own institutional legacy:

- Standing Observers;
- Observers; and
- Ad hoc Observers.[115]

[109] Ibid.

[110] ICH, Articles of Association, art 8.

[111] Chapter 2 Section III B.

[112] ICH, International Council for Harmonisation of Technical Requirements for Pharmaceuticals for Human Use – Rules of Procedure of the Assembly, Version 8.0, Approval by the Assembly on 19 November 2019, 7.

[113] Commission Decision C(2015) 7256 final, Preamble 8.

[114] Chapter 2 Section III B.

[115] ICH, Articles of Association, art 15.

According to the ICH Articles of Association, the World Health Organisation (WHO) and the International Federation of Pharmaceutical Manufacturers & Associations (IFPMA) are the Standing Observers.[116] While the WHO always had observer status before the ICH reform, the role of the International Federation of Pharmaceutical Manufacturers Associations (IFPMA) pre-reform was less clearly circumscribed. The IFPMA, a collective organisation of all national/regional research-based pharmaceutical company associations, in the early days of the ICH was one of the co-sponsors of the Conference[117] and Steering Committee Member,[118] thus on equal footing with the six founding parties. However, the role of the IFPMA, apart from hosting the ICH Secretariat, had diminished over time and its main role became keeping the national industry associations informed about the ICH process.[119]

Besides the fixed category of Standing Observers, the status of 'Observer' can be granted to legislative and administrative authorities, supranational bodies and international organisations regulating pharmaceuticals; as well as Regional Harmonisation Initiatives regulating pharmaceuticals.[120] In these cases, the observer status is granted 'on the basis of their contribution or benefit to the ICH'.[121] Additionally, observer status can be granted to international pharmaceutical industry organisations, as a pre-stage to membership.[122] Finally, international organisation which are affected by ICH guidelines can become observers, where they or their members are not yet represented as members or observers in the ICH.[123]

The admission of observer status is decided on by the Assembly, after the Management Committee has reviewed the application and drafted a recommendation.[124] Observers will be able to attend the meetings of the ICH Assembly without voting rights.[125] They will not, however, automatically have the right to appoint experts to the Working Groups, but can only do so where this is approved by the Management Committee.[126] A special status is accorded to the Standing Observers, who in addition to the attendance of the Assembly can also attend the Management Committee and will maintain the right to nominate experts for the Working Groups.[127] In December 2020, observer status has been

[116] Ibid, art 16.
[117] P D'Arcy and D Harron (eds), *Proceedings of the First International Conference on Harmonisation – Brussels 1991* (Belfast: The Queen's University Belfast, 1992) xxii.
[118] Ibid, xix.
[119] Interview with an official of the EFPIA, conducted in Brussels on 17 February 2015, notes on file with the author, Interview with two officials of the European Commission, conducted in Brussels on 17 February 2015, notes on file with the author.
[120] ICH, Articles of Association, art 17(1)(a) and (b).
[121] Ibid.
[122] Ibid, art 17(1)(c).
[123] Ibid, art 17(1)(d).
[124] Ibid, art 19(1).
[125] Ibid, art 17(2).
[126] Ibid, art 17(3).
[127] Ibid, art 16.

granted to 17 legislative or administrative authorities, six Regional Harmonisation Initiatives, one International Pharmaceutical Industry Organisation, and six International Organisations with an Interest in Pharmaceuticals.[128]

Moreover, the Articles of Association introduced the category of Ad-hoc Observers, which are invited by the Assembly or Management Committee to participate in the Assembly meetings.[129] The Rules of Procedure of the Assembly in this regard specify that this category includes 'entities or bodies … that have not applied for or do not fulfil the criteria for Observership'.[130] The invitations for Ad-hoc Observers to participate in an Assembly meeting will be restricted to specific meetings and the number of Ad-hoc Observers will be kept limited.[131]

III. THE ICH: INSTITUTIONAL STRUCTURE

After having established the membership and observer rules of the ICH, this section will look more closely at the institutional structure and how the different membership categories laid out above lead to diverging rights and obligations with the institutions. In order to provide some context to the current institutional structure, it should be mentioned that the ICH pre-reform was constituted by a Steering Committee and the Working Groups composed of experts.[132] The Steering Committee was formed by representatives of the six founding members, which maintained oversight of the harmonisation process at large and retained the power to finally endorse the guidelines. However, the governance of the harmonisation process as tasks of the Steering Committee was separated from the process of forming the scientific consensus in the Expert Working Groups.

This two-tier structure allowed the ICH to consult very specific expertise in one topic by drawing on a network of experts from the respective members, while the governance of the ICH and management decisions are dealt with in

[128] A list of observers is available via: www.ich.org/page/members-observers. In December 2020 these were: the respective legislative or administrative authorities of Argentina, India, Cuba, Mexico, Israel, Colombia, Jordan, Moldova, Lebanon, Kazakhstan, Malaysia, Iran, Russia, South Africa, Armenia, Saudi Arabia and Australia; and the following Regional Harmonisation Initiatives: APEC, ASEAN), EAC, GHC), PANDRH, and SADC. International Industry Organisations: APIC. International Organisations with an Interest in Pharmaceuticals: CIOMS, EDQM, IPEC, USP, PIC/S, and the Bill and Melinda Gates Foundation.

[129] ICH, International Articles of Association, art 18.

[130] ICH, Rules of Procedure of the Assembly, 21.

[131] Ibid.

[132] Lindström-Gommers and Mullin (2019) 926. For analysis of the ICH institutional structure before the reform see for example: B Dorbeck-Jung, 'Challenges to the Legitimacy of International Regulation: The Case of Pharmaceuticals Standardisation', in A Føllesdal, R Wessel and J Wouters (eds), *Multilevel Regulation and the EU: The Interplay between Global, European and National Normative Processes* (Leiden: Martinus Nijhoff Publishers, 2008) 51–71; Katsikas (2011); Contrera (1994–1995).

a separate dedicated part of the institutional structure.[133] The main change brought about by the reform is the abolition of the Steering Committee as the main governing body of the ICH, and its replacement with a Management Committee and an Assembly of ICH Members. The Assembly is the central decision-making body in the ICH and the Management Committee is responsible for administrative and managerial tasks. However, the two-tier structure of separating the management, governance and decision-making in the Management Committee and the Assembly from the forming of scientific consensus on specific guidelines in Expert Working Groups is maintained. Article 21 of the Articles of Association now lists the bodies of the Association as the Assembly, the Management Committee, the MedDRA Management Committee, the ICH Secretariat and the Auditors.[134] The Expert Working Groups do not form bodies of the Association according to the Articles of Association, which might be due to the fact that they are created and abolished with respect to the execution of a specific task, such as the drafting of a new ICH guideline.

A. The Assembly

The Assembly is the 'overarching body of the Association',[135] consisting of representatives of all ICH members.[136] Moreover, the Standing Observers and Observers attend the Assembly, where they can actively participate in this discussion and voice their opinion,[137] while lacking voting rights.[138] It elects a Chair and Vice-Chair for a period of two years with possible re-election.[139] The Chair can only be elected from among the Founding Regulatory Members, the Standing Regulatory Members or the Regulatory Members of the Management Committee, whereas the Vice-Chair can be elected amongst the Founding Regulatory Members, the Standing Regulatory Members or the Regulatory Members of the Assembly.[140] Thus, in any case, the Chair and Vice-Chair will be representatives of a regulatory member as opposed to industry representatives.

The Assembly is the central organ of the ICH and its tasks are laid down in article 23 of the Articles of Association: it decides on the adoption, amendment or withdrawal of guidelines, as well as the selection of new topics for harmonisation. From an organisational perspective it is important as it has

[133] S Röttger-Wirtz, 'Independence under threat – the role of private actors in the setting of global pharmaceutical standards and resulting challenges for European public law' (2018a) 24 *European Public Law* 433, 440.
[134] ICH, Articles of Association, art 20.
[135] Ibid, art 23.
[136] Ibid, art 22. Each member is entitled participate in the meetings with two representatives, not counting the Chair and Vice-Chair (ICH, Articles of Association, art 25).
[137] ICH, Rules of Procedure of the Assembly, 21.
[138] ICH, Articles of Association, arts 16 and 17.
[139] Ibid, art 24(6).
[140] Ibid.

the competence to adopt and amend the Articles of Association, and is able to dissolve the Association. Furthermore, the Assembly appoints the elected members to the Management Committee and has the competence to dismiss both Elected and Permanent Management Committee Representatives. It is also the main decision-making body with regard to the admission or refusal of applications for ICH membership and observer status, and also their exclusion. As far as the ICH finances are concerned, the Assembly determines the membership fees, appoints and dismisses the auditors, and approves the annual accounts as well as the ICH's budget for the coming fiscal year. The Assembly has important control functions, as it approves the annual report of ICH activities drafted by the Management Committee and will discharge the activities of the other bodies of the Association. In addition to that, it approves the annual work plan as well as the multi-annual strategic plan, and is responsible for approving cooperation with other organisations.

The Assembly takes its decision by consensus.[141] Only where the Assembly fails to reach a decision by consensus will it vote on the decision, with each member being assigned one vote.[142] The required majority will differ with regard to the types of decision: for example, a three-quarter majority, which must include the votes of each Founding Regulatory Members, is necessary to amend the Articles of Association.[143] For some decisions, only the votes of the various regulatory members will be counted, thus excluding the industry members.[144] The Assembly meets annually at a minimum, or additionally where this is decided by the Management Committee.[145] According to the Rules of Procedure of the Assembly, two meetings per year in spring and autumn have been agreed, as was the case prior to the reform.[146]

B. The Management Committee

The Management Committee has been entrusted with the 'operational aspects' and specifically the 'administrative and financial matters' of the ICH.[147] In this respect, the Management Committee has extensive competences in the management and administration of the ICH.[148] The Management Committee submits recommendations and proposals for Assembly decisions, including the annual work plan and multi-annual strategic plan, as well as recommendations regarding the membership and observer applications. It decides which member will

[141] Ibid, art 26(2).
[142] Ibid.
[143] Ibid, art 26(3).
[144] Ibid, art 26(5) and (6).
[145] Ibid, arts 24 (1) and (5).
[146] ICH, Rules of Procedure of the Assembly, 23.
[147] ICH, Articles of Association, art 36(1).
[148] Ibid, art 36(2).

host the Assembly meetings, and prepare as well as convene those meetings. Thus, although the Assembly is the main decision-making body of the ICH, the Management Committee has a strong influence on the decisions taken and is tasked with their preparation. It also makes proposals and recommendations on financial matters, such as the draft budget, to be decided on by the Assembly. In terms of the standard setting, the Management Committee is responsible for supervising the Working Groups, with regard to an efficient harmonisation process and high-quality guidelines. It also makes recommendations for harmonisation topics and proposals on the adoption, amendment or withdrawal of ICH guidelines.

The Management Committee is composed of a total of up to 28 members, whereas up to 16 are Permanent Management Committee Representatives and 12 are Elected Management Committee Representatives.[149] The Permanent Management Committee Representatives represent the Founding Regulatory Members, Founding Industry Members and Standing Regulatory Members. This essentially covers all of the members who were parties to the ICH pre-reform – EU, US and Japanese regulators, industry representatives, as well as Health Canada and Swissmedic. They are entitled to two Permanent Management Committee Representatives per member.[150] Additionally, the Assembly select up to 12 Elected Management Committee Representatives: eight Elected Management Committee Representatives, representing four Regulatory Members with two representatives each, and four Elected Management Representatives representing two Industry Members.[151] All Management Committee Representatives are expected to act in the interest of the member they represent, while they are also asked to act in the interest of the Association.[152]

The Management Committee meets whenever necessary, but at least whenever the Assembly is meeting, either face to face, by phone or through video conference.[153] A representative of a Permanent Regulatory Member chairs the Management Committee. Alongside the members, the WHO and IFPMA will attend the Management Committee as Permanent Observers with two delegates each.[154]

The main decision-making principle in the Management Committee is consensus; however, qualified majority voting will be adhered to where reaching consensus on a decision fails.[155] The votes will be cast per member, which means that the two representatives per member will have one vote to exercise jointly. Although the precise voting requirements differ with regard to the type of

[149] Ibid, art 28(3).
[150] Ibid.
[151] Ibid. In order to be eligible for election the members have to fulfil certain conditions: ICH, Articles of Association, arts 30 and 31.
[152] Ibid, art 35(3).
[153] Ibid, art 37.
[154] Ibid, art 28(4).
[155] Ibid, art 38.

decision that has to be taken, the joint votes cast by the Permanent Management Committee Representatives appointed by the Founding Regulatory Members have to be included in the required majority.[156]

C. Other ICH Bodies: MedDRA Management Board, ICH Secretariat and Auditors

The Medical Dictionary for Regulatory Activity (MedDRA) produced and managed by the ICH lays down the standard medical terminology for international use, which is applicable through all stages of a medicinal product, from development to the monitoring of products on the market.[157] Thus, whereas the ICH guidelines lay down scientific requirements like testing procedures, the MedDRA harmonises the terminology used by regulators and industry in these guidance documents, applications and in other communication. The task of the MedDRA Management Board, composed of up to two representatives of each Founding Regulatory Members, Founding Industry Members and Standing Regulatory Members, as well as two representatives of the Medicines and Healthcare Products Agency of the UK,[158] is to coordinate and control the MedDRA activities.[159] The WHO may participate in the meetings with two delegates as observers.[160]

The ICH Secretariat carries out the daily management of the ICH, including assistance to the Management Committee in the preparation of the budgets and supporting any sub-committees or working groups, as well as the coordination of ICH activities.[161] Moreover, the Secretariat represents the ICH externally, whereas the Management Committee decides on the power of signature.[162] A Director, who is supervised by the Management Committee, heads the Secretariat.[163] The Secretariat has an important coordinative role within the ICH for the harmonisation process.[164] Its role in ensuring that the harmonisation process moves forward, and preparing the meetings, is key to facilitating progress in harmonisation where the members are active in so many organisational entities. Before the ICH reform, the Secretariat of the ICH was hosted by the IFPMA in Geneva, although as a separate entity from the IFPMA

[156] Ibid, art 38(5), (6) and (7).
[157] Available via: www.meddra.org/about-meddra/vision.
[158] ICH, Articles of Association, arts 43 and 44.
[159] Ibid, art 42.
[160] Ibid, art 43(3).
[161] Ibid, art 55.
[162] Ibid, art 55(1).
[163] Ibid, art 54(1).
[164] Interview with two officials of the European Commission, conducted in Brussels on 17 February 2015, notes on file with the author; Interview with two officials of the European Medicines Agency, conducted in London on 23 March 2015, notes on file with the author; Interview with an official of the EFPIA, conducted in Brussels on 17 February 2015, notes on file with the author.

as such and instructed by the ICH Steering Committee.[165] However, as the ICH Secretariat has an important function in coordinating the ICH process, it drew critical attention that the Secretariat was hosted by the IFPMA, the global industry representation, and was not an independent body. With the reform, the institutional role of the ICH Secretariat has changed and it is now a body of the Association.[166] Under the new Articles of Association the ICH provides the salaries of the Secretariat and its Director.[167]

The final ICH body listed the Articles of Association are Auditors, which are assigned the annual audit of the financial statements of the ICH under Swiss law and accounting principles.[168] This task is assigned to an auditing firm subject to appointment by the Assembly for a period of two years with the possibility of dismissal at any time.[169] A written report of the annual audit is provided to the Assembly.[170]

D. The Working Groups

The Working Groups do not appear as bodies of the ICH in the Articles of Association, however, they play a central role in the ICH as they are responsible for drafting the respective scientific guidelines. These Working Groups take the form of: Expert Working Group (EWG); Implementation Working Group (IWG); or Informal Working Group. The Expert Working Groups (EWGs) draft new ICH guidelines and coordinate scientific and technical aspects of a specific harmonisation topic, working towards scientific consensus in the matter.[171] Implementation Working Groups (IWGs) develop Q&A documents, which are meant to assist the implementation of the Guidelines.[172] Informal Working Groups are established before the formal start of harmonisation activities and develop the Concept Paper and Business Plan for an upcoming harmonisation topic.[173] An Informal Working Group is established whenever the Assembly decides to approve a new topic for an ICH guideline, while an Expert Working Group will be established, after approval of the Concept and Business Paper developed by the Informal Working Group.[174]

[165] Interview with two officials of the European Commission, conducted in Brussels on 17 February 2015, notes on file with the author.
[166] ICH, Articles of Association, art 21.
[167] Ibid, art 54.
[168] Ibid, art 57.
[169] Ibid, art 56.
[170] Ibid, art 57.
[171] ICH, Standard Operating Procedure of the ICH Working Groups, 6.
[172] Ibid, 7.
[173] Ibid, 7.
[174] Ibid, 12.

The Working Groups do not have a fixed meeting rhythm, since they carry out most of their work through writing and teleconferences, only meeting in person where this is necessary in conjunction with Assembly meetings, if approved by the Management Committee.[175] The composition of the EWGs and IWGs is determined when a new group with new experts is established. Each member is allowed to appoint one expert for each Working Group,[176] whereas the Founding Regulatory Members are required to appoint one expert and may appoint two.[177] Standing Observers and Observers are also allowed to nominate one expert for participation in a Working Group,[178] subject to approval of the Management Committee for representative of the Standing Observers.[179] For the EU, the members are usually appointed from the experts of the CHMP or the CHMP working groups, and are occasionally also nominated from EMA staff.[180] The positions taken by these experts at the ICH working group level are reconfirmed within the scientific EMA committees and their working groups, who will discuss the topics at an EU level as the discussion progresses at the global level.[181]

Within each group, a Regulatory Chair is appointed by the Regulatory Members of the Management Committee, to represent the Regulatory Members.[182] The Regulatory Chair will ensure that the consensus-building process is streamlined according to the scope of the harmonisation, and will be executed according to the agreed upon deadlines.[183] A Rapporteur will be appointed by the Assembly from among the representatives of any members; however, if the Rapporteur is an industry representative, a regulatory representative will replace this Rapporteur in Step 2b of the decision-making process.[184] The Rapporteur is appointed to coordinate the scientific work of the group and draft the documents.[185]

[175] Ibid, 22.

[176] ICH, Articles of Association, art 9(2)(b), art 10(2)(b), art 11(3)(d), and art 12(2)(d); ICH, Standard Operating Procedure of the ICH Working Groups, 16.

[177] ICH, Articles of Association, art 8(3)(d); ICH, Standard Operating Procedure of the ICH Working Groups, 16.

[178] ICH, Articles of Association, art 16(2)(b) and art 17(3). ICH, Standard Operating Procedure of the ICH Working Groups, 16.

[179] ICH, Articles of Association, art 17(3).

[180] Interview with two officials of the European Commission, conducted in Brussels on 17 February 2015, notes on file with the author; interview with two officials of the European Medicines Agency, conducted in London on 23 March 2015, notes on file with the author.

[181] Interview with two officials of the European Commission, conducted in Brussels on 17 February 2015, notes on file with the author; Interview with two officials of the European Medicines Agency, conducted in London on 23 March 2015, notes on file with the author; Interview with an official of the EFPIA, conducted in Brussels on 17 February 2015, notes on file with the author.

[182] ICH, Standard Operating Procedure of the ICH Working Groups, 19ff.

[183] Ibid, 20f.

[184] Ibid, 20.

[185] Ibid, 21f.

IV. THE STANDARD-SETTING PROCESS

From the inception of the ICH in 1990 until the reform, the ICH formed the scientific consensus in Expert Working Groups and took its decision on the adoption of the guidelines in the Steering Committee, consisting of the regulators of the EU, US and Japan, as well as the industry representatives of these members.[186] The Steering Committee agreed if there was consensus, and subsequently the three regulatory parties would sign on the guidelines for adoption in their regions. As the Steering Committee decisions were taken by consensus, the industry used to be an equal partner in the decision-making process and essentially a co-regulator. Therefore, in the literature the pre-reform ICH standard-setting process has been described as 'negotiated rule-making', which allows the regulated industry to participate directly and on eye-level with the regulators in the decision-making efforts.[187] Moreover, if one of the industry association representatives in the Steering Committee had objections, for example because the final draft was diverging too far from the Expert Working Group draft as agreed upon between the parties, the regulatory parties could re-submit the draft to the EWG for renewed consideration.[188] Thus, the industry representatives had to agree to the adoption of the guideline and also had the opportunity to renegotiate any changes. The reformed ICH standard-setting procedure curtailed industry influence on the standard-setting.

A. The Selection of Topics for Harmonisation

Standard-setting in the ICH occurs through the Formal ICH Procedure in five steps.[189] Before the actual five-step process begins, a topic for harmonisation has to be selected. This starts with a member or an observer proposing a topic to the Management Committee.[190] The decision on whether a topic is adopted for harmonisation is a prerogative of the Assembly, which receives a recommendation from the Management Committee.[191] This means that the choice of a new harmonisation topic is subject to two decision-making stages: a decision on a

[186] The information of the ICH standard-setting process before the reform has been removed from the ICH website. A copy of the ICH Procedures – Endorsed by the ICH Steering Committee on 10 June 2015 is on file with the author. For an account of the pre-reform ICH standard-setting process see. Contrera (1994–1995); Bahri and Tsintis (2005); Spina (2011).

[187] Contrera (1994–1995); M Rizzi, 'Non-Measurable Negotiations: The EU between Transnational Regulation of Pharmaceuticals and Private Law' in M Cremona and H Micklitz, *Private Law in the External Relations of the EU* (Oxford: Oxford University Press, 2016).

[188] Bahri and Tsintis (2005) 379.

[189] ICH, Standard Operating Procedure of the ICH Working Groups, 28. Next to the Formal ICH Procedure used for new guidelines, the ICH also knows procedures for drafting Q&A documents, as procedures for revisions, maintenance and correction of ICH documents.

[190] ICH, Standard Operating Procedure of the ICH Working Groups, 11.

[191] ICH, Articles of Association, arts 23 (1)(r) and art 36(2)(g).

recommendation by the Management Committee, and a decision on the adoption of a topic for harmonisation by the Assembly. The Management Committee adheres to consensus decision-making and only shifts to voting where consensus cannot be obtained.[192] Where the Management Committee has to vote on a recommendation regarding a proposed harmonisation topic, a two-thirds majority of votes cast including the votes by the representatives of the Founding Regulatory Members is necessary.[193] Where a two-thirds majority is not obtainable, the decision will be taken by unanimity of the representatives of the Founding Regulatory Members.[194]

Also, the decision of the Assembly on a topic proposed for harmonisation is in principle taken by consensus,[195] which means that all members take part in the discussions.[196] However, where consensus cannot be achieved the Assembly has to take a vote. In this case, a simple majority of the votes exercised by the Founding Regulatory Members, Standing Regulatory Members and Regulatory Members, which needs to include the votes of all Founding Regulatory Members, will be decisive for the adoption of a new topic for harmonisation.[197] This decision-making procedure in the Assembly means that industry members will not be able to prevent the choice of a topic for harmonisation. The fact that the regulators will ultimately decide on the harmonisation topic is justified in the Rules of Procedure of the Assembly, by stating that 'regulators have the ultimate responsibility to ensure the protection of public health and have the responsibility to issue regulatory guidelines'.[198] Nonetheless, the Articles of Association oblige the members with voting rights on the selection of new harmonisation topics to 'in good faith, consider the opinions expressed by other Members'.[199]

Where a proposed topic is chosen for harmonisation, an Informal Working Group is established to develop a Concept Paper, which entails a statement of the perceived problem, and outlines the issues that a harmonisation should resolve.[200] Moreover a Business Plan, providing an overview of the costs and benefits of adopting a topic for harmonisation, is developed in the Informal Working Group for a new topic.[201] The Concept Paper and Business Plan are subject to endorsement by the Management Committee.[202] When the Concept Paper and Business Plan are approved, an Expert Working Group is established and the five-step decision-making procedure starts. Within the procedure, the members are responsible for making sure that any requirement internal to the

[192] ICH, Articles of Association, art 38(4).
[193] Ibid, art 38(7).
[194] Ibid.
[195] ICH, Articles of Association, art 26(2).
[196] ICH, Rules of Procedure of the Assembly, 28.
[197] ICH, Articles of Association, art 26(5).
[198] ICH, Rules of Procedure of the Assembly, 28.
[199] ICH, Articles of Association, art 26(5).
[200] ICH, Standard Operating Procedure of the ICH Working Groups, 13.
[201] Ibid, 14.
[202] Ibid, 10.

member's regulatory framework, like the assessment through legal counsels in that member's organisation or other internal approval processes, are carried out correctly and without delaying the ICH process.[203]

B. The ICH Five Step Standard-Setting Procedure

In *Step 1* scientific consensus on the harmonisation topic is formed. The Expert Working Group works towards a consensus in the form of a 'Technical Document' for the respective topic assigned to them and based on the Concept Paper.[204] A Rapporteur will draft the technical document based on the consultations carried out with the experts in the Working Group.[205] As the Management Committee has the task of overseeing the Working Group process, the EWG will regularly provide work plans to the Management Committee, and will inform the Management Committee about issues that are arising and which may obstruct the achievement of consensus or delay the process.[206] Moreover, the Regulatory Chair and the Rapporteur will also be invited to attend the Assembly for this agenda item, to report about the harmonisation process.[207] Where an agreement on the topic is reached in the Working Group, the members of the EWG sign a 'Step 1 Experts Sign-off sheet' and set up the 'Step 1 Technical Document' which is submitted to the Assembly.[208] If consensus cannot be reached the Management Committee may extend the timeline of adoption, ask for a Technical Document that sets out different alternatives, itself provide guidance on how to resolve the dispute or ask for a decision of the Assembly, or suspend the harmonisation.[209]

In *Step 2*, the scientific consensus expressed in the Technical Document is confirmed by the Assembly.[210] In *Step 2a* the members of the Assembly have to be in agreement that there is scientific consensus and, at this stage, the views of all members including the members representing industry are taken into account for the consensus.[211] However, '(i)n the unlikely situation where consensus cannot be reached, the Assembly will proceed to voting' in order to adopt the Final Technical Document by majority.[212] This Final Technical Document then will be developed into a Draft Guideline. Whereas the industry experts in the respective Working Group are fully part of the development and may serve as Rapporteur of the Technical Document until *Step 2a*, the development of the Draft Guideline in *Step 2b* is regulator-driven. If initially the Rapporteur

[203] Ibid, 28.
[204] Ibid, 28.
[205] Ibid.
[206] Ibid.
[207] Ibid.
[208] Ibid, 29.
[209] Ibid.
[210] Ibid.
[211] ICH, Rules of Procedure of the Assembly, 28f.
[212] ICH, Standard Operating Procedure of the ICH Working Groups, 29.

was an industry member, from *Step 2b* the regulatory members need to appoint the Rapporteur.[213] However, the experts nominated by the Founding Industry Members and Industry Members remain members of the Working Group and participate in the process.[214] *Step 2b* is concluded by the endorsement of the Draft Guideline through the Assembly, for which only the views of the members representing regulators are taken into account for the consensus.[215] Again, where consensus fails, the Regulatory Members of the Assembly can adopt the Draft Guideline by majority vote.[216] After *Step 2*, the Draft Guideline will be published on the ICH website.[217]

Step 3 is characterised by a public consultation procedure. The Draft Guideline is submitted to the regulatory authorities of the ICH Members for public consultation according to their national procedures.[218] Comments on the Draft Guideline can be submitted to the regulatory authorities according to the usual national procedure. In the EU, it will be published as a draft CHMP Guideline, the CHMP being the Committee for Human Medicinal Products within the EMA.[219] In addition, the draft is published by the ICH Secretariat for comments by Industry Associations and other Regulatory authorities.[220] The comments are forwarded to the EWG, which will consider and discuss them and subsequently draft a revised version of the Draft Guidelines, the 'Step 3 Expert Draft Guideline', subject to sign-off by experts of the ICH Regulatory Members.[221]

At *Step 4*, the adoption of the ICH Guideline follows. Like the adoption of a new topic for harmonisation, the adoption of a finalised guideline is also subject to two decision-making stages: a decision on a recommendation by the Management Committee, and a decision on the adoption of the guideline by the Assembly.[222] First, the Management Committee will adopt a recommendation on the adoption of a guideline. Again, the core decision-making principle is consensus.[223] Where this cannot be reached, a two-thirds majority of votes cast is necessary to adopt a decision, whereas the two-thirds majority must include the votes by the representatives of the Founding Regulatory Members.[224] Should a two-thirds majority not be obtainable, the decision will be taken by unanimity of the representatives of the Founding Regulatory Members.[225] The decision

[213] Ibid, 30.
[214] Ibid.
[215] Ibid.
[216] Ibid.
[217] Ibid.
[218] Ibid, 31.
[219] The role of the EMA in the implementation of the ICH guidelines in the EU will be discussed in Chapter 4. A closer examination of the public consultation procedure is provided in Chapter 6.
[220] ICH, Standard Operating Procedure of the ICH Working Groups, 31.
[221] Ibid, 31f.
[222] Ibid, 32.
[223] ICH, Articles of Association, art 38(4).
[224] Ibid, art 38(7).
[225] Ibid.

of the Assembly on the adoption of a guideline is also, in principle, taken by consensus, with only the members representing regulators considered to be relevant for the forming of the consensus.[226] Where voting takes place, a simple majority of the votes exercised by the Founding Regulatory Members, Standing Regulatory Members and Regulatory Members, which needs to include the votes of all Founding Regulatory Members, will be necessary for the adoption of an ICH guideline.[227] Thus, the Founding Industry Members and the Industry Members are excluded from the voting.

Step 5 consists of regulatory implementation by the regulatory members.[228] The regulatory authorities will report the implementation measures taken to the Assembly and these will be published on the ICH website by the Secretariat.[229]

V. CONCLUSION: THE REFORMED ICH IN PERSPECTIVE

Since its inception in 1990, the ICH has become a pivotal source of global pharmaceutical standards. It has progressively evolved from a rather *ad hoc*, informal meeting-based harmonisation forum to become a Swiss association with an elaborate institutional structure and decision-making processes. Thus, throughout its history the ICH has undergone considerable formalisation. The recent reform of the ICH was intended to open up ICH membership to the national regulators and international industry associations affected by the guidelines and to make the ICH more regulator-driven, clarifying the distinct roles of industry and regulators.

With regard to enabling a truly global membership, the ICH has now opened up for other regulatory authorities or industry associations to become ICH members (or at least observers). However, joining the ICH is subject to strict conditions of prior participation in ICH meetings and Working Groups, as well as progressive implementation of the existing ICH guidelines.[230] While the ICH was conscious that joining should not be made impossible, it also ensured that the requirements would 'not be too low either given that ICH membership is considered to bring with it integrity and recognition'.[231] Furthermore, new ICH members do not join the Association on an equal footing to the original members. Both Regulatory Founding Members and Industry Founding Members have maintained a privileged status in the ICH. They are guaranteed participation in the Management Committee, which gives them significant steering power, while only 12 out of the 28 seats can be filled by the new Regulatory and Industry Members subject to election by the Assembly.

[226] ICH, Rules of Procedure of the Assembly, 29.
[227] ICH, Articles of Association, art 26(6).
[228] ICH, Standard Operating Procedure of the ICH Working Groups, 32.
[229] Ibid, 33.
[230] See also: Seuba (2018) 481.
[231] Lindström-Gommers and Mullin (2019) 929.

Also, where decision-making is concerned not all members have the same prerogatives:[232] where decisions are taken by vote, the Founding Regulatory Parties both in the Management Committee and the Assembly have a prominent position, as their votes are required to achieve a decision-making majority. Thus, while the new members do have a say in the decision-making process and contribute to the consensus forming, where decisions have more conflict potential and have to be voted on, their say is less than that of the founding members. As expressed by Lindström-Gommers and Mullin: 'The founding members of the ICH were thus entrusted the maximum of rights and obligations in the association as they committed to making the biggest contribution to the Association and taking the ultimate responsibility for ensuring the continuity of ICH activities.'[233]

Furthermore, the reform aimed to address the role of the industry in the ICH, and especially it aimed to ensure that the regulatory authorities were in the lead in the standard-setting process. Concerning its overall institutional structure, after the reform the ICH is defined by the cooperation of public and private (mostly industry) parties, which habitually undertake joint decision-making, and characterised by shared rights and responsibilities between the actors. It is still a public-private partnership.[234] While the ICH from 1990 until recently operated with an equilibrium of three regulatory members and three industry members, at the time of writing 11 regulatory members and six industry members take part in the ICH. The aim of the reform was to make the ICH more regulator-focused and to open up to other regulators, while also providing room for including other industry associations that are affected by ICH guidelines. However, the focus seems to be on an extension of regulatory members rather than industry members, as also becomes evident from the ICH website: 'More involvement from regulators around the world is *welcomed and expected* … This is matched by the *possibility* of wider inclusion of global industry sectors affected by ICH harmonisation.'[235] Nonetheless, public as well as private parties participate in the two main governing bodies. In the Assembly each member is entitled to up to two representatives, which guarantees the participation rights of both public and private bodies.[236] In the Management Committee consisting of 28 Members, 10 representatives will be industry representatives and 18 will be regulatory members, which means that although there is representation of industry interests in the Management Committee, the majority of the members will be public members representatives.

[232] See also: Seuba (2018) 481.
[233] Lindström-Gommers and Mullin (2019) 929.
[234] For a discussion of public-private partnerships as a type of global standard-setting bodies see Chapter 2 Section II B iv.
[235] ICH, Press Release – ICH announces organisational changes as it marks 25 years of successful harmonisation, Geneva, 26 October 2015 (emphasis added), available via: www.ich.org/page/press-releases.
[236] ICH, Articles of Association, art 24.

With regard to the standard-setting process as such, the process has become more regulator-driven. While all Members and Observers can propose a topic for harmonisation, the decision on the adoption of a topic for harmonisation is then taken by the Assembly, upon recommendation of the Management Committee. In the initial step of choosing a topic for harmonisation, the industry representatives in the Management Committee take part in the decision-making on the recommendation. In the Assembly the views of the industry are taken into account for forming a consensus. However, the Founding Industry Members and Industry Members are excluded from voting if consensus cannot be reached. Moreover, where the scientific consensus in form of a Technical Document is agreed upon, for decisions in *Step 2b* regarding the adoption of a Draft Guideline and *Step 4* regarding the adoption of a final ICH guidelines, the industry representatives' views are not taken into account for the forming of consensus in the Assembly. Founding Industry Members and Industry Members are also excluded from voting if consensus on the adoption cannot be achieved. In the Management Committee too, which adopts a recommendation for the Assembly on the adoption of a guideline, the industry representatives are excluded from voting if consensus cannot be achieved.

While the industry influence on key decision-making steps in the guideline adoption process has been abolished, this has not changed the significant influence of the industry on the forming of the content of the guidelines, which takes place on the level of the Expert Working Groups. Thus, whereas the decision-making process might now be more regulator-driven and any possibility of the industry representing members to block the adoption of guidelines has been removed, the substance of the guidelines still comes into being in a co-regulatory effort between regulatory and industry experts.[237] The ICH will still be characterised by its public-private membership, with a co-regulatory decision-making process, as well as the sharing of expertise and financial resources of the regulators and the industry associations, although the reform has had an impact on the position of the industry within the ICH.

Finally, it should be noted that the ICH reform has only been concluded recently, at a point where after 25 years of harmonisation, the ICH had already adopted a large catalogue of harmonised guidelines, which have already been implemented in many regions of the world and have to be accepted by incoming members.[238]

[237] Röttger-Wirtz (2018a) 443.
[238] Seuba (2018) 478.

4

The Implementation of ICH Standards in the European Union

As shown in the previous chapter, the ICH guidelines constitute recommendations, which after the adoption on ICH level require implementation into national and regional regulatory systems, while the guidelines as such lack legally binding force. This chapter will provide a detailed account of the effects of ICH guidelines on the European regulatory framework for pharmaceuticals. It will analyse how precisely they are implemented, and how ICH standards affect this regulatory framework beyond their mere implementation. This analysis will show how deeply the norms set at the ICH level permeate EU regulation. In this regard, this chapter exemplifies how global standards, which are voluntary soft law measures when characterised in international law, shape the reality of risk regulation in the EU in practice.

I. A CLOSER LOOK AT THE ICH GUIDELINES

The aim of the ICH is to harmonise the regulatory requirements that have to be fulfilled in order to obtain marketing authorisations for pharmaceuticals in the different regulatory systems around the world. Like the EU,[1] most countries around the world require an authorisation of medicinal products, based on proof of their quality, safety and efficacy, before they can be marketed. On the one hand, the ICH standards address the regulatory authorities that are members of the ICH, where they will be used to determine the information required in the marketing authorisation applications and constitute evaluation criteria. On the other hand, they regulate the activities of the pharmaceutical industry, which will have to make sure their products and production as well as testing processes will conform to ICH guidelines, in order to get them authorised in the countries that use those standards.

[1] See Chapter 1.

A. The Four ICH Guideline Categories

Currently over 60 ICH guidelines have been adopted[2] – an 'impressive' result according to participants in the process.[3] The ICH categorises the guidelines into quality, safety and efficacy topics, reflecting the core criteria for scientific assessment in the marketing authorisation procedure for medicinal products.[4] In addition to these three categories, a 'multidisciplinary' category was created for topics that do not fit well into (only) one of the above categories.

As the name suggests, *quality guidelines* contain methods to ensure the quality of a pharmaceutical product. For example, they are concerned with establishing test methods to guarantee that the products maintain the same quality throughout their shelf-life. The Q1A guideline contains testing standards establishing the duration, temperature and humidity under which the shelf-life of a product is tested.[5] This is complemented with the Q1B guideline for testing the photostability of new substances, ie whether exposure to light will have an effect on their quality.[6] Moreover, there are guidelines dealing with the impurities in drug substances (Q3A-D)[7] and establishing guidance for testing new drug substances (Q6A[8] and Q6B[9]). Importantly, the manufacturing of pharmaceuticals is also harmonised through the Q7 guideline, dealing with Good Manufacturing Practice.[10]

The *safety guidelines* address potential risks in the form of toxic effects of the product. Topics harmonised include, for example, carcinogenicity studies (S1A-S1C)[11] establishing rules for testing on cancer-causing properties, and

[2] The adopted guidelines can be found on the ICH website: www.ich.org/page/ich-guidelines.

[3] F Sauer, 'Preface', in J van de Laan and J DeGeorge (eds), *Global Approach in Safety Testing – ICH Guidelines Explained* (New York: Springer, 2013) vii.

[4] B Kuhnert, 'ICH at 20: An overview' (2011) 3 *Drug Information Association Global Forum* 17, 17.

[5] ICH, ICH Harmonised Tripartite Guideline – Stability Testing of New Drug Substances and Products Q1A(R2), 6 February 2003.

[6] ICH, ICH Harmonised Tripartite Guideline – Stability Testing: Photostability Testing of New Substances and Products – Q1B, 6 November 1996.

[7] ICH, ICH Harmonised Tripartite Guideline – Impurities in New Drug Substances Q3A(R2), 25 October 2006; ICH, ICH Harmonised Tripartite Guideline – Impurities in New Drug Products Q3B(R2), 2 June 2006; ICH, ICH Harmonised Tripartite Guideline – Impurities: Guideline for Residual Solvents Q3C(R6), 9 November 2016; ICH, ICH Harmonised Tripartite Guideline – Guideline for Elemental Impurities Q3D (R1), 22 March 2019. The ICH in July 2020 started work on Q3E on Impurities: Assessment and Control of Extractables and Leachables for Pharmaceuticals and Biologics.

[8] ICH, ICH Harmonised Tripartite Guideline – Specifications: Test Procedures and Acceptance Criteria for New Drug Products: Chemical Substances Q6A, 6 October 1999.

[9] ICH, ICH Harmonised Tripartite Guideline – Specifications: Test Procedures and Acceptance Criteria for Biotechnological/Biological Products Q6B, 10 March 1999.

[10] ICH, ICH Harmonised Tripartite Guideline – Good Manufacturing Practice Guide for Active Pharmaceutical Ingredients Q7, 10 November 2000.

[11] ICH, ICH Harmonised Tripartite Guideline – Guideline on the Need for Carcinogenicity Studies of Pharmaceuticals S1A, 29 November 1995; ICH, ICH Harmonised Tripartite Guideline – Testing for Carcinogenicity of Pharmaceuticals S1B, 16 July 1997; ICH, ICH Harmonised Tripartite Guideline – Dose Selection for Carcinogenicity Studies of Pharmaceuticals S1C(R2), 27 October 1994.

genotoxicity studies (S2)[12] concerned with testing for negative effects on genetic material. Tests on whether a drug will cause birth defects or might have a negative effect on fertility are also established in an ICH guideline (Reproductive Toxicology S5).[13] Moreover, a special guideline has been established for the safety of biotechnological products (S6).[14]

Efficacy guidelines address clinical trials to be conducted in order to obtain a marketing authorisation for a medicinal product. Clinical trials are the phase in the drug development process where the drug is tested on humans. Various aspects of clinical trials are regulated in ICH guidelines, such as the definition of terminology used to collect and report the results of clinical trials (for example, a harmonised definition of Adverse Event or Adverse Drug Reaction), in the ICH E2A Guideline.[15] Moreover, the ICH has agreed on a Good Clinical Practice Guidance (E6), which is meant to ensure that the results are reliable, and that the participants in clinical trials are adequately protected through establishing 'an international ethical and scientific quality standard for designing, conducting, recording and reporting trials'.[16] The E6 guideline is currently under review, in order to address innovation in clinical trial design and especially the use of new data sources.[17] The E5 Guideline on Ethnic Factors in Clinical Trials Data has also been an important contribution to pharmaceutical standards as it facilitates the acceptance of clinical trials conducted in a country that is not the country where marketing authorisation is requested.[18] This is highly relevant as it significantly reduces the number of clinical trials it is necessary to conduct. Agreement on this issue was complicated through the fact that in drug regulation, 'factors relating to the genetic and physiologic (intrinsic) and the cultural and environmental (extrinsic) characteristics of a population'[19] need to be taken into account.

Interestingly, the efficacy guidelines not only contribute to the regulation of data necessary for the marketing authorisation of pharmaceuticals, but also contribute significantly to the harmonisation of pharmacovigilance requirements. Pharmacovigilance is concerned with gathering data on, analysing, and reacting

[12] ICH, ICH Harmonised Tripartite Guideline – Guidance on Genotoxicity Testing and Data Interpretation for Pharmaceuticals Intended for Human Use S2(R1), 9 November 2011.

[13] ICH, ICH Harmonised Tripartite Guideline – Detection of Toxicity to Reproduction for Medicinal Products & Toxicity to Male Fertility S5(R3), 18 February 2020. See: Jordan (1992), p. 494.

[14] ICH, ICH Harmonised Tripartite Guideline – Preclinical Safety Evaluation of Biotechnology-Derived Pharmaceuticals S6(R1), 16 July 1997.

[15] ICH, ICH Harmonised Tripartite Guideline – Clinical Safety Data Management: Definitions and Standards for Expedited Reporting E2A, 27 October 1994.

[16] ICH, ICH Harmonised Tripartite Guideline – Guideline for Good Clinical Practice E6(R2), 9 November 2016, 1.

[17] ICH, Final Concept Paper ICH E6(R3): Guideline for Good Clinical Practice Dated 17 November 2019.

[18] ICH, ICH Harmonised Tripartite Guideline – Ethnic Factors in the Acceptability for Foreign Clinical Data E5(R1), 5 February 1998.

[19] Ibid, 1.

to adverse effects of pharmaceuticals when they are already being marketed.[20] Although the E2A on definitions and standards for expedited reporting is concerned with adverse drug reactions in the clinical trials conducted before the marketing of a product,[21] it has also been applied to pharmacovigilance activities after the marketing authorisation has been granted.[22] With the E2D guideline on post-approval safety data management, the ICH adopted a guideline explicitly devoted to the post-authorisation phase.[23] Overall, the ICH has been very influential in the pharmacovigilance processes of its members.[24]

Finally, as a fourth type of ICH standard, the *multidisciplinary guideline* category is a 'catch-all' that encompasses guidelines which do not fit into a single of the above described categories. Here, the most relevant guidelines are the M4 guidelines establishing the Common Technical Document (CTD),[25] a harmonised format for the marketing authorisation application.

Where during the first ICH conference, the harmonisation started with defining the very basics of data collection conditions, such as defining what is 'room temperature', it soon moved towards establishing detailed standards for clinical trials and addressing challenging issues such as ethnical differences in drug response.[26] The ICH has set out to harmonise the regulatory requirements for marketing authorisations; however, many of these standards also affect the research and development process of pharmaceuticals, as they have to be adhered to in the development of the medicine before an authorisation can even be requested.[27] For example, by means of guidelines such as the ICH S6 Preclinical Safety Evaluation of Biotechnology-Derived Pharmaceuticals,[28] or the development of a guideline for Nonclinical Biodistribution Considerations for Gene Therapy Products which has been endorsed as a topic for harmonisation

[20] G Castle and B Kelly, 'Global Harmonization is Not All that Global: Divergent Approaches in Drug Safety' (2008) 63 *Food and Drug Law Journal* 601, 601; A Spina, 'The Regulation of Pharmaceuticals Beyond the State: EU and Global Administrative Systems', in E Chiti and B Mattarella (eds), *Global Administrative Law and EU Administrative Law* (Heidelberg: Springer, 2011) 255.

[21] ICH, ICH Harmonised Tripartite Guideline – Clinical Safety Data Management: Definitions and Standards for Expedited Reporting E2A, 27 October 1994.

[22] P Bahri and P Tsintis, 'Pharmacovigilance-related topics at the level of the International Conference on Harmonisation (ICH)' (2005) 14 *Pharmacoepidemiology and Drug Safety* 377, 379.

[23] ICH, ICH Harmonised Tripartite Guideline – Post-Approval Safety Data Management: Definitions and Standards for Expedited Reporting E2D, 12 November 2003. This guideline is currently being revised.

[24] Bahri and Tsintis (2005).

[25] Section II D.

[26] D Vogel, 'The Globalization of Pharmaceutical Regulation' (1998) 11 *Governance* 1.

[27] See: Chapter 1; X Seuba, 'International harmonization of pharmaceutical standards: trade, ethics and power', in G Burci and B Toebes, *Research Handbook in Global Health Law* (Cheltenham: Edward Elgar, 2018); G Bache, M Flear and T Hervey, 'The Defining Features of the European Union's Approach to Regulating New Health Technologies', in M Flear, A Farrell, T Hervey, and T Murphy (eds), *European Law and New Health Technologies* (Oxford: Oxford University Press, 2013).

[28] ICH, ICH Harmonised Tripartite Guideline – Preclinical Safety Evaluation of Biotechnology-Derived Pharmaceuticals S6(R1), 12 June 2011.

in 2019,[29] the ICH significantly shapes the development of highly innovative medicinal products.[30]

ICH standards apply to the full 'cycle of innovation'[31] of medicinal products from non-clinical, pre-clinical and clinical research, the marketing authorisation requirements as such, through to the manufacturing stage of active substances as well as finished pharmaceuticals and also include the market surveillance in terms of pharmacovigilance.[32] In particular, Good Clinical Practice (GCP) developed by the ICH has been discussed in this context. It has been praised as having ensured the protection of trial subjects and quality of trial data, and ultimately enabling the increase of multiregional clinical trials for new medicinal products.[33] At the same time criticism has been voiced: as it provides detailed guidance on the documentation of the trials and the management of clinical trials data, it is questioned as to how far this actually protects the participants of the trials.[34] It is also argued that the GCP creates a (sometimes unnecessarily) high administrative burden, negatively affecting the development of pharmaceuticals in non-commercial settings and in countries with a newly arising pharmaceutical industry and/or limited regulatory capacity.[35]

B. The Legal Status of ICH Guidelines upon Adoption

The ICH has adopted a significant number of guidelines, extensively harmonising the regulatory requirements for pharmaceuticals around the world. However, once these standards are adopted on ICH level, what is their legal status and what obligations for the ICH members follow from the adoption? While the ICH guidelines lack legally binding force,[36] the Articles of Association lay down

[29] ICH, Concept Paper S12: Nonclinical Biodistribution Considerations for Gene Therapy Products, Dated 18 November 2019.

[30] See also: Bache, Flear and Hervey (2013) 15.

[31] Ibid, 12.

[32] Bahri and Tsintis (2005).

[33] See: J Molzon et al, 'The Value and Benefits of the International Conference on Harmonisation to Drug Regulatory Authorities: Advancing Harmonization for Better Public Health' (2011) 89 *Clinical Pharmacology & Therapeutics* 503, 508; L Lindström-Gommers and T Mullin, 'International Conference on Harmonization: Recent Reforms as a Driver of Global Regulatory Harmonization and Innovation in Medical Products' (2019) 105 *Clinical Pharmacology & Therapeutics* 926, 927.

[34] E Jackson, *Medical Law – Text, Cases, and Materials*, 5th edn (Oxford: Oxford University Press, 2019) 527.

[35] See in this regard: World Health Organization, The Impact of Implementation of ICH Guidelines in Non-ICH Countries, Report of a WHO Meeting 13–15 September 2001 (Geneva), Regulatory Support Series No 9, WHO/EDM/QSM/2002.3; A Berman, 'The Distributional Effects of Transnational Pharmaceutical Regulation', (2012b) CTEI Working Paper, CTEI-2012-01; M Flear, 'Charting a roadmap towards membership and formal voice in global bioethics standard-setting: Health research and the case of the International Council on Harmonisation' (2018) *Medical Law International* 157.

[36] ICH, International Council for Harmonisation of Technical Requirements for Pharmaceuticals for Human Use – Rules of Procedure of the Assembly, Version 8.0, Approval by the Assembly on 19 November, 11.

that the Founding Regulatory Members, the Standing Regulatory Members, and the Regulatory Members 'are expected to implement all ICH Guidelines in accordance with the applicable Rules of Procedure'.[37] The Founding Industry Members will 'actively support and encourage the compliance by the Founding Industry Member and/or its affiliated members with the ICH Guidelines',[38] and the Industry Members will 'actively support and encourage the compliance with the ICH Guidelines that the Industry Member or its affiliated members are regulated or affected by'.[39] Thus, the members representing regulators should implement the guidelines, while the members representing industry associations are responsible for promoting the use of ICH guidelines in the associations and the companies they represent. However, the Articles of Association do not contain a legally binding obligation for the members to implement ICH guidelines and characterise the guidelines as 'recommendations towards achieving greater harmonisation'.[40]

As Fernand Sauer, former Executive Director of the EMA and founding member of the ICH explains: 'ICH has no authority to impose regulatory requirements … It can only advise regulators and regulated on scientific issues.'[41] This voluntary nature of the ICH guidelines is also highlighted by the fact that the ICH has no internal enforcement mechanism to address incorrect or a lack of implementation. It is provided that where in exceptional circumstances a Regulatory Member only implements a guideline partially or cannot implement the guideline, it has to inform the ICH Secretariat and provide justifications.[42] However, no legal consequences are attached to missing or only partial implementation. Nonetheless, standards gain their effectiveness not from hierarchical coercion, but more from the horizontal cooperation process through which they are adopted.[43] In this regard, they constitute soft law, which means that they introduce certain obligations which (indirectly) affect the legal situation of a variety of actors. They are capable of constraining the freedom to act of the parties that agreed on the measure, conditioning their actions through their authority, thereby often reducing the possibility to deviate to mere fiction.[44] This is also true for the standards set in the ICH process.

[37] ICH, Articles of Association, art 8(4) for Founding Regulatory Members, art 10(4) for Standing Regulatory Members, and art 11(5) for Regulatory Members.

[38] ICH, Articles of Association, art 9(3)(b).

[39] Ibid, art 12(3)(b).

[40] Ibid, art 3(a).

[41] Sauer (2013) viii.

[42] ICH, Rules of Procedure of the Assembly, 12.

[43] Chapter 2 Section I B; See also: H Röhl, 'Internationale Standardsetzung', in C Möllers, A Vosskuhle and C Walter (eds), *Internationales Verwaltungsrecht – Eine Analyse Anhand von Referenzgebieten* (Tübingen: Mohr Siebeck, 2007) 321; C Möllers, 'Transnationale Behördenkooperation – Verfassungs- und Völkerrechtliche Probleme Transnationaler Administrativer Standardsetzung' (2005) 65 *Zeitschrift für ausländisches öffentliches Recht und Völkerrecht* 351.

[44] A von Bogdandy, P Dann and M Goldmann, 'Developing the Publicness of Public International Law', in A von Bogdandy, R Wolfrum, J von Bernstorff, P Dann and M Goldmann (eds), *The Exercise of Public Authority by International Institutions: Advancing International Institutional Law* (Heidelberg: Springer, 2010) 11f.

It is the commitment of the ICH regulatory parties to implement the guidelines endorsed in the ICH process that has contributed to the success of the ICH over the years.[45] The fact that implementation was reliably carried out by the three original regulatory parties to the ICH before the reform has built a system of mutual trust.[46] A Commission official has described this commitment as a 'gentlemen's agreement': once the regulator signs off the guideline at *Step 4*, this regulator has committed to implementing the guideline.[47] Thus, the guidelines are not implemented due to a legal obligation, but rather due to a political commitment and group dynamic that has built up over the years. Therefore, although there is no legal obligation for the ICH members to implement the guidelines, the guidelines become *de facto* binding through the participation of ICH members in the process. In essence they are self-binding on the members.

After the ICH reform, the membership of the ICH has been broadened and new regulators will join the ICH as Regulatory Members. As explained, these members should also implement the ICH guidelines according to the Articles of Association.[48] However, the new Regulatory Members are not expected to have implemented all ICH guidelines before they apply for membership. Instead, a gradual implementation of the guidelines is envisaged in three stages according to the importance of the guidelines. First, in order to be eligible for the application to become a Regulatory Member, the 'Tier 1 Guidelines' Q1, Q7 and E6 have to be implemented by the respective regulator or the members of a Regional Harmonisation Initiative.[49] Where the application is successful and a regulator or Regional Harmonisation Initiative becomes a Regulatory Member, they will submit a plan with timeframes to implement the 'Tier 2 Guidelines' E2A, E2B, E2D, M4 and M1, aiming for implementation within five years.[50] The rest of the guidelines, the 'Tier 3 Guidelines', should be implemented 'in the near term and as soon as possible'.[51] Therefore, although the flawless implementation rate of the ICH prior to the reform is presumably endangered by the enlarged ICH membership, the reform process includes a structured approach to leading new members into implementing all ICH guidelines. The ICH is currently working on a better understanding of the level of implementation of the ICH guidelines amongst its members, and has carried out a survey amongst regulatory authorities and companies, showing that the guidelines are adequately implemented

[45] Source: https://www.ich.org/page/mission. Also confirmed by the Commission: Interview with two officials of the European Commission, conducted in Brussels on 17 February 2015, notes on file with the author.

[46] Interview with two officials of the European Commission, conducted in Brussels on 17 February 2015, notes on file with the author.

[47] Interview with two officials of the European Commission, conducted in Brussels on 17 February 2015, notes on file with the author.

[48] ICH, Articles of Association, art 11.

[49] ICH, Rules of Procedure of the Assembly, 11.

[50] Ibid, 12.

[51] Ibid.

and adhered to by the Founding and Standing Regulatory Members and implementation was in process by the Regulatory Members and Observers.[52]

Overall, the ICH has a very successful history with regard to the implementation of its guidelines. The original three regulatory members have implemented all ICH guidelines, and their implementation even in non-member countries eventually led to the ICH reform. Consensus as a core principle in the decision-making process has contributed significantly to the successful implementation of adopted guidelines in the past. Before the reform, a guideline was only adopted when every regulatory party was satisfied with the consensus, and therefore the regulatory parties were also willing to implement it.[53] The dialogue within the standard-setting process and decision-making by consensus are central to understanding the operation of the harmonisation process and its success.[54] The ICH guidelines are a product of negotiated rule-making, which means that the parties are more willing to accept the norms, since they have contributed to their development.[55] After the ICH reform, consensus remains the main decision-making principle; however, the Articles of Association provide that where consensus cannot be achieved voting will take place in both the Management Committee and the Assembly.[56] Whether this will affect the implementation of the guidelines can only be evaluated in the future, when enough experience with regard to the new decision-making practice has been gathered. Moreover, it is not yet clear whether the voting on the adoption of a guideline will be a regular occurrence or if it will remain a rare exception.

Apart from consensus as a trigger for implementation, other factors should be considered too. In the very scientific and technical area of pharmaceutical regulation in particular, the agreement on a standard as commonly accepted by the regulatory authorities and industry 'represents de facto a limitation of the discretionary power of administrative bodies at national level to deviate from the standards or to present a different assessment without a sound justification'.[57] This is caused by the scientific expertise represented in the ICH, which lends high persuasive power to a consensus of these highly qualified experts. Indeed, in general, international harmonisation through bodies like the ICH is often respected because these bodies are equipped with the leading experts in the respective fields, which gives their guidelines a high level of

[52] ICH, CRIS – 2019 Project Report Monitoring the Adequacy of Implementation and Adherence to ICH guidelines, available via: https://www.ich.org/page/ich-guideline-implementation.

[53] Interview with two officials of the European Commission, conducted in Brussels on 17 February 2015, notes on file with the author.

[54] P Lezotre, *International Cooperation, Convergence and Harmonization of Pharmaceutical Regulations – A Global Perspective* (Oxford: Academic Press Elsevier, 2014) 61; Spina (2011) 263.

[55] J Contrera, 'The Food and Drug Administration and the International Conference on Harmonisation: How Harmonious Will International Pharmaceutical Regulations Become?' (1994–1995) 8 *The Administrative Law Journal* 927, 937.

[56] Chapter 3.

[57] Spina (2011) 263.

scientific authority.[58] The high scientific quality has been attested to the ICH in a World Health Organization (WHO) report.[59] This high scientific value provides the guidelines with authority and acceptance amongst ICH members as well as non-ICH members.

II. IMPLEMENTING GLOBAL STANDARDS IN THE EU: THE INTEGRATION OF ICH STANDARDS IN EU PHARMACEUTICAL LAW

The ICH has successfully shaped and harmonised the regulatory requirements for the marketing authorization of pharmaceuticals in the regulatory systems of its members and even beyond. How these standards interact with a regulatory framework will be shown in the following sections, which examine the implementation of the ICH standards in the EU.

A. The Implementation of Global Standards in EU Law: The General Framework

Before examining the implementation of ICH standards in the EU in detail, it is important to understand that the non-binding nature of global standards has consequences for their implementation, as the standards will require a connecting measure ('*Bindungselement*') to be incorporated into a regulatory framework.[60] In this regard, for the implementation of global standards into the European framework in principle two routes are open: implementation through binding Union legislation, and implementation via EU administrative soft law measures.

The first route is implementation through a binding legislative measure on an EU level and in this regard, three different routes to legislative implementation can be distinguished: (i) *the binding static reference* to a certain standard in force at the time of implementation; (ii) a *dynamic binding reference*, where a general reference to a certain standard or standard setting-body also includes future developments of this standard or new norms adopted by the standard-setting body; and (iii) an *obligation to take into account* (as opposed to being bound by) a certain standard or rules of a certain standard-setting body.[61]

[58] J Wouters and S Verhoeven, 'Regulation and Globalization: Interaction between International Standard-Setting Agencies and the European Union, in D Geradin, R Muñoz, and N Petit (eds), *Regulation Through Agencies in the EU: A New Paradigm of European Governance* (Cheltenham: Edward Elgar, 2006) 261.

[59] World Health Organization, The Impact of Implementation of ICH Guidelines in Non-ICH Countries, 15.

[60] P Müller-Graff, 'Das "Soft Law" der Europäischen Organisationen' (2012) 1 *Europarecht* 18, 27.

[61] Müller-Graff (2012) 28; M Ruffert, '§17 Rechtsquellen und Rechtsschichten des Verwaltungsrechts', in W Hoffmann-Riem, E Schmidt-Aßmann and A Voßkuhle (eds), *Grundlagen des Verwaltungsrechts Band I* (München: Beck, 2012) 1212ff.

Thus, implementation in options (i) and (ii) leads to a legal enforcement of the global standards, making them a part of EU law through implementation in an EU legislative measure as well as implementing or delegated act. In option (i), this is achieved by either absorbing the standards into the regulatory framework though literal transposition or through making reference to the standard in force at the time in binding legislation.[62] This is for example the case where the Codex Alimentarius Commission sets a maximum residue level (MRL), determining how much residue of a certain chemical, like a pesticide, is acceptable on food, and the EU subsequently prescribes this MRL in legislation.[63] The second variation, the dynamic reference, means that a standard or the output of a certain standard-setting body is referenced in binding legislation, not only with regard to the standards as adopted at the time the legislative measure is adopted, but also in opening the EU framework for future amendments or new standards. This is exemplified in the Tobacco Products Directive, which refers to certain ISO standards for measuring the emission of cigarettes in terms of tar, nicotine and carbon monoxide, while not integrating the precise standards at time of adoption and stating that the measurements should be based on the relevant, internationally accepted ISO standards.[64] This would mean that subsequent changes to the ISO standards referred to are automatically also recognised. While dynamic reference thus allows for maintaining the legislation up to date in terms of scientific requirements, it also means that changes in the global standards are not normatively reviewed in the EU before becoming applicable.[65]

The third variation, an obligation to take into account certain standards, is the more common implementation method with regard to standards, at least in the field of risk regulation. Regulation (EC) 178/2002, which is known as the 'General Food Law', exemplifies this variant, as Article 5(3) contains an obligation to take international standards into account whenever new food legislation is drafted and adopted in the EU. It does not, however, necessarily lead to the full transposition of the standard. The General Food Law for example allows for the deviation from international standards 'where such standards or relevant parts

[62] For a discussion of the implementation through legislative measures and soft law – placing an emphasis on the difference between references and incorporation see: A Volpato and M Eliantonio, 'The contradictory approach of the CJEU to the judicial review of standards: a love-hate relationship?' in M Eliantonio and C Cauffman (eds), *The Legitimacy of Standardisation as a Regulatory Technique: A Cross-disciplinary and Multi-level Analysis* (Cheltenham: Edward Elgar Publishing, 2020).

[63] See eg: Commission Regulation (EU) 2019/977 of 13 June 2019 amending Annexes II and IV to Regulation (EC) No 396/2005 of the European Parliament and of the Council as regards maximum residue levels for aclonifen, Beauveria bassiana strain PPRI 5339, Clonostachys rosea strain J1446, fenpyrazamine, mefentrifluconazole and penconazole in or on certain products, [2019] OJ L159/1.

[64] Directive 2014/40/EU of the European Parliament and of the Council of 3 April 2014 on the approximation of the laws, regulations and administrative provisions of the Member States concerning the manufacture, presentation and sale of tobacco and related products and repealing Directive 2001/37/EC, [2014] OJ L127/1, art 4 and preamble (11).

[65] See also: Volpato and Eliantonio (2020) 97f.

would be an ineffective or inappropriate means for the fulfilment of the legitimate objectives of food law, or where there is a scientific justification, or where they would result in a different level of protection from the one determined as appropriate in the Community'.[66]

Apart from these three variations of the first route of implementation of global standards through legislative measures, the second route maintains the soft law character of global standards after implementation in the EU: implementation via administrative guidelines. Such 'soft administrative rule-making'[67] is gradually gaining importance in the EU's regulatory framework, as was seen with regard to pharmaceutical regulation in Chapter 1. As administrative bodies frequently use soft law measures to further clarify legislative requirements, reference to global standards or their literal reproduction are adopted as EU soft law, in order to clarify and further define technical and scientific requirements in EU law. This is also the implementation method used for ICH standards, as will be explained in the following section.

B. The Implementation of ICH Guidelines in the EU: Adoption by the EMA

In the previous chapter, the five-step decision-making procedure leading to the adoption of ICH guidelines, culminating in the implementation of guidelines in the ICH regions, was explained.[68] After the adoption of the ICH guideline on the global level (*Step 4*), the regulatory parties are politically committed to implementing the guidelines into their regulatory framework (*Step 5*). The regional implementation takes place according to national or regional procedures applicable to the respective regulatory parties. For example in the US, this entails the publication of a notice by the Food and Drug Administration (FDA) with the text of the ICH guideline in the Federal Register,[69] while in Japan, the guidelines will be published in English and Japanese on the website of the Pharmaceuticals and Medical Devices Agency (PMDA) together with an implementation date.[70] In the EU, ICH guidelines are implemented through adoption

[66] Regulation (EC) No 178/2002 of the European Parliament and of the Council of 28 January 2002 laying down the general principles and requirements of food law, establishing the European Food Safety Authority and laying down procedures in matters of food safety, [2002] OJ L31/1, art 5(3).

[67] L Senden and A van den Brink, 'Checks and Balances of Soft EU Rule-Making', European Parliament – Directorate General for Internal Policies Study (2012) PE 462.433.

[68] Chapter 3 Section IV.

[69] Lezotre (2014) 49. For more detail on the US implementation ICH guidelines see: J Molzon, 'The Value and Benefit of the International Conference on Harmonisation (ICH) to Drug Regulatory Authorities: Advancing Harmonization for Better Public Health', in J van de Laan and J DeGeorge (eds), *Global Approach in Safety Testing – ICH Guidelines Explained* (New York: Springer, 2013) 26f.

[70] Lezotre (2014) 49.

by the Committee for Medicinal Products for Human Use (CHMP), thereby becoming EMA guidelines.[71] After adoption by the CHMP, these administrative guidelines are published on the website of the EMA, together with the other EMA administrative soft law guidelines.

The adoption of ICH guidelines through the EMA, rather than adoption through the European Commission, corresponds to the EU internal distinction between scientific as opposed to regulatory guidelines: as the ICH guidelines are of a scientific nature defining quality, safety and efficacy criteria, they are implemented by the EMA.[72] The EMA is responsible for the adoption of scientific guidance, and specifically the CHMP, as the main scientific committee for human pharmaceutical products, is well equipped for the adoption of these guidelines as it applies these guidelines on a day-to-day basis. Furthermore, the CHMP is involved during the drafting process of the ICH guidelines, as the ICH topics form part of the work programme of the CHMP's working parties and groups.[73] Moreover, within the ICH Expert Working Groups, the EU is generally represented by experts from the CHMP.[74]

In general, the adoption of guidelines by the EMA follows a 10-step process, which has been applicable since 2005:

- Step 1 of drafting a guideline is the choice of a topic in the responsible scientific committee, working party or inspection group.
- In step 2 a rapporteur and in some cases a co-rapporteur are appointed by the respective body to be responsible for the respective topic.
- Step 3 consists of the drafting of a concept paper by the respective body, which will identify the matters that have to be addressed in the guideline without necessarily providing solutions. This concept paper will contain an 'Impact Assessment' anticipating the effects of the guideline on public health and also on the interested parties and involved regulatory authorities.
- The concept paper will then be adopted by the responsible scientific committee (step 4) and published on the EMA website for a two to three month long public consultation, unless there is urgency in developing the guideline or it only concerns editorial changes to an existing guideline.
- Taking the received comments into account, the rapporteur then produces a draft guideline (step 5), which will be considered by the relevant working parties, the committees and the EMA secretariat. Should the relevant

[71] ICH, 'The Value and Benefits of ICH to Drug Regulatory Authorities', November 2010, 9; S Vamvakas, 'EU Perspectives on ICH', in J van de Laan and J DeGeorge (eds), *Global Approach in Safety Testing – ICH Guidelines Explained* (New York: Springer, 2013) 17.

[72] On the distinction see Chapter 1 Section III.

[73] Vamvakas (2013) 16. Also confirmed in an interview with two officials of the European Medicines Agency, conducted in London on 23 March 2015, notes on file with the author.

[74] Interview with two officials of the European Commission, conducted in Brussels on 17 February 2015, notes on file with the author; Interview with two officials of the European Medicines Agency, conducted in London on 23 March 2015, notes on file with the author.

working party chairs, the EMA secretariat and the respective scientific committee chairs deem it necessary, it is possible to organise a meeting with interested parties as well.

- At the point where the draft guideline sufficiently represents the view of the members of the respective working party or other responsible group, the draft guideline is submitted to the appropriate organ indicated in the legal basis, which will adopt the draft guideline for a three to six month long public consultation (step 6).
- Following the public consultation process (step 7), the designated working party or other group prepares a final version of the guideline (step 8), with consideration of the comments, and submits it to the relevant scientific committee or other body for adoption.
- Step 9 then consists of the adoption of the guideline in the relevant scientific committee or other responsible body and its publication on the EMA website.
- Regarding the implementation (step 10), if the guideline does not include an implementation deadline, it will become operational six months after adoption.[75]

According to the guideline adoption procedure communicated by the EMA, some of these EMA guidelines find their origin in existing legislative requirements, new technical and scientific developments, measures following on from international activities, or cooperation with other regulatory authorities, or even proposals made by interested parties.[76] The ICH and its counterpart for veterinary medicinal products, the VICH (International Cooperation on Harmonisation of Technical Requirements for Registration of Veterinary Products) are specifically mentioned as 'international activities' in the procedure document.[77] Thus, the EMA in this procedure document presents the ICH guidelines as 'inspiration' for the topic search in the adoption of CHMP guidelines.

However, it needs to be clarified that when they are adopted by the CHMP, the ICH guidelines do not follow the normal guideline adoption procedure with different drafting steps and public consultation, but are only endorsed. In the spirit of harmonisation, this endorsement of course means that the guidelines are not to be changed in the implementation process. In essence, the 10-step guideline adoption procedure applicable to the EMA guidelines is replaced by the ICH five-step adoption procedure on the global level, which is then followed by the formal adoption of the guidelines by the CHMP. The Rules of Procedure adopted by the ICH Assembly after the reform also stress that 'to achieve true

[75] European Medicines Agency, Procedure for European Union Guidelines and Related Documents Within the Pharmaceutical Legislative Framework, EMEA/P/24143/2004 Rev 1 corr, 18 March 2009, 8f.

[76] Ibid, 9.

[77] Ibid.

international harmonisation, it is important that ICH guidelines are adequately implemented in as consistent manner by all ICH regulators'.[78] Therefore, 'direct references'[79] are proposed as the preferred method for implementation and it is stressed that adding or omitting requirements defeats the harmonisation purpose of the guidelines.[80]

The EMA guidelines, and therefore also the implemented ICH guidelines, usually enter into force six months after their adoption.[81] Where the CHMP has adopted the ICH guidelines, their legal status is identical to the EMA guidelines, which do not originate in the ICH process.[82] They, therefore, can also be regarded as 'quasi-binding' and have the same practical as well as indirect legal effects on individuals, Member States and the EMA (as adopting body) as were identified for pharmaceutical guidelines in general.[83] The implemented ICH guidelines even 'replace existing guidelines on the subjects covered'.[84]

C. The Role of ICH Guidelines in the Administrative Rule-Making of the EMA

In order to better understand the interaction of the implemented ICH guidelines with the EU pharmaceutical regulation, it is revealing to examine the guidelines published by the EMA on its website. In March 2015, of the 337 EMA scientific guidelines in force, 63 are implemented ICH guidelines adopted by the CHMP.[85] This amounts to a share of 19 per cent of all scientific guidelines published by the EMA. Thus, roughly a fifth of the guidelines clarifying the legislative requirements of quality, safety and efficacy in the Union originate at the global level in the ICH.

The influence of ICH guidelines is not evenly distributed throughout the categories of guidelines. In this regard, however, it should be noted that the guideline categorisation differs between the ICH and the EMA; while the ICH recognises four categories of guidelines (quality, safety, efficacy and multidisciplinary), the EMA operates a different categorisation (quality, biological, non-clinical, clinical efficacy and safety, and multidisciplinary).[86] Generally, the quota of ICH originating guidelines is higher in the categories of quality and safety than in the

78 ICH, Rules of Procedure of the Assembly, 12.
79 Ibid, 11.
80 Ibid, 12.
81 EMA, EMEA/P/24143/2004 Rev 1 corr, 9.
82 Vamvakas (2013) 17.
83 Chapter 1 Section III.
84 EMA, EMEA/P/24143/2004 Rev 1 corr, 9.
85 The research reflects the status of guidelines on 19 March 2015 as published on the website of the EMA (www.ema.europa.eu). The guidelines were counted, excluding other documents like reflections papers, Q&As or Addenda. An effort was made to count every guideline only once, even if it was presented in more than one section of the website.
86 As presented on the website of the EMA in March 2015.

category of efficacy.[87] In 2015, an assessment of the guidelines published on the EMA website revealed that 14 out of 57 EMA quality guidelines originated in the ICH.[88] In the area of biological medicines 7 out of 56 guidelines are implemented ICH guidelines, whereas in the area of non-clinical guidelines 19 out of 43 guidelines are implemented ICH guidelines. A low share of implemented ICH guidelines is found in the categories of clinical efficacy and safety, whereas out of 125 EMA guidelines only 14 originate in the ICH. In the category of multidisciplinary guidelines, only 2 of the 49 EMA guidelines are implemented ICH guidelines. However, 7 ICH originating guidelines are not included in any of the above categories on the EMA website. Thus, the influence of the ICH guidelines on European regulation is very much dependent on the category of guidelines concerned. (See Figure 1.)

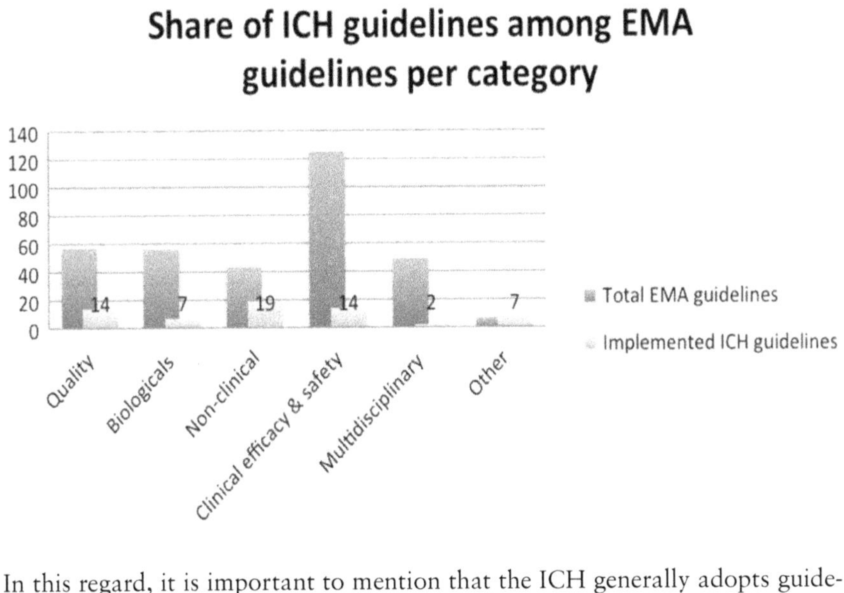

In this regard, it is important to mention that the ICH generally adopts guidelines, which are to be applied to all therapeutic classes of drugs.[89] In contrast, the EMA has adopted a multitude of guidelines tailored to specific therapeutic classes, namely classes of drugs categorised by the way they work or their chemical structure. Thus, in some areas, there might be an overarching ICH guideline

[87] Interview with two officials of the European Medicines Agency, conducted in London on 23 March 2015, notes on file with the author.

[88] The research reflects the status of guidelines on 19 March 2015 as published on the website of the EMA (www.ema.europa.eu) (see n 85 above). The categories reflect the categorisation on the EMA website.

[89] Lezotre (2014) 52; I Schneider, *Das Kooperationsprinzip im Vorfeld der Arzneimittelzulassung – Zum national und Europarechtlichen Rahmen des Zusammenwirken von Potentiellen Antragsstellern und Zulassungsbehörden* (Frankfurt am Main: Peter Lang Europäischer Verlag der Wissenschaften, 2003).

supplemented by EMA guidelines applying to specific therapeutic classes of medicines.[90]

In order to understand the interaction between the guidelines originating in the EMA and the implemented ICH guidelines, references to ICH guidelines in the guidelines originating in EMA should also be taken into account. In March 2015, out of the 274 guidelines originating in the EMA, 195 in some way refer or make reference to ICH guidelines.[91] This means that 71 per cent of the guidelines originating in the EMA include references to ICH guidelines. Therefore, the overarching majority of EMA originating guidelines do refer to ICH guidelines, either in a very general way or pointing to specific guidelines.

With regard to more general reference, a large number of EMA originating guidelines state that they should be read in conjunction with either ICH guidelines in general or specific ICH guidelines listed. Example 1 consists of a very general reference to other legal and soft law measures including ICH guidelines that should be read in conjunction with the respective EMA origination guideline. In example 2, the reference also provides that the EMA originating guidelines should be read in conjunction with legal and soft law measures including ICH guidelines; however, here the relevant ICH guidelines are specifically mentioned. Lastly, example 3 is a reference in the text of the guideline, which refers to a specific ICH guideline.

Example 1: General reference

'This document should be read in conjunction with Directive 2001/83/EC (as amended) and all relevant CHMP and ICH Guidelines.'

From: Guideline on Carcinogenicity Evaluation of Medicinal Products for the Treatment of HIV Infection (EMEA/CHMP/194898/2006)

Example 2: General reference but specifically identified ICH guidelines

'This guideline has to be read in conjunction with the introduction and general principles of the Annex I to Directive 2001/83 as amended.

Pertinent elements outlined in current and future EU and ICH guidelines, should also be taken into account, especially those listed below:

- Dose-Response Information to Support Drug Registration (ICH E4)

[90] Vamvakas (2013) 16. Vamvakas explains that for example in the area of clinical development, the ICH has established the general requirements, while the CHMP has adopted guidelines on the investigation of drugs in specific therapeutic fields such as cancer or diabetes.

[91] The research reflects the status of guidelines on 19 March 2015 as published on the website of the EMA (www.ema.europa.eu). The guidelines published were searched (Ctrl+F) for references to 'ICH' and 'International Conference on Harmonisation' (at this time the name was not yet changed to 'International Council on Harmonisation').

- Statistical Principles for Clinical Trials (ICH E9)
- Choice of Control Group and Related Issues in Clinical Trials (ICHE10)
- Points to consider on an Application with
  1) Meta-analyses
  2) One pivotal study (CPMP/EWP/2330/99)
- Studies in Support of Special Populations: Geriatrics (ICH E7 CHMP/ICH/379/95) and related Q&A document (EMA/CHMP/ICH/604661/2009)
- Reflection paper on the extrapolation of results from clinical studies conducted outside the EU to the EU-population (EMEA/CHMP/EWP/692702/2008)
- Note for guidance on antiarrhythmics (CPMP/EWP/237/95)
- Addendum to the Guideline on antiarrhythmics on atrial fibrillation and atrial flutter (EMA/CHMP/EWP/213056/2010).'

From: Guideline on clinical investigation of medicinal products for prevention of stroke and systemic embolic events in patients with non-valvular atrial fibrillation (EMA/CHMP/341363/2014).

Example 3: Text reference to specific ICH guidelines

'When the cell substrate is obtained by recombinant DNA technology, a description of the expression system used for the production of antibodies should be in accordance with relevant guidelines, especially "Production and Quality Control of medicinal products derived by recombinant DNA technology" (3AB1A), and the relevant ICH guidelines Q5A (viral safety), Q5B (expression constructs) and Q5D (cell substrates).'

From: Guidelines on Development, Production, Characterisation and Specifications for Monoclonal Antibodies and Related Products (EMA/CHMP/BWP/532517/2008).

All three types of references demonstrate that the EMA originating guidelines are also interrelated with the guidelines developed at the ICH level. Thus the scientific guidance of the EMA, whether originating in the agency itself or the ICH, has to be regarded as an integrated system of norms, with interrelated guidance documents.

Moreover, there are also EMA originating guidelines which explicitly state that they were adopted due to a gap in ICH harmonisation. These are indicators of the fact that general ICH guidelines are often supplemented by EMA guidelines geared to specific cases. One example is to be found in the EMA guideline on impurities in antibiotics, which extensively explains the need to adopt a specific guideline for antibiotics although impurities are harmonised by the ICH:

Example 4: Reference to ICH guideline to be supplemented by EMA guideline

'Antibiotics active substances currently on the market are produced by fermentation, by fermentation followed by one or more synthetic steps (semi-synthetic substances) or by chemical synthesis. Fermentation processes are, in comparison to synthetic processes, more variable and less controllable, so the impurity profile of an active substance whose manufacturing process involves fermentation may be more complex and less predictable than that of a purely synthetic product. For this reason fermentation products and semi-synthetic substances are not included in the scope of the ICH Q3 and the VICH GL10/GL11 guidelines, which set thresholds for the identification, reporting and qualification of related impurities in active substances manufactured by chemical synthesis.

This guideline has been developed in order to provide guidance on how specifications for related impurities in antibiotics that are fermentation products or semi-synthetic substances derived from fermentation products, and are therefore not included in the scope of the (V)ICH guidelines mentioned above, should be set.'

From: Guideline on setting specifications for related impurities in antibiotics (EMA/CHMP/CVMP/QWP/199250/2009 corr).

Thus, ICH guidelines account for a share of 19 per cent of all EMA guidelines. Although this number is substantial, it does not accurately reflect the full impact of ICH guidelines in the EU. As the ICH guidelines cover harmonised rules for all medicinal products, these ICH guidelines often form the basis for further EMA guidelines for specific therapeutic classes and 71 per cent of EMA guidelines contain references to ICH guidelines. Therefore, implemented ICH guidelines form an important part of the scientific guidance of the EMA, and the implemented ICH guidelines together with the EMA originating guidelines form an integrated system of governance of pharmaceutical products through soft law measures.

D. The Common Technical Document

When assessing the impact of the ICH on European pharmaceutical regulation one major ICH work product must be mentioned specifically: the Common Technical Document (CTD), which establishes the format for the marketing authorisation application. The impact of the CTD on European pharmaceutical regulation is significant, as it has streamlined the data requirements of regulatory authorities and set one common standard format to which all the pharmaceutical companies have to adhere. It has been qualified as possibly the 'most significant new achievement of the ICH'[92] and even 'one of the most ambitious and successful international harmonisation activities ever undertaken'.[93] The acceptance of the CTD as a mandatory or highly recommended format is remarkable since it is a sign of the willingness to harmonise the information required for a marketing authorisation. Nonetheless, it should be pointed out that the first module of the CTD is still region specific and contains administrative as well as prescribing information that is still diverging in the three regions.[94] Through the introduction of the CTD, the drafting of marketing authorisation applications has become less work-intensive for the applicants, as the laborious process of reformatting the application for every region can be omitted.[95] The CTD and its electronic version eCTD has opened the door to 'near simultaneous submission for new review of medicinal products … and earlier access for patients around the world'.[96]

The CTD itself is established by four ICH guidelines,[97] which, like the other ICH guidelines, have been adopted by the EMA.[98] However, since the mandatory format for the marketing authorisation in the EU was contained in Annex 1 of Directive 2001/83/EC this Annex had to be amended.[99] The CTD consists of five modules. The first module contains administrative information being addressed to the respective regulatory authority where the marketing authorisation is applied, for example with regard to labelling. The other four modules contain an overall introduction and summary as well as data concerning the quality of the product, nonclinical study reports and clinical study reports.[100]

[92] J Lee, 'What is Past is Prologue: The International Conference on Harmonization and Lessons Learned from European Drug Regulations Harmonization' (2005) 26 *University of Pennsylvania Journal of International Economic Law* 151, 180.

[93] J Molzon, 'The International Conference on Harmonization Common Technical Document – Global Submission Format?' (2005) 60 *Food and Drug Law Journal* 447, 450.

[94] Ibid, 449.

[95] ICH, The Value and Benefits of ICH to Drug Regulatory Authorities, 2.

[96] Lindström-Gommers and Mullin (2019) 927.

[97] ICH, ICH Tripartite Guideline – Organisation of the Common Technical Document for the Registration of Pharmaceuticals for Human Use M4 (R4), 5 June 2016; ICH, ICH Tripartite Guideline – The Common Technical Document for the Registration of Pharmaceuticals for Human Use: Quality – M4Q(R1) Quality, 12 September 2002; ICH, ICH Tripartite Guideline – The Common Technical Document for the Registration of Pharmaceuticals for Human Use: Safety – M4S(R2), 20 December 2002; ICH, ICH Tripartite Guideline – The Common Technical Document for the Registration of Pharmaceuticals for Human Use: Efficacy – M4E(R2), 15 June 2016.

[98] EMA, CPMP/ICH/2887/99; CPMP/ICH/2887/99-Quality; CPMP/ICH/2887/99-Safety; CPMP/ICH/2887/99-Efficacy.

[99] Commission Directive 2003/63/EC of 25 June 2003 amending Directive 2001/83/EC of the European Parliament and of the Council on the Community code relating to medicinal products for human use, [2003] OJ L159/46.

[100] Molzon (2005) 449.

In essence, the CTD serves as guidance regarding which ICH guidelines apply to the corresponding part of the marketing authorisation. While ICH guidelines have harmonised a wide field of requirements for the registration of medicinal products, what the CTD does is to put them into order in one consistent document, forming the dossier that companies have to submit to obtain marketing authorisation.

Furthermore, the CTD facilitates the exchange of information amongst regulatory authorities.[101] However, this format should not only be seen as a formal requirement, but indeed has an influence on the way the review of marketing authorisations is exercised.[102] The development of the CTD was complicated by the fact that the harmonisation of the format also required looking into the content of the marketing authorisation applications, to ensure that the terms used had the same meaning in the regions.[103] Thus, with the CTD the ICH developed a 'common regulatory language'.[104] Moreover, putting the information submitted by the applicant into a specific order shapes the review process and makes it more efficient.[105]

Ultimately, Lee sees the common format as a possible step towards mutual recognition of marketing authorisations.[106] Indeed, when comparing the development of the CTD to the history of pharmaceutical regulation in the EU,[107] similarities become apparent. In the history of EU integration, the harmonisation of the marketing authorisation application provided a basis for the mutual acceptance of marketing authorisations, as well as for the scientific data required in order to demonstrate the quality, safety and efficacy of a medicinal product. However, there are obstacles to mutual recognition of marketing authorisation between the ICH regions, mostly because it does not seem to be politically possible yet due to the loss of sovereignty connected to such a development.[108] Moreover, this would require substantial changes in the legislative framework.[109]

[101] Molzon et al (2011) 504. This was also confirmed in an interview with two officials of the European Medicines Agency, conducted in London on 23 March 2015, notes on file with the author.

[102] Molzon et al (2011) 507; Y Julliet, 'CTD – A Tool for Global Development and Assessment' (2011) 3 *Drug Information Association Global Forum* 25.

[103] Julliet (2011).

[104] Kuhnert (2011) 18.

[105] Molzon (2013) 26.

[106] Lee (2005) 181. See also: K Purnhagen, 'The Challenge of Globalization in Pharmaceutical Law – Is an International Drug Approval System Modeled after the European System Worth Considering?' (2008) 63 *Food and Drug Law Journal* 623. Purnhagen discusses the possibility of establishing a system based on the European decentralised procedure on the global level.

[107] Chapter 1 Section I.

[108] Interview with an official of the EFPIA, conducted in Brussels on 17 February 2015, notes on file with the author. Interview with two officials of the European Commission, conducted in Brussels on 17 February 2015, notes on file with the author. Interview with two officials of the European Medicines Agency, conducted in London on 23 March 2015, notes on file with the author.

[109] This point was raised in the interviews with the EMA officials as well as the EMA's Legal Department. Interview with two officials of the Legal Department of the European Medicines Agency, conducted in London on 23 March 2015, notes on file with the author; interview with two officials of the European Medicines Agency, conducted in London on 23 March 2015, notes on file with the author.

Although a mutual recognition of marketing authorisations between the ICH parties is not currently planned, the CTD has certainly contributed to the feasibility of future developments into this direction.

III. THE INFLUENCE OF ICH GUIDELINES ON LEGISLATION, COMMISSION GUIDELINES AND THE COURT OF JUSTICE

As the previous sections have shown, the implementation of ICH guidelines takes place through the adoption of administrative soft law measures in the form of EMA guidelines, which form an important part of the EMA scientific guidance. This section will examine the influence of the ICH guidelines beyond the EMA. Indeed, ICH guidelines have an impact on other acts like Commission guidelines, and even legislative measures, as the following analysis will demonstrate. Moreover, it examines whether ICH guidelines might also have an influence on the judiciary, looking at the use of ICH guidelines in the Court of Justice.

A. The ICH Influence on Commission Guidelines

As shown in Chapter 1, not only does the EMA adopt guidance measures, but also the Commission has published an extensive soft law framework for the governance of medicinal products in the form of regulatory guidelines.[110] Although the ICH guidelines are implemented as EMA guidelines, they can also affect the guidance developed by the Commission. First, the Commission guidelines make references to CHMP guidelines implementing ICH guidelines in some instances. This can be seen in the field of clinical trials, where the CT-3 guideline states that this guidance 'is to be read in conjunction with, in particular: … the Note for guidance on clinical safety data management: Definition and standards for expedited reporting ("note for guidance ICH E2A").'[111] In a footnote to this provision, reference is made to the CPMP/ICH/377/95.

Moreover, at least in one instance there is evidence that a Commission guideline has been changed on the basis of an ICH guideline. In the regulation of Good Manufacturing Practice (GMP), in addition to binding legislative measures, the Commission adopted the EU Guidelines for Good Manufacturing Practice for Medicinal Products for Human and Veterinary Use. Chapter 1 of Volume 4 deals with the Pharmaceutical Quality System. On the cover page it is stated that amendments to this chapter have been made according to the ICH

[110] Chapter 1 Section III.

[111] European Commission, Communication from the Commission – Detailed guidance on the collection, verification and presentation of adverse event/reaction reports arising from clinical trials on medicinal products for human use ('CT-3'), (2011/C 172/01), 1.4 (9).

Q10 guideline, leading also to a change in the title of the Chapter.[112] Thus, the ICH guidelines evidently also influence the European Commission guidelines in the EU framework of pharmaceutical regulation.

B. The ICH Influence on EU Pharmaceutical Legislation

Apart from the implementation of ICH guidelines through the CHMP in the form of soft law administrative guidelines, ICH harmonisation can also have an impact on legislation.[113] This is remarkable as the EU's core pharmaceutical legislation, laid down in Directive 2001/83/EC and Regulation (EC) 726/2004, does not share the same obligation to take international standards into account in the drafting of legislation concerning medicinal products as can be found, for example, in the General Food Law.[114]

The ICH Q7 guideline on Good Manufacturing Practice (GMP) is exemplary for showing the influence of ICH standards on legislation.[115] Directive 2001/83 had to be amended in the aftermath of the agreement at the ICH on Good Manufacturing Practice, which not only regulates Good Manufacturing Practice for the finished medicinal product, but also applies to the starting materials used. The requirements of Good Manufacturing Practice were extended to starting materials for pharmaceutical products in in Article 46(f) of Directive 2001/83.[116] Moreover, Article 47 of the Directive was amended, to delegate power to the Commission to adopt a renewed GMP guideline. This lead to the adoption of Volume 4 of 'The Rules Governing Medicinal Products in the European Union', through which the Commission implemented ICH Q7. Thus, ICH Q7 broadened the scope of the Good Manufacturing Practice legislation in the EU and, additionally, led to the adoption of a new soft law measure by the Commission.

The ICH E6 guideline on Good Clinical Practice (GCP) was also very influential on the regulation of clinical trials in the EU.[117] In this case, the E6 guideline influenced Directive 2001/20/EC regulating clinical trials in Europe.[118]

[112] European Commission, EudraLex, The Rules Governing Medicinal Products in the European Union Volume 4 EU Guidelines for Good Manufacturing Practice for Medicinal Products for Human and Veterinary Use Chapter 1 Pharmaceutical Quality System, SANCO/AM/sl/ddg1.d.6(2012)860362, p. 1.

[113] Molzon et al (2011) 508; Vamvakas (2013) 16.

[114] Section II A.

[115] Molzon et al (2011) 508.

[116] The amendment was carried out via: Directive 2004/27/EC of the European Parliament and of the Council of 31 March 2004 amending Directive 2001/83/EC on the Community code relating to medicinal products for human use, [2004] OJ L136/34.

[117] For a detailed discussion see: Flear (2018).

[118] Directive 2001/20/EC of the European Parliament and of the Council of 4 April 2001 on the approximation of the laws, regulations and administrative provisions of the Member States relating to the implementation of good clinical practice in the conduct of clinical trials on medicinal products for human use, [2001] OJ L121/34.

The Directive largely took over the definitions and general principles established in the ICH guideline, often even literally, and created an institutional framework and procedure applicable in the EU to structure clinical trials accordingly. The Good Clinical Practice Commission Directive 2005/28/EC, reflects the provisions from the ICH E6 guideline on general good clinical practice principles in Section 1.[119] The Commission Directive then continues with the establishment of a European procedure for the authorisation of the manufacturing or import of the medicine to be investigated in a clinical trial, as well as procedures for the inspection of clinical trials. This has to be read together with the clinical trials guidance established by the EMA, which includes ICH guidance.[120] So the influence of ICH guidelines in the regulation of clinical trials runs as a common thread through the overall legal and administrative framework for clinical trials. As Flear points out: 'Although formally non-binding, the ICH's guidelines have "hard" legal effect in the EU.'[121]

The Clinical Trial Directive was criticised for creating too high an administrative burden, especially in case of multi-country trials as harmonisation between the Member States was not fully achieved.[122] These concerns, together with calls for transparency with regard to clinical trials data, led to the revision of the legislation and the adoption of the Clinical Trials Regulation (CTR).[123] The CTR is far more detailed than Directive 2001/20/EC,[124] which makes tracing ICH generated norms in the Regulation more difficult. However, in the CTR the EU seems to have emancipated itself from the literal transposition of ICH definitions. Yet, in the Preamble of the Regulation the ICH and its clinical trial guidelines are referred to in the sense that they should 'be taken appropriately into account for the application of the rules set out in this Regulation, provided that there is no other specific guidance issued by the Commission and that those guidelines are compatible with this Regulation'.[125] Therefore, the influence of the ICH on the clinical trials still seems to persist.

Moreover, the ICH was very influential concerning the development of the EU's paediatric legislation, which aims at increasing clinical trials involving chil-

[119] Commission Directive 2005/28/EC of 8 April 2005 laying down principles and detailed guidelines for good clinical practice as regards investigational medicinal products for human use, as well as the requirements for authorisation of the manufacturing or importation of such products, [2005] OJ L91/13.

[120] Flear (2018) 170f.

[121] Flear (2018) 171.

[122] Jackson (2019) 529; Regulation (EU) No 536/2014 of the European Parliament and of the Council of 16 April 2014 on clinical trials on medicinal products for human use, [2014] OJ L158/1, Premable 4.

[123] Regulation (EU) No 536/2014. At the time of writing the Regulation has not yet become applicable, as applicability depends on the functioning of the Clinical Trials Information System (CTIS), which currently is still hampered by technical difficulties.

[124] See: M Rizzi, 'Simple, Safe and Transparent (?): Preliminary Reflections on the Proposal for a New EU Regulation of Clinical Trials' (2013) 4 *European Journal of Risk Regulation* 534.

[125] Regulation (EU) No 536/2014, preamble 43.

dren in order to ensure more availability of medicines for this population group and increasing insights into the adequate dosage for children.[126] While in the past, only a very small number of medicines were available and sufficiently labelled for use in children, the US in the 1990s started to develop measures to encourage paediatric research.[127] In 1998, supported by the European Commission,[128] the ICH started developing what became ICH guideline E11 Clinical Investigation of Medicinal Products in the Pediatric Population in 2000,[129] which lays down standards for developing safe, ethical an efficient clinical trials in children. Subsequently the EU adopted its Paediatric Regulation in the European Union in 2006, which created obligations to carry out clinical trials in children subject to exceptions and set up the Paediatric Committee within the EMA to assess the proposed studies.[130] In this regard, the Preamble of the Regulation states: 'The Paediatric Committee should follow existing Community requirements, including Directive 2001/20/ EC, as well as International Conference on Harmonisation (ICH) guideline E11 on the development of medicinal products for the paediatric population, and it should avoid any delay in the authorisation of medicinal products for other populations deriving from the requirements for studies in the paediatric population.'[131] Thus the deliberations in the ICH were an important step towards the initiation of legislative action in the EU, and the legislative measure adopted enhanced the importance of the ICH guideline for the trial development.

Conclusively, the impact of ICH guidelines in the EU's regulatory framework for pharmaceuticals in some cases extends beyond the soft law implementation via the EMA administrative guidelines, to exert an influence on the Commission's pharmaceutical guidelines and even legislative provisions. This finding is important as it shows that, beyond implementation through EMA guidelines, the effects of the ICH shape pharmaceutical legislation in the EU even where this is less visible and careful comparison of the texts might be required in order for it to be detected.

[126] For a discussion see: Hervey and McHale (2015) 334ff.

[127] M Turner, M Catapano, S Hirschfeld and C Giaquinto, 'Global Research in Paediatrics. Paediatric drug development: the impact of evolving regulations' (2014) 73 *Advanced drug delivery reviews* 2; J Zisowsky, A Krause and J Dingemanse, 'Drug Development for Pediatric Populations Regulatory Aspects' (2010) 2 *Pharmaceutics* 364; A Mulberg and T Cripps, 'Global Harmonization of Pediatric Drug Development: Critical for Progress for Developing Safe and Effective Therapeutic Agents for Children' (2019) *Current Therapeutic Research* 109.

[128] EMA, The European paediatric initiative: History of the Paediatric Regulation (EMEA/17967/04 Rev 1), 2.

[129] The most recent version is: ICH, ICH Harmonised Guideline – Clinical Investigation of Medicinal Products in the Pediatric Population E11(1), 18 August 2017.

[130] Regulation (EC) No 1901/2006 of the European Parliament and of the Council of 12 December 2006 on medicinal products for paediatric use, [2006] OJ L378/1. See further Turner, Catapano, Hirschfeld and Giaquinto (2014); Zisowsky, Krause and Dingemanse (2010); Mulberg and Cripps (2019).

[131] Regulation (EC) No 1901/2006, preamble 8.

C. The ICH Influence on the Court of Justice: Implemented ICH Guidelines used in Court

The previous sections of this chapter have demonstrated the extensive influence of ICH standards on pharmaceutical regulation in the EU with regard to hard and soft law. However, the influence of global standards in some instances extends beyond the administrative and legislative regulation to the judiciary,[132] this is exemplified in the area of foodstuffs through the extensive use of Codex Alimentarius standards through the Court of Justice.[133] With regard to pharmaceuticals, such a practice of references of the Court to ICH standards has not developed until now. A search of the Court's curia database does not reveal any instances of the Court relying on ICH standards in its case law.[134] Nonetheless, in two Court orders related to the access of documents in clinical trials data, the ICH is mentioned. The Court in these instances only reproduces a statement of the EMA: that scientific guidelines governing clinical trials are also published by the ICH.[135] This statement has not been subject to further discussion in the order and remains merely additional information.

Nonetheless, depending on how the standard is implemented in the EU, the Court could use global standards either directly or indirectly: Whereas the direct use of standards would entail that the Court makes reference to the global standard as such, indirect references in this regard are cases where the Court relies on EU soft or hard law measure implementing a global standard. With indirect references, it is difficult to recognise whether the Court is actually relying on a

[132] Müller-Graff (2012) 29.

[133] For example, in the *Beer Purity* case (Case 178/84 *Commission v. Germany*, ECLI:EU:C:1987:126), the Court made clear that in judging whether a restriction to the free movement of goods is justified under the public health exemption, it takes into account 'international scientific research', specifically mentioning the Codex. In the area of food safety, it is a well-established practice that the Court uses Codex standards as interpretative aid. (See: M Masson-Matthee, *The Codex Alimentarius Commission and Its Standards* (The Hague: TMC Asser Press, 2007) 103ff.) The Court also used the Codex to assess national administrative measures such as the classification of foodstuffs, as exemplified by the *Sachsenmilch* case regarding the question of classification of mozzarella cheese. (Case 196/05 *Sachsenmilch v Oberfinanzdirektion Nürnberg*, ECLI:EU:C:2006:383, para 29.)

[134] Search of the official CJEU website (http://curia.europa.eu), for text references to 'ICH' or 'International Conference on Harmonisation' and 'International Council for Harmonisation', last verified on 24 April 2016.

[135] Order of the President of the General Court of 25 April 2013 in Case T-44/13 R *AbbVie v EMA*, ECLI:EU:T:2013:221, para 66; Order of the President of the General Court of 25 April 2013 in Case T-73/13 R *InterMune UK and Others v EMA*, ECLI:EU:T:2013:222, para 52. Paragraph 52 of the *InterMune* Order states: '... The EMA adds that scientific guidelines on clinical trials, including clinical safety and clinical study reports, are also published following agreement on a harmonised approach between Europe, Japan and the United States of America by the International Conference on Harmonisation of Technical Requirements for Registration of Pharmaceuticals for Human Use. The EMA further states that it provides guidelines for non-clinical trials of medicinal products, intended for pharmacology, pharmacokinetics and toxicology.' The *AbbVie* paragraph is worded in a similar way.

global standard. It must first be established whether the European measure the Court is using as an interpretative tool actually originates in a global standard.

For ICH standards, as their implementation takes place through EMA guidelines, it is worthwhile to look into the case law on pharmaceuticals in the EU and to assess whether the Court is using soft law measures as an interpretative aid in its case law. In the area of pharmaceutical regulation, one of the best-known cases in which the Court used non-binding measures to rule on a dispute is the *Chemische Fabrik Kreussler* case, which dealt with the distinction between cosmetic and medicinal products.[136] The Court affirmed that a guidance document, which was drafted by the Commission together with the Member States on the distinction in question, can be taken into account by national courts, and was in fact relied upon by the Court itself in the case.[137] According to the Court the guidance document, although not legally binding, 'may provide useful information for the interpretation of the relevant provisions of European Union law and therefore contribute to ensuring that they are applied uniformly'.[138]

There are several other instances in which the Court relied on Commission or agency guidelines in order to interpret the law applicable to disputes it was called to adjudicate. A very prominent role was played by an EMA note for guidance in the *Artegodan* case, dealing with the withdrawal of marketing authorisations by the Commission.[139] The Commission decision was based on an assessment of the EMA, which in turn relied on a CPMP note for guidance. This guideline, adopted after the products had been authorised, introduced a change in the evaluation criteria for the benefit/risk assessment of medicines treating obesity,[140] stating that '(t)herapeutic efficacy for treating obesity requires a significant and long-term lowering of body weight (of at least one year)'.[141] This change in scientific evaluation of the efficacy of such products led to a withdrawal of their marketing authorisations, since the benefit/risk assessment based on this new criterion was considered negative for the products concerned.[142] The Court in *Artegodan* goes into detail in assessing whether the guideline indeed changes the evaluation criteria and whether this change is based on new scientific data, which would justify the withdrawal of a marketing authorisation.[143]

[136] Case C-308/11 *Chemische Fabrik Kreussler v Sunstar Deutschland*, ECLI:EU:C:2012:548. In this case the guideline subject to discussion was not one of the Eudralex Commission regulatory guidelines discussed in Chapter 3, but a Guideline by DG Enterprise and Industry regulating medical devices.

[137] Ibid, paras 25–27 and 29.

[138] Ibid, para 25. The Court in this paragraph reaffirms the introduction of the respective guideline.

[139] Joined cases T-74/00, T-76/00, T-83/00, T-84/00, T-85/00, T-132/00, T-137/00 and T-141/00 *Artegodan GmbH and Others v Commission of the European Communities*, ECLI:EU:T:2002:28. The note for guidance in question was the CPMP Note for Guidance on clinical investigation of drugs used in weight control (CPMP/EWP/281/96).

[140] Ibid, paras 162 and 164.

[141] Ibid, para 39.

[142] Ibid, paras 203 and 209.

[143] Ibid, paras 211–16.

It came to the conclusion that it did not establish a new criterion for assessing the efficacy of the medicinal products in question.[144] The Court also concluded that a mere change in the scientific evaluation, without new scientific data, does not justify a withdrawal.[145] Thus, in this case the assessment of the guideline led the Court to finding a breach of EU law with regard to the Commission Decisions, leading to their annulment.[146]

Also in the *Novartis* case, a preliminary ruling concerning the UK marketing authorisation of generic medicinal products – medicines that are equivalent to authorised products – the Court referred back to the 'Notice to Applicants' to define in which cases the generic authorisation procedure could be used.[147] Moreover, in the *Nycomed* case permission to omit the otherwise mandatory submission of a paediatric investigation plan, a so-called waiver, was denied. Here, the applicant Nycomed Danmark ApS relied amongst others on a Commission guideline.[148] Nycomed referred to a guideline to support its argument concerning the interpretation of concept of 'disease or condition for which the medicinal product is intended'.[149] The Court subsequently used the same guideline to prove the applicant's interpretation wrong.[150] The guideline used in the case does contain references to the ICH E11 guideline; however, this is only for the purpose of defining the age classification in the paediatric population, and not with regard to the disputed concept.[151]

In none of the above-mentioned cases apart from the *Nycomed* case were the guidelines relied upon by the Court implemented ICH guidelines, and nor did they contain ICH references. Although in the *Nycomed* case the guideline did contain ICH references these were not disputed in court. Thus, for now, to the best of knowledge of the author, there is no case where an indirect reliance on ICH standards by the Court can be proven. However, the possibility of indirect reliance exists. As established before, European soft law governing

[144] Ibid, para 212.

[145] Ibid, para 211.

[146] Ibid, paras 220 and 221.

[147] Case C-106/01 *Novartis Pharmaceuticals UK Ltd v The Licensing Authority established by the Medicines Act 1968*, ECLI:EU:C:2004:245, para 53.

[148] Case T-52/09 *Nycomed Danmark v EMA*, ECLI:EU:C:2011:83. (The guideline in question was: European Commission, Commission Communication – Guideline on the format and content of applications of agreement or modification of a paediatric investigation plan and request for waivers or deferrals and concerning the operation of the compliance check and on criteria for assessing significant studies ([2008] OJ C243/1).)

[149] Ibid, para 78. (The disputed concept is to be found in Regulation (EC) No 1901/2006, Art 11(1)(b).)

[150] Ibid, para 79.

[151] European Commission, Commission Communication – Guideline on the format and content of applications of agreement or modification of a paediatric investigation plan and request for waivers or deferrals and concerning the operation of the compliance check and on criteria for assessing significant studies, [2008] OJ C243/1, point 2.1, 2.5.1.2, 2.5.5.1 and 2.5.5.4. In these points the guideline refers to the ICH E 11 guideline with regard to the age group classification contained in the guideline and the timing of the measures.

pharmaceuticals is heavily influenced by the ICH standards, and the Court relies on this soft law in the form of Commission and EMA guidelines in order to judge disputes. Where the guidelines would be implemented ICH guidelines or where they contain ICH references, this could amount to the use of ICH guidelines through the Court. Such a direct or indirect reference to an ICH guideline through the Court would then certainly 'amplify' the legal effects of the originally non-binding norm.

IV. CONCLUSION: ICH GUIDELINES AS INTEGRAL PARTS OF THE EU REGULATORY FRAMEWORK FOR PHARMACEUTICALS

This chapter has established that although the guidelines developed by the ICH are soft law, forming recommendations of a global standard-setting body, in practice they are implemented without fail in the EU. Within the EMA's scientific guidance, these implemented ICH standards play an important role and account for about a fifth of the total guidelines adopted by the agency. However, it is difficult to truly separate between ICH originating guidelines and the guidelines originating in the EMA, as together they form an integrated governance system with interconnected guidelines. Whereas the ICH guidelines apply to all therapeutic classes, the EMA has adopted a multitude of guidelines for specific therapeutic classes, such as specific rules for medicines treating a certain illness, or groups of medicines working in a specific way. The large majority of the EMA originating guidelines make references to ICH guidelines and should be applied together with these. Moreover, alongside the individual guidelines, the ICH has shaped the format of marketing authorisation applications through the introduction of the CTD. In addition to relieving the marketing authorisation applicants from the re-drafting of the application for every region, the CTD has also improved the exchange of information between the regulatory authorities.

Moreover, it was shown that beyond the implementation of the ICH guidelines as EMA guidelines, the standards set on the global level also have an effect on European pharmaceutical legislation and the soft law measures established by the European Commission. In the regulation of Good Manufacturing Practice and Good Clinical Practice, the adoption of ICH guidelines has led to the broadening of the scope of legislation, and some legislative acts contain (often literal) transpositions of ICH norms. In the Paediatric Regulation, the discussions in the ICH were a catalyst for legislative action in the EU and the respective guideline shapes the standards for clinical trials involving children in the EU.

Moreover, it has been shown that ICH guidelines are referenced to in Commission guidelines and that such regulatory guidelines have been amended to conform to ICH standards. In addition to these effects on the legislative and administrative rules applying to pharmaceuticals in the EU, it was also argued that global standards are used as an interpretative aid in front of the Court, either directly or indirectly. While such a practice cannot currently be proven for the pharmaceutical standards developed by the ICH, it was shown that soft law measures are relied upon by the Court in the interpretation of pharmaceutical law and, therefore, the potential route to (the indirect) use of global pharmaceutical standards in EU case law is open.

Thus, ICH standards substantially shape the regulation of pharmaceuticals on the agency level and also affect Commission soft law and even legislation. Furthermore, they can serve as an interpretative aid in front of the Court. When looking beneath their soft law 'cover', these standards are powerful tools in the regulation of pharmaceuticals and integral parts of the EU pharmaceutical law and policy.

Part II

5

Questioning the Legitimacy of Global Standards

THE PREVIOUS PART of this book examined the important role that global standards play in the risk regulation of the EU in general and, specifically, how the pharmaceutical standards set by the ICH shape significant aspects of the regulation of quality, safety and efficacy of medicines in the European Union. This impact on EU risk regulation also means that global standards and the processes through which they are developed require in-depth scrutiny.

To quote the political scientist Michael Zürn: 'the more international institutions intervene in formerly national issues, the more they will be confronted with questions regarding their legitimacy'.[1] The fact that standard-setting on the global level is often exercised remotely from public control, and through negotiation between non-elected experts and government officials, generates severe legitimacy concerns.[2] The transposition of regulatory competences to the transnational level tends to create gaps in the legitimacy of these global structures, a phenomenon that Jürgen Habermas calls '*Legitimitätslücken*' ('legitimacy gaps').[3] Therefore, this chapter will look at the legitimacy questions raised by global standard setting, developing a framework for the examination of the legitimacy of implementing ICH guidelines in the EU in the following chapters.

I. WHY SHOULD THE LEGITIMACY OF GLOBAL STANDARDS BE EXAMINED?

Examining legitimacy means questioning why people follow certain commands or rules, that is, asking: 'Why, actually, do people obey authority?'[4] It is associated

[1] M Zürn, 'Global Governance and Legitimacy Problems' (2004) 39 *Government and Opposition* 260, 277.

[2] P Nanz and J Steffek, 'Global Governance, Participation and the Public Sphere' (2004) 39 *Government and Opposition* 314, 315; D Kerwer, 'Rules that Many Use: Standards and Global Regulation' (2005) 18 *Governance* 611, 620ff.

[3] J Habermas, 'Die Postnationale Konstellation und die Zukunft der Demokratie', in J Habermas, *Die Postnationale Konstellation – Politische Essays* (Frankfurt am Main: Suhrkamp Verlag, 1998) 109.

[4] S Kalberg (ed), *Max Weber – Readings and Commentary on Modernity* (Malden: Blackwell, 2005) 174.

with justifying the ability to take decisions that are binding and, therefore, employ public authority.[5] One might therefore ask whether it is even relevant to examine the legitimacy of global standards, being scientific and technical soft law norms. However, as shown in Part I of this book, although global standards like ICH guidelines are voluntary measures, in practice these are very effective regulatory measures, which are implemented in national/ regional regulatory frameworks, and which the regulated actors adhere to.[6] Thus, emphasising the non-binding nature of global standards does not accurately reflect their regulatory impact upon closer assessment, as standards can very well constitute an exercise of authority which requires legitimation.

This view is also supported by the 'International Public Authority'[7] scholarship of the Max Planck Institute, which proposes that 'any kind of governance activity by international institutions, be it administrative or intergovernmental, should be considered as an exercise of international public authority *if* it determines individuals, private associations, enterprises, states, or other public institutions'.[8] It is deemed irrelevant whether the measure in question is legally binding or not.[9] As discussed previously, standards do address the regulated industry and ultimately affect individuals. Where these standards regulate public or private persons, this constitutes an exercise of public authority. Furthermore, consumers are affected by the quality and safety of products as regulated through standards. As these individuals cannot rely on the protection of their rights through national constitutional and administrative law any more, questions of legitimacy also become increasingly relevant for global governance structures.[10]

In addition, global standards are not necessarily as technical or purely scientific as they are depicted. Risk regulation measures such as global standards often transcend mere questions of technicalities or science, entailing

[5] R Wolfrum, 'Legitimacy in International Law', in R Wolfrum (ed), *The Max Planck Encyclopedia of Public International Law* (Oxford: University Press Oxford, 2016), article last updated March 2011, available via: opil.ouplaw.com/home/EPIL.

[6] Chapter 2.

[7] A von Bogdandy, R Wolfrum, J von Bernstorff, P Dann and M Goldmann (eds), *The Exercise of Public Authority by International Institutions: Advancing International Institutional Law* (Heidelberg: Springer, 2010); M Goldmann, *Internationale öffentliche Gewalt – Handlungsformen internationaler Institutionen im Zeitalter der Globalisierung* (Heidelberg: Springer, 2015).

[8] A von Bogdandy, P Dann and M Goldmann, 'Developing the Publicness of Public International Law', in A von Bogdandy, R Wolfrum, J von Bernstorff, P Dann and M Goldmann (eds), *The Exercise of Public Authority by International Institutions: Advancing International Institutional Law* (Heidelberg: Springer, 2010) 5 (emphasis in original).

[9] Ibid, 12.

[10] H Hofmann, 'Dealing with Trans-Territorial Executive Rule-Making' (2013) 78 *Missouri Law Review* 423, 435 and 440; J Mendes, 'EU Law and Global Regulatory Regimes: Hollowing Out Procedural Standards?' (2012) 10 *International Journal of Constitutional Law* 988, 1015; C Möllers, 'Transnationale Behördenkooperation – Verfassungs- und Völkerrechtliche Probleme Transnationaler Administrativer Standardsetzung' (2005) 65 *Zeitschrift für ausländisches öffentliches Recht und Völkerrecht* 351, 384.

policy decisions.[11] Sheila Jasanoff, an influential Science and Technologies Studies scholar, explains that 'regulatory standard-setting involves significant measures of political choice and judgment'[12] and that '[s]aftey standards, in particular always entail associated questions of political significance: safety for whom, against what, and to what extent?'[13] To take the example of the ICH E1 guideline,[14] the guideline develops standards for safety testing of drugs intended for long-term use, laying down norms on how long and on how many people the drugs in question have to be tested.[15] This standard needs to balance the required amount of safety data against faster access to the product, and also considerations of monitoring adverse effects in the pharmacovigilance systems.[16] It requires the balancing of diverging scientific opinions on when a product is 'safe (enough)' and taking decisions with an impact on health care policy.

The policy dimension of standard setting is also exemplified by the ICH guidelines on clinical trials,[17] in which placebo-controlled trials are advocated over trials with a control group that receives another comparable medicinal product.[18] This entails an important choice concerning the definition of the efficacy of a medicinal product: is it sufficient if the product has a curative effect, or should it be superior to existing treatment? This has ethical implications with regard to the control group, which receives a placebo instead of an actual cure without knowing. It will entail implications for the health care system in general, as it means that products that are actually inferior to existing ones can be on the market.[19]

[11] G Majone, 'Science and Trans-Science in Standard Setting' (1984) 9 *Science, Technology, & Human Values* 15; S Jasanoff, 'Epistemic Subsidiarity – Coexistence, Cosmopolitanism, Constitutionalism' (2013) 4 *European Journal of Risk Regulation* 133; Habermas (1998) 165.

[12] Jasanoff (2013) 133.

[13] S Jasanoff, 'Constitutions of Modernity: Science, Risk and Governable Subjects', in M Weimer and A de Ruijter, *Regulating Risks in the European Union – The Co-production of Expert and Executive Power* (Oxford: Hart, 2017) 29.

[14] See also: S Röttger-Wirtz, 'Independence under threat – the role of private actors in the setting of global pharmaceutical standards and resulting challenges for European public law' (2018) 24 *European Public Law* 433, 443f.

[15] ICH, ICH Harmonised Tripartite Guideline – The Extent of Population Exposure to Assess Clinical Safety for Drugs Intended for Long-Term Treatment of Non-Life-Threatening Conditions (E 1), 27 October 1994.

[16] See: S Dagron, 'Global Harmonization through Public-Private Partnership: The Case of Pharmaceuticals', Instituto di Ricerche sulla Pubblica Amministrazione, Global Administrative Law Working Papers (2012), IRPA GAL Working Paper 2012/2, 14f.

[17] See Chapter 4. For a more detailed discussion of the choices made see: G Bache, M Flear and T Hervey, 'The Defining Features of the European Union's Approach to Regulating New Health Technologies', in M Flear, A Farrell, T Hervey, and T Murphy (eds), *European Law and New Health Technologies* (Oxford: Oxford University Press, 2013); X Seuba, 'International Harmonization of Pharmaceutical Standards: Trade, Ethics and Power', in G Burci and B Toebes, *Research Handbook in Global Health Law* (Cheltenham: Edward Elgar, 2018) 476f.

[18] See also: L Wallach, 'Accountable Governance in the Era of Globalization – The WTO, NAFTA and International Harmonization of Standards' (2001–2002) 50 *Kansas Law Review* 823, 861.

[19] E Mossialos, M Mrazek and T Walley, 'Regulating Pharmaceuticals in Europe: an Overview', in E Mossialos, M Mrazek and T Walley (eds), *Regulating Pharmaceuticals in Europe: Striving for Efficiency, Equity and Quality* (Maidenhead: Open University Press, 2004) 7.

Overall, it has been argued that the ICH guidelines in the value choices made leans towards 'trade-oriented choices, upholding rapid access to market and free flow of products with health protection as somewhat subsidiary goal'.[20] It is debated in the literature whether the ICH harmonisation has led to an increase of protection of public health through higher standards as some participants in the process argue.[21] Or whether it has led to lowering regulatory standards, especially with regard to reporting of adverse drug reactions, clinical trial requirements and toxicological studies, in order to decrease the burden on companies and ensure faster market access.[22] Thus, apart from the clarification of technical details, the standard-setting process also has the potential to entail and influence broader policy choices. In particular it is the choices made in situations where science will not exclusively resolve the question of what is required for a product to be safe, which compels a standard-setting body to take these decisions. The institutional structure of the standard-setting bodies and the processes which they carry out influence such value choices. Therefore, global standard-setting requires legitimation.

II. WHAT CONSTITUTES LEGITIMACY ON THE GLOBAL LEVEL?

Legitimacy has been defined and assessed by many authors in different ways and in relation to different entities.[23] However, the application of traditional

[20] M Rizzi, 'Non-Measurable Negotiations: The EU between Transnational Regulation of Pharmaceuticals and Private Law', in M Cremona and H Micklitz, *Private Law in the External Relations of the EU* (Oxford: Oxford University Press, 2016) 283. See also: J Abraham and T Reed, 'Trading Risks for Markets: The International Harmonization of Pharmaceuticals Regulation' (2001) 1 *Health, Risk and Society* 113.

[21] See eg: P D'Arcy and D Harron (eds), *Proceedings of the First International Conference on Harmonisation – Brussels 1991* (Belfast: The Queen's University Belfast, 1992); D Vogel, 'The Globalization of Pharmaceutical Regulation' (1998) 11 *Governance* 1; L Lindström-Gommers and T Mullin, 'International Conference on Harmonization: Recent Reforms as a Driver of Global Regulatory Harmonization and Innovation in Medical Products' (2019) 105 *Clinical Pharmacology & Therapeutics* 926. See generally for the controversies: D Katsikas, 'International Conference on Harmonization of Technical Requirements for the Registration of Pharmaceutical Products', in T Hale and D Held (eds), *Handbook of Transnational Governance – Institutions & Innovations* (Cambridge: Polity Press, 2011) 92. It should be noted that such higher standards in itself are also contested as they might have exclusionary effects on developing countries: Dagron (2012); A Berman, 'The Distributional Effects of Transnational Pharmaceutical Regulation' (2012b) CTEI Working Paper, CTEI-2012-01; M Flear, 'Charting a Roadmap Towards Membership and Formal Voice in Global Bioethics Standard-Setting: Health Research and the Case of the International Council on Harmonisation' (2018) *Medical Law International* 157.

[22] C Hodgkin, 'International Harmonisation – The Need for Transparency' (1996) 9 *International Journal of Risk & Safety in Medicine* 195; J Abraham, 'The Pharmaceutical Industry as a Political Player' (2002) 360 *The Lancet* 1498; Abraham and Reed (2001); J Abraham and T Reed, 'Progress, Innovation and Regulatory Science in Drug Development: The Politics of International Standard-Setting' (2002) 32 *Social Studies of Science* 337.

[23] For an overview of the theoretical works on legitimacy: D Bodansky, 'Legitimacy in International Law and International Relations', in J Dunoff and M Pollack (eds), *Interdisciplinary Perspectives on International Law and International Relations – The State of the Art* (Cambridge: Cambridge

instruments to determine the legitimacy of state power – such as the constitutional principles of a state, legality, constitutional rights, democratic decision-making and control, checks and balances of powers and judicial review – fail with regard to international governance, as they cannot merely be reproduced outside of the nation state.[24] Especially in a national context, legitimation is connected to the democratic legitimacy of the entity that exercises public authority.[25] Democratic legitimacy operates on the presumption that sovereign people are the sole source of legitimacy.[26] Therefore, on the global level, one comes to the conclusion that 'legitimacy of governance beyond the nation-state cannot be but deficient'.[27] This is based on a lack of global *demos* as an essential precondition for democracy.[28] Apart from that, other essential elements of democracy (such as direct elections) are absent on the global level.[29] Therefore, global governance has been argued to suffer from a 'democratic deficit'.[30]

In the specific case of global standards, the normative question of legitimacy is complex to assess.[31] Governance through global standards constitutes an example of Weiler's regulatory layer, which in essence forms a system of '(g)overnance without government and without the governed – ie. polity',[32] since a democratic basis for this decision-making as found in national systems is

University Press, 2013). For further reading on legitimacy of international bodies see eg: I Hurd, 'Legitimacy and Authority in International Politics' (1999) 53 *International Organization* 379; R Keohane, 'Global Governance and Legitimacy' (2011) 18 *Review of International Political Economy* 99; M Livermore, 'Authority and Legitimacy of Global Governance: Deliberation, Institutional Differentiation, and the Codex Alimentarius' (2006) 81 *New York University Law Review* 766. For a discussion of EU legitimacy see eg: F Scharpf, *Governing in Europe – Effective and Democratic?* (Oxford: Oxford University Press, 1999).

[24] B Dorbeck-Jung, 'Challenges to the Legitimacy of International Regulation: The Case of Pharmaceuticals Standardisation', in A Føllesdal, R Wessel and J Wouters (eds), *Multilevel Regulation and the EU: The Interplay between Global, European and National Normative Processes* (Leiden: Martinus Nijhoff Publishers, 2008) 55; R Mayntz, 'Legitimacy and Compliance in Transnational Governance', MPIfG Working Paper 10/5 (2010) 9.

[25] Mayntz (2010) 8; J Weiler, 'The Geology of International Law – Governance, Democracy and Legitimacy' (2004) 64 *Zeitschrift für ausländisches öffentliches Recht und Völkerrecht* 547; N Hachez and J Wouters, 'A Glimpse at the Democratic Legitimacy of Private Standards: Assessing the Public Accountability of Global G.A.P.' (2011) 14 *Journal of International Economic Law* 677.

[26] Mayntz (2010) 8.

[27] Mayntz (2010) 9.

[28] Bodansky (2013) 330; A Buchanan and R Keohane, 'The Legitimacy of Global Governance Institutions' (2006) 20 *Ethics and International Affairs* 405, 416.

[29] Mayntz (2010) 9; Livermore (2006) 780.

[30] R Dahl, 'Can International Organizations be Democratic? A Skeptic's View', in I Shapiro and C Hacker-Cordón (eds), *Democracy's Edges* (Cambridge: Cambridge University Press, 1999).

[31] See: J Black, 'Constructing and Contesting Legitimacy and Accountability in Polycentric Regulatory Regimes' (2008) 2 *Regulation & Governance* 137, 149; C Devaux, 'The Experts in the Elaboration of the Cape Town Convention: Between Authority and Legitimacy' (2013) 19 *European Law Journal* 843, 846. On the legitimacy of global governance in general: T Risse, 'Transnational Governance and Legitimacy', in A Benz and Y Papadopoulos (eds), *Governance and Democracy – Comparing National, European and International Experiences* (Oxon: Routledge, 2006); Mayntz (2010); Keohane (2011).

[32] Weiler (2004) 560.

largely absent. This lack of democratic basis is even more pronounced where this regulatory activity or standard-setting body is not established by law, be it national, supranational or international.[33] The views on what provides legitimacy beyond democracy are diverse, a multitude of approaches sometimes overlapping and contradicting each other. Bodansky for instance mentions factors such as legality, democratic accountability, expertise or even factors such as tradition or religion, as forming different conceptions of legitimacy.[34] In governance theory, in such cases legitimacy is derived from the interaction of public and private interests in decision-making.[35] Habermas argued for legitimacy through deliberation,[36] where the exercise of authority is legitimised by discourse, enabling the public to express its opinion and contribute to the will-formation.[37]

With regard to global standards, the legitimacy of global standard-setting often draws on the rhetoric of efficiency and effectiveness in addressing global risks.[38] The catalysts of global public, private and public-private standard-setting are the globalisation of trade and the increasing complexity and interconnection of risks. The regulatory cooperation of administrative bodies on the global level essentially aims at more regulatory efficiency, while the incorporation of private parties is based on a need for their expertise. These claims of efficiency are invoked to legitimise global standards, justifying the shift of regulatory decision-making to the global level. Such emphasis on efficiency and its subsequent use as legitimating factor is a very familiar form of argumentation to EU law and policy scholars, as it has been intensely debated in the analysis of the legitimacy of the EU.[39] Scharpf's distinction between input and output legitimacy, established as general democracy theory in 1975[40] and later applied to the EU,[41] is well known and often relied on in this regard. As Scharpf's theory addresses the question of legitimacy of entities beyond the national level that cannot rely on democratic legitimacy like a democratic nation state, it also appears to provide a framework for the analysis of the legitimacy of global standard-setting bodies.

[33] Black (2008) 138.

[34] Bodansky (2013) 324.

[35] J Ponce Solé, 'The History of Legitimate Administration in Europe', in M Ruffert (ed), *Legitimacy in European Administrative Law: Reform and Reconstruction* (Groningen: European Law Publishing, 2011a).

[36] Habermas (1996).

[37] Habermas (1996) 135.

[38] See: von Bogdandy, Dann and Goldmann (2010) 8; S Quack, 'Law, Expertise and Legitimacy in Transnational Economic Governance: An Introduction' (2010) 8 *Socio-Economic Review* 3, 10; Devaux (2013) 852ff, C Cutler, 'The Legitimacy of Private Transnational Governance: Experts and the Transnational Market for Force' (2010) 8 *Socio-Economic Review* 157.

[39] See eg: V Schmidt, 'Democracy and Legitimacy in the European Union Revisited: Input, Output *and* "Throughput"' (2013) 61 *Political Studies* 2; G Majone, 'Europe's "Democratic Deficit": The Question of Standards' (1998) 4 *European Law Journal* 5; A Moravcsik, 'In Defence of the "Democratic Deficit": Reassessing Legitimacy in the European Union' (2002) 40 *Journal of Common Market Studies* 603; A Menon and S Weatherill, 'Transnational Legitimacy in a Globalising World: How the European Union Rescues its States' (2008) 31 *West European Politics* 397.

[40] F Scharpf, *Demokratietheorie Zwischen Utopie und Anpassung* (Konstanz: Universitätsverlag Konstanz, 1970).

[41] Scharpf (1999).

According to this theory, input legitimacy refers to 'government by the people' meaning that policy choices reflect the will of the governed,[42] and 'refers to the participatory quality of the process leading to laws and rules as ensured by the "majoritan" institutions of electoral representation'.[43] Input legitimacy as defined by Scharpf, therefore, looks at legitimacy from the perspective of the democratic basis of an authority in a wider than just electoral sense. It includes the participatory openness of a political system, giving those with a broad array of interests access to determine how society is governed. However, input legitimacy presupposes a 'pre-existing collective identity'[44] of the governed, expressing their will through elections and participatory features. Such a collective identity is based on 'commonalities of history, language, and culture'[45] and, therefore, not existing or even envisaged on the global level. Therefore, by its nature, global standard-setting will suffer from a defect in terms of input legitimacy, regardless of whether it might be performed by open and participatory means. In fact, instead of a growing collective identity, an establishment of epistemic communities can be observed on the global level, building clusters of experts in separate regulatory sectors.[46] This 'sectoralisation' is problematic in terms of input legitimacy as it leads to an increased dependency of the administration on its regulated industry and facilitates decision-making in a very narrow technical or scientific context, where the greater political and democratic context is disregarded.[47] The regulation of specific sectors becomes decoupled from an open democratic discourse in society.

Moreover, looking closely at participatory mechanisms in global standard-setting bodies reveals that the participation of private parties in global standard-setting is often dominated by industry participation, with other societal interests mostly lacking a prominent role in decision-making on the global level.[48] An explanation for this phenomenon might be that civil society interests are more diffuse than industry interests and, therefore, more demanding to organise.[49] Additionally, participation in regulatory processes presupposes a high level of expertise, financial as well as in human resources.[50] For example,

[42] Ibid, 6.
[43] Schmidt (2013), 3.
[44] Scharpf (1999) 10.
[45] D Bodansky, 'The Legitimacy of International Governance: A Coming Challenge for International Environmental Law?' (1999) 93 *The American Journal of International Law* 596, 622f.
[46] On epistemic communities see: P Haas, 'Introduction: Epistemic Communities and International Policy Coordination' (1992) 46 *International Organization* 1.
[47] Möllers (2005) 379.
[48] W Mattli, 'The Politics and Economics of Institutional Standards Setting: An Introduction' (2001) 8 *Journal of European Public Policy* 328, 331.
[49] A Herwig, 'The Contribution of Global Administrative Law to Enhancing the Legitimacy of the Codex Alimentarius Commission', in O Dilling, M Herberg and G Winter (eds), *Transnational Administrative Rule-Making – Performance, Legal Effects and Legitimacy* (Oxford: Hart Publishing, 2011) 197.
[50] Ibid; Dorbeck-Jung (2008) 56.

although the ICH is viewed as having broad 'epistemic legitimacy' in the sense that the standards are scientifically respected, 'political legitimacy' based on a broad involvement of stakeholders seems to be lacking.[51] Also, although the Codex Alimentarius Commission which allows for international non-governmental organisations (NGOs) to be invited as observers,[52] it has been pointed out that problems remain regarding the overwhelming industry dominance within the stakeholders' granted observer status.[53] Thus, global standard-setting is often regarded as flawed in its input legitimacy due to a lack of common identity of the governed, a removal of decision-making from a democratic to a narrow administrative reasoning, and participatory structures that are unbalanced and do not sufficiently incorporate all stakeholders.

Nevertheless, Scharpf's argument is that even though input legitimacy is required for a legitimised political system, eventual flaws can be counterbalanced by high output legitimacy.[54] Thus, Scharpf developed another perspective that assessed legitimacy concentrating on the 'output' of a political system. Based on 'governance for the people', output legitimacy reviews the legitimacy of an authority based on 'its capacity to solve problems requiring collective solution'.[55] In contrast to input legitimacy, the focus is less on a common identity as a basis of authority, but more on a common interest as a yardstick for legitimacy.[56] Output legitimacy essentially refers to the ability to effectively solve a problem in common interest while preventing the abuse of power, which would dilute the achievement of the common interest and render a political system less efficient.[57] By means of problem solving capacity decisions attain *ex post* legitimacy.[58]

When assessing the legitimacy of global standards in Scharpf's terms the core question will be whether a strong output legitimacy of these standards could justify their lack of democratic basis. However, 'the common interest' that output legitimacy refers to is not straightforward in standard-setting in the area of risk regulation. It implies that these regulatory decision-making processes have a 'correct' outcome, solving the question of risk regulation with a 'better or worse answer.'[59] However, in risk regulation it is by no means certain

[51] A Berman, 'The Public-Private Nature of Harmonisation Networks' (2011) CTEI Working Paper, CTEI-2011-06, 55.

[52] Livermore (2006) 781f.

[53] M Masson-Matthee, *The Codex Alimentarius Commission and Its Standards* (The Hague: TMC Asser Press, 2007) 275f.

[54] Scharpf (1999) 10f.

[55] Ibid, 11.

[56] Ibid.

[57] Ibid, 13.

[58] M Schäferhoff, S Campe and C Kaan, 'Transnational Public-Private Partnerships in International Relations: Making Sense of Concepts, Research Frameworks, and Results' (2009) 11 *International Studies Review* 451, 465.

[59] Bodansky (1999) 620.

that problems do have (only) one correct solution, as convincingly argued by Majone: '(f)ar from being an almost mechanical process safely relegated to technicians, the setting of health, safety and environmental standards is in reality a microcosm in which conflicting epistemologies, regulatory philosophies, national traditions, social values, and professional attitudes are faithfully reflected'.[60] Accordingly, standard-setting should not be viewed as a process of applying scientific knowledge, but involves choices regarding the methodology, the approach to risk regulation in general (for example, how risk averse is a regulatory system?),[61] and to a certain degree also 'scientific tradition'.[62] As output legitimacy means that the process in question is devoted to acting in a common interest to guarantee a 'decent standard of living',[63] in a pluralistic society and in the face of complex risks, the regulator cannot define the general interest in isolated procedures, but needs to consider diverse interests.[64]

Where only the effectiveness of a regulatory system is considered, the question of legitimacy is placed in the hands of the actors that are powerful enough to determine which outcomes they perceive to efficiently mitigate a certain risk.[65] Therefore, especially in the context of global regulatory standards, legitimisation solely through the efficiency and output of the process turns into a circular argument.[66] In order to define an effective solution to the regulatory problem and have a legitimate output, input legitimacy is presupposed.[67] In the words of Weiler: 'a legitimacy powerfully skewed to results and away from process, based mostly on outputs and only to a limited degree on inputs, is a weak legitimacy and sometimes none at all'.[68] Accordingly, the narrative of efficiency and the output legitimacy of global standard-setting do not provide a sufficient basis for its legitimacy. Where input legitimacy is bound to fail in providing a workable framework on the global level and also output legitimacy in terms of efficiency does not provide a convincing basis for legitimacy, it is necessary to look at the role of law, and particularly administrative law, in the provision of legitimacy to global standards, as will be argued in the following.[69]

[60] Majone (1984).

[61] See also: E Fisher, *Risk Regulation and Administrative Constitutionalism* (Oxford: Hart, 2010) 7.

[62] Majone (1984) 16.

[63] Ponce Solé (2011a) 158.

[64] Ibid, 159.

[65] Hachez and Wouters (2011) 685.

[66] See: Risse (2006) 191f.

[67] Mayntz (2010) 11. Mayntz, however, argues that norms for technical appliances or pharmaceuticals do not need democratic legitimation due to their basis in a sound science. (See: Mayntz (2010) 12.) As argued previously in this research, the author does not agree with this presumption, as science will not always be able to provide a clear answer to the regulatory problems addressed in these standards.

[68] Weiler (2004) 562.

[69] See also: Bodansky (2013) 330.

III. ADMINISTRATIVE LAW AND GLOBAL STANDARDS

As risk regulation, and the setting of regulatory standards for the protection of health and the environment, is essentially an administrative task and national and regional regulators are important actors in global standard-setting,[70] it is only logical to analyse the role of administrative law in the legitimacy of global standard-setting processes. In democratic states, legitimacy of administrative actions is based on compliance with the administrative law of the respective legal system.[71] In this regard, administrative law provides legal-rational legitimacy to administrative action. Max Weber conducted a well-established theorization of legitimacy, providing for three types of legitimacy: traditional, charismatic and legal-rational.[72] Weber's theory of legal-rational legitimacy places an emphasis on how the norms come into being, basing their legitimacy on the fact that they were created through a proper enactment procedure – 'proper' here referring to a whole, socially accepted, system of norms – which leads to the rules being in the common interest and justified.

A. Administrative Law for Global Standard-Setting Bodies

Through accountability of the administration to the legislature in a chain of delegation, administrative law on the national level ensures the democratic legitimacy of administrative action.[73] These administrative actions are legitimised by a legal mandate with powers subject to delimitations, such as through restraining delegation from the legislature to the administration, often through constitutional as well as secondary law, subject to control through judicial review and parliamentary oversight.[74] Therefore, the administration can rely on the 'transmission belt' of administrative law in order to legitimise its actions.[75] Administrative law fulfils essentially three functions: it ensures the proper working of the separation of powers in the institutional structure of a state; it protects the rights of the subjects of administrative decisions; and it contributes to democratic legitimacy through regulating public participation in the decision-making process.[76] These functions overlap with the gaps in the frameworks for

[70] Chapter 2 Section II A.

[71] Ponce Solé (2011a) 158.

[72] M Weber, *Wirtschaft und Gesellschaft – Grundriss der Verstehenden Soziologie*, 5th edn (Tübingen: Mohr Siebeck, 1972); Kalberg (2005) 190ff.

[73] B Kingsbury, N Krisch and R Stewart, 'The Emergence of Global Administrative Law' (2005) 68 *Law and Contemporary Problems* 15, 30.

[74] Herwig (2011) 189; Fisher (2010) 23.

[75] R Stewart, 'The Reformation of American Administrative Law' (1975) 88 *Harvard Law Review* 1669, 1675; R Stewart, 'Administrative Law In The Twenty-First Century' (2003) 78 *New York University Law Review* 437; C Harlow, 'Composite Decision-Making and Accountability Networks: Some Deductions from a Saga' (2013) 32 *Yearbook of European Law* 3, 4.

[76] See also: von Bogdandy, Dann and Goldmann (2010) 9; E Schmidt-Aßmann, 'The Internationalization of Administrative Relationships as a Challenge for Administrative Law Scholarship', in

legitimacy discussed previously. Administrative law could give a formalised structure to the regulatory cooperation and could discipline the *ad hoc* development of standard-setting bodies through procedural standards.[77] Through the development of administrative norms applicable to global standard-setting, a legal framework could be developed that would clearly define the currently very complex institutional structures and decision-making processes. Its mechanisms would provide protection to the rights of individuals and contribute to the legitimation of the global standard-setting bodies.[78]

However, can administrative law be applied beyond the nation state to global standard-setting processes? Does administrative law provide accepted procedural standards for global administrative action, or more specifically for global standard-setting? Is this form of legitimation transferable to the global level, lacking separate legislative, judicial and executive powers? Currently no established legal framework or administrative law is applicable to global governance mechanisms. Although the legitimacy of these bodies has been criticised, the gap in the law regulating them creates a legal vacuum, meaning that they are not facing claims of illegality as there simply is no law applying to them.[79] However, in the legal scholarship, the development of a legal framework regulating global administrative bodies is recognised.

In his extensive work on the cooperation of administrative bodies on the global level, Tietje points to a very long tradition in German scholarship, arguing for the existence of an international administrative law (*Internationales Verwaltungsrecht*), dating back to the works of Lorenz von Stein in the mid-19th century.[80] Traditionally, international administrative law is characterised as describing the body of law that regulates the collusion of national laws, in situations where administrative activities have a foreign link, serving as public law counterpart to private international law.[81] However, 'international administrative law' is undergoing a reconceptualisation as administrative law originating on the international level, which encompasses three different bodies of law: the law applicable to administrative institutions on the global level; the international law that has an impact on national administrative legal orders; and, finally, the

A von Bogdandy, R Wolfrum, J von Bernstorff, P Dann and M Goldmann (eds), *The Exercise of Public Authority by International Institutions: Advancing International Institutional Law* (Heidelberg: Springer, 2010) 947.

[77] Möllers (2005) 384.

[78] M Ruffert, 'Perspektiven des Internationalen Verwaltungsrechts', in C Möllers, A Vosskuhle and C Walter (eds), *Internationales Verwaltungsrecht – Eine Analyse Anhand von Referenzgebieten* (Tübingen: Mohr Siebeck, 2007) 410.

[79] von Bogdandy, Dann and Goldmann (2010) 20.

[80] C Tietje, *Internationalisiertes Verwaltungshandeln* (Berlin: Duncker & Humblot GmbH, 2001) 50ff.

[81] M Ruffert and S Steinecke, *The Global Administrative Law of Science* (Heidelberg: Springer, 2011) 20; Schmidt-Aßmann (2010) 960. The leading literature in this interpretation of international administrative law is: K Neumeyer, *Internationales Verwaltungsrecht – Vol. IV: Allgemeiner Teil* (Zürich: Verlag für Recht und Gesellschaft, 1936).

law that governs the cooperative multilevel administrative processes.[82] International administrative law in this sense does not form a coherent body of positive law – at least not at the moment – but is rather a body of law 'in the making'.[83] The scholarship in international administrative law carries out a an analysis of different reference areas (*Referenzgebiete*)[84] – such as environmental law[85] or migration law[86] – identifying the legal consequences of the globalised administrative activity in this specific area of law, from a national, supranational and international perspective.[87] The approach is to pinpoint emerging international administrative law in the respective areas, as well as to study its interaction with national administrative law, followed by a comparison of the findings obtained in the reference areas in order to synthesise a common legal framework of international administrative law.[88]

A comparable debate has been developed by the global administrative law (GAL) scholarship.[89] Global administrative law takes the growing interaction of administration on the global level as a starting point, mapping the complex interconnected structures of regulatory bodies and informal transnational groups.[90] It includes a variety of subjects beyond what is traditionally understood in the national context as administration, examining international organisations, institutions and networks as well as hybrid public-private bodies.[91] It is argued that in this context democratic legitimacy cannot be derived from a

[82] Schmidt-Aßmann (2010) 960f.

[83] C Möllers and J Terhechte, '§40 Europäisches Verwaltungsrecht und Internationales Verwaltungsrecht', in J Terhechte (ed), *Verwaltungsrecht der Europäischen Union* (Baden-Baden: Nomos, 2011) 1439; Ruffert (2007).

[84] Möllers and Terhechte (2011) 1443; C Möllers, 'Internationales Verwaltungsrecht – Eine Einführung in die Referenzanalyse', in C Möllers, A Vosskuhle and C Walter (eds), *Internationales Verwaltungsrecht – Eine Analyse Anhand von Referenzgebieten* (Tübingen: Mohr Siebeck, 2007) 5f.

[85] W Durner, 'Internationales Umweltverwaltungsrecht', in C Möllers, A Vosskuhle and C Walter (eds), *Internationales Verwaltungsrecht – Eine Analyse Anhand von Referenzgebieten* (Tübingen: Mohr Siebeck, 2007); M Rossi, 'Europäisiertes internationales Umweltverwaltungsrecht', in C Möllers, A Vosskuhle and C Walter (eds), *Internationales Verwaltungsrecht – Eine Analyse Anhand von Referenzgebieten* (Tübingen: Mohr Siebeck, 2007).

[86] J Bast, 'Internationalisierung und De-Internationalisierung der Migrationsverwaltung', in C Möllers, A Vosskuhle and C Walter (eds), *Internationales Verwaltungsrecht – Eine Analyse Anhand von Referenzgebieten* (Tübingen: Mohr Siebeck, 2007); N Krisch, 'Das Migrationsrecht und die Internationalisierung des Verwaltungsrechts', in C Möllers, A Vosskuhle and C Walter (eds), *Internationales Verwaltungsrecht – Eine Analyse Anhand von Referenzgebieten* (Tübingen: Mohr Siebeck, 2007).

[87] Ruffert (2007) 411; Möllers (2007) 3f.

[88] Schmidt-Aßmann (2010) 963; Möllers (2007) 5.

[89] See eg; Kingsbury, Krisch and Stewart (2005) 30; N Krisch and B Kingsbury, 'Introduction: Global Governance and Global Administrative Law in the International Legal Order' (2006) 17 *The European Journal of International Law* 1; B Kingsbury and L Casini, 'Global Administrative Law Dimensions of International Organizations Law' (2009) 6 *International Organizations Law Review* 319; S Cassese (ed), *Research Handbook on Global Administrative Law* (Cheltenham: Edward Elgar, 2016).

[90] Kingsbury, Krisch and Stewart (2005) 17.

[91] Ibid.

state-centred chain of accountability,[92] as the global interactions form a distinct 'global administrative space'.[93] Therefore, the GAL project is working towards the identification of 'mechanisms, principles, practices, and supporting social understandings that promote or otherwise affect the accountability of global administrative bodies, in particular by ensuring they meet adequate standards of transparency, participation, reasoned decision, and legality, and by providing effective review of the rules and decisions they make'.[94] Whereas international administrative law operates a strictly legal approach to the subject, global administrative law can be seen as the legal counterpart to global governance theories,[95] often borrowing from political science methodologies.[96] Through a deductive approach, the project carries out case studies of global governance bodies to identify the emerging principles of a global administrative law.

Kingsbury, Krisch and Stewart identified three mechanisms through which global administrative law is currently formed: (i) national mechanisms applied to hold global administrative bodies accountable; (ii) measures adopted by global bodies themselves applying to their procedure; and (iii) measures adopted by global bodies regulating the domestic implementation of their norms.[97] The main procedural principles[98] identified as currently emerging in global administrative practice are:

- procedural participation: affected persons should have their views taken into account.[99] This principle can be divided into the right to participate in the formation of norms and the right to be heard.[100] However, it is recognised that these participation rights are only developing in some areas;[101]
- transparency: encompassing both decisional transparency and access to information.[102] This is defined as 'a governance of information, including demands for active transparency and access to information, but also demands for confidentiality and privacy, and for legal or political controls on the gathering and use of policy-shaping information'.[103] With regard to transparency,

[92] Ibid, 26.
[93] Ibid, 25ff.
[94] Ibid, 17. See also: B Kingsbury, 'The Administrative Law Frontier in Global Governance' (2005) 99 *Proceedings of the Annual Meeting of the American Society of International Law* 143.
[95] Kingsbury (2005). See also: Ruffert (2007) 403.
[96] Möllers and Terhechte (2011) 1440; K Ladeur, 'Die Internationalisierung des Verwaltungsrechts: Versuch einer Synthese', in C Möllers, A Vosskuhle and C Walter (eds), *Internationales Verwaltungsrecht – Eine Analyse Anhand von Referenzgebieten* (Tübingen: Mohr Siebeck, 2007) 375.
[97] Kingsbury, Krisch and Stewart (2005) 31f.
[98] The GAL project also developed some emerging substantive principles for administrative decision- making (proportionality, means-ends rationality, avoidance of unnecessarily restrictive means, legitimate expectations). See: Kingsbury, Krisch and Stewart (2005) 26.
[99] Kingsbury, Krisch and Stewart (2005) 37.
[100] S Cassese, 'Administrative Law without the State? The Challenge of Global Regulation' (2005) 37 *International Law and Politics* 663, 690f.
[101] Kingsbury, Krisch and Stewart (2005) 38.
[102] Ibid.
[103] Kingsbury and Casini (2009) 325.

the GAL project points to several attempts to increase the transparency of formal and informal bodies on the international level;[104]

- reasoned decisions: with regard to a requirement to give reasons, in practice this is rather weak.[105] Cassese additionally identifies the 'right to decisions based upon scientific and testable data',[106] which could be brought under the right to reasoned decision in the sense of providing a scientifically sound basis;
- review: as containing the right to review either by national authorities, national courts or tribunals at the international level;[107]
- accountability: first, as an overarching concept for all the above principles,[108] but also in a narrower sense as affecting the liability and immunity of international organisations.[109]

However, filling in these emerging principles with concrete norms for global administrative law remains a difficult task. While GAL has served to map and provide a framework for very complex governance structures, its normative claim is delimited by the fact that 'the global legal space is still too diverse, and GAL principles display too great a variety of features, depending on the sectors where they are applied'.[110] It largely refrains from defining the substantive content of global administrative law beyond the level of identifying these general principles.[111] Möllers therefore criticised the case study approach, arguing that it does not allow for the substantiation of a more general normative claim.[112] Conversely, the desirability of a fixed set of global administrative rules is questioned, advocating a 'pluralistic' framework of global administrative law with a multitude of normative systems, which interact in constant competition.[113] Whether one adheres to this pluralist logic, or rather argues for the benefits of a unified administrative law system on the global level,[114] it becomes clear that a major difficulty in assessing or enhancing the legitimacy of global governance

[104] Kingsbury, Krisch and Stewart (2005) 38.
[105] Ibid, 39.
[106] Cassese (2005) 691.
[107] Kingsbury, Krisch and Stewart (2005) 39f.
[108] Krisch and Kingsbury (2006) 4f; Kingsbury (2005) 143.
[109] Kingsbury and Casini (2009) 325.
[110] L Casini, 'Beyond drip-painting? Ten years of GAL and the emergence of a global administration' (2015) 13 *International Journal of Constitutional Law* 473, 477.
[111] Kingsbury, Krisch and Stewart (2005) 29.
[112] C Möllers, 'Ten Years of Global Administrative Law' (2015) 13 *International Journal of Constitutional Law* 469.
[113] See most prominently: N Krisch, 'The Pluralism of Global Administrative Law' (2006) 17 *European Journal of International Law* 247. See also: C Harlow, 'Global Administrative Law: The Quest for Principles and Values' (2006) 17 *European Journal of International Law* 187, 207ff.
[114] For a very good account of the debate between pluralism and constitutionalism see: G de Búrca, 'The European Court of Justice and the International Legal Order after *Kadi*' (2010) 51 *Harvard International Law Journal* 1, 31ff. For a critique of a pluralist approach to global administrative law see: Herwig (2011) 200.

and global standard-setting through the application of global administrative law, is the question of which benchmarks are to be applied and on which basis such norms do or should develop.

B. Assessing the Legitimacy of Global Standard-Setting Bodies through Administrative Law: A Problem of Sources

Both the global and international administrative law scholarships provide testimony of an emerging administrative law governing the globalisation of administrative action. While this might prove to be a route towards establishing a framework for the assessment of the legal-rational legitimacy of global governance, neither 'international administrative law' nor 'global administrative law' currently form an established area of law or could point out a detailed body of norms applicable to administrative bodies on the global level.[115] Therefore, although the scholarship on the development of a global administrative law is a helpful contribution to the legal debate surrounding the phenomenon of global governance, a myriad of questions remain about its content and potential sources.[116]

The GAL scholarship pleads against developing the content of global administrative law based on national administrative law,[117] based on several arguments. First, it is pointed out that most national administrative laws are based on the delegation of power from the parliament to the administration and a connected chain of accountability.[118] Thus, the transposition of national administrative law to the global level is essentially discarded, due to the fundamental differences in the institutional structure and overall context on the global level.[119] Furthermore, it is argued that national administrative law is usually concerned with binding decisions directed against individuals, which – although a phenomenon also on the rise at the global level – is not always the case for global decisions, which are more often directed to states.[120] Also, it is reasoned that national judicial review mechanisms, granting standing for the individual, are difficult to achieve at the global level.[121]

However, while the general principles of global administrative law can be argued to form progressively a global administrative law, their manifestation

[115] Kingsbury, Krisch and Stewart (2005) 31.

[116] Harlow (2006); D Esty, 'Good Governance at the Supranational Scale: Globalizing Administrative Law' (2005–2006) 115 *Yale Law Journal* 1490, 1561f.

[117] Kingsbury, Krisch and Stewart (2005) 51. However, there are also examples of GAL scholars advocating to take inspiration from domestic law. See in particular: R Stewart, 'U.S. Administrative Law: A Model for Global Administrative Law?' (2005) 68 *Law and Contemporary Problems* 63.

[118] Kingsbury, Krisch and Stewart (2005) 53f.

[119] Ibid.

[120] Ibid, 54.

[121] Ibid.

is rather fragmented. They develop in different modes in the respective bodies, making it difficult to form a coherent benchmark for a phenomenon as diverse as global standard-setting. Thus, for the purposes of this book, they allow for an assessment of the ICH standard-setting process with regard to principles such as transparency and participation in very broad terms, without however, establishing concrete benchmarks as to when a process for instance would be regarded as transparent or transparent enough. In this regard, the international administrative law approach allows for more systematic access, as the administrative activity on the global level is always analysed in the context of its interaction with an established system of administrative law.[122]

Although direct transposition of national administrative law to the global level might not be feasible or desirable,[123] it is important to draw on established legal frameworks to find stimulus for the development of global administrative law. This is especially true as global administrative activities do find their way back into the (supra-)national legal system – for example in the implementation of global standards – which means that the analysis of global practices in the context of established legal systems is necessary and valuable. Thus, without taking inspiration from national or supranational administrative law, developing international law to address the governance challenges is not practicable.[124] This, however, should not be understood to advocate that one specific administrative law of a nation state or a region should be transposed to the global level. It is fully acknowledged that practices can be derived from many administrative law frameworks and that a 'westernisation' of administrative law with a global reach should be avoided.[125]

IV. APPLYING THE PERSPECTIVE OF EUROPEAN ADMINISTRATIVE LAW

With the previous section in mind, this section and the other chapters in this Part of the book, relying on an approach of 'intradisciplinary exchange in legal studies',[126] propose that inspiration can be drawn from EU administrative law in order to study international administrative actors in general and the ICH

[122] Möllers (2007) 3.

[123] Legrand for example contends that it is impossible to transplant law, as law is per definition a culturally-situated phenomenon, meaning that while rules can be transplanted they lose their original meaning (see: P Legrand, 'The Impossibility of Legal Transplants' (1997) 4 *Maastricht Journal of European and Comparative Law* 111). For a more nuanced account of the debate surrounding legal transplants see: D Nelken, 'The Meaning of Success in Transnational Legal Transfers' (2001) 19 *Windsor Yearbook of Access to Justice* 349.

[124] von Bogdandy, Dann and Goldmann (2010) 24; Möllers (2005) 385; Schmidt-Aßmann (2010) 959.

[125] Harlow (2006). For a critique of global administrative law in this regard see: F Spagnuolo 'Diversity and pluralism in earth system governance: Contemplating the role for global administrative law' (2011) 70 *Ecological Economics* 1875.

[126] von Bogdandy, Dann and Goldman (2010) 24.

specifically, without disregarding the differences between the EU, which operates as a supranational organisation between international organisations and national states, and the global administrative space.[127] This is not a claim that the administrative framework in the EU would grant an optimum of legitimacy,[128] but rather that useful practices identified at the EU level might also contribute to the improvement of processes on a global level.

On the one hand, this inspiration drawn from European administrative law can contribute to filling the general principles of an emerging global (or international)[129] administrative law with concrete procedural rules.[130] Taking EU administrative law as inspiration for an emerging a global administrative law allows for parallels with the evolution of EU administrative law, which faced similar problems in establishing its administrative order above the national level and away from classic forms of democratic legitimacy.[131] EU administrative law has also developed with a strong orientation towards general principles.[132] The general principles conceived of in this way have become the core criteria for assessing the actions of the European administration.[133] These principles have been developed and defined, especially through jurisprudence, based on the practice in the Member States and policy-specific EU norms.[134]

Interestingly, the EU as an organisation also seems to have a vision of exporting its own good governance norms: Article 3(5) TEU provides that the EU shall

[127] See: E Chiti, 'EU and Global Administrative Organizations', in E Chiti and B Mattarella (eds), *Global Administrative Law and EU Administrative Law* (Heidelberg: Springer, 2011).

[128] For discussion of EU administrative law and legitimacy especially in the regulatory context including existing gaps see eg: G Majone, 'The Regulatory State and Its Legitimacy Problems' (1999) 22 *West European Politics* 1; D Curtin, *Executive Power of the European Union – Law, Practice and the Living Constitution* (Oxford: Oxford University Press, 2009); M Weimer and A de Ruijter, *Regulating Risks in the European Union – The Co-production of Expert and Executive Power* (Oxford: Hart Publishing, 2017); M Scholten and A Brenninkmeijer, *Controlling EU Agencies – The Rule of Law in a Multi-jurisdictional Legal Order* (Cheltenham: Edward Elgar, 2020).

[129] In the following, the term global administrative law refers to administrative law on the global level rather than explicitly to the GAL scholarship.

[130] See also: Möllers and Terhechte (2011); M Savino, 'EU "Procedural" Supranationalism: On Models for Global Administrative Law', paper presented at NYU Global Forum on 13 December 2006; E Chiti and B Mattarella (eds), *Global Administrative Law and EU Administrative Law* (Heidelberg: Springer, 2011). More generally geared towards the democratisation of international organizations: A von Bogdandy, 'The European Lesson for International Democracy – The Significance of Articles 9 to 12 EU Treaty for International Organizations' (2012) 23 *European Journal of International Law* 315. See also Lin, who applies lessons learned from European Food Safety Authority to the global level: C Lin, 'The European Food Safety Authority in Global Food Safety Governance: A Participant, a Benchmark, and a Model', in A Alemanno and S Gabbi (eds), *Foundations of EU Food Law and Policy* (Farnham: Ashgate, 2014b).

[131] See: E Schmidt-Aßmann, *Das allgemeine Verwaltungsrecht als Ordnungsidee – Grundlagen und Aufgaben der verwaltungsrechtlichen Systembildung*, 2nd edn (Heidelberg: Springer, 2006).

[132] H Trute, '§6 Die demokratische Legitimation der Verwaltung', in W Hoffmann-Riem, E Schmidt-Aßmann and A Voßkuhle (Eds.), *Grundlagen des Verwaltungsrechts Band I* (München: Beck, 2012) 414ff; Schmidt-Aßmann (2010) 959.

[133] H Hofmann, J Schneider and J Ziller, 'The Research Network on European Administrative Law's Project on EU Administrative Procedure – Its Concepts, Approaches and Results' (2014) 7 *Review of European Administrative Law* 45, 47.

[134] Ibid.

contribute to 'the development of international law'. Moreover, in the field of external actions the Treaties specifically mention Article 21 TEU: '2. The Union shall define and pursue common policies and actions, and shall work for a high degree of cooperation in all fields of international relations, in order to: … (h) promote an international system based on stronger multilateral cooperation and good global governance.' Also, in the White Paper on European Governance the European Commission declares that: '(t)he Union should seek to apply the principles of good governance to its global responsibilities. It should aim to boost the effectiveness and enforcement powers of international institutions.'[135]

On the other hand, it needs to be stressed that where European regulators are bound to EU procedural rules, the fact that they carry out their regulatory activity in a global body rather than internally in the EU does not *per se* mean that they can sidestep these rules.[136] Apart from the possible contribution to establishing procedural rules for administrative action on the global level, another argument for analysing such global administrative activities from a European administrative law perspective is that these global activities work their way through to the EU level, as the implementation of global standards in the EU demonstrates. Where the global measure is received in the EU through implementation – like it is the case for the standards of the ICH[137] – the legitimacy of this can be questioned, given that the global administrative body has not been subject to the same procedural rules that would have to be followed in the EU in adopting the measure.[138] A legitimacy review at the EU level could perform a 'gatekeeper'[139] function, as it forms the 'entrance level' for standards into European as well as national risk regulation frameworks.[140] Devaux argues that the EU could perform a 'legitimacy test … with which the EU would evaluate whether a transnational norm deserves its support or not',[141] through an administrative procedure in which the legitimacy of a norm that is to be implemented in the EU is assessed. Core criteria in this assessment could be the application of EU administrative law, which is applicable to comparable instruments on the EU level.

The clash between procedural rules on the global and EU level is exemplified in the *Kadi* case, where the claimant targeted a regulation originating in

[135] European Commission, European Governance – A White Paper, COM(2001) 428 final, OJ 287, 12 October 2001, 5.

[136] J Mendes, 'Rule of Law and Participation: A Normative Analysis of Internationalized Rulemaking as Composite Procedures' (2014) 12 *International Journal of Constitutional Law* 370, 396.

[137] Chapter 4.

[138] Mendes (2014) 372; Stewart (2005) 69; H Röhl, 'Internationale Standardsetzung', in C Möllers, A Vosskuhle and C Walter (eds), *Internationales Verwaltungsrecht – Eine Analyse Anhand von Referenzgebieten* (Tübingen: Mohr Siebeck, 2007) 328.

[139] The term is borrowed from: J Scott, 'International Trade and Environmental Governance: Relating Rules (and Standards) in the EU and WTO' (2004) 15 *European Journal of International Law* 307.

[140] Röhl (2007) 337.

[141] Devaux (2013) 862.

an UN Security Council Resolution on the basis of the right to property, to a fair hearing and the right to effective judicial review.[142] The Court in that case declared that 'the obligations imposed by an international agreement cannot have the effect of prejudicing the constitutional principles of the EC Treaty'.[143] Arguably, the *Kadi* case is very special due to its anti-terrorism context, and as it concerned the protection of fundamental rights rather than procedural administrative law standards. However, the Court in that ruling stressed the autonomy of the EU legal order and the rights this order protects.[144] Mendes convincingly argued that the values of transparency, participation and good governance are enshrined in the Treaty and therefore form part of the constitutional order of the Union, which is used by the Court in its judicial review.[145] Therefore, where the *Kadi* reasoning is applied to the measures implementing global standards in the EU, it could serve as an argument for questioning such measures, where the standard-setting process from which they originate does not conform to administrative law and good governance norms applicable in the EU. As Curtin and Eckes have explained, the Court in *Kadi* made 'an attempt to stop the executive from hollowing-out the rule of law from above'.[146] Indeed, where the Court is willing to set aside EU rules implementing binding international law in the form of a Security Council Resolution, a similar logic could be applied to measures implementing global standards.

What remains problematic about the approach of applying EU administrative law to global standards – in terms of the development of a global administrative law – is that different constituencies will simultaneously apply their administrative law to the same global activity. This potentially leads to conflicting approaches to administrative law on the global level. Therefore, the enforcement of national or European administrative law targeting global actions entails the danger of breaking up the idea of one global administrative law into a kaleidoscope of national norms differing from state to state.[147] However, the alternative currently seems to be a lack of any formalised procedural constraints at all, which creates a complete vacuum of legal protection. How a conflict arising out of the simultaneous application of diverging and even opposing administrative laws can be overcome is exemplified by the ICH. As Lindström-Gommers and Mullin explain in the context of the ICH reform:[148] '... public demands for

[142] Joined cases C-402 and 415/05P *Kadi & Al Barakaat International Foundation v Council and Commission*, ECLI:EU:C:2008:461.

[143] Ibid, para 285.

[144] de Búrca (2010) 5.

[145] Mendes (2012) 1010.

[146] D Curtin and C Eckes, 'The *Kadi* Case: Mapping the Boundaries between the Executive and the Judiciary in Europe' (2008) 5 *International Organizations Law Review* 365, 369.

[147] Kingsbury, Krisch and Stewart (2005) 56; M Herberg, 'Global Governance Networks in Action: The Development of Toxicological Test Methods at the OECD', in O Dilling, M Herberg and G Winter (eds), *Transnational Administrative Rule-Making – Performance, Legal Effects and Legitimacy* (Oxford: Hart Publishing, 2011) 84.

[148] For more on the reform see Chapter 3.

the assurance of government integrity and transparency had increased in several developed regions … Reflecting these considerations, for example, in 2010, the European Commission conveyed concerns about the current role of industry in this international initiative … Although this concern regarding clear lines of control for the regulators in all guideline work was initially met with some reservation in the Steering Committee, it was acknowledged as legitimate by the other ICH regulators.'[149] Thus, the ICH reform provides an example of how the Commission, based on concerns of acting against own procedural standards, has initiated the reform of a global standard-setting body through deliberation amongst the involved actors. Although, as will be made clear in Chapter 6, the reform of the ICH has not brought it completely in line with EU administrative law.

A. Procedural Standards Derived from European Administrative Law

Having argued for the application of EU administrative law to global standards, it is now time to look closer at the procedural principles that are relevant for standard-setting on the EU level and as will be argued therefore also on the global level. Although there is a broad array of administrative law provisions, this section looks only at those which could be applicable to procedural questions related to risk regulation through standard-setting. Discussions on substantive principles – such as for example proportionality – are left aside, as are the principles that apply to the taking of binding decisions directed towards individuals through the administration, as they are not applicable in standard-setting.[150] It also has to be acknowledged that at this point EU administrative law is not thoroughly and comprehensively codified. To a large extent it is developed by the Court of Justice's rulings on general principles.[151] While a uniform EU law on administrative procedures, advocated for quite some time in literature[152]

[149] Lindström-Gommers and Mullin (2019) 927.

[150] In general the following principles form the core of European administrative law: the rule of law and specifically the margin of appreciation left to the administrative, equality, non-discrimination, proportionality, the protection of legitimate expectations, legal certainty and the right to a fair administrative procedure. See: J Schwarze, *EU Administrative Law* (London: Sweet and Maxwell, 2006) cxi.

[151] Schwarze (2006) cxi; H Hofmann and A Türk, 'An Introduction to EU Administrative Governance', in H Hofmann and A Türk (eds), *EU Administrative Governance* (Cheltenham: Edward Elgar, 2006) 2; S Kadelbach, 'EU Administrative Law and the Law of the Europeanized Administration', in C Joerges and R Dehousse (eds), *Good Governance in Europe's Integrated Market* (Oxford: Oxford University Press, 2002).

[152] P Craig, H Hofmann, J Schneider and J Ziller (eds), *ReNEUAL Model Rules on EU Administrative Procedure* (Oxford: Oxford University Press, 2017); Hofmann, Schneider and Ziller (2014); P Craig, 'A General Law on Administrative Procedure, Legislative Competence and Judicial Competence' (2013) 19 *European Public Law* 503; A Meuwese, Y Schuurmans and W Voermans, 'Towards a European Administrative Procedure Act' (2009) 2 *Review of European Administrative Law* 3.

and by the European Ombudsman,[153] is now also being requested by the European Parliament,[154] the provisions applying to EU action are currently scattered over a large variety of sources, from hard law to soft law provisions and the case law of the Court. A full description of these norms is beyond the scope of this section, but it will provide an introduction to the core norms applicable to standard-setting in the administrative context.[155]

The starting point of assessing administrative actions is Article 1(2) TEU, which states that 'decisions are taken as openly as possible' in the EU. Moreover, Article 2 TEU provides that the EU is based – amongst others – on the principles of democracy and the rule of law. These principles apply to all EU institutions, not just the administrative actors, and find further illustration in the provisions of Articles 9 to 12 TEU, the following of which are relevant for administrative action:

- Article 10(3) TEU: the right of citizens to take part 'in the democratic life of the Union', as well as the openness of decisions.
- Article 11 TEU:
  - the right of citizens as well as representative organisations to express their opinion and enter into discussion regarding all EU action (para 1);
  - and the duty of institutions to 'maintain an open, transparent and regular dialogue' with these actors (para 2);
  - furthermore, it contains an obligation for the Commission to 'carry out broad consultations with parties concerned in order to ensure that the Union's actions coherent and transparent' (para 3).

Thus, the core values of participation and transparency derive from the principle of democracy, combining to form the principle of openness.[156] In this regard, the principle of transparency refers to the right of individuals to obtain documents, but also to an obligation to make documentation more readily available to the public at large.[157] In general, the principles of participation and transparency should be read as a commitment to open up the decision-making process to comprehension and overview by the general public, besides their function

[153] European Ombudsman, The European Code of Good Administrative Behaviour, available via: europa.eu/!Gx99WU.

[154] European Parliament, European administrative procedure law, Resolution of 15 January 2013, 2012/2024 INL, P7_TA(2013)0004; European Parliament, A regulation for an open, efficient and independent European Union administration, Resolution of 9 June 2016, 2016/2610 RSP, P8_TA(2016)0279.

[155] For a more detailed discussion see for example: F Bignami, 'Three Generations of Participation Rights Before the European Commission' (2004) 68 *Law and Contemporary Problems* 61; J Mendes, *Participation in EU Rule-Making – A Rights-Based Approach* (Oxford: Oxford University Press, 2011a); A Alemanno, 'Unpacking the Principle of Openness in EU Law: Transparency, Participation and Democracy' (2014) 39 *European Law Review* 72.

[156] Alemanno (2014) 81.

[157] Bignami (2004) 71; Alemanno (2014) 82.

of providing rights such as the access to documents for individuals.[158] These general European constitutional principles apply across all policy areas and activities of the European administration.[159]

In the evolution of European administrative law, the increasing emphasis on the various dimensions of openness is clearly linked to the pursuit of legitimacy and democracy.[160] According to the Court, openness 'enables citizens to participate more closely in the decision-making process and guarantees that the administration enjoys greater legitimacy and is more effective and more accountable to the citizen in a democratic system'.[161] While the presumed contribution to legitimacy of the principle of openness is subject to vivid debate in scholarship,[162] the constitutionalisation of these principles in the Treaties, and their growing use in the Court, have been argued to provide a basis for enhancing the democratic legitimacy of the EU. This is of course dependent upon their application in practice, and potentially also in their further shaping through the Court and the legislator.[163]

In addition, norms of good governance have contributed to shaping administrative procedures. In 2001, as a response to a lack of trust and interest of European citizens in the actions of the EU – not only in the context of risk regulation – the European Commission published a White Paper on European Governance, addressing the legitimacy challenges it was facing and proposing changes on the basis of the principles of good governance.[164] Relying on the core values of democracy and the rule of law, the Commission identifies five – sometimes overlapping – principles of good governance: 'openness, participation, accountability, effectiveness and coherence'[165] and proposed several actions to enforce these principles. Good governance norms are also established in the Treaty with Article 15(1) TFEU: '(i)n order to promote good governance and ensure the participation of civil society, the Union's institutions, bodies, offices and agencies shall conduct their work as openly as possible'. This openness also includes a right to access to documents (Article 15(3) TFEU), which is also to be found in Article 42 of the Charter, and which has been further implemented through the Access to Documents Regulation.[166]

[158] Hofmann, Schneider and Ziller (2014) 51.

[159] Ibid, 46.

[160] Alemanno (2014) 82f.

[161] Joined cases C-39/05P and C-52/05P *Kingdom of Sweden and Maurizio Turco v Council*, ECLI:EU:C:2008:374, para 45.

[162] See eg. Mendes (2011a); D Curtin and A Meijer, 'Does Transparency Strengthen Legitimacy?' (2006) 11 *Information Polity* 109; B Kohler-Koch and C Quittkat (eds), *De-Mystification of Participatory Democracy* (Oxford: Oxford University Press, 2013).

[163] Alemanno (2014); D Curtin, H Hofmann and J Mendes, 'Constitutionalising EU Executive Rule-Making Procedures: A Research Agenda' (2013) 19 *European Law Journal* 1.

[164] European Commission, European Governance – A White Paper, COM(2001) 428 final, OJ 287, 12 October 2001, 1–29.

[165] Ibid, 10.

[166] Regulation (EC) No 1049/2001 of the European Parliament and of the Council of 30 May 2001 regarding public access to European Parliament, Council and Commission documents, [2001] OJ L145/ 43.

But do these procedural standards also apply to standards and comparable soft law measures within the EU? With regard to the principle of transparency, including access to documents, there is no provision in the treaties that would indicate that it is only applicable to legislative acts.[167] The Access to Documents Regulation also provides for access to documents which are broadly defined as 'content whatever its medium (written on paper or stored in electronic form or as a sound, visual or audiovisual recording), concerning a matter relating to the policies, activities and decisions falling within the institution's sphere of responsibility'.[168]

Regarding the principle of participation, Article 11 TEU does not provide a limit to the applicability of the principle concerning soft law.[169] However, with regard to Article 11(3) TEU, the duty to conduct public consultations is limited to the Commission. According to the Commission's consultation guideline, in conjunction with its impact assessment guideline, there is no obligation to do so – although the Commission occasionally carries out consultations for soft law acts.[170] Article 15 TFEU is addressed to 'the Union's institutions, bodies, offices and agencies' and provides that these should work as openly as possible to facilitate the participation of civil society; in contrast, the participation provisions of Article 11(1) and (2) TEU only explicitly apply to the institutions and, thus, not to agencies. Therefore, it seems that while Article 15 TFEU imposes an obligation of openness to all EU bodies, the obligation to maintain a dialogue with civil society and the consultation obligations do not apply to all EU bodies. However, Article 11 TEU does connect participation to democracy, which is a founding principle of the Union according to Article 2 TEU.[171] Thus, although no specific duty to facilitate participation in agencies arises from the Treaty, the general commitment to democracy in the EU does apply to agencies. In this spirit they should not bar the participation of civil society.

In this regard, secondary legislation introduces consultation obligations that also apply to other actors and types of measures. For example, the General Food Law, the founding regulation of the European Food Safety Authority (EFSA), provides for the conduct of an 'open and transparent public consultation, directly or through representative bodies, during the preparation, evaluation and revision of food law, except where the urgency of the matter does not allow it'.[172] This means that both the Commission and EFSA are obliged to

[167] See also: L Senden and A van den Brink A, 'Checks and Balances of Soft EU Rule-Making', European Parliament – Directorate General for Internal Policies Study (2012) PE 462.433.

[168] Regulation (EC) No 1049/2001, art 3(a).

[169] See also: Senden and van den Brink (2012) 28ff.

[170] Ibid; European Commission, Towards a reinforced culture of consultation and dialogue – General principles and minimum standards for consultation of interested parties by the Commission, COM(2002) 704 final, Brussels, 11 December 2002.

[171] J Mendes, 'Participation and the Role of Law after Lisbon: A Legal View on Article 11 TEU' (2011b) 48 *Common Market Law Review* 1849, 1853f.

[172] Regulation (EC) No 178/2002 of the European Parliament and of the Council of 28 January 2002 laying down the general principles and requirements of food law, establishing the European Food Safety Authority, and laying down procedures in matters of food safety, [2002] OJ L31/1, art 9.

execute public consultation procedures in the evaluation and revision through law, regulation and administrative measures.[173] Indeed stakeholder participation in agencies – established as non-majoritarian expert bodies following quite a technocratic logic of being 'at the expense of democratic legitimacy'[174] – is especially important. Some agencies have therefore created advisory fora and stakeholder groups,[175] and some have also adopted consultation procedures, which are comparable to the procedure adopted by the Commission.[176]

In the search for administrative law applicable to standard-setting, the right to good administration, which is found in Article 41 of the Charter of Fundamental Rights, also has to be mentioned.[177] Amongst rights that address the protection of individuals in administrative decision-making procedures in which they are concerned, it contains the duty of administrators to give reasons for their decisions, which is one of the necessary characteristics of a transparent administrative process. Although Article 41 of the Charter is geared towards single-case decision-making, the Court has also applied it in the broader context of non-legislative rule-making, where it has been used as a criterion for the legality review of non-legislative measures.[178]

In the aforementioned provisions, the focus of procedural administrative legitimacy is laid on participation and transparency. However, the Treaties provide in Article 298(1) TFEU that 'the institutions, bodies, offices and agencies of the Union shall have the support of an open, efficient and independent European administration'. In the same vein, the Court has also contributed to the definition of EU administrative law. The well-known *Pfizer* case is key to understanding the European risk regulation framework.[179] This case established that risks must be assessed by scientific experts consulted on the basis of the 'principles of excellence, independence and transparency'.[180] While efficiency and excellence are legally difficult to assess in matters of risk regulation,[181] this means that the independence of administrative actors is a core principle in the assessment of legitimacy of administrative action, in addition to transparency

[173] J Mendes, 'Administrative Law Beyond the State: Participation at the Intersection of Legal Systems', in E Chiti and B Mattarella (eds), *Global Administrative Law and EU Administrative Law* (Heidelberg: Springer, 2011c).

[174] Senden and van den Brink (2012) 46.

[175] H Hofmann, G Rowe and A Türk, *Administrative Law and Policy of the European Union* (Oxford: Oxford University Press, 2011).

[176] Mendes (2011b) 1853f.

[177] See: J Ponce Solé, 'EU Law, Global Law and the Right to Good Administration', in E Chiti and B Mattarella (eds), *Global Administrative Law and EU Administrative Law* (Heidelberg: Springer, 2011b).

[178] H Hofmann and B Mihaescu, 'The Relation between the Charter's Fundamental Rights and the Unwritten General Principles of EU law: Good Administration as the Test Case' (2013) 9 *European Constitutional Law Review* 73, 87. See for example: Joined cases C-154/04 and C-155/04 *Alliance for Natural Health*, ECLI:EU:C:2005:449, para 82.

[179] Case T-13/99 *Pfizer Animal Health v Council*, ECLI:EU:T:2002:209.

[180] Ibid, para 159.

[181] Section II.

and participation, especially in the field of risk regulation. In this respect, independence should be understood both in an inter-institutional sense as well as referring to independence from the regulated industry.[182]

Following on from the analysis above, the core principles identified as main focal points of EU administrative law that could be applied to the assessment of global standard-setting procedures are:

- participation,
- transparency, and
- independent expertise.[183]

Applying these general principles in the legitimacy assessment of global standards implemented in the EU requires the assessment of policy sector-specific rules, applying to administrative bodies like the Commission and agencies in a specific regulatory field such as pharmaceuticals regulation.[184] One needs to evaluate the policies and practices of the EU administrative actors in order to uncover how the Treaty principles are applied in specific policy areas. It has been pointed out that some of the agencies founding regulations provide procedural rules such as consultation requirements. Internal rules and the policies that agencies set themselves need to be taken into account for a comprehensive picture. For example, the Treaty provision on access to documents provides that '[e]ach institution, body, office or agency shall ensure that its proceedings are transparent and shall elaborate in its own Rules of Procedure specific provisions regarding access to its documents'.[185] Generally, the transparency policies of regulatory agencies are diverse due to their different regulatory fields and task. In a study regarding the proceduralisation of rule-making powers, Chiti shows that where agencies are mandated to adopt binding implementing rules, there is a tendency to lay down certain basic procedural rules that are applied either in the founding regulation or in rules of procedure.[186] In soft law activities, the degree of proceduralisation is lower. However, where procedures applicable to soft law are established, they seem to mirror the rules applicable to binding measures, with a strong basis in the principles of participation and transparency.[187]

[182] E Vos, 'European Agencies and the Composite EU Executive', in M Everson, C Monda and E Vos (eds), *European Agencies In Between Institutions and Member States* (Alphen aan den Rijn: Kluwer Law International, 2014) 37.

[183] For a similar approach see: Röhl (2007) 339; M Ruffert, '§17 Rechtsquellen und Rechtsschichten des Verwaltungsrechts', in W Hoffmann-Riem, E Schmidt-Aßmann and A Voßkuhle (eds), *Grundlagen des Verwaltungsrechts Band I* (München: Beck, 2012), 1214; M Eifert, '§19 Regulierungsstrategien', in W Hoffmann-Riem, E Schmidt-Aßmann and A Voßkuhle (eds), *Grundlagen des Verwaltungsrechts Band I* (München: Beck, 2012) 1353.

[184] On the importance of policy specific rules in EU administrative law see: Hofmann, Schneider and Ziller (2014) 46f; Hofmann (2009) 50.

[185] Art 15(3) TFEU.

[186] E Chiti, 'European Agencies' Rulemaking: Powers, Procedures and Assessment' (2013) 19 *European Law Journal* 93, 101.

[187] Ibid, 101f.

V. CONCLUSION: IN SEARCH OF LEGITIMACY

Legitimacy was introduced as a multi-faceted concept that, beyond the notion of democracy, can contain a variety of procedural and substantive factors which have to be applied to the body in question according to its context, taking into account how the body exercises authority, and on which level of the complex interactions of governance it is established. Accordingly, governance through global standard-setting raises questions of legitimacy, which cannot be answered in terms of traditional national or international law. These legitimacy questions, however, are important to consider since these standards – irrespective of their voluntary nature – are adhered to and implemented in national or regional regulatory frameworks, and ultimately have an effect on the rights and duties of individuals.

It has been shown that the input legitimacy on the global level is often flawed by procedures that are neither transparent nor open to the participation of all concerned actors, thus failing to compensate for the lack of democratic legitimacy. While standards are argued to be legitimised through their efficiency and effectiveness in addressing risks globally, this logic of legitimisation via output legitimacy meets its limits where, as in the case of risk regulation, there is not necessarily a 'good' or 'most effective' solution to a regulatory problem. Instead a verdict on the efficiency and effectiveness of a certain standard will very much depend on methodological choices or the perception of risks in certain societies, which means that output legitimacy cannot provide a sufficient basis of legitimisation for risk regulation standards.

In the context of these debates, applying EU administrative law to the standard-setting processes on the global level was proposed as a technique to assess the legal-rational legitimacy derived from the conformity with administrative law. Whereas currently no established international or global administrative law exists, its evolution has become the object of recent scholarly interest. This has made a very valuable contribution in identifying core principles as they are forming. However, global administrative law currently cannot provide a sufficient basis for a detailed substantive assessment of global standard-setting activities. Therefore, it is argued that EU administrative law can serve as a source of inspiration for the development of administrative rules on the global level. Although counterintuitive at first, applying EU administrative law to global standard-setting bodies like the ICH is imperative from an EU law perspective given the effects that these standards have in the European risk regulation framework. Thus, as well as increasing the legitimacy of EU implementation of global standards, an EU administrative law perspective can contribute to establishing a framework to assess and improve the legitimacy of the global standard-setting process itself.

With regard to the application of EU administrative law to the global standard-setting processes, three relevant core principles were identified: transparency, participation and independent expertise. However, it was also pointed out that although EU administrative law – like the evolving global administrative law – is largely based on general principles, these principles have been proceduralised differently in the respective policy areas, as well as through their formalisation in the Treaties and case law. Thus, where the legitimacy of global standards is assessed against EU administrative law benchmarks, an in-depth study of the policy area concerned is required. This realisation is put into practice in the following chapters, which are devoted to the legitimacy analysis of global pharmaceutical standards set by the ICH and their implementation in the EU.

6

Examining the Legitimacy of the ICH Standard-Setting Procedure and Uploading EU Administrative Law

THE PREVIOUS CHAPTER proposed the application of procedural norms developed by EU administrative law for assessment of the legitimacy of global standard-setting bodies. Following this line of argument, this chapter will examine whether the procedure through which ICH pharmaceutical standards are adopted lives up to the administrative law principles that comparable measures originating in the EU would have to fulfil. In this respect, the administrative and good governance principles of participatory openness, transparency and independent expertise have been identified as core benchmarks in examining the standard-setting procedure.

Even if participation (Article 10(3) and 11 TEU), transparency (Articles 10(3) and 11 TEU, Article 15 TFEU), and independent expertise (Article 298(1) TFEU, 'open efficient and independent European administration') are principles enshrined in the EU Treaties, their content is not clarified in detail at this constitutional level. Most administrative procedures are regulated in a policy-specific way, in legislation and also by means of rules of procedures set by the respective bodies.[1] This leads to a 'patchwork blanket'[2] of procedural rules applicable to administrative action in the EU. Therefore, applying a European perspective to participation, transparency and independent expertise in the ICH process, requires a specific assessment of what procedural standards are applicable in the guideline development process of the European Medicines Agency, by analogy. This is based on the fact that ICH standards are implemented in the EU in the form of EMA guidelines and that EU-originating scientific guidelines comparable to those of the ICH are adopted by the EMA.

This chapter will not only compare the procedural standards applicable and identify potential legitimacy gaps in the ICH procedure, but, as it was argued

[1] Chapter 5.

[2] L Senden and A van den Brink, 'Checks and Balances of Soft EU Rule-Making', European Parliament – Directorate General for Internal Policies Study (2012) PE 462.433, 67.

that EU norms can contribute to the formation of global administrative law and can improve the legitimacy of the ICH, it will also provide recommendations for policies and practices that can be 'uploaded' from the EMA standard-setting procedure to the ICH level.[3] The chapter therefore addresses legitimacy concerns from several different perspectives simultaneously. On the one hand, the EU as an implementing regulatory system should be concerned about the legitimacy of pharmaceutical standards set on the global level as they become an integral part of the EU regulatory framework. On the other hand, where the procedural policies and practices applied in the EU are 'uploaded' to the ICH, this might contribute to the ICH as a body on the global level being able to address legitimacy challenges arising from an emerging global administrative law.

I. THE PRINCIPLE OF PARTICIPATION

Participation, as aptly defined by Mendes, is to be understood as 'procedural intervention of natural and legal persons whose substantive rights and interests are potentially affected by … regulatory measures, irrespective of the form in which the latter are adopted'.[4] In the following analysis, attention is paid to both institutionalised forms of participation, where the stakeholder forms an integral part of the institutional structure and the decision-making process, and other, less formalised forms of participation. Beyond the state level most bodies, as they are not electorally legitimised, have to rely on other means to increase their legitimacy, such as inclusive participation of all relevant stakeholders.[5] Nevertheless, the influence that can be exerted through participation is subject to limitations as 'it is the right to be heard, not the right to decide'.[6] Along with a potential contribution to legitimacy, the participation of stakeholders in the decision-making process serves the accountability of the decision-makers as well as the quality of the decisions taken.[7]

[3] 'Uploading' as used in the research refers to the transposition of norms from one regulatory level to another. For a similar use of the term 'uploading' see: A Batory, 'Uploading as Political Strategy: the European Parliament and the Hungarian Media Law Debate' (2014) 30 *East European Politics* 230; K Howell, 'Uploading, Downloading and European Integration: Assessing the Europeanisation of UK Financial Services Regulation' (2004) 6 *Journal of International Banking Regulation* 53; J Connolly, 'Europeanization, Uploading and Downloading – The Case of Defra and Avian Influenza' (2008) 23 *Public Policy and Administration* 7.

[4] J Mendes, *Participation in EU Rule-Making – A Rights-Based Approach* (Oxford: Oxford University Press, 2011a) 25.

[5] B Dorbeck-Jung, 'Challenges to the Legitimacy of International Regulation: The Case of Pharmaceuticals Standardisation', in A Føllesdal, R Wessel and J Wouters (eds), *Multilevel Regulation and the EU: The Interplay between Global, European and National Normative Processes* (Leiden: Martinus Nijhoff Publishers, 2008) 55.

[6] C Möllers, 'European Governance: Meaning and Value of a Concept' (2006) 43 *Common Market Law Review* 313, 321.

[7] J Steffek and M Ferretti, 'Accountability or "Good Decision"? The Competing Goals of Civil Society Participation in International Governance' (2009) 23 *Global Society* 37.

A. Assessing the Principle of Participation in the ICH Standard-Setting Process

As has been argued in this book,[8] the ICH is to be characterised as a public-private partnership, granting extensive rights and decision-making influence to pharmaceutical industry associations. Therefore, it provides for a particularly interesting study of participatory mechanisms at the global level, given that the participation of industry stakeholders in the regulatory process is an integral feature of its institutional structure. However, the participatory rights of other stakeholders are not so inherent in the ICH institutional structure, leading to the question whether the ICH participatory mechanisms allow for a balanced input from all relevant stakeholders.

From its inception the ICH was construed as a partnership between regulators and representatives of the research-based pharmaceutical industry. This partnership, and with it, the institutionalised participation of industry in the ICH standard-setting process has persisted after the ICH reform. As established in Chapter 3, both the institutional structure and decision-making process allow for considerable participation by pharmaceutical industry representatives. Pharmaceutical industry associations are members of the ICH, represented in the two main governing bodies, the Assembly and the Management Committee.[9] Moreover, they nominate experts for the Expert Working Groups,[10] granting them considerable influence on the content of ICH guidelines. Although industry representatives do not have a final say in the adoption of the guidelines since the reform, they still contribute significantly to the scientific consensus that shapes the content of the guidelines.[11] Thus, the participation of the research-based industry in the process is not limited to an advisory role or the provision of scientific data, industry representatives take an active part in determining the content and scope of the ICH guidelines. Therefore, the ICH has enabled the pharmaceutical industry to directly engage with regulators in the standard-setting process, 'influencing health care and economic decisions at the highest levels of government'.[12] The desirability of establishing the ICH as a body composed of regulators and industry is attributed to the benefits this cooperation brings for the regulators, ultimately enabling them to carry out their task not only as protectors of industrial interests, but also as guardians of public health.[13] Indeed, the collaboration with industry ensures that standards are set

[8] Chapter 3.

[9] Chapter 3 Section III.

[10] Chapter 3 Section IV.

[11] Chapter 3 Section V.

[12] D Kidd, 'The International Conference on Harmonization of Pharmaceutical Regulations, the European Medicines Evaluation Agency, and the FDA: Who's Zooming Who?' (1996) 4 *Indiana Journal of Global Legal Studies* 183, 186.

[13] A Spina, 'The Regulation of Pharmaceuticals Beyond the State: EU and Global Administrative Systems', in E Chiti and B Mattarella (eds), *Global Administrative Law and EU Administrative Law* (Heidelberg: Springer, 2011) 264; A Berman, 'Informal International Lawmaking in Medical

in line with the latest developments in pharmaceutical research and opens up larger resources than the public authorities could provide. This arguably enables the protection of public health through standards based on the highest expertise.

However, especially given the field in which the ICH is operational – pharmaceutical regulation, where the declared aim is a symbiosis of the protection of public health and industrial interests, which do not always overlap – the powerful representation of industrial interests in the regulatory process has attracted a lot of criticism.[14] This is especially precarious, given that the conflicted independence is an integral feature of the ICH as a public-private partnership between regulators and the regulated industry. The role of industry stakeholders as co-regulators in the ICH should be seen in a broader context of increasing influence of the regulated industry on regulatory processes in general, where 'commercial interests that were once regarded to be, at best, "troublesome"' in character, have been recast as "stakeholder" …'.[15] Where the role of private industry actors has been redefined from being subjected to regulation to becoming active participants in the regulatory process, potential conflicts of interests are an integral feature. This will be subject to further discussion in the section devoted to the independence of expertise.[16]

This is not to suggest that industry involvement is *per se* undesirable or that concerns of public health are always opposing industrial interest. Arguably, no pharmaceutical producer aims to market harmful products. Moreover, for the experts involved in the ICH process, their scientific reputation is at stake as well.[17] However, opening up public processes to participation of commercial interest requires mechanisms ensuring the transparency of these processes, which will be addressed later in this chapter.[18] At the same time they demand a counter-balancing of industry representation through participation of the non-commercial interest representatives that the regulation seeks to protect.[19] This is

Products Regulation', in A Berman, S Duquet, J Pauwelyn, R Wessel and J Wouters (eds), *Informal International Lawmaking: Case Studies* (The Hague: Torkel Opsahl Academic Publishers, 2012c) 353–93.

[14] J Abraham, 'The Pharmaceutical Industry as a Political Player' (2002) 360 *The Lancet* 1498; J Abraham and T Reed, 'Trading Risks for Markets: The International Harmonization of Pharmaceuticals Regulation' (2001) 1 *Health, Risk and Society* 113; J Abraham and T Reed, 'Progress, Innovation and Regulatory Science in Drug Development: The Politics of International Standard-Setting' (2002) 32 *Social Studies of Science* 337.

[15] M van Asselt, M Everson and E Vos, 'The European Union Put to the Test: The Quest for Politics', in M van Asselt, M Everson and E Vos (eds), Trade, Health and the Environment – The European Union Put to the Test (Oxon: Routledge/Earthscan, 2014) 12.

[16] Section II.

[17] A Berman, 'The Public-Private Nature of Harmonisation Networks' (2011) CTEI Working Paper, CTEI-2011-06, 55.

[18] Section III.

[19] C Scott, 'Standard-Setting in Regulatory Regimes', in R Baldwin, M Cave and M Lodge (eds), *The Oxford Handbook of Regulation* (Oxford: Oxford University Press, 2010) 116; C Möllers, 'Transnationale Behördenkooperation – Verfassungs- und Völkerrechtliche Probleme Transnationaler Administrativer Standardsetzung' (2005) 65 *Zeitschrift für ausländisches öffentliches Recht und Völkerrecht* 351, 385; Pereira R, 'Why Would International Administrative Activity Be Any Less

particularly relevant as by balancing the input of those affected by the decision-making, participation facilitates the safeguarding of all interests protected by risk regulation policies.[20] It is all the more important given that in its mandate the ICH acknowledges that the standards it sets aim to protect public health. As the setting of regulatory standards is not only a technical/scientific but also a political exercise,[21] balanced stakeholder participation is needed to facilitate democratic decision-making. In order to counteract the risk of capture, an equal representation of various interests in the decision-making is required.[22] Thus, the incorporation of diverse views in the regulation mechanisms through a system of stakeholder participation is essential to legitimate risk regulation, especially in the case of pharmaceuticals.

It should be clarified that addressing questions of stakeholder participation on the global level is subject to the presumption that direct and individual participation of citizens in global standard-setting bodies is unlikely to occur, due to a lack of capacity in terms of expertise, finance and organisational capacity.[23] Thus, participation will take place in an imperfect form through civil society organisations such as non-governmental organisations (NGOs) and collective bodies.[24] Even for organised civil society, due to financial constraints participation in global decision-making is more difficult, and they are in a comparative disadvantage due to industrial interest representation.[25] In the context of pharmaceutical standards, concerned NGOs like doctors or healthcare professional associations as well as patient or consumer groups can be identified as relevant stakeholders. It needs to be acknowledged, however, that the democratic legitimation effect of NGO participation is mitigated by the fact that participation on the global level is often only available to groups which have a specific interest and are highly organised, which means that they do not necessarily represent the interest of the general public.[26] The participation of organised civil society

Legitimate? – A Study of the Codex Alimentarius Commission', in A von Bogdandy, R Wolfrum, J von Bernstorff, P Dann and M Goldmann (eds), *The Exercise of Public Authority by International Institutions: Advancing International Institutional Law* (Heidelberg: Springer, 2010) 569.

[20] J Mendes, 'Rule of Law and Participation: A Normative Analysis of Internationalized Rulemaking as Composite Procedures' (2014) 12 *International Journal of Constitutional Law* 370, 379.

[21] M Everson and E Vos, 'The Scientification of Politics and the Politicization of Science', in M Everson and E Vos (eds), *Uncertain Risks Regulated* (Oxon: Routledge/Cavendish, 2009) 8.

[22] J Ponce Solé, 'The History of Legitimate Administration in Europe', in M Ruffert (ed), *Legitimacy in European Administrative Law: Reform and Reconstruction* (Groningen: European Law Publishing, 2011a).

[23] See also: C Devaux, 'The Experts in the Elaboration of the Cape Town Convention: Between Authority and Legitimacy' (2013) 19 *European Law Journal* 843, 855; Steffek and Ferretti (2009) 42.

[24] Mendes (2011a) 119.

[25] Mendes (2011a) 124; A Herwig, 'The Contribution of Global Administrative Law to Enhancing the Legitimacy of the Codex Alimentarius Commission', in O Dilling, M Herberg and G Winter (eds), *Transnational Administrative Rule-Making – Performance, Legal Effects and Legitimacy* (Oxford: Hart Publishing, 2011) 187.

[26] R Mayntz, 'Legitimacy and Compliance in Transnational Governance', MPIfG Working Paper 10/5 (2010) 10; Möllers (2006) 321.

in global standard-setting processes, like the ICH guideline-setting procedure, can take the form of either the institutionalised participation in the process itself, the form of membership or to a lesser extent through obtaining observer status, or a more externalised influence through providing comments in a public consultation procedure.

Granting ICH membership to NGOs would be the prime mechanism to ensure participation of private, non-commercial stakeholders. However, contrary to the extensive rights granted to the industry associations in the ICH, no civil society or professionals representation group has membership status. The ICH Articles of Association limit the possibility of obtaining membership to industry and regulatory bodies.[27] The only institutionalised form of participation left for stakeholders other than industry associations is, therefore, observership. In the reform process, providing observer status to interested stakeholder organisations was considered.[28] This is also confirmed by Lindström-Gommers and Mullin, who state that '… there was also some consideration of the value in allowing other international organizations active in the pharmaceutical sector as observers in the ICH'.[29] And indeed, the first ICH Articles of Association adopted include the possibility for '(i)nternational organisations with an interest in pharmaceuticals on the basis of their contribution or benefit to the ICH' to obtain observer status, subject to the decision of the Assembly which acts upon recommendation of the Management Committee.[30] However, subsequently this possibility was limited as 'the need to be inclusive needed to be balanced against ensuring a smooth functioning of the Association'.[31] Due to the high number of applications for observership the criteria were redefined.[32] This means that now this option is only open to international organisations which are affected by the ICH guidelines, meaning that they 'are expected to comply with ICH guideline(s) by the competent regulatory authorities'.[33] This excludes broader societal representation NGOs.

Furthermore, observer status is inferior to full membership, as it does not provide for voting rights. With regard to participation in Expert Working Groups

[27] ICH, International Council for Harmonisation of Technical Requirements for Pharmaceuticals for Human Use – Articles of Association, Adopted by the ICH Founding Members at ICH Inaugural Assembly on 23 October 2015, Approved by the Assembly on 19 November 2019, arts 11 and 12.

[28] Interview with two officials of the European Commission, conducted in Brussels on 17 February 2015, notes on file with the author.

[29] L Lindström-Gommers and T Mullin, 'International Conference on Harmonization: Recent Reforms as a Driver of Global Regulatory Harmonization and Innovation in Medical Products' (2019) 105 *Clinical Pharmacology & Therapeutics* 926, 930.

[30] ICH, International Council for Harmonisation of Technical Requirements for Pharmaceuticals for Human Use – Articles of Association, Adopted by ICH Founding Members at ICH Inaugural Assembly on October 23, 2015, art 17(1)(d), 17(2).

[31] Lindström-Gommers and Mullin (2019) 930.

[32] Ibid.

[33] ICH, International Council for Harmonisation of Technical Requirements for Pharmaceuticals for Human Use – Rules of Procedure of the Assembly, Version 8.0, Approval by the Assembly on 19 November 2019, 19.

the rules are quite complex. Whereas the Articles of Association grant observers the right to appoint experts subject to approval of the Management Board,[34] the Rules of Procedure which frame the decision of the Board provide that the size of the Working Groups shall not exceed 25 to 30 members,[35] and assessing the rules of how the members are chosen it becomes evident that Observers in the 'international organisation with an interest in pharmaceuticals' have very low priority in the nomination order of preference.[36] Overall, obtaining observer status would, however, allow stakeholders to closely follow the harmonisation measures proposed throughout the decision-making process, and to provide comments directly during the Assembly meetings, enabling them to actually monitor how their comments are dealt with. As well as full observer status, it could also be conceivable that stakeholders could attend specific meetings under the status of Ad-hoc Observers, which was created through the adoption of the ICH Articles of Association in 2015. Ad-hoc Observer status depends upon invitation through the Assembly or Management Committee.[37] Any natural or legal person can become an Ad-hoc Observer; however, they are only invited for specific meetings.[38]

At the time of writing observer status has been granted to six international organisations regulated or affected by ICH guidelines: the Bill & Melinda Gates Foundation, the Council for International Organizations of Medical Sciences (CIOMS), the European Directorate for the Quality of Medicines & Health Care (EDQM), the International Pharmaceutical Excipient Council (IPEC), the Pharmaceutical Inspection Co-operation Scheme (PIC/S), and the United States Pharmacopeia (USP).[39] The CIOMS is an NGO established jointly by the World Health Organization (WHO) and UNESCO representing the biomedical scientific community, while the other organisations are engaged in the drafting of pharmacopoeias which are reference works for drug specifications (EDQM, USP) or, represent producers, distributors and users of pharmaceutical excipients (IPEC), thus all organisations engaged in the production of pharmaceuticals in the broader sense. The PIC/S is concerned with coordinating Good Manufacturing Practice inspections.[40] Hence, only the CIOMS, representing healthcare professionals, and the Gates foundation, which aims to reduce poverty and improve healthcare, represent stakeholders beyond the pharmaceutical industry or regulators. Thus, broader civil society still lacks significant representation as observers in the ICH, especially when compared to industrial interests. While some claim that the apparent exclusion of other societal interests

[34] ICH, Articles of Association, art 17(3).
[35] ICH, Rules of Procedure of the Assembly, 33.
[36] Ibid, 33–34.
[37] ICH, Articles of Association Articles, art 18.
[38] ICH, Rules of Procedure of the Assembly, 21.
[39] See: www.ich.org/page/members-observers.
[40] Chapter 2 Section II B ii.

in pharmaceutical regulation was steered by the pharmaceutical industry,[41] the budgetary constraints that public interest advocacy groups possibly also face have an impact on their inability to establish themselves as a major global political force as the industry successfully did.[42] In this context, the question would be whether they would have the financial means to participate in the process by attending the bi-annual ICH week, including covering the travelling costs.[43]

Accordingly, through the ICH reform process, institutionalised participation has been opened up for non-industry stakeholders. However, if the commitment to balanced participation is taken seriously, health interests groups should be able to obtain full membership rights, thereby making the institutional structure of the ICH truly representative of its dual mandate: the protection of public health and industry interests. Since granting observer status does not provide them with a right to vote, this can only counterbalance the industries' membership rights to a certain extent. Finally, it should also be mentioned that the representation of public health interests in the ICH procedure is secured indirectly through the regulatory authorities and their dual mandate to promote public health while also paying due attention to industrial interests.

When considering other, less institutionalised mechanisms of stakeholder participation in the ICH standard-setting process, the primary possibility for participation by non-commercial stakeholders in the current ICH process is the public consultation in the third step of the ICH standard-setting process.[44] The consultation is carried out through the regulatory authorities with ICH membership applying their public consultation mechanisms, and through the ICH website. Being open to everyone interested, comments can be provided to the regulatory authorities of the three regions or the ICH Secretariat. However, the public consultation takes place only after the scientific consensus is formed and shortly before the adoption of the guideline, which is quite late in the process. It is questionable how much effect the comments will have at this late stage of the guideline procedure and whether the parties are truly open to deviate from the position they have already negotiated.[45] The harmonisation procedure foresees that the comments received through the public consultation will be discussed in the Expert Working Group.[46] Nonetheless, from an external perspective it is not possible to track whether this indeed happens and to what extent. This hinders the meaningful provision of comments by stakeholders

[41] Abraham (2002) 1500.

[42] See: also: Dorbeck-Jung (2008) 56.

[43] Interview with an official of the EFPIA, conducted in Brussels on 17 February 2015, notes on file with the author.

[44] For the ICH five-step decision-making procedure see Chapter 3 Section IV B.

[45] For a similar criticism see: M Flear, 'Charting a roadmap towards membership and formal voice in global bioethics standard-setting: Health research and the case of the International Council on Harmonisation' (2018) *Medical Law International* 157, 167.

[46] ICH, International Council for Harmonisation of Technical Requirements for Pharmaceuticals for Human Use – Standard Operating Procedure of the ICH Working Groups, 31.

as they receive no feedback enabling them to engage in active discussions. It certainly has a demotivating effect, as the impact of the comments is not visible and is uncertain.[47] Therefore, although the public consultation procedure opens the door to participation of societal interest, the possibilities for actual influence on the procedural outcome conveyed through this are limited.

Conclusively, the participatory mechanisms in the ICH operate mainly in favour of the participation of industrial interest, whereas other stakeholders only have limited access to the standard-setting. These heavily imbalanced participation options fall short of the overall aim of pharmaceutical regulation, which consists of the protection of public health as well as the consideration of economic interests. This is unfortunate as the incorporation of all relevant interests, along with bringing legitimacy benefits, also contributes to the factual acceptance of standards in practice. It also helps to substantially improve them, as doctors and patients in particular provide practical knowledge that can benefit the rule-making.[48] For instance, the ICH Guideline on Good Clinical Practice, which is concerned with clinical trials from a scientific but also an ethics perspective (such as through requiring the establishment of independent ethics committees), has been developed largely without the involvement of patient and consumer or professional groups, leading to criticism of this practice by the respective non-profit groups.[49]

It is, therefore argued by some authors that the involvement of industry without representation of other interests is highly problematic, as the efficiency of the ICH might be owed to the marginalisation of non-industrial interests.[50] Although in principle, cooperation with private stakeholders can certainly have a positive influence on the quality of decision-making, due to the expertise provided by private profit and nonprofit parties, it becomes an obstacle to legitimate regulation if private interests become factually synonymous with commercial interests, and are not counterbalanced with sufficient involvement of other interested parties.

B. Comparison with the EU: EMA and the Principle of Participation

Having established the shortcomings in the participatory mechanisms at the ICH level, it is now time to look at participation rights and opportunities in EU pharmaceutical regulation. The guideline drafting procedure as applied by

[47] See also: J Mendes, 'EU Law and Global Regulatory Regimes: Hollowing Out Procedural Standards?' (2012) 10 *International Journal of Constitutional Law* 988, 1013.

[48] M Livermore, 'Authority and Legitimacy of Global Governance: Deliberation, Institutional Differentiation, and the Codex Alimentarius' (2006) 81 *New York University Law Review* 766, 780.

[49] WHO, 'International Harmonization of Regulatory Activities: Future Options' (2000) 14(3) WHO Drug Information 147.

[50] J Abraham and G Lewis, *Regulating Medicines in Europe: Competition, Expertise and Public Health* (London: Routledge, 2000) 138.

the European Medicines Agency will be looked at specifically in order to evaluate the findings with regard to the ICH from an EU perspective. Participatory openness is enshrined in the Treaties through Articles 10 and 11 of the TEU as well as Article 15 TFEU, making it a general European constitutional principle. Article 11 TEU contains an obligation for open and regular dialogue and contains the duty for the Commission to hold stakeholder consultations. While this duty does not extend to agencies, Article 15 TFEU does require agency work to be open in order to facilitate civil society participation. Together with the fact that Article 11 TEU links participation to democracy, a founding value of the EU, this means that agencies are not free to disregard the participation requirement established by the general principles of EU law.[51] Accordingly, the European Parliament's proposal for an EU administrative procedure law stresses the importance of a balanced approach to stakeholder participation, as it explicitly requires that the EU's 'administration shall guarantee a fair balance between different types of citizens' interests (business, consumer and other)'.[52]

Stakeholder participation is enshrined in the institutional structure of the EMA. In the EMA Management Board, two members represent patients' organisations and, additionally, the board includes one representative of a doctor's association and one representative of a veterinarian's association, which provides these representatives with considerable influence on the work of the agency.[53] In addition, patients' and consumers' organisations have representatives in several EMA Committees (the Committee for Orphan Medicinal Products (COMP), the Paediatric Committee (PDCO), the Committee for Advanced Therapies (CAT) and the Pharmacovigilance and Risk Assessment Committee (PRAC)).[54] Furthermore, health care professionals are represented in the Paediatric Committee (PDCO), the Committee for Advanced Therapies (CAT), and the Pharmacovigilance and Risk Assessment Committee (PRAC).[55]

This participatory openness is also reflected in the founding regulation of the EMA, which provides that the Management Board has to 'develop appropriate contacts between the Agency and the representatives of industry, consumers and patients and the health professions',[56] which may take the form of 'the participation of observers in certain aspects of the Agency's work, under conditions

[51] Chapter 5.

[52] European Parliament, Resolution of 15 January 2013 with recommendations to the Commission on a Law of Administrative Procedure of the European Union (2012/2024(INL)), P7_TA(2013)0004, Recommendation 3. See also: E Vos, 'EU Agencies and Independence', in D Ritleng (ed), *Independence and Legitimacy in the Institutional System of the European Union* (Oxford: Oxford University Press, 2016) 214f.

[53] Regulation (EC) No 726/2004 laying down Community procedures for the authorisation and supervision of medicinal products for human and veterinary use and establishing a European Medicines Agency, [2004] OJ L136/1, art 65.

[54] EMA, Revised framework for interaction between the European Medicines Agency and patients and consumers and their organisations, EMA/637573/2014, 16 October 2014, 3.

[55] EMA, Revised framework for interaction between the European Medicines Agency and healthcare professionals and their organisations, EMA/89918/2016, 16 December 2016, 4.

[56] Regulation (EC) No 726/2004, art 78(1).

determined beforehand by the Management Board'.[57] All these policies have to be developed in agreement with the Commission.[58] Moreover, the EMA's Scientific Committees and their working parties and advisory groups 'shall in general matters establish contacts, on an advisory basis, with parties concerned with the use of medicinal products, in particular patient organisations and health-care professionals' associations'.[59] Thus, in its general activities the agency is obliged to maintain contacts with it stakeholders, and has institutionalised the participation of stakeholders in several ways.

The Agency has adopted a 'Revised framework for interaction between the European Medicines Agency and healthcare professionals and their organisations'[60] as well as a 'Revised framework for interaction between the European Medicines Agency and patients and consumers and their organisations',[61] both of which are in accordance with the 'European Medicines Agency (EMA) stakeholder relations management framework'[62] adopted in 2016. Nowadays the EMA has established a network of healthcare professionals associations as well as the so-called Healthcare Professionals Working Party (HCPWP).[63] This working party provides a forum for the dialogue between the professionals' associations and the agency including its Committees, also providing feedback on various aspects of the agencies' work.[64] The Patients' and Consumers' Working Party (PCWP), which has been operational since 2006, is contributing to the work of the agency and its Committees through recommendations, together with a network of patients' and consumers' organisations.[65] Thus, the agency has made significant efforts to provide participation opportunities for civil society actors. In contrast to the ICH, here the participation of non-industry interests is institutionally strengthened, whereas the industry involvement is less formalised.[66] Therefore, whereas mechanisms for stakeholder involvement often run the risk of favouring those with high expert capacity and financial resources such as the regulated industry,[67] the EMA has set up a framework to actively support less powerful civil society actors in their participation efforts.

As the ICH guidelines become EMA guidelines after implementation, it is relevant to examine how EMA guidelines are adopted when they do not originate in the ICH process but solely in the EMA itself, and what role stakeholders play

[57] Ibid.
[58] Ibid.
[59] Regulation (EC) No 726/2004, art 78(2).
[60] EMA, EMA/89918/2016.
[61] EMA, EMA/637573/2014.
[62] EMA, European Medicines Agency (EMA) stakeholder relations management framework, EMA/48651/2016, 16 June 2016.
[63] EMA, EMA/89918/2016, 3.
[64] Ibid, 9.
[65] EMA, EMA/637573/2014, 6ff.
[66] EMA, Framework for interaction between the European Medicines Agency and industry stakeholders, EMA/591272/2014, 2 October 2015.
[67] Senden and van den Brink (2012) 47.

in the adoption of these EMA originating guidelines. As far as the Commission is concerned, Article 31(4) of Regulation 726/2004 provides that when drafting guidelines establishing the form of marketing authorisation applications, the Commission should work together with the agency, Member States and interested stakeholders. Regulation 726/2004 does not contain a similar provision for the adoption of EMA guidelines; however, the EMA has adopted an elaborate guideline adoption procedure.[68]

In the 10-step guideline drafting process by the EMA, stakeholder participation is mainly facilitated through public consultation. In step 4, a concept paper, which contains the matters that have to be addressed and the expected impact of the guideline on regulators, regulatees and interested parties, is released for a two to three month public consultation.[69] The PCWP will help develop the proactive consultation with patient's and consumer's associations.[70] The comments received will be taken into account in the guideline drafting process in step 5.[71] Then, once the draft guideline has been developed by the working party and is adopted by the responsible committee or other EMA organ, it is released for public consultation again for a period of three to six months.[72] The comments are subsequently discussed in a drafting group and will be published on the consultation website (unless issues of commercial confidentiality arise or the authors object to the publication).[73] Furthermore, the rapporteur prepares an overview of comments received and includes notes on whether the comments have been taken into account or not, which will also be published and remain accessible through the archive of the EMA website.[74] Moreover, throughout the process, meetings might be organised with stakeholders for further discussions.[75]

The main difference of the EMA procedure when compared to the ICH procedure is the two-stage public consultation procedure in the process. As the EMA, after incorporating the comments received in the first consultation round, opens up the document for public consultation again, stakeholders can give feedback on the implementation of their comments. This encourages a dialogue between the regulator and the private interest stakeholders. Moreover, the EMA publishes a summary overview of the comments received including short responses to them, which shows that the comments have indeed been considered, and it also provides a short explanation for why they have been incorporated or not. This makes the public consultation more transparent,

[68] European Medicines Agency, Procedure for European Union Guidelines And Related Documents Within the Pharmaceutical Legislative Framework, EMEA/P/24143/2004 Rev. 1 corr, 18 March 2009, p 9f. For a full description see Chapter 4 Section II B.

[69] EMEA/P/24143/2004 Rev 1 corr, 11.

[70] Ibid.

[71] Ibid.

[72] Ibid, 12.

[73] Ibid, 13.

[74] Ibid.

[75] Ibid, 9f.

as who has provided which comments becomes visible.[76] This stands in sharp contrast to the ICH guideline adoption procedure where, once the comments are submitted to the ICH, they leave no trace that could be followed by external stakeholders. The EMA facilitates the involvement of patients, consumers and healthcare professionals, mainly through their respective organisations, both in its institutional structure and the specific guideline drafting procedure, while the ICH only provides very limited participation mechanisms. It has, however, been pointed out that the ICH process is already very cumbersome through the consensus requirement, and that additional steps, such as publishing a summary with responses to comments – which again would have to be agreed upon by consensus – would be counterproductive.[77]

When the EMA implements the ICH guidelines, these procedural efforts to facilitate stakeholder involvement are not made. The public consultation procedure in the EU is carried out by the EMA, but it does not follow all the steps of its own guideline adoption procedure. While the EMA publishes summaries of the comments of its public consultations and short responses to them, it does not do so systematically with regard to the public consultations on draft ICH guidelines. Recently, the EMA has been publishing comments it has received during the public consultation on ICH guidelines, but without any feedback given that the EMA only forwards the comments to the ICH.[78] Still, this very welcome increase of transparency only concerns the comments received by the EMA. It is unclear if other ICH parties are also publishing the comments or whether they plan to do so. Crucially, the ICH itself neither provides access to the comments received by its regulator members and submitted directly to the ICH, nor does it provide any reasons or feedback for either taking into account or disregarding comments.

Overall, significant differences between the participatory openness for stakeholders can be identified between the drafting of ICH guidelines and the drafting of analogous guidelines adopted by the EMA in the purely EU-based procedure, both with regard to institutionalised forms of stakeholder participation and in the public consultation procedures. The response to comments the EMA received in the process of adopting its own guideline procedure is very remarkable. Confronted with the suggestion that more industry involvement should be facilitated, similar to the ICH mode of decision-making, the EMA stressed the need to consider all relevant stakeholders and not just industry interests, stating:

> The procedure takes over many aspects of the ICH/VICH model. However it does not propose to systematically involve industry in all steps of the process, nor does it

[76] See also: Mendes (2012) 1013.

[77] Interview with two officials of the European Commission, conducted in Brussels on 17 February 2015, notes on file with the author.

[78] See eg: EMA, Overview of comments received by EMA on 'ICH guideline E17 on general principles for planning and design of multi-regional clinical trials – Step 2b', EMA/CHMP/ICH/453276/2016, 10 February 2017.

> propose that industry would draft guidelines. In view of the need to have a harmonised position among all 25-member states, systematic early involvement of industry would not be appropriate. ... Overall there are plenty of opportunities for industry to comment. Drafting suggestions from industry are always welcomed but careful consideration has also to be given to equal treatment of all relevant interested parties during the procedure.[79]

It is remarkable that, according to the EMA, early industry involvement without balancing it with the participation of other interest representatives is not acceptable in the procedure harmonising the standards on the EU level. At the same time it is established practice in the harmonisation of standards on the global level, which once they are implemented, have the same status as other EMA guidelines in the Member States. Whereas implemented ICH guidelines and guidelines originating in the agency itself are not distinguished in the pharmaceutical regulatory framework, their drafting process varies considerably from the perspective of participation.

C. Uploading EU Administrative Law: The Principle of Participation

The previous analysis has shown that the institutional and procedural differences between the ICH and the EU standard-setting work to the detriment of civil society and public health interests on the global level. On the ICH level, non-commercial stakeholders, in contrast to industry associations, are excluded from membership. They are limited to observer status. Moreover, the ICH public consultation procedure shows several disadvantages for stakeholder participation when compared to the EU procedure. Lessons can be learned from the EMA guideline adoption procedure that could lead to more balanced stakeholder participation in the ICH. First of all, the EMA has institutionalised the participation of the often less powerful non-commercial stakeholders in its internal bodies and in the guideline adoption procedure. Opening up the ICH observer status to potential access by NGOs was a first step in this direction. However, overall, the participation of stakeholders could be promoted through establishing a specialised body within the ICH – comparable to the EMA PCWP or the Healthcare Professionals' Working Party – actively engaging and liaising with healthcare professionals and consumer organisations.

Effective stakeholder participation might then also require the provision of funding possibilities for NGO members to counterbalance the financial disadvantage they have in comparison to industry. The process of setting 'European standards' by private bodies could provide an example.[80] Concerns regarding

[79] EMA, Overview of comments received on draft guideline procedure for EU guidelines and related documents within the pharmaceutical legislative framework, EMEA/125817/2004.

[80] Chapter 2.

the lack of stakeholder participation in the creation of European standards by private standard-setters were addressed by funding stakeholder organisations through the EU budget, where these stakeholder organisations subsequently participate in the development of European standards.[81] Thus, it might be conceivable that with its membership financed budget the ICH could set aside resources to fund stakeholder organisations representing private interests such as professionals, patients or civil society organisations. However, this would also make these stakeholders dependent on the partially industry-financed ICH budget, which might compromise their independence.

When it comes to more procedural aspects, what certainly can be improved on the basis of the EMA guideline adoption procedure is the public consultation process carried out by the ICH. The fact that draft guidelines are opened for consultation at two different steps in the EMA procedure, whereas the first round of consultation is carried out early in the adoption process, facilitates more meaningful interaction with interested stakeholders. This could be carried out in the ICH standard-setting procedure by submitting the concept paper that is adopted at the start of a harmonisation activity to an additional public consultation procedure. Moreover, the ICH should centrally publish a summary of all comments received in the public consultation, including the ones it has received directly as well as the ones received by the regulatory members. Such a summary would benefit from short responses as to the position of the ICH towards the comments received, as this would assure stakeholders that their comments have been taken into account and also enable a dialogue between the ICH and the stakeholders, ultimately facilitating a learning process on both sides.

It was pointed out that the fact that the ICH is established as a regulator-industry partnership means that naturally the context in which participation is discussed is fundamentally different from the EU context, where the EMA is discussing the guidelines as a public body. What, however, can be deduced from EU administrative law is that participation should be open to all interested stakeholders. Against this background, truly balanced participatory openness would require that membership of the ICH should be opened up to stakeholders other than industry.

II. THE PRINCIPLE OF INDEPENDENT EXPERTISE

Expertise and resources offered by industry often constitute the trigger for regulating in the form of a public-private partnership in order to address the complex risks faced by society today.[82] Based on the presumption that integrating the technical and scientific knowledge of experts into regulatory processes

[81] Regulation (EU) No 1025/2012 of the European Parliament and of the Council of 25 October 2012 on European standardisation, [2012] OJ L316/12, art 5.

[82] Chapter 2 Section II A.

is necessary for efficient regulation, these experts are supposed to contribute their knowledge in a manner that is 'objective, neutral and independent'.[83] In a scientific and technical area such as that of pharmaceuticals, industry attracts highly skilled experts and, by conducting the research necessary for drug development, industry experts have the finger on the pulse of time when it comes to innovation.[84] By including the pharmaceutical industry in a harmonisation process the regulators get access to information of which they otherwise would not be aware.[85]

The reliance on industry expertise can become problematic as 'the borderlines between the pursuit of commercial self-interest and the provision of expertise are often blurred'.[86] This is especially critical since it is widely acknowledged that risk regulation, although presented as based solely on science, is highly porous for various other influences.[87] As explained in the previous chapter, even scientific assessments of risk depend on value and methodological choices.[88] Thus, although the epistemic legitimacy of global standard-setting bodies is often a reason for their success,[89] their expertise should not be regarded as detached from the potential influences that these bodies might be subject to. In terms of good governance values and legitimate standard-setting, participants in the decision-making process should be prevented from benefitting from steering the regulation into a certain direction.[90] Therefore, the independence requirement is closely related to the participation of stakeholders, and specifically of industry representatives, as discussed in the previous section. It also extends to the regulatory participants in the standard-setting process, and whether they are independent or have personal interests in the pharmaceutical industry.

A. Assessing the Principle of Independent Expertise in the ICH Standard-Setting Process

The independence of expertise within the ICH, as a partnership between the regulators and the pharmaceutical industry, leads to challenges *per se* in terms of

[83] Devaux (2013) 848.

[84] See also: Berman (2011) 22ff.

[85] Interview with two officials of the European Medicines Agency, conducted in London on 23 March 2015, notes on file with the author.

[86] S Quack, 'Law, Expertise and Legitimacy in Transnational Economic Governance: An Introduction' (2010) 8 *Socio-Economic Review* 3, 10.

[87] S Jasanoff, 'Epistemic Subsidiarity – Coexistence, Cosmopolitanism, Constitutionalism' (2013) 4 *European Journal of Risk Regulation* 133, 133.

[88] Chapter 5 Section II.

[89] As Berman points out, the ICH is viewed as having broad 'epistemic legitimacy' in the sense that the standards are scientifically up to speed, which explains their global influence. See Berman (2011) 55.

[90] D Esty, 'Good Governance at the Supranational Scale: Globalizing Administrative Law' (2005-2006) 115 *Yale Law Journal* 1490, 1524ff.

independence given that the standard-setting process heavily relies on the input of the regulated industry. Prohibiting industry experts from taking part in the standard-setting process within the ICH system, in order to ensure the scientific objectivity of the standards, would of course go against the entire underlying logic of this public-private partnership. In this regard, where public-private partnerships allow for co-regulation by the regulated industry, there is an inherent risk that the rules agreed upon might be intentionally debilitated by those who would have to comply with them in the first place.[91]

However, whereas the integration of industry expertise in the ICH process is inherent in its organisational structure and decision-making process, it is noticeable that in the ICH no effort is undertaken to address potential conflicts of interest through any means other than a full prohibition of industry participation in the ICH process. In his speech during the first International Conference on Technical Harmonisation, Commissioner Bangemann presented the ICH as a forum where 'real experts can express the true scientific needs and the regulators can benefit from the clear unbiased view of these international experts'.[92] Given the role of the industry as an important partner in the ICH decision-making process, with no restrictions with regard to experts who might have commercial interests in the harmonisation topic at stake, this statement is a rather naïve perspective on expertise.

Since the ICH reform, industry representatives are prohibited from voting on the adoption of a new topic in the Assembly and are also excluded from the final decision-making when the guidelines are adopted.[93] However, in the Expert Working Groups, which establish the content of the guidelines, there is no conflict of interest policy which would require experts to declare their interests and attach consequences to existing conflicts. Realising that in the public-private standard-setting bodies the parameter should not be whether there are conflicts of interest, but rather how they are dealt with, the following questions arise: are the affiliations and interests of the experts involved communicated within the body? Are they communicated to the outside world? Is any consequence attached to conflicts of interest of individual experts participating in the forming of scientific consensus?

Admittedly, dealing with conflicts of interest in public-private settings is challenging. However, a transparent handling of existing interests at least is a prerequisite for legitimate standard-setting. The representatives participating in the Assembly and the Management Committee are listed on the ICH website,

[91] T Börzel and T Risse, 'Public-Private Partnerships: Effective and Legitimate Tools of International Governance?', in E Grande and L Pauly (eds), *Complex Sovereignty: On the Reconstruction of Political Authority in the 21st Century* (Toronto: University of Toronto Press, 2007) 210.

[92] M Bangemann, 'Welcome Address by Mr Martin Bangemann', in P D'Arcy and D Harron (eds), *Proceedings of the First International Conference on Harmonisation – Brussels 1991* (Belfast: The Queen's University Belfast, 1992) 5.

[93] Chapter 3 Section IV.

including a short CV with their affiliation.[94] This is important, given that some members representing industry associations are directly employed by pharmaceutical companies. Until very recently, the membership of the working groups was not made public, and therefore it was not revealed who had been involved in the drafting of the guidelines and in what way the expert might have had an interest in interfering with the harmonisation outcome.[95] In October 2017, the ICH started making the membership of ongoing ICH Expert Working Groups public.[96] While this does improve transparency, it also should be noted that what is published are the names of the experts and the ICH Members/Observers that have nominated them. This means that if an industry organisation such as the European Federation of Pharmaceutical Industries and Associations (EFPIA) nominates an expert, who will often be employed in one of its member companies, the employing company is not revealed.

Leaving aside the communication of possible conflicts to the outside world, from the information publicly available there also seems to be no internal policy on conflicts of interest. One could for example think about whether the affiliation of individual experts in the working groups is communicated to the other members, so that everyone in the discussion is aware that opinions might have to be evaluated in the light of the person's (employer's) interests. Moreover, the criteria of choice for experts could define that certain personal or financial interests in the harmonisation topic might prevent participation of an expert. However, the Standard Operating Procedures for the ICH Working Groups document does not reveal any criteria in this regard.[97]

Whether the experts with industry interest have indeed been successful in influencing ICH standards in a direction they desired is difficult to establish without extensive regulatory and scientific expertise. While such a lowering of standards is debated,[98] Abraham and Reed claim that there have been several instances where the ICH has opted for the less strict standard within the regulatory options available.[99]

[94] The overviews are available at: www.ich.org.

[95] Dorbeck-Jung (2018) 66.

[96] ICH, Press Release – ICH releases finalised, draft Guidelines and publishes working party membership for first time, 16 October 2017, available via: www.ich.org/page/press-releases. See also: Lindström-Gommers and Mullin (2019) 930.

[97] ICH, Standard Operating Procedure of the ICH Working Groups, 16. It is mentioned that founding Industry members and Industry Members can nominate 1 expert each (no criteria mentioned). And that additionally, that: 'Founding Industry Members, Industry Members, Industry Standing Observer and Industry Observers of ICH may collectively as a group nominate up to 3 additional experts, by coordinating amongst themselves the nomination from a pool of designated industry experts amongst their associations. In this coordination, efforts should be made to identify the best possible experts across concerned industry sectors while at the same time make efforts to have experts from regions outside of the 3 Founding Members to achieve appropriate diversity in representation of industry perspectives'.

[98] See Chapter 5 Section I.

[99] Abraham (2002) 1500.

B. Comparison with the EU: EMA and the Principle of Independent Expertise

The independence of expertise is an important value in the EU administrative law governing risk regulation.[100] Article 298 TFEU provides for an 'open, efficient and independent European administration'. Also in the *Pfizer* case, which was very influential on the EU's risk regulation, the Court required that risks must be assessed by experts based on the 'principles of excellence, independence and transparency'.[101] The Code of Good Administrative Behaviour as developed by the Ombudsman, requires officials to 'be impartial and independent'[102] and to 'abstain from … any preferential treatment on any grounds whatsoever'.[103] A similar provision is also included in the European Parliament's proposed EU administrative procedure law.[104] The EMA, with a reference to the Code of Good Administrative Behaviour of the Ombudsman, has adopted its own Code of Good Administrative Behaviour,[105] which states that:

> The staff of the Agency shall be impartial and independent, and respect principles of scientific integrity. They shall abstain from any arbitrary action adversely affecting members of the public or the Agency's stakeholders, as well as from any preferential treatment on any grounds whatsoever. The staff of the Agency shall not be guided by any outside influences of whatever kind, including political or national influences, or by personal interests. They shall abstain from being involved in the taking of a decision on a matter concerning their own interests, or those of their family, relatives, and/or friends. In performing their role within the context of the Agency's work scientific independence shall be ensured.[106]

Independence of expertise is a prerequisite for creating legitimate standards, therefore, European agencies have to maintain independence from political influence through other EU institutions as well as from Member States, but also from players in the respective regulated field.[107] As a core principle in risk regulation, independence from the regulated industry has also been enshrined in European pharmaceutical legislation. Article 62(3) of Regulation 726/2004

[100] For a detailed analysis of independence with regard to EU agencies see: Vos (2016).

[101] Case T-13/99 *Pfizer Animal Health v Council*, ECLI:EU:T:2002:209, para 159.

[102] European Ombudsman, The European Code of Good Administrative Behaviour, art 8, available via: europa.eu/!Gx99WU.

[103] Ibid.

[104] European Parliament, Resolution of 15 January 2013 with recommendations to the Commission on a Law of Administrative Procedure of the European Union (2012/2024(INL)), P7_TA(2013)0004, Recommendation 3.

[105] EMA, The European Medicines Agency Code of Good Administrative Behaviour, EMA/264257/2013, 1 September 2013.

[106] Ibid, 4.

[107] E Vos, 'European Agencies and the Composite EU Executive', in M Everson, C Monda and E Vos (eds), *European Agencies In Between Institutions and Member States* (Alphen aan den Rijn: Kluwer Law International, 2014) 37. For the EMA experts this is enshrined in Regulation (EC) No 726/2004, arts 61(6), 63.

prohibits members of the EMA's Management Board, committee members, and external experts consulted by the agency from having any financial or other interest in the pharmaceutical industry. One should, however, also mention that in the past the EMA has been criticised for conflicts of interest, especially by the European Parliament.[108] It has since updated its conflict of interest policy extensively. Nonetheless, ensuring independence, especially from commercial interests, is very much a continuous learning process for the EMA and in the EU in general. Thus, also in the EMA, the handling of conflicts of interest still leaves room for improvement. The agency has acknowledged its difficulty in balancing a strict conflict of interest policy with finding the much-needed expertise.[109]

With regard to the members of the scientific committee and external experts interests have to be declared and published in a register.[110] This concerns direct interests (such as employment with, consultancy to, or an advisory role for a pharmaceutical company, as well as financial interests or intellectual property rights)[111] as well as indirect interests (such as being a principal investigator, or clinical trial investigator, working for an institution or organisation sponsored by the industry).[112] According to a standard operating procedure for scientific meetings, these declarations are assessed before every meeting in order to assign the necessary restrictions and to inform all meeting participants about the conflict of interest status of the participants.[113] The conflict of interest rules apply to all members of the scientific committees including the alternates, and to experts, explicitly regarding all activities of the agencies, including the drafting of guidelines.[114] Additionally, similar rules have applied to all staff members of the agency since 2012, committing them to fill out their declarations of interest.[115]

Especially interesting for the discussion in relation to the ICH is how the EMA deals with experts, committee members or staff members that have declared conflicts of interest. Here, an EMA policy has been put into place, assigns a risk level to respective person according to which the activities of the person in the

[108] European Parliament, Decision of 10 May 2012 in Discharge in Respect of the Implementation of the Budget of the European Medicines Agency for the Financial Year 2010, (C7-0281/2011 – 2011/2220 [DEC]).

[109] EMA, Best expertise vs conflict of interests: Striking the right balance, Report from the public workshop hosted by the European Medicines Agency in London on 6 September 2013, EMA/548247/2013, 2.

[110] EMA, Policy 044 – European Medicines Agency policy on the handling of competing interests of scientific committees' members and experts, EMA/MB/89351/2020, 11 June 2020, 1.

[111] Ibid, 5–7.

[112] Ibid, 7–8.

[113] EMA, Standard operating procedure: Arrangements for handling of conflicts of interest for EMA scientific meetings, SOP/EMA/0126, 8 October 2012.

[114] EMA, EMA/MB/89351/2020, 2.

[115] EMA, The European Medicines Agency Code of Conduct, EMA/385894/2012 rev.1, 16 June 2016; EMA, Decision on rules relating to Articles 11, 11a and 13 of the Staff Regulations concerning the handling of declared interests of staff members of the European Medicines Agency and candidates before recruitment, EMA/259494/2016, Rev. 4, 5 October 2020.

EMA work are restricted.[116] Current employment or financial interest within the pharmaceutical industry is incompatible with participating in the work of the agency.[117] For all other declared conflicts of interest, the participation of the respective person might be restricted depending on the declared interest in question and the role of the person concerned in the process.[118] This could take the form of excluding someone from procedures regarding a specific product, or allowing the person to take part in the discussion but not the final deliberation. The policy even takes into account whether close family members are working in the pharmaceutical industry and imposes restrictions on persons where this is the case.[119] Where a committee member or expert with restrictions has taken part in a meeting this will be recorded in the minutes of the meeting which are published on the website, which increases the transparency of conflicts.[120]

C. Uploading EU Administrative Law: Independent Expertise

It is important to again underline the core value of the principle of independent expertise, especially for pharmaceutical regulation, which has the inherent aim of protecting public health as a common good. Nonetheless it also needs to be acknowledged that the expertise required for carrying out these regulatory tasks often requires relying on experts who are either current or former employees of the pharmaceutical industry. Therefore, a system of identifying and addressing these conflicts is important, especially in this regulatory area.

Applying the EMA conflict of interest system to the ICH would mean that standard-setting based on consensus in partnership with industry would be prevented by the conflicted interest of the industry representatives involved. Thus, it is inherent to the public-private partnership that conflicts of interest with regard to the participants from the industry associations will arise.[121] Resolving this would require excluding the industry associations from membership. This would therefore fundamentally restructure the ICH's public-private character. Although this could be regarded as essential from the perspective of the core principle of independence, in practice this does not seem likely to occur in the near future, given the legacy of the ICH.

Still, lessons can be learned from the EMA's conflict of interest policy in a situation where the aim would be to maintain the public-private partnership.

[116] EMA, EMA/MB/89351/2020.

[117] Ibid, 11.

[118] Ibid, 11–12.

[119] Ibid, 8.

[120] Ibid, 13.

[121] See also: S Röttger-Wirtz, 'Independence under threat – the role of private actors in the setting of global pharmaceutical standards and resulting challenges for European public law' (2018) 24 *European Public Law* 433.

Publicly accessible conflict of interest declarations would make conflicts visible to the other ICH members as well as external stakeholders. This would at least make the industrial interests in the development of a specific guideline more transparent. Thus, a first step to enhancing the ICH's approach to conflicts of interest would be to make them visible, internally and externally, with declarations of interest of everyone taking part in the ICH activities publicly available on the website. Moreover, it would also be necessary to make visible which meetings certain persons with conflicted interests have participated in.

Nonetheless, it has to be concluded that the core nature of the ICH as a hybrid body stands in irreconcilable contrast to the conflict of interest policies as applied to guidelines developed by the EMA itself. This could be mitigated through a more transparent conflict of interest policy, but the fundamental problem remains, leading to serious concerns with regard to the legitimacy of the ICH standards. It also undermines the rules applicable within the EMA, given that the ICH guidelines are implemented by the EMA and treated like EMA-originating guidelines.

III. THE PRINCIPLE OF TRANSPARENCY

Transparency is a prerequisite for citizens to be able to understand government action and to facilitate meaningful contestation.[122] Transparent decision-making processes are imperative to the exercise of public control.[123] However, although transparency is deemed to be a very important component and in fact a prerequisite of legitimate decision-making, it should not easily be assumed that transparency leads to democratic legitimacy. It should rather be regarded as a starting point for the participation of civil society and democratic control.[124] It can be achieved through a variety of mechanisms, encompassing clear information about decision-making processes and the topic subject to debate, access to documents and reason-giving requirements, as well as information on who is participating in a decision-making process.[125] Such transparency mechanisms can be used passively by providing the information only where this is requested, or actively through providing information without prior request, for example by publishing it on the website of the institution involved.[126]

[122] P Craig, *EU Administrative Law* (Oxford: Oxford University Press, 2012) 356f.

[123] R Grant and R Keohane, 'Accountability and Abuses of Power in World Politics' (2005) 99 *American Political Science Review* 29, 39.

[124] D Curtin and A Meijer, 'Does Transparency Strengthen Legitimacy?' (2006) 11 *Information Polity* 109, 120; Möllers (2006) 319.

[125] A Alemanno, 'Unpacking the Principle of Openness in EU Law: Transparency, Participation and Democracy' (2014) 39 *European Law Review* 72, 82.

[126] Curtin and Meijer (2006) 113; Alemanno (2014) 75ff.

A. Assessing the Principle of Transparency in the ICH Standard-Setting Process

In the early years of the ICH procedure and especially before the rise of the internet, information on the ICH and its procedures was very sparse. In his article from 1995, Contrera sees a weakness in the ICH regulatory process in its transparency, as the only possibility of obtaining information on the harmonisation activities were the public consultations through the national/regional authorities.[127] He suggested that the ICH was keeping the public uninformed about its activities, based on the rather dated view of the patient being better kept ignorant of health matters, leaving their regulation to the experts.[128] However, a lot has changed in the past 25 years and the approach to transparency within the ICH has evolved, at least partially. With regard to the ICH reform, the Press Release announcing the organisational changes stated that: '(t) he reforms strengthen ICH as the leading platform for global pharmaceutical regulatory harmonisation, and one that brings together *in a transparent manner* all key regulatory authorities and industry stakeholders.'[129]

Nowadays the main publication tool and source of information is the website which is run by the ICH secretariat.[130] Any interested member of the public can find information on the ICH's history and membership, as well as the ICH's founding documents in the form of Articles of Association and the Rules of Procedure of the bodies. Moreover, information on the core of the ICH work (that is, the guidelines as a final result of the standard-setting process) are made accessible to the public. For the guidelines which have reached step 5 in the procedure, leading to implementation in the national or regional pharmaceutical regulation, the website provides information on the measure through which the guideline is implemented by the respective members. Besides publishing information on the website, the ICH also uses meetings to make its activities known. It holds ICH Public Events as an initiative to increase transparency in the ICH process and to inform non-members about ongoing proceedings.[131]

Overall, the transparency regarding current ICH activities has increased. The Steering Committee Meeting Reports have been published since 2005. However, in the course of the reform process they were removed from the website, together with most information about the institutional set-up and working documents

[127] J Contrera, 'The Food and Drug Administration and the International Conference on Harmonisation: How Harmonious Will International Pharmaceutical Regulations Become?' (1994–1995) 8 *The Administrative Law Journal* 927.

[128] Ibid.

[129] ICH, Press Release – ICH announces organisational changes, 26 October 2015 (emphasis added), available via: www.ich.org/page/press-releases.

[130] www.ich.org.

[131] www.ich.org/page/ich-public-events.

of the ICH before the reform. After the reform, the ICH has started publishing the minutes of the Management Committee meetings and summary reports of teleconferences,[132] as well as agenda papers and minutes of the Assembly meetings.[133] In this regard, the Rules of Procedure of the Assembly state that the minutes of the Assembly meetings, which are made available on the ICH website, will not only provide a summary record of the discussion, but may also contain information on possible dissenting views.[134] In particular, if decisions are not taken by consensus, but the Assembly proceeds to vote, the minutes will indicate how the individual members voted and should reflect the discussion that has taken place.[135] This could indeed increase the transparency of the decision-making, at least with regard to the selection of guidelines topics and the adoption of final guidelines.

Additionally, the transparency of the ICH process has been increased through the current reform as the ICH now also publishes an annual report as well as yearly work plans and multi-annual strategic plans.[136] The annual report provides an overview of the main activities of the association and its respective bodies, including the key decisions of the Assembly and the Management Committee, as well as an overview of all ICH Working Groups and the anticipated next steps in the decision-making process of the guidelines they are preparing. The annual work plan covers ICH activities in terms of harmonisation, procedures, strategy, and operations, providing for the activity that has to be undertaken in the different categories, which body is responsible, and the anticipated timeline. The multi-annual strategic plan provides an overview on activities in the longer perspective, albeit in a very general and abstracted way. These documents certainly improve the transparency of the overall development of the ICH as an organisation and upcoming harmonisation activities, but even more so in general governance terms.

Nonetheless, one of the main traits of transparency is to make public who has taken part in the decision-making process. As discussed, the membership of the Working Parties remains opaque with regard to the precise interests of the industry members.[137] This constitutes a transparency problem as industry involvement in the guideline drafting process cannot be traced. Moreover, although the transparency of the ICH has increased generally and importantly, the guidelines as end products of the harmonisation process are accessible, what persists is a lack of 'decisional transparency' in the guideline drafting process.[138]

[132] www.ich.org/page/management-committee.
[133] www.ich.org/page/assemblyreports.
[134] ICH, Rules of Procedure of the Assembly, 30f.
[135] Ibid.
[136] To be accessed via: http://www.ich.org/about/work-plans-reports.html.
[137] Section II A.
[138] See also: S Dagron, 'Global Harmonization through Public-Private Partnership: The Case of Pharmaceuticals', Instituto di Ricerche sulla Pubblica Amministrazione, Global Administrative Law Working Papers (2012), IRPA GAL Working Paper 2012/2, 19.

The consensus forming process in the Expert Working Groups remains opaque and no information is available which could give more indications as to how the scientific consensus was reached and which arguments were discussed.

As pointed out in the section addressing participation in the ICH, a transparency problem also exists with regard to the public consultation procedure.[139] While public consultations are easily accessible, the biggest transparency lacuna is the omission of publication of the comments received by the ICH, or summaries thereof, and the reasons why they have or have not been taken into account. Publication of these comments would contribute to a better understanding of the consensus formed and would also give the ICH the opportunity to give reasons for its decisions, ultimately increasing the legitimacy of its standards. In addition, the fact that comments or summaries are not published also conceals who has taken the opportunity to actually comment via this procedure. According to an interview carried out with EMA officials, the parties providing comments vary greatly depending on the topic both with regard to ICH guidelines and EMA originating guidelines. The main respondents are usually from industry, as well as healthcare professionals or patients' organisations, as well as other interest groups.[140]

Therefore, the overall picture on transparency of the ICH is mixed. While the importance of transparency and communication to the public for the legitimacy of standard-setting appears to be recognised by the ICH members, there are still flaws with regard to making information available that would facilitate the comprehension of the decision-making process, and would provide an insight into the scientific debate undertaken in the standard-setting process. These transparency flaws are amplified, as they need to be evaluated in combination with the imbalanced participation and lack of conflict of interest procedures identified in the previous sections.

B. Comparison with the EU: EMA and the Principle of Transparency

Transparency forming part of the principle of openness in the EU is regarded as a central democratic value.[141] According to Article 1 TEU the Union is committed to take 'decisions … as openly as possible'. In Article 15 TFEU it is specified that 'institutions, bodies, offices and agencies shall conduct their work as openly as possible' to foster good governance and facilitate participation. It is, furthermore, also specifically demanded from the European administration through Article 298 TFEU. This transparency commitment is to be understood to relate

[139] Section I A.

[140] Interview with two officials of the European Medicines Agency, conducted in London on 23 March 2015, notes on file with the author.

[141] Chapter 5. For a good overview of the principle of transparency in the EU see: Craig (2012) 356–66.

to access to documents (Article 15(3) TFEU, Article 42 Charter), which is specified in the access to document Regulation 1049/2001 (EC) as a right for every Union citizen, as well as legal or natural persons which reside in the Union or have a registered office there, subject to certain procedures and conditions.[142] The Regulation is not directly applicable to agencies as such, but has been made applicable to the EMA in its founding regulation.[143] However, the transparency commitment of the Union extends beyond the passive provision of information upon request, to include active duty to open up the decision-making processes in the EU as provided for in Article 15(1) TFEU.

Again, in order to specifically define the content of the principle of openness, the policy that the respective EU body has established must be looked at, since no overall framework applies. The EMA has been subject to Ombudsman criticism with regard to its transparency in a case from 2010, concerning an access to documents request.[144] However, since then it has 'substantially broadened'[145] its transparency policy. The main transparency mechanism for the active provision of information with regard to the EMA is its website which provides information on the mandate and work of the agency as well as a search option to get information on specific medicines.[146] The website provides extensive information and is directed not only towards industry and other experts, but also makes an effort to address the general public. It provides information on the agency structure and introduces the staff working in the higher management level, as well as providing access to their declarations of interest. Importantly, the membership of the Committee for Medicinal Products for Human Use (CHMP) and other scientific committees, including the declarations of interest for these members, is made accessible via the website. In order to provide more insight into the work of the CHMP, the agendas of the meetings as well as minutes of the meeting are made available. However, the information provided by agendas, meeting minutes and work plans does not go beyond the information that an ICH guideline was worked on or adopted. However, unlike in the ICH, the membership of the organs involved in the drafting process is known. Through the public list of European experts, the conflict of interest declarations as well as the CVs of the experts involved in the guidelines drafting process are accessible.

With regard to the EMA's scientific guidelines, the homepage has one section specifically devoted to 'scientific guidelines' introducing the tasks of the

[142] Regulation (EC) No 1049/2001 of the European Parliament and of the Council of 30 May 2001 regarding public access to European Parliament, Council and Commission documents, [2001] OJ L145/43.

[143] Regulation (EC) No 726/2004, art 73.

[144] European Ombudsman, Decision of the European Ombudsman closing her inquiry into complaint 1877/2010/FOR against the European Medicines Agency, 2 December 2013.

[145] Senden and van den Brink (2012) 45; See also: European Ombudsman, Ombudsman applauds European Medicines Agency's new transparency policy, Press Release No 22/210, 01 December 2010.

[146] www.ema.europa.eu.

agency and providing access to the procedure for the adoption of guidelines.[147] There, the EMA publishes the finalised, adopted guidelines on its website and even has a specific section for guidelines originating in the ICH.[148] Moreover, as discussed in Section I the consultation procedure means that the internal process of finding scientific consensus will become visible at two occasions before the adoption of the final guideline. Additionally, comments received in the consultation procedure will be published on the website, and synthesised into a document that points out the main comments and explains the agencies' position on them. Therefore, with regard to the 'decisional transparency', the EMA procedure provides significant advantages in transparency of the procedure, leading to the adoption of a guideline.

C. Uploading EU Administrative Law: Transparency

Overall, it has to be concluded once again that the EMA's approach to transparency in the guideline drafting process provides significant advantages over the transparency in the ICH process. The procedural standards in the EU with regard to transparency are at a higher level than at the ICH. Although the EMA guideline drafting process does not have institutionalised industry involvement, it is additionally ensured that the interests of the participating members of the scientific Committees are transparent.

Therefore, what can be learned from the EMA guideline drafting procedure, and the transparency requirements, with regard to consulted scientific experts in the EU in general is as follows: it is inherent for the legitimacy of a scientific guideline to know who has taken part in the decision-making process. In particular, it is important to know how private interests might have influenced the opinions voiced by respective experts. Apart from transparency about who is consulted, the scientific discussion itself becomes more transparent in two key ways: through the publication of drafts in two steps of the public consultation process, and through the publication of comments, together with reasoning on how they were integrated into the draft or why they were not.

IV. DISCUSSING REMEDIES: THE INTRODUCTION OF EX-ANTE AND EX-POST PROCEDURES IN THE PROCESS OF IMPLEMENTATION

The flaws that have been identified with regard to stakeholder participation, independent expertise and transparency are imported into the European

[147] www.ema.europa.eu/en/human-regulatory/research-development/scientific-guidelines.

[148] www.ema.europa.eu/en/human-regulatory/research-development/scientific-guidelines/ich-guidelines.

regulatory framework through the implementation of the ICH guidelines through the EMA. Thus, along with suggesting the 'uploading' of lessons learned from the application of EU administrative law, one might also ask which role the implementation in the EU could play in mitigating some of the problems identified on ICH level.

One way to counterbalance legitimacy gaps in the adoption process of a standard on a global level would be the introduction of an implementation procedure on the European level allowing for the safeguarding of European procedural standards. One could, for example, imagine applying the full procedure applicable to the drafting of EMA guidelines to ICH guidelines, instead of merely endorsing them through the agency. This would include a renewed discussion of the scientific content of the norms in the respective scientific bodies of the agency and an additional public consultation procedure. However, introducing such an implementation procedure is only a theoretical possibility, as it is obstructed by the fact that once the standard is adopted on the global level its content cannot be changed, as otherwise the standard would not lead to the envisaged global harmonisation. Therefore, any *ex post* procedures on the European level, like applying the European style public consultation procedure, would be merely window-dressing as the guideline as adopted on the ICH level could not be changed.

Rather than applying an *ex post* procedure, one could also imagine safeguarding procedural standards *ex ante*, through preparatory procedures in the EU before the standard is set on the global level. One procedural mechanism that could be applied on a European level, to provide stakeholders with more ways to participate and to influence the work of the ICH, would be to systematically hold preliminary discussions of ICH standards with stakeholders in open meetings while the drafting process in the ICH is still underway. The existing means of stakeholder participation in the EMA, for example the stakeholder working parties, could be used as channels to disseminate information on ICH standards and to identify interested stakeholders who could participate in public ICH preparation meetings.

However, although this might improve the participation of stakeholders other than industry, it would probably only provide a mechanism to be used by European-based stakeholder groups and – similarly to the consultation procedure already in place – also does not grant stakeholders direct access to the discussions in the ICH. Given that the guidelines will be subject to discussion on the ICH level afterwards, there is also no guarantee that the input provided by stakeholders on the EU level would persist throughout the discussions in the ICH. Finally, such an *ex ante* approach would only address the gaps in participation of other stakeholders, while issues such as the independence of experts involved in the ICH and the transparency of the ICH process cannot be addressed through EU measures. Thus, *ex ante* mechanisms in the EU will only mitigate the flaws in the ICH process to a certain degree.

V. CONCLUSION: UNDERMINING AND UPLOADING PROCEDURAL STANDARDS

With regard to participation, independent expertise, and transparency, this chapter has shown that when measuring the ICH standard-setting process against benchmarks of EU administrative law, flaws in the ICH's institutional structure, governance and decision-making procedures persist. This is despite the fact that, like other global bodies, the ICH is increasingly trying to improve its procedural legitimacy.

In terms of participation, the ICH retains a heavy industry bias in its member structure whilst largely excluding the representation of other interests in the decision-making procedure. It is highly questionable whether such an institutional set-up can really live up to the mandate of protecting public health. This structural problem of the institutionalisation of industry interests is aggravated by the lack of independent expertise, which could be remedied through a conflict of interest policy. Moreover, a recurring problem in the discussion of the ICH decision-making process is the lack of decisional transparency, as public control cannot be exerted on the forming of scientific consensus.

This chapter has argued that procedural norms can be 'uploaded' from EU administrative law, especially with the principles of participation, independent expertise and transparency. Concerning stakeholder participation, the institutional structures and procedural rules supporting weaker stakeholders as used by the EMA could provide inspiration for the ICH decision-making process. Regarding the principle of independent expertise, it was shown that as a public-private partnership the ICH is as such irreconcilable with the requirement of independent expertise applicable to administrative activities in the EU. In the absence of a fundamental re-organisation of the ICH, what could be transposed to the global level, however, are conflict of interest policies that make potential and existing conflicts of interest visible. Finally, a gap in the decisional transparency of the ICH was identified. The transparency of the EMA committees and other scientific bodies could serve as inspiration for the ICH, and could contribute to forming a norm for decisional transparency in international administrative law.

Regardless of the procedural flaws identified, the ICH standards are implemented into the EU regulatory framework and have the same status as other EMA guidelines. Thus, the procedural standards applicable in the EU, which are consistently not lived up to in the ICH process, are bypassed through the outsourcing of standard-setting to the global level. This creates a two-tier system of procedural protection in the guideline drafting process, creating a distinction between the different origins of a guideline, whereas the *de facto* effects of these guidelines on the institutions, Member States, natural and legal persons remains the same.

Finally, it is clear that neither *ex-ante* nor *ex-post* procedures in the process of implementing global standards can fully remedy the legitimacy deficits identified. However, an *ex-ante* procedure would at least enhance the input of EU stakeholders.

7

Global Pharmaceutical Standards as a Challenge for EU Law: Remedies within the EU

WHEREAS THE PREVIOUS chapter analysed the legitimacy of the ICH standard-setting procedure by applying the perspective of EU administrative law, showing that global standards implemented by the EU are 'hollowing out'[1] procedural rules applicable to the same type of guidance documents on the European level, this chapter will address existing accountability mechanisms within the EU, applicable to the bodies that implement the ICH standards: the EMA and the European Commission.

The underlying reason for examining EU accountability structures is twofold: on the one hand, the question from the perspective of EU law is whether these accountability mechanisms could mitigate the legitimacy flaws that the implementation of ICH guidelines causes in the EU regulatory framework for pharmaceuticals. On the other hand, this is also important because the respective accountability fora where they would contest the implementation of ICH guidelines could act as a catalyst for change.[2] This could facilitate the 'uploading' of EU administrative law as discussed in the previous chapter, but it could also lead to a rethinking of the role of global standards in EU law in general.

One of the most established conceptualisations of accountability is provided by Bovens, defining accountability as the relationship between an actor and an accountability forum, characterised by the obligation of the actor to provide explanations and justifications for its activities. The forum is then entitled to ask for further information and can ultimately pass judgement, which might entail consequences for the actor.[3] Such an accountability relationship can be established between actors and different types of fora, distinguishing

[1] J Mendes, 'EU Law and Global Regulatory Regimes: Hollowing Out Procedural Standards?' (2012) 10 *International Journal of Constitutional Law* 988.

[2] The term catalyst is borrowed from: J Scott and S Sturm, 'Courts as Catalysts: Rethinking The Judicial Role in New Governance' (2007) 13 *The Columbia Journal of European Law* 565.

[3] M Bovens, 'Analysing and Assessing Accountability: A Conceptual Framework' (2007) 13 *European Law Journal* 447, 450.

between political, legal, administrative, professional and social accountability.[4] This chapter will analyse the political accountability and judicial accountability within the EU of the EU actors that take part in the ICH process, and that are responsible for the implementation of ICH standards in the EU: ie the EMA and to a certain degree the European Commission.[5]

In this regard, it needs to be acknowledged from the outset that this chapter exclusively examines EU accountability mechanisms while the ICH membership is broader and the domestic accountability mechanisms of other ICH members might also contribute to the enhanced legitimacy of the ICH. Further research is required to identify the effect of the interaction of the different accountability regimes on the global level, and within the ICH member states and regions, on the accountability of the ICH. However, as this book focuses on the impact of the ICH guidelines on the regulatory framework of the EU, it will only examine the EU accountability mechanisms. In this regard, it will also examine the juridification of the implementation of global standards in an EU administrative procedure act.

I. POLITICAL ACCOUNTABILITY WITHIN THE EU FOR GLOBAL PHARMACEUTICAL STANDARDS: A REMEDY WITH LIMITS

This section will enquire whether *ex post* political accountability mechanisms at the EU level are applicable to the Commission and the EMA, with regard to the reception of ICH standards in the EU. In this regard, accountability of the European actors within the ICH can be one legitimating factor, counterbalancing legitimacy flaws identified in the ICH process. In the following paragraphs, referring to accountability as a relationship consisting of information, questioning, judging and sanctioning stages,[6] it will be examined whether other EU institutions are sufficiently informed about the standard-setting in the ICH process, and whether they could interfere and eventually mitigate the legitimacy gaps that have been identified by this research. To provide an example: one could argue that through the accountability of the Commission and EMA for the implementation of ICH standards towards the European Parliament, the democratic legitimacy of the reception of ICH standards in the EU regulatory framework would be enhanced. Nonetheless, it needs to be acknowledged that political accountability itself is subject to certain limitations. In the example chosen, for instance, the legitimacy challenges the European Parliament is itself facing should also be acknowledged.[7] Moreover, although the accountability

[4] M Bovens, D Curtin and P 't Hart, 'Studying the Real World of EU Accountability: Framework and Design', in M Bovens, D Curtin and 't Hart P (eds), *The Real World of EU Accountability – What Deficit?* (Oxford: Oxford University Press, 2010).

[5] Chapter 4.

[6] Bovens (2007) 450.

[7] See prominently: J Weiler, U Haltern and F Mayer, 'European Democracy and its Critique' (1995) 18 *West European Politics* 4.

of executive actors like the Commission and European agencies is increasingly being studied,[8] there is still a need for further empirical research on the exercise of control. In particular, the complex question of how different accountability mechanisms interact – how they reinforce but also hinder each other – and also how political and judicial accountability can supplement each other require more attention.[9]

A. Reporting Obligations: The Commission and the European Medicines Agency

The basis for accountability is the provision of information, and in this regard both the European Commission and the EMA are subject to reporting obligations and publish annual activity reports. With regard to the European Commission, the annual activity reports adopted by DG SANTE could function as a source of information on the Commission's activities in the ICH. For example, the 2019 DG SANTE activity mentions the ICH, stating that 'DG SANTE promotes EU health and safety standards for pharmaceuticals at global level through the International Council for Harmonisation of Technical Requirements for Registration of Pharmaceuticals for Human Use (ICH) which helps increase EU-extra trade'.[10] The 2015 report, for instance, also referred to the ICH reform, stating that: 'The reorganisation of the International Conference on Harmonisation of Technical Requirements for Registration of Pharmaceuticals for Human Use (ICH) was finalised. This will increase the participation of key partners and promote the recognition of ICH guidelines as international standards.'[11] Arguably, statements like those do not provide much detail on EU involvement in the ICH and the effect of ICH guidelines on the regulatory framework of the EU. And indeed, according to Curtin, these reports are to be regarded more as an internal accountability mechanism, providing an account of administrative and managerial issues.[12]

The EMA is subject to an obligation to submit annual reports on its activities to the European Parliament, the Council, the Commission, the Economic and

[8] See eg: D Curtin, *Executive Power of the European Union – Law, Practice and the Living Constitution* (Oxford: Oxford University Press, 2009); M Busuioc, *European Agencies: Law and Practice of Accountability* (Oxford: Oxford University Press, 2013); M Scholten, *The Political Accountability of EU and US Independent Regulatory Agencies* (Leiden: Brill Nijhoff, 2014); M Scholten and A Brenninkmeijer, *Controlling EU Agencies – The Rule of Law in a Multi-jurisdictional Legal Order* (Cheltenham: Edward Elgar, 2020).

[9] M Scholten, M Maggetti and Y Papadopoulos, 'Towards a comprehensive system of controls for EU agencies', in M Scholten and A Brenninkmeijer, *Controlling EU Agencies – The Rule of Law in a Multi-jurisdictional Legal Order* (Cheltenham: Edward Elgar, 2020).

[10] European Commission, 2019 Annual Activity Report Directorate General for Health and Food Safety Ref. Ares(2020)2355142 – 04/05/2020, 10.

[11] European Commission, 2015 Annual Activity Report Directorate General for Health and Food Safety, Ref. Ares(2016)1611103 – 05/04/2016, 9.

[12] Curtin (2009) 257.

Social Committee, the Court of Auditors and the Member States.[13] Moreover, the EMA also drafts an annual work programme which is forwarded to the European Parliament, the Council, the Commission and the Member States.[14] These reports and work programmes are available on the website of the agency.[15] The EMA work programmes over the last years mention the ICH amongst other international organisations and forums with which the EMA collaborates.[16] In 2016 there was also an additional paragraph on the ICH reform.[17] Sometimes specific ICH activities are mentioned; for example the work programme for 2016 lists 'Promote application of harmonised international standards' as an objective for the EMA under 'Additional objectives and activities'. There is an objective to 'Provide technical and scientific contribution to the development of an addendum to the ICH statistical principles guideline E9 and of an addendum to the ICH Paediatrics guideline E11, relating to the design and analysis of clinical trials', as well as: 'Provide technical and scientific contribution to the development of ICH safety guidelines (Carcinogenicity assessment document evaluation for ICH S9)'.[18] The annual activity reports contain Annexes that list adopted EMA guidelines and include a specific section listing the ICH guidelines as adopted by the EMA.[19]

However, whether the work programmes and the annual reports provided by the Commission and the EMA are an effective means to control the activities of the EU executive with regard to its activities in the ICH and the implementation of the ICH standards in the EU can be questioned. The information in these documents is very general and usually does not extend beyond mentioning that the Commission or the EMA participated in the ICH or in very significant activities such as the ICH reform. It is questionable whether such reports subsequently trigger a closer examination of the Commission and EMA activities through other European institutions such as the Parliament. Empirical research has shown that representatives of the Agencies in general, while acknowledging

[13] Regulation (EC) No 726/2004 laying down Community procedures for the authorisation and supervision of medicinal products for human and veterinary use and establishing a European Medicines Agency, [2004] OJ L136/1, arts 64(3), 65(10).

[14] Regulation (EC) No 726/2004, arts 64(3), 65(9).

[15] Via: www.ema.europa.eu/en/about-us/annual-reports-work-programmes.

[16] See eg: EMA, Final programming document 2020-2022, EMA/9529/2020, 110. For earlier mentions see eg: EMA, Work Programme 2015, 18 December 2014, EMA/773839/2014 Rev 1, 45; EMA, Work Programme 2014, 12 December 2013, EMA/695772/2013, 35.

[17] EMA, Work Programme 2016, 5 July 2016, EMA/92499/2016 Rev 1, 48f. On p 49 the work programme states: 'Reforms to ICH – now called the International Council for Harmonization – will come fully into force in 2016, allowing for a broader global membership and strengthening ICH as the leading platform for global pharmaceutical regulatory harmonisation. The Agency plays an important role in supporting the European Commission by coordinating the EU expertise and contribution to the work of ICH.'

[18] EMA, Work Programme 2016, 5 July 2016, EMA/92499/2016 Rev 1, 26.

[19] See eg: EMA, Annexes – 2019 annual report of the European Medicines Agency EMA/115760/2020, 25.

the relevance of these reports, 'are generally reluctant to regard it as a powerful instrument of parliamentary accountability'.[20]

B. The Council and the European Parliament

As explained in Chapter 1, the adoption of scientific guidelines serves to clarify the legislative requirements of quality, safety and efficacy of medicinal products. Therefore, this section will examine whether the Commission and the EMA remain accountable to the Council and the Parliament as the EU's legislators, in their adoption of guidelines and, therefore, also the implementation of ICH guidelines. As indicated in the previous section, the Council and the European Parliament are kept informed about the ICH activities of the Commission and the EMA through the reports and work programmes. Thus, in principle they can serve as an accountability forum for the EU's involvement in the ICH. However, so far, no occasion where the Council or the Parliament would have interfered with the ICH activities of the Commission and the EMA can be identified.

The Commission has informed the Council Working Party on Pharmaceuticals and Medical Devices with regard to the reform of the ICH.[21] However, it is not clear from the agenda documents if the Working Party also provided input or whether it was simply informed. Thus, at the least the Council was informed on major institutional changes in the ICH. However, no accountability relationship between the EMA and the Council regarding its ICH tasks appears to be in place, and accountability for specific ICH guideline implementations therefore tends to be weak. This finding is in accordance with the conclusion drawn by the general research carried out on the accountability of EU agencies, showing that the Council in general is not keen on holding agencies to account.[22] As far as the day-to-day implementation of ICH guidelines is carried out by the EMA, this process seems to fall below the Council's radar.

Still, especially through the EU budget procedure, both the Council and the Parliament have the possibility of acting as an accountability forum.[23] Especially given that the ICH will now be membership financed, and therefore the Commission will have to pay a membership fee for participation in the ICH,[24]

[20] Busuioc (2013) 119.

[21] See for example: Council of the European Union – General Secretariat, Notice of Meeting and Provisional Agenda – Working Party on Pharmaceuticals and Medical Devices Friday 19 July 2013, CM 3637/13. The agenda item is: 'International Conference on Harmonisation of Technical Requirements for Registration of Pharmaceuticals for Human Use (ICH) – Outcome of the discussions on the reform of the ICH at the meeting in La Hulpe, Belgium 1-6 June 2013 – Information from the Commission'.

[22] M Chamon, *European Agencies – Legal and Political Limits to the Transformation of the EU Administration* (Oxford: Oxford University Press, 2016) 319.

[23] Arts 314 and 319 TFEU.

[24] See Chapter 3.

the budgetary procedure might prove to be a viable route for the Council and the Parliament to hold the EU representatives in the ICH accountable. Indeed, the European Parliament has over the course of time increasingly acted as an accountability forum for the Commission and also the European agencies.[25] The European Parliament appoints the Commission,[26] and may ask questions to the Commission and organise debates with the Commission.[27] In addition, the annual report of the Commission is discussed in Parliament.[28] Moreover, any Member of the European Parliament can ask written questions to the Commission, which has to reply in writing.[29]

As far as the European agencies are concerned, in the past the Parliament used to omit detailed discussion of the annual reports or questionings of the agency directors; however it has recently adopted the practice of inviting the directors for hearings.[30] Therefore, the EMA Executive Director will appear regularly before the European Parliament Committee on Environment, Public Health and Food Safety (ENVI).[31] In addition, the founding regulation foresees that prior to the formal appointment of a new EMA Executive Director, the candidate will be heard by the Parliament.[32] Although MEPs do not have the right to submit written questions to the agencies directly, it is possible to address a question for an agency to the Commission, which then forwards the question. However, it will be the Commission that drafts the official written answer, which is also made public, while the response of the agency remains concealed.[33] Thus, the European Parliament could indeed function as an accountability forum with regard to the ICH activities of the Commission and the EMA. Nonetheless, currently it does not seem to live up to this function. A search of the Parliament website shows that the ICH was only mentioned in two written questions to the Commission.[34] However, none of these questions directly concerned ICH activities as such, or the European participation in the setting of, or implementation of, ICH standards, but were concerned with the Falsified Medicines Directive and the use of animal testing for pharmaceutical products.[35]

Should the European Parliament decide to hold EU actors in the ICH accountable, it would have considerable sanctioning power. In conjunction with

[25] Curtin (2009) 260.
[26] Art 17(7) TEU.
[27] Art 230 TFEU; Framework Agreement on relations between the European Parliament and the European Commission, [2010] OJ L204/47.
[28] Arts 233 and 249(2) TFEU.
[29] See: European Parliament, Rules of Procedure, 9th Parliamentary term, February 2020, Rule 138.
[30] Curtin (2009) 260.
[31] Busuioc (2013) 129. See eg: European Parliament, Committee on the Environment, Public Health and Food Safety, Draft Agenda Meeting 7 and 8 November 2016, ENVI(2016)1107_1.
[32] Regulation (EC) No 726/2004, art 64(1).
[33] Chamon (2016) 322.
[34] According to a search of the term 'ICH' on the European Parliament website: www.europarl.europa.eu/plenary/en/parliamentary-questions.html.
[35] European Parliament, Parliamentary Question (E-004699-13), 26 April 2013; European Parliament, Parliamentary Question (E-0561/06), 15 February 2006.

the growing dialogue between the Commission and the Agencies on the one side, and the Parliament on the other side, a strengthening in terms of sanctioning power of the Parliament in this accountability relationship can be seen. The Parliament's sanctioning power extends to dismissing the Commission as whole[36] – a very harsh sanction, that is unlikely to be used to hold the Commission accountable for flaws in the legitimacy of the ICH standard-setting process. Through an inter-institutional agreement between the Parliament and the Commission, it is possible for the Parliament to request the Commission President to ask a Commissioner to resign.[37] Moreover, the Parliament has to discharge the Commission budget.[38] However, these possibilities are also rather harsh and it is doubtful whether they would be used to hold the Commission accountable for participating in a global standard-setting initiative that does not live up to European procedural standards. As far as agencies are concerned, the most important accountability and sanctioning tool for the Parliament is the budgetary procedure. And indeed, the Parliament has used its budgetary powers to hold EMA accountable. In the past, the Parliament has used the budgetary discharge procedure to address issues beyond the financial management of the EMA,[39] by postponing the discharge to hold the agency accountable for structural problems, such as concerns with regard to the independence of experts.[40] The Parliament also uses the resolutions it adopts in the discharge procedure to criticise the EMA, as it did in 2014, asking the EMA to ensure transparency with regard to clinical trials data.[41]

Thus, while both the Council and the Parliament could potentially act as accountability forums with regard to the EU participation in setting ICH standards and their subsequent implementation, they have not yet taken on this role. One hurdle might be the rather sparse information that is provided by the Commission and EMA in their reports. However, it is also questionable whether a seemingly technical process on the global level will attract the attention of the Council and the Parliament.[42]

[36] Arts 17(8) TEU and 234 TFEU.

[37] Framework Agreement on relations between the European Parliament and the European Commission, [2010] OJ L 204/47.

[38] Art 329 TFEU.

[39] For example in the budgetary discharge procedure for the year 2014, the Parliament asked the EMA to ensure transparency with regard to clinical trials data. See: European Parliament, Resolution of 28 April 2016 with observations forming an integral part of the decision on discharge in respect of the implementation of the budget of the European Medicines Agency for the financial year 2014, (2015/2171(DEC)).

[40] European Parliament, Decision of 25 October 2011 on discharge in respect of the implementation of the budget of the European Medicines Agency for the financial year 2009, (C7-0233/2010 – 2010/2173(DEC)); European Parliament, Decision of 10 May 2012 in Discharge in Respect of the Implementation of the Budget of the European Medicines Agency for the Financial Year 2010, (C7-0281/2011 – 2011/2220 (DEC).

[41] European Parliament, Resolution of 28 April 2016 with observations forming an integral part of the decision on discharge in respect of the implementation of the budget of the European Medicines Agency for the financial year 2014 (2015/2171(DEC)).

[42] Scholten, Maggetti and Papadopoulos (2020).

C. The Pharmaceutical Committee

Another European body that has the potential to contribute to the accountability of the activities of the EU administration in the ICH is the Pharmaceutical Committee, which is an advisory committee to the Commission composed of senior members of the Member States' administrations and which is chaired by the Commission.[43] Consistently, the Commission reports on the progress of ICH guidelines in this committee, and has also discussed the reform of the ICH on several occasions.[44] However, whether this committee indeed functions as an effective accountability forum has to be questioned, since earlier research has shown that the membership of the Pharmaceutical Committee overlaps with the membership of the EMA Management Board.[45] Moreover, again in this case it is unclear whether the committee is only informed or if it provides input and acts as a viable forum of dialogue and contestation. However, further empirical research is needed in order to analyse the role of the Pharmaceutical Committee as an accountability forum for the Commission and also the EMA. In any case, no sanctioning mechanism is available for the committee to hold the Commission to account with regard to its ICH activities.

D. The Ombudsman and the Court of Auditors

The European Ombudsman, which is responsible for the investigation of the maladministration of EU bodies, could serve as an accountability forum for the Commission's and EMA's involvement in the ICH.[46] Complaints may be made by every natural or legal person residing or having its registered office in a Member State.[47] Furthermore, the Ombudsman can also act on its own initiative or upon a complaint made by a Member of Parliament.[48] The Ombudsman has held the Commission and the EMA accountable in several instances. The pronounced interest of the Ombudsman in increasing transparency in the field of pharmaceutical regulation has been exemplified by the recent Ombudsman's dialogue with the EMA about the transparency of clinical trials data.[49]

[43] Council Decision 75/320/EEC of 20 May 1975 setting up a pharmaceutical committee, [1975] OJ L147/23.

[44] See eg: European Commission, 74th meeting of the Pharmaceutical Committee, 17 March 2015, PHARM 686, Agenda Item 4a International Conference for Harmonisation of Technical Requirements for Registration of Pharmaceuticals for Human Use (ICH), Presentation of the European Commission 'ICH Reform State-of-play and next steps', 17 March 2015.

[45] E Vos, *Institutional Frameworks of Community Health and Safety Regulation – Committees, Agencies and Private Bodies* (Oxford: Hart Publishing, 1999) 227.

[46] Art 228(1) TFEU, art 24 TFEU and art 43 Charter of Fundamental Rights (CFR).

[47] Art 228(1) TFEU, art 43 CFR.

[48] Art 228(1) TFEU.

[49] European Ombudsman, Decision on own-initiative inquiry OI/3/2014/FOR concerning the partial refusal of the European Medicines Agency to give public access to studies related to the approval of a medicinal product, 8 June 2016; European Ombudsman, Decision on own-initiative

However, the Ombudsman recommendations do not have legal force or binding effect.[50] The process of investigation and the recommendation drafted by the Ombudsman certainly provides a route to deliberation, acting as a less proceduralised accountability forum.[51] Moreover, the Ombudsman reports to the European Parliament about the instances of maladministration identified.[52] Therefore, the Ombudsman seems to be a suitable accountability forum, not for the ICH procedure as such, but to review the EU participation in the ICH as well as the implementation of the ICH standards.

The Commission and the EMA are also subject to budgetary control by the Court of Auditors,[53] which has the task of auditing the EU budget and the expenditure of the bodies, offices and agencies of the European Union.[54] While the Court of Auditors will report to the European Parliament and Council, it has no sanctioning power of its own and a negative statement of the Court of Auditors does not bind the Parliament and Council in the budget procedure.[55] Still, it has the power of naming and shaming, as the reports are published in the Official Journal.[56] However, with regard to the ICH, the Court of Auditors mandate is limited to financial accountability, which thus would only allow a review of the budgetary implications of EU participation in the ICH. However, the Court of Auditors has already shown its willingness to hold agencies accountable even beyond strictly budgetary issues through drafting a report on the management of conflicts of interest in selected European agencies.[57] Nonetheless, neither the European Ombudsman nor the Court of Auditors have served as accountability forum with regard to the EU's involvement in the ICH or the implementation of ICH standards in the EU pharmaceuticals regulatory framework.

E. EMA Management Board

Besides these external accountability mechanisms, the EMA is also subject to an internal accountability system, as the Executive Director is accountable to the EMA Management Board.[58] This Management Board is composed of one

inquiry OI/3/2014/FOR concerning the partial refusal of the European Medicines Agency to give public access to studies related to the approval of a medicinal product, Press release No 6/2016, 10 June 2016.

[50] H Hofmann, G Rowe and T Türk, *Administrative Law and Policy of the European Union* (Oxford: Oxford University Press, 2011) 788.

[51] Curtin (2009) 271.

[52] Art 228(1) TFEU.

[53] Regulation (EC) No 726/2004, art 68.

[54] Art 287 TFEU.

[55] Art 287 TFEU. For a detailed discussion of administrative accountability to the Court of Auditors see: Hofmann, Rowe and Türk (2011) 728–35.

[56] Art 287 TFEU.

[57] E Vos, 'EU Agencies and Independence', in D Ritleng (ed), *Independence and Legitimacy in the Institutional System of the European Union* (Oxford: Oxford University Press, 2016) 222.

[58] Regulation (EC) No 726/2004, art 64.

representative of each Member State and two representatives each of the Commission and the European Parliament. In addition, the Council, in consultation with the Parliament, appoints two representatives of patients' organisations, as well as a representative of a doctors' association and of a veterinarians' association, based on a list drawn up by the Commission.[59]

As the name suggests, the Management Board serves as an accountability forum for the general management of the agency and not scientific specificities.[60] Thus, while the Management Board could hold the EMA Executive Director accountable for the general policies underlying the EMA's involvement in the ICH, as well as the general system of implementation of ICH guidelines through the EMA, it is not an efficient accountability forum to assess the implementation of specific ICH guidelines. However, the effectiveness of the accountability of European agencies towards their Management Boards also strongly depends on the committed preparation of the members of the Board and the level of information they receive.[61]

There is currently no indication that the Management Board has taken issue with the role of the EMA in the ICH or the implementation of ICH standards. Moreover, the ultimate sanctioning power of the Management Board, the removal of the Executive Director, is dependent on the proposal of the Commission.[62] It also seems to be a rather misplaced sanction, given that the EMA essentially takes part in the ICH on the Commission's request and not based on the decision of its Executive Director.[63]

F. A Lacuna of Political Accountability?

The previous analysis has shown that although several European institutions and bodies could function as accountability fora with regard to the participation of the Commission and EMA in the global standard-setting process, and also the implementation of the ICH standards in the EU, in practice these mechanisms are not used to hold the respective actors to account in a meaningful way. Especially with regard to the Council and the Parliament, which would have the opportunity to be informed and also to exercise sanctioning power, the setting of regulatory standards seems to fall below the radar. This might be explained by the fact that as legislators these bodies have delegated the adoption of pharmaceutical guidelines to the Commission and the EMA.[64] So far, most of these institutions do not seem to exercise systematic control in terms of

[59] Ibid, art 65.

[60] European Court of Auditors, Management of Conflict of Interest in selected EU Agencies, Special Report 15/2012. See also: Vos (2016) 218.

[61] Busuioc (2013).

[62] Regulation (EC) No 726/2004, art 64(1).

[63] Chapter 3 Section II C.

[64] Chapter 1 Section III.

the reception of global standards in general, or ICH standards specifically, in the EU. However, this might of course change where they become aware of problems caused, say due to a scandal regarding a medicine that had to be withdrawn, where ICH standards would not have sufficiently protected the safety of patients. Such 'fire alarms'[65] might lead to increased accountability.

Nonetheless, more systematic accountability mechanisms should be applicable for how regulatory guidelines are generated by the Commission and the EMA, to ensure that the basic procedural norms of European administrative law are respected. In general, further research is certainly required about the accountability of the European administration when it acts globally and implements global standards into the EU regulatory framework. The introduction of specific accountability mechanisms could be proposed for the participation of the EU administration in the setting of global regulatory standards, and their ensuing implementation into the EU regulatory framework, given that global standards influence many regulatory areas. However, this needs to be imbedded in the general discussion about improving the accountability of the EU executive.

II. LEGAL ACCOUNTABILITY: JUDICIAL REVIEW OF ICH GUIDELINES WITHIN THE EU

Examining the potential of judicial review through the Court of Justice to address the legitimacy deficits of the ICH guidelines is certainly counterintuitive, as the Court does not have jurisdiction over global bodies such as the ICH. What this section will assess, however, is whether the Court could review the use of the implemented standards in the European Union, including questions regarding their (global) origin. It was set out in Chapter 5 that in the *Kadi* case[66] the Court looked beyond the EU measure when assessing a Regulation based on a UN Security Council Regulation, and assessed the underlying UN procedure and its compliance with fundamental rights protection in the Union. A similar logic could be applied with regard to the ICH guidelines and their implementing measures in the EU. The Court would then examine the implementation of ICH standards through the EMA, and question whether these standards live up to the procedural requirements that have to be fulfilled for such administrative guidance measures in the EU.

Effective judicial protection is important as it offers protection to individuals affected by the guidelines, as well as having a more general accountability function in terms of *ex post* control.[67] Raised at many points in this book before, the

[65] Scholten, Maggetti and Papadopoulos (2020) 318.

[66] Joined cases C-402 and 415/05P *Kadi & Al Barakaat International Foundation v. Council & Commission*, ECLI:EU:C:2008:461. See: Chapter 5 Section IV.

[67] S Prechal and R Widdershoven, 'Principle of effective judicial protection', in M Scholten and A Brenninkmeijer, *Controlling EU Agencies – The Rule of Law in a Multi-jurisdictional Legal Order* (Cheltenham: Edward Elgar, 2020) 80.

distinction between hard law and soft law is also central to the assessment of the access to judicial review of administrative guidelines.[68] As the ICH guidelines are implemented in the form of EMA guidelines on the European level, the question of judicial reviewability is mainly connected to the reviewability of EMA guidelines.

A. Judicial Review of the Legality of EMA Guidelines Implementing ICH Guidelines

The competences of the Court with regard to the legality review are laid down in Article 263 TFEU, the act of annulment procedure. Within this review system, the range of reviewable measures is limited to 'legislative acts' as well as 'acts of the European Parliament and the European Council intended to produce legal effects vis-à-vis third parties'.[69] The review power of the Court also encompasses 'acts of bodies, offices or agencies of the Union intended to produce legal effects vis-à-vis third parties'.[70] Central entry points for access to judicial review are thus the authorship of the act as well as its legally binding nature or the intention to produce legal effects vis-à-vis third parties. With regard to the authorship of the measures in question, the ICH guidelines as they are adopted by the Committee for Medicinal Products for Human Use (CHMP) are attributed to the EMA. As Article 263 TFEU since the Lisbon Treaty also encompasses 'agencies' amongst the bodies and institutions subject to judicial review, the authorship criterion is, in principle, fulfilled.[71] As the EMA implements the ICH guidelines literally,[72] the authorship of the adopted guideline lies *de facto* with the ICH, while *de iure* – through the CHMP adoption – it is transformed into an act of the agency.

The key to whether the EMA guidelines will be amenable to judicial review is thus the question of whether they are legally binding or produce legal effects. Guidelines are 'atypical instruments'[73] in the sense that they are not mentioned within the range of legally binding instruments available to the EU institutions as laid down in Article 288 TFEU. Still, it is important to assess whether these guidelines are capable of producing legal effects towards third parties. As for guidance documents, the question of judicial reviewability in the light of

[68] Ibid, 94ff. for a more general debate concerning effective judicial protection against agencies' soft law.

[69] Art 263(1) TFEU.

[70] Ibid.

[71] The inclusion of agencies in art 263 TFEU is a codification of previous case law of the Court (Case 294/83 *Les Verts v Parliament*, ECLI:EU:C:1986:166; Case T-411/06 *Sogelma v EAR*, ECLI:EU:T:2008:419).

[72] Chapter 4 Section II B.

[73] A Alemanno, 'A Meeting of Minds on Impact Assessment – When Ex Ante Evaluation Meets Ex Post Judicial Control' (2011)17 *European Public Law* 485, 493.

these considerations is not sufficiently clarified for Commission nor for agency guidelines.[74] The soft law nature of a measure, in the jurisprudence of the Court, does not generally exclude legal effects. In the words of the *Grimaldi* judgment, the Court acknowledged that a recommendation, although non-binding, 'cannot therefore be regarded as having no legal effect'.[75] In *Grimaldi* this legal effect concerned the duty of Member States to take the recommendation in question into account.[76] Whether a measure has legal effect is determined by its substance and not necessarily through its form.[77]

One important factor in establishing legal effect is the procedural stage at which a measure is adopted. This is exemplified by an action brought against a scientific opinion of the EMA, which constitutes a preparatory step towards the marketing authorisation granted by a Commission Decision. In the *Olivieri* case the action was dismissed and the opinion declared not to be subject to judicial review due to its preparatory nature.[78] However, guidelines are not a preparatory step in a procedure leading to a binding outcome; with adoption of the guidelines the administrative procedure has ended. Thus, these guidelines cannot be qualified as preparatory documents, which would preclude judicial review.

According to research by Stefan, in the area of competition law the Court has acknowledged the binding legal effects of soft law measures in over 600 instances.[79] Still, these acknowledged legal effects are usually only in the form of a self-binding effect on the body drafting the guidance document and not a binding effect vis-à-vis third parties, with the Court relying on general principles of law like legitimate expectations as well as legal certainty and transparency.[80] Overall, however, the record of judicial review of guidance documents is mixed. The Court has, for example, declined to accept legal effect of a Commission guideline that was declared to be an 'internal guideline', due to its administrative-coordinative nature, which accordingly fell short of granting rights or imposing obligations on third parties.[81] However, research by Scott showed that the Court has acknowledged legal effects of guidance documents,[82]

[74] J Scott, 'In Legal Limbo: Post-Legislative Guidance as a Challenge for Administrative Law' (2011) 48 *Common Market Law Review* 329, 339.

[75] Case C-322/88 *Grimaldi*, ECLI:EU:C:1989:646, para 18.

[76] Ibid, para 16.

[77] Case 22/70 *Commission v Council (ERTA)*, ECLI:EU:C:1971:32, para 42; Case 60/81 *IBM v Commission*, ECLI:EU:C:1981:264, para 9.

[78] Case T-326/99 *Nancy Fern Olivieri v Commission*, ECLI:EU:T:2003:351, para 53.

[79] O Stefan, *Soft Law in Court: Competition Law, State Aid, and the Court of Justice of the European Union* (Alphen aan den Rijn: Kluwer, 2013). These include judgments as well as orders and opinions.

[80] O Stefan, 'European Union Soft Law: New Developments Concerning the Divide Between Legally Binding Force and Legal Effects' (2012) 75 *The Modern Law Review* 865, 893; O Stefan, 'Helping Loose Ends Meet? The Judicial Acknowledgement of Soft Law as a Tool of Multi-Level Governance' (2014) 21 *Maastricht Journal of European and Comparative Law* 359.

[81] Case C-443/97 *Spain v Commission*, ECLI:EU:C:2000:190, para 28.

[82] Scott (2011) 341.

where they (i) introduce an obligation that is not found in the relevant legislation;[83] (ii) are of decisional character in the sense that they lay down how legal obligations will be applied where the institution has discretion;[84] or (iii) are binding upon the Member States due to legislation.[85] Still, overall Scott pointed out that these cases are exceptional and guidance documents commonly will not be eligible to judicial review.[86]

One therefore has to assess whether the clarification of the legislative requirements of quality, safety and efficacy laid down in the guidelines might be qualified as introducing new obligations. Scott convincingly argued that '(w)hen the underlying legal obligation takes the form of an only vaguely defined framework norm, it will frequently be impossible to make a clear determination of where the boundaries of existing obligation begin and end'.[87] Indeed, without performing an assessment of the content of all EMA guidelines implementing ICH standards, it seems that the EMA guidelines provide the technical specifications of what quality, safety and efficacy of medicinal products entail, and which methods can be used to prove them, rather than creating additional obligations. Generally, the technical nature of these documents seems to impair the ability of the Court to assume review responsibilities.[88]

Moreover, where the Court has resorted to the reasoning of a judicial review due to newly imposed obligations, a crucial factor is the imperative wording of the measures.[89] As discussed before, the EMA guidelines come with a disclaimer that underlines their voluntary nature and the possibility to deviate, while the language used in the guidelines cannot be qualified as imperative.[90] A statement published by the EMA indicates that an intention to produce legal effects is lacking: 'Within the framework of the pharmaceutical legislation, scientific guidelines do not have legal force and the definitive legal requirements are those outlined in the relevant Community legislative framework (Directives, Regulations, Decisions etc.) as well as appropriate national rules.'[91] Although the Court is willing to look beyond such legal disclaimers, taking this together with the fact that the language of the guidelines is not imperative, overall, in the light

[83] Example provided by Scott: Case C-366/88 *France v Commission* (Internal instructions), ECLI:EU:C:1990:348.

[84] Example provided by Scott: Case T-374/04 *Germany v Commission*, ECLI:EU:T:2007:332.

[85] Example provided by Scott: Case C-311/94 *IJssel-Vliet Combinatie BV v Minister van Economische Zaken*, ECLI:EU:C:1996:383.

[86] Scott (2011) 329.

[87] Ibid, 342.

[88] E Korkea-aho, 'Better Judicial Review? EU Courts and the Smart Regulation Agenda in Implementing Chemicals Regulation' (2012) 6 *Legisprudence* 397, 413.

[89] Scott (2011) 340. See: Case C-325/91 *France v Commission*, ECLI:EU:C:1993:245, para 14; Case C-366/88 *France v Commission (Internal instructions)*, ECLI:EU:C:1990:348.

[90] See: Chapter 1 Section III B.

[91] EMA, Status of EMEA scientific guidelines and European Pharmacopoeia monographs and chapters in the regulatory framework applicable to medicinal products, EMEA/42371/2008, 11 September 2008 – corr.

of the current jurisprudence in all likelihood legal effects of EMA guidelines will be excluded.

Legal effect of a guidance document might also be based on its decisional nature in indicating how the institution will apply its discretion, even where the intention to produce legal effect is lacking. The Court has ruled that guidelines can have legal effects: by publishing the guidelines the institution limits its own discretion to deviate when it takes the decisions directed at individuals that are governed by these guidelines.[92] As was pointed out in Chapter 1, the EMA guidelines do have legal effect on the agency itself.[93] Nevertheless, Article 263 TFEU is very specific in requiring legal effect vis-à-vis third parties in order to subject acts of agencies to judicial review. Thus, the legal effects of the guidelines with regard to the drafting body are not sufficient to trigger review under Article 263 TFEU.

The core principle with regard to judicial review is that 'an action for annulment is available in the case of all measures adopted by the institutions, whatever their nature or form, which are intended to have legal effects'.[94] Looking at this more closely, the intention of the drafting body is relevant. Whether the act brings about a change in the legal position of a third party depends on the imperative nature of the language used. As pointed out before, the guidelines are published with a disclaimer and although the website states that the EMA 'strongly encourages'[95] compliance with these guidelines, a legal obligation is not conveyed by the agency. Looking at the Good Manufacturing Practice guideline, for example, the language is not perceived as imperative as the document is characterised as 'intended to provide guidance', or 'intended to help'; it is clarified that 'the term "should"', which is used consistently throughout the guideline, 'indicates recommendations'.[96] Therefore, an intention to produce legal effects vis-à-vis third parties cannot be deduced.

In Chapter 1 it was shown that the guidelines are reinforced through legislation and are presented as marking the route to obtaining a marketing authorisation by communicating what, in the view of the agency, are acceptable methods to prove the quality, safety and efficacy of a medicinal product.[97] Although it is possible to deviate from the guidelines, this needs to be duly justified, entailing a shift in the burden of proof.[98] Nonetheless, currently, at least, the Court does not seem to be open to such arguments. The Court ruled in the case of *Chemische Fabrik Kreussler*, with regard to a Commission guidance

[92] Case T-374/04 *Germany v Commission*, ECLI:EU:T:2007:332, para 114.
[93] See Chapter 1 Section III.
[94] Case C-57/95 *France v Commission*, ECLI:EU:C:1997:164, para 7.
[95] https://www.ema.europa.eu/en/human-regulatory/research-development/scientific-guidelines (emphasis added).
[96] EMA, Note for Guidance on Good Manufacturing Practice for Active Pharmaceutical Ingredients, November 2000, CPMP/ICH/4106/00, 5.
[97] Chapter 1 Section III.
[98] Chapter 1 Section III.

document on medical devices, that a 'guidance document …, which is not one of the legal acts of the European Union referred to in Article 288 TFEU, cannot be of a legally binding nature or enforceable against individuals'.[99] The Court thus simply brushed aside the question of capability to produce *de facto* legal effects without closer assessment.

Still, in a preliminary ruling procedure under Article 267 TFEU, the *Fra.bo* case, the Court took an interesting stance about technical standards set by private standard-setters in Germany.[100] The system allowed for proving compliance with its conditions through a different procedure, rather than obtaining certification via the standard-setter. Despite this, the Court was convinced that the other procedure was not used in practice, due to procedural ambiguities and additional costs. The Court thus ruled that 'the DVGW, by virtue of its authority to certify the products, in reality holds the power to regulate the entry into the German market of products'.[101] Although the situation in this case differs from the question on whether the standards in EMA guidelines can have legal effects, the Court expressed its consciousness of the quasi-legal effects of standardisation on trade. Whether the Court would be inclined to adopt a parallel approach in the judicial review under Article 263 TFEU and for risk regulation standards is unclear, and will require clarification in front of the Court. However, as was shown with regard to the guidelines adopted by the CHMP, the industry is more inclined to follow the guidelines than to justify deviation.[102] Thus, in principle an analogy could be drawn here,[103] which would mean that legal effect might be attributed to EMA guidelines.

To conclude, whether EMA guidelines would be viewed as producing legal effects, and, therefore, fall under the review possibilities of Article 263 is unclear. However, in all likelihood the Court would currently deny judicial review responsibilities due to the lack of legal effects of these guidelines. Overall, there exists a 'mismatch between the actual effects of soft law and the readiness of the CJEU to acknowledge them'.[104]

Even if an EMA guideline would be qualified as a reviewable act, the procedure under Article 263 TFEU has limited standing as only privileged applicants (being the Members States, the European Parliament, the Council or the Commission) have the unlimited capacity to challenge an act. None of these privileged applicants have shown an interest in challenging an EMA guideline implementing an ICH guideline. Judicial review could be an interesting option

[99] Case C-308/11 *Chemische Fabrik Kreussler & Co. GmbH v Sunstar Deutschland GmbH*, ECLI:EU:C:2012:548, para 23.

[100] Case C-171/11 *Fra.bo SpA v Deutsche Vereinigung des Gas- und Wasserfaches eV (DGVW)-Technisch Wissenschaftlicher Verein*, ECLI:EU:C:2012:45.

[101] Ibid, para 31.

[102] Chapter 1 Section III.

[103] For a more in-depth discussion see: S Röttger-Wirtz, 'Standardisation of health products in search of legitimacy: rethinking judicial review?', in M Eliantonio and Cauffman, *The Legitimacy of Standardization as a Regulatory Technique in the EU* (Cheltenham: Edward Elgar, 2020b).

[104] Stefan (2014) 367.

for pharmaceutical companies or non-governmental organisations that do not agree with the guideline. However, for non-privileged applicants, access to judicial review is limited through the strict standing requirements of the Court established in the *Plaumann* case, which require an applicant which is not one of the privileged applicants, but another natural or legal person, to prove that the measure in question is of direct and individual concern to that applicant before access to judicial review is granted.[105] This means that natural or legal persons, such as a pharmaceutical company or a stakeholder group, can only in very limited circumstances challenge a legislative measure and the mandate to participate in the ICH contained therein. Although heavily criticised, the *Plaumann* criteria has so far largely prevented legal challenges brought by non-privileged applicants.[106]

The introduction of judicial review of 'regulatory acts' under Article 263(4) TFEU, which only requires direct effect and no further implementing measures, also does not benefit the position of a private party wanting to challenge an EMA guideline. It is not entirely clear if guidelines would indeed qualify as a regulatory act. The court defined regulatory acts as 'acts of general application apart from legislative acts'.[107] Although the guidelines are acts of general nature not adopted in accordance with a legislative procedure under Article 289 TFEU, many ambiguities with regard to the concept of regulatory acts persist. More importantly, however, the adoption of an EMA guideline as such does not directly affect the legal situation of a private party; this only happens through its application in the marketing authorisation procedure. Even if a marketing authorisation is rejected due to non-compliance with a guideline, it is the actual decision of the Commission refusing to grant a marketing authorisation that will be the act that changes the legal position and, thus, forms the act that should be challenged.

B. Judicial Review through other Means: Challenging Binding Decisions

As an alternative option to challenging EMA guidelines directly, in some cases EMA guidelines can be part of the challenge to a binding decision of the Commission. This logic of assessment of an act through the assessment of another act is

[105] Case C-25/62 *Plaumann & Co v Commission of the European Economic Community*, ECLI:EU:C:1963:17.

[106] Criticism of the requirements of direct and individual concern is and inter alia voiced by: A Arnull, 'Private Applicants and the Action for Annulment since *Codorniu*' (2001) 38 *Common Market Law Review* 7; P Craig, 'Legality, Standing and Substantive Review in Community Law' (1994) 14 *Oxford Journal of Legal Studies* 507; C Harlow, 'Towards a Theory of Access for the European Court of Justice' (1992) 12 *Yearbook of European Law* 213.

[107] Case T-18/10 *Inuit Tapiriit Kanatami and Others v Parliament and Council*, ECLI:EU:T:2011:419; Case T-262/10 *Microban International Ltd and Microban (Europe) Ltd v European Commission*, ECLI:EU:T:2011:623; Case C-583/11 *Inuit Tapiriit Kanatami and Others v Parliament and Council*, ECLI:EU:C:2013:625.

exemplified in the *Artegodan* case, where the withdrawal of marketing authorisations through several Commission decisions was challenged.[108] In this case the Court acknowledged that the review of the Commission decision did require looking beyond the decision to its scientific base, which was a Committee for Proprietary Medicinal Products (CPMP) opinion.[109] It then continued to assess whether the CPMP in its opinion provided sufficient reason for its decision and the transparency of the process, which 'ensures that the substance in question has undergone a detailed and objective scientific assessment'.[110] As pointed out in Chapter 4, in this case the Court also looked into the substance of a CPMP note for guidance relevant to the case.[111] Thus, while the CPMP opinion itself was not amenable to judicial review, it was assessed on its procedural qualities since it provided the scientific basis for a contested binding measure.

A similar situation could also occur in case of the ICH guidelines, as the following discussion of the *Acino* case will show.[112] The dispute between the company Acino AG and the European Commission surrounded the recall of the drug Clopidogrel due to irregularities in an Indian manufacturing site, which amounted to a breach of the Good Manufacturing Practice prescribed in the EU. The inspection report showed that 70 protocols (manufacturing standards) had been manipulated and, furthermore, other Good Manufacturing Practice requirements such as those relating to the equipment used, the premises in which the manufacturing was conducted, and the cleaning of both equipment and premises were not followed in the factory. Due to the danger of contamination or cross-contamination, the factory was removed from the list of sites authorised to manufacture Clopidogrel. The marketing authorisation of the medicine was suspended and concerned products manufactured in the factory had to be recalled. Thus, due to its non-compliance with Good Manufacturing Practice, the marketing authorisations had to be changed as the factory was removed from the sites that were allowed to manufacture the drug.

The Good Manufacturing Practice applicable in European pharmaceutical law is enshrined in a variety of legislative and non-legislative measures, whereas some of the requirements have their origin in ICH guidelines.[113] Whether non-compliance with ICH Good Manufacturing Practice requirements (in their implemented form) were also among the breaches that led to the closure of the Indian factory is not clear from the case, and is difficult to reenact as the Court

[108] Joined cases T-74/00, T-76/00, T-83/00, T-84/00, T-85/00, T-132/00, T-137/00 and T-141/00 *Artegodan GmbH and Others v Commission of the European Communities*, ECLI.EU:T:2002:283, para 39.

[109] Ibid, paras 198 and 199.

[110] Ibid, para 200.

[111] Chapter 4 Section III C.

[112] Case T-539/10 *Acino AG v Commission*, ECLI:EU:T:2013:110. The case has been appealed: Case C-269/13P *Acino AG v Commission*, ECLI:EU:C:2014:255.

[113] Chapter 4 Section II B.

did not go into detail on which Good Manufacturing Practice norms exactly had been breached. However, the technical requirements regarding Good Manufacturing Practice, including cleaning of the equipment and premises, are subject to ICH guidelines. In the *Acino* case the applicant did not contest the validity of the Good Manufacturing Practice as such, but rather the consequences that the Commission – relying on the CHMP – drew from the non-compliance, namely the change of the marketing authorisation and the order for recall of the products. It is, however, conceivable that an applicant could contest the validity of the applied norms. One reason could be the origin in ICH guidelines, which would force the Court to look into the process of establishing ICH guidelines. In the *Artegodan* case the Court clarified that the scope of its review would cover whether 'the consultation of the CPMP is *inter partes* and transparent, it ensures that the substance in question has undergone a detailed and objective scientific assessment, based on a comparison of the most representative scientific opinions …'.[114] In this regard, for example the involvement of potentially conflicted industry experts in the ICH standard-setting process, this would certainly leave room to argue that the standards do not represent the outcome of an objective scientific assessment. Also, the legitimacy gaps related to stakeholder participation and transparency could be raised before the Court under this logic.

However, even if the Court would indeed be ready to extend the *Artegodan* logic to EMA guidelines and thereby look at their formal legality – which then would need to include taking into account the ICH decision-making procedure where the EMA guidelines are essentially ICH guidelines – the review would be incidental and limited only to the cases of a decision that finds its explicit base in an implemented ICH guideline. Moreover, it is highly questionable whether the Court would indeed reach out and closely examine the decision-making procedure at the ICH level. In the *Kadi* case, the Court felt entitled to look into the UN origin of the contested measure and assess alleged procedural flaws. However, in *Kadi* the claims concerned the infringement of fundamental rights of individual persons, whereas in the case of ICH guidelines, the flaws are more of an administrative nature and do not directly infringe individual rights.

Therefore, the judicial review of binding measures does not provide a satisfactory solution in order to address the procedural deficits of ICH guidelines that are implemented in the EU. The analysis has thus shown that under the current judicial review mechanisms the Court currently will not provide for judicial review of the ICH-based norms, apart from the very incidental cases where binding decisions will be based on EMA implemented ICH guidelines. Even in these cases the probability of an in-depth consideration of the ICH

[114] Joined cases T-74/00, T-76/00, T-83/00, T-84/00, T-85/00, T-132/00, T-137/00 and T-141/00 *Artegodan GmbH and Others v Commission of the European Communities*, ECLI:EU:T:2002:283, para 200.

process is low. Although the Court in *Fra.bo* seems open to acknowledging the *de facto* effects of standards, it does not seem ready to generally open up to such logic, and as a consequence admit the judicial review of scientific and technical standards.

As long as a judicial grappling with the legitimacy flaws in measures such as the implemented ICH norms is lacking and the Court turns a blind eye on these instruments, substantial parts of the risk regulation framework will escape the enforcement of the EU's commitment to participatory openness, transparency and the independent scientific expertise on which it bases its decisions. This also means that the Court loses the possibility of actively shaping the procedural legitimacy of soft law.[115] Moreover, this limited judicial review fails to acknowledge the actual effects of guidelines on the institutions, the Member States, individuals and even the Court itself, as assessed in the previous chapter. Given these effects, the guidance measures should be subject to judicial review. Thus, in keeping the distinction between hard and soft law with regard to Court access, the reality of increasingly unclear borders between hard and soft law is ignored in practice.[116] In their seminal article of 2007 Scott and Sturm find a different role for European courts in general and the Court of Justice specifically, depicting it as a 'catalyst'.[117] They emphasise the ability of the Court to promote norms of participation, reason-giving, expertise as well as transparency and accountability.[118] This judicial review is then meant to enhance the legitimacy of governance mechanisms through 'shared values justifying the elaboration and implementation of public norms'.[119] In this regard, calls for judicial review of various types of soft law mechanisms have been voiced frequently in the literature.[120]

III. A BROADER PERSPECTIVE: GLOBAL STANDARDS AS A CHALLENGE FOR EUROPEAN LAW – THE POTENTIAL FOR JURIDIFICATION

This book has shown that legitimacy flaws derive from the implementation of global pharmaceutical standards failing to live up to essential EU administrative law principles. As shown in this chapter this is also not sufficiently counterbalanced by political or judicial accountability mechanisms. Moreover, the participation of the European actors – in this case the Commission and the EMA – in global standard-setting bodies is not sufficiently regulated in the Treaties and is subject to diverse degrees of regulation in the respective

[115] Stefan (2014) 366; Scott (2011) 349ff.
[116] Stefan (2014) 368.
[117] Scott and Sturm (2007).
[118] Ibid., 565.
[119] Ibid., 567.
[120] See amongst others: Scott (2011); Senden (2003), Stefan (2014); L Senden, 'Soft Post-Legislative Rulemaking: A Time for More Stringent Control' (2013) 19 *European Law Journal* 57.

sectoral secondary legislation. Overall, the limits to global activities of the EU administration, and the procedural rules applicable to these activities, are non-transparent and incoherent.

However, as Chapter 2 has shown, global standards are also implemented in European regulation in a large variety of other areas. Yet, the implementation of these global standards and the participation of the EU administration in global standard-setting initiatives are not expressly regulated in EU law, while as the example of the ICH standards has shown, there is need for a more comprehensive regulation of the interaction between global standards and EU risk regulation. What has become clear in the general analysis of the role of European actors in global standard-setting carried out in Chapter 2 is that there is no clear mandate for the Commission to participate in global standard-setting initiatives. It has been shown that only in the case of standard-setting in international organisations and binding legal agreements, does the Treaty provide answers to whether the EU is competent to act externally and who should act on behalf of the EU.[121] Beyond the remit of traditional international law the boundaries of the Commission's mandate to participate are less clear, which is the case for many standard-setting initiatives that are not established as international organisations or through binding international agreements. Moreover, whereas the mandate for the EMA as well as other agencies can be located in their founding regulations, it is rather superficial, without providing for procedural rules or limitations with regard to the bodies in which the agencies participate or their role in implementing global standards. The complex regulatory structures with diverse types of global standard-setting bodies, as well as the specific position of the EU – which in many areas shares the competence for external action with the Member States – certainly complicate the development of clear legal mandates. Moreover, as was shown in this chapter, the accountability mechanisms in place for the participation of the Commission and European agencies should be further developed, to account for the important role that global standards play in EU regulatory frameworks.

A juridification of the participation of European administration in global standard-setting bodies, and procedural rules on the acceptability of global standards received in the EU, could address the legitimacy flaws caused by the current situation. Juridification should be understood as a 'process through which an activity becomes subjected to legal regulation or more detailed legal regulation'.[122] This is exemplified in the field of 'European standards' developed under the New Approach.[123] Since the inception of the New Approach in 1985

[121] Chapter 2 Section III B.

[122] L Blichner and A Molander, 'Mapping Juridification' (2008) 14 *European Law Journal* 36, 42. See also: J Habermas, *The Theory of Communicative Action – Volume 2* (Boston: Beacon Press, 1987) 359.

[123] H Schepel, 'The New Approach to the New Approach: The Juridification of Harmonized Standards in EU Law' (2013) 20 *Maastricht Journal of European and Comparative Law* 521.

the Commission has, for example, worked towards increasing stakeholder participation possibilities for consumer representatives, and the transparency of the standard-setting process in the private bodies that develop the European standards.[124] The procedure of setting European standards has been juridified through the adoption of Regulation 1025/2012 on European standardisation.[125] Basic procedural requirements on transparency and stakeholder participation are now laid down in the regulation, such as Article 5 stating that standardisation organisations need to 'encourage and facilitate an appropriate representation and effective participation of all relevant stakeholders' and specify procedural stages such as 'the technical discussion on proposals' in which stakeholder participation is to be encouraged.[126]

The existing rules with regard to the EU's interplay with global standards, just like EU administrative law in general, are very fragmented. Administrative bodies like the Commission and agencies are bound to the specific procedural rules established in the respective regulatory field such as pharmaceuticals regulation.[127] Of course the rules applicable to EU administrative actors in principle also guide their activities on the global level,[128] and therefore, the core principles of participation, transparency and independent expertise apply to internal as well as external activities. However, one needs to look into the rules and practices of the European administrative actors in order to uncover how the treaty principles are applied in specific policy areas. Additionally, these sector-specific rules are drafted for the internal regulatory and administrative tasks, while often ignoring the global activities of these bodies. In the face of globalisation, the fragmented nature of EU administrative law causes problems. The existing internal divergence in procedural standards runs the risk of further sectoralisation. The administrative authorities of one regulatory branch (namely pharmaceuticals) cooperate with their counterparts globally, establishing not only vertically split administrations,[129] but also establishing their own sector-specific global cooperation practices.

A unified European law regulating administrative procedures could address this fragmentation. As pointed out in Chapter 5, the EU does not currently dispose

[124] H Schepel, *The Constitution of Private Governance – Product Standards in the Regulation of Integrating Markets* (Oxford: Hart, 2005) 242ff; E Vos, *Institutional Frameworks of Community Health and Safety Regulation – Committees, Agencies and Private Bodies* (Oxford: Hart Publishing, 1999) 289ff.

[125] Regulation (EU) No 1025/2012 of the European Parliament and of the Council of 25 October 2012 on European standardization, OJ L316/12.

[126] Regulation (EU) No 1025/2012, art 5.

[127] See also further Chapter 5 Section IV.

[128] J Mendes, 'Rule of Law and Participation: A Normative Analysis of Internationalized Rulemaking as Composite Procedures' (2014) 12 *International Journal of Constitutional Law* 370, 396.

[129] C Möllers, 'Transnationale Behördenkooperation – Verfassungs- und Völkerrechtliche Probleme Transnationaler Administrativer Standardsetzung' (2005) 65 Zeitschrift für ausländisches öffentliches Recht und Völkerrecht 351, 379.

over an Administrative Procedure Act, although the European Parliament[130] and the European Ombudsman have undertaken initiatives.[131] However, where the EU would adopt such an act, it could introduce provisions on the participation of European administrative bodies in global administrative bodies. It could establish rules regarding the implementation of global standards through administrative measures, which would safeguard the procedural standards applicable in the EU, where the decision-making power is outsourced to the global level. In a way that is comparable to the juridification of European standards, where basic rules for transparency and participation in the standard-setting process are laid down in a Regulation, a European administrative procedure act could set basic rules for global standards received in the EU. The EU could perform a legitimacy test before integrating norms that are developed externally into its regulatory framework.[132] Deriving such basic procedural rules would require a comparative study of the interface of global standards with various areas of European regulation. Therefore, this book is not the right place to indicate such common rules. However, the analysis in Chapter 6 has already uncovered certain principles and norms against which global standards can be assessed in the area of pharmaceuticals. The rules and practices identified in this research regarding balanced participation, public consultations, conflict of interest and transparency could form a starting point for developing general minimum standards, which could be incorporated into an EU act of administrative procedure.

Where the European administrative procedure act should provide a meaningful tool to address the implementation of global standards, it also has to cover the development of administrative soft law, given that – as in the case of the ICH – the adoption of such guidance documents might be the route to implementing global standards. The proposal attached to the European Parliament Resolution in 2016 includes 'administrative activities of the Union's institutions, bodies, offices and agencies', while only excluding legislative as well as judicial procedures, and 'the adoption of non-legislative acts directly based on the Treaties, delegated acts or implementing acts'.[133] Therefore, the proposal as drafted by the Parliament would cover the drafting of EMA guidelines.

[130] European Parliament, European administrative procedure law, Resolution of 15 January 2013, 2012/2024 INL, P7_TA(2013)0004; European Parliament, A regulation for an open, efficient and independent European Union administration, Resolution of 9 June 2016, 2016/2610 RSP, P8_TA(2016)0279.

[131] European Ombudsman, The European Code of Good Administrative Behaviour, available via: europa.eu/!Gx99WU.

[132] See also: C Devaux, 'The Experts in the Elaboration of the Cape Town Convention: Between Authority and Legitimacy' (2013) 19 *European Law Journal* 843, 862.

[133] European Parliament, A regulation for an open, efficient and independent European Union administration, Resolution of 9 June 2016, 2016/2610 RSP, P8_TA(2016)0279, art 2. The ReNEUAL project at this point does not call for application of its rules to administrative soft law (P Craig, H Hofmann, J Schneider and J Ziller (eds), *ReNEUAL Model Rules on EU Administrative Procedure* (Oxford: Oxford University Press, 2017).

The Commission has not used its right of legislative initiative with regard to a European Administrative Procedure Act and it is not certain if it might cover the adoption of administrative guidance. However, this research has shown that soft law standards form an important part of the regulatory framework. Neglecting them in a law governing European administrative procedures means that a large part of administrative activity will not be covered, although it has (indirect) legal effects on the regulated individuals in practice. Moreover, as argued above, the adoption of an EU Administrative Procedure Act would provide the EU with a chance to remedy the challenges posed by global standards, and their implementation in the EU.

IV. CONCLUSION: ACCOUNTABILITY GAPS AND JURIDIFICATION

In this chapter it became clear that the political accountability of EU administrative actors participating in global standard-setting and implementing global standards in the EU can contribute to enhancing the legitimacy of using ICH standards in the EU. However, it is currently not used as an effective remedy. Although it was shown that the Council and the European Parliament especially would have available efficient accountability mechanisms, the rather complex technical and scientific issue of pharmaceutical standards falls below the legislators' accountability 'radar'.

Other bodies also fail to fill this gap, as the Pharmaceutical Committee would have the required expertise, but not the sanctioning power. The Ombudsman and the Court of Auditors have not made use of their – arguably more limited – powers to hold the Commission or the EMA accountable with regard to their ICH activities. In this regard, this research has raised the question of whether specific political accountability mechanisms for the global regulatory activities of the EU administration might be beneficial.

Moreover, it was shown that, currently, legal accountability through judicial review of implemented ICH guidelines is lacking, as due to their non-binding nature the EMA guidelines are not subject to systematic legality review. Incidentally, they may become subject to judicial review where they form the scientific basis of a challengeable act. However, this only provides for an incomplete accountability framework – if any at all. With this, the Court misses an important opportunity to acknowledge the *de facto* legal effect of administrative guidance and the global standards which it can implement.

In a broader approach, it was proposed that the participation of EU administrative actors in global standard-setting bodies and the implementation of global standards in the EU should be subjected to general juridification in an EU administrative procedure law. In this regard, while the norms identified in Chapter 6 can form a starting point, future research is required to identify common standards addressing global standards from the perspective of various sectors of European regulation.

Conclusion

THE QUESTIONS 'WHO makes the rules that ensure the quality, safety and efficacy of pharmaceuticals on the EU market? And how are these rules determined?' have instructed the analysis carried out in this book. What it has revealed are complex multilevel interactions between the EU and global standard-setting bodies, such as the International Council on Harmonisation.

Risk regulation increasingly takes place on the global level, due to the interconnected markets and the complexity of risks faced by society today. Standards are often set through the cooperation of domestic regulators, and the administration gains importance as a global actor. Within standard-setting there is also increasing reliance on another actor at the global level: private parties. In this regard, public interest non-governmental organisations (NGO) or private economic actors such as businesses and private organisations either take part in standard-setting or set standards on their own. These actors perform their standard-setting tasks in four different types of bodies: (i) international organisations, (ii) transnational regulatory networks, (iii) private standard-setting bodies, and (iv) public-private partnerships. Within these bodies regulators and/or private actors work together in various degrees of cooperation and formalisation.

Where such standards are developed on the global level, they are mainly addressed to regulators for implementation into the domestic frameworks. However, through this implementation they then also affect private actors as second level addressees. Thus, although global standards do not constitute legally binding measures, they can be soft law in the sense that they can give rise to (indirect) legal effects. Indeed, irrespective of their voluntary nature, global standards have proven to be very effective regulatory measures and can become *de facto* binding based on their origin in regulatory cooperation, their epistemic legitimacy and sometimes also due to reinforcement through law. However, this causes challenges with regard to the legitimacy of global standards as the classical forms of legitimation in democratic nation states are left behind.

I. PHARMACEUTICAL REGULATION IN A GLOBALISED WORLD

The book discussed the regulatory framework applicable to pharmaceuticals in the European Union, which evolved with the introduction of a marketing authorisation requirement as the core of pharmaceutical law, as well as subsequent proceduralisation and extensive harmonisation of the regulatory requirements concerning quality, safety and efficacy. What has been emphasised is the prominent role of non-binding measures in the form of EMA and European Commission guidelines in the governance of pharmaceuticals on the European level. While legislation will set out the overarching lines of the regulatory policies and the procedures to execute them, they require further scientific and technical details, which are then elaborated on in post-legislative guidance documents.

These guidance documents have been used extensively in the regulation of pharmaceuticals, harmonising the regulatory requirements in the centralised, decentralised and national marketing authorisation procedures and they constitute soft law, creating (indirect) legal effects.

Although they are not legally binding, they have to be taken into account in drafting the marketing authorisation applications according to Annex 1 of Directive 2001/83/EC and Article 6(1) of Regulation (EC) 726/2004. The guidelines are usually adopted on an explicit basis in the legislation and have been qualified by the EMA itself as 'quasi-binding'. They can only be deviated from by marketing authorisation applicants upon provision of a justified reason and, therefore, these guidelines present which studies are acceptable to prove the quality, safety and efficacy of a medicinal product from a scientific point of view. In practice, the leeway for marketing authorisation applicants to deviate from the guidelines is rather small. The high costs involved in pharmaceutical development certainly deter companies from risking deviation from the established standards given the shifting burden of proof. Moreover, these guidelines also affect Member States as the guidelines work through into the national marketing authorisation procedures. Finally, the adoption of guidelines has a self-binding effect on the adopting body, derived from the principles of equal treatment, legitimate expectations and legal certainty.

However, it has been shown that the guidance setting the requirements concerning the quality, safety and efficacy does not necessarily originate in the EU bodies, but to a large extent is set on the global level, where the International Council on Harmonisation has become the leading global source for pharmaceutical standards. This body, originally established by the regulators and representatives of the research-based pharmaceutical industry of the US, EU and Japan, has successfully harmonised the marketing authorisation requirements with regard to the quality, safety and efficacy of pharmaceuticals in these three regions and beyond. Through its recent reform, it has opened up membership to other regulators and industry associations, while the six founding members still retain considerable privileges.

As this book has shown, the ICH can be qualified as a public-private partnership, characterised by the participation of regulatory and industry representatives on all institutional levels. In this regard, the ICH heavily depends on the expertise provided by both industry and regulators in order to form the guidelines. It, therefore, epitomises the increasing institutional diversity of interaction at the global level and, through the membership rights it grants to industry representatives, the rise of private actors in global governance. Steps have been undertaken in order to better distinguish the role of industry and regulators in the ICH process. The members representing industry cannot prevent the choice of a topic for harmonisation in a voting procedure in the Assembly. They will not be considered for the consensus or for voting on the final adoption of a guideline in the Assembly. Nonetheless, while the process has therefore become more regulator-driven, industry representatives still take part in the forming of the scientific consensus in the Expert Working groups, and can exert substantial influence on the content of the ICH guidelines. Thus, the relationship between industry and regulators in the ICH can be qualified as co-regulation.

These guidelines are not legally binding on the ICH members. However, the members are politically committed to implement the standards. This commitment together with the firm basis of the guidelines in consensus as well as their recognition as state-of-the-art standards has led to the success of the ICH. Currently over 60 guidelines are adopted by the ICH and all of them are implemented in the regulatory framework of the Founding Regulatory Members, while Standing Regulatory Members and new Regulatory Members are also expected to implement the standards in the near future. Thus, although there is no legal obligation to implement the guidelines, they become *de facto* binding on the members. The analysis has shown that 19 per cent, thus approximately one fifth, of the EMA guidelines originate in the ICH. Importantly, these ICH guidelines are usually applicable to all therapeutic classes of drugs, while the EMA guidelines often address specific therapeutic classes. Thus, the ICH guidelines will often provide the overarching standards, while additional EMA guidelines will supplement these ICH guidelines for more specific therapeutic classes. Once the ICH guidelines are implemented into the regulatory framework of the EU, through adoption by the Committee for Medicinal Products for Human Use (CHMP) in the EMA, they have the same legal status as guidelines originating in the EMA, ie being 'quasi-binding'. While the share of ICH guidelines within the EMA guidelines is not equally distributed amongst the different guideline categories (quality, biological, and so on), it was shown that there is also a significant degree of interaction between the guidelines originating in the EMA and the ICH guidelines. It was also established that over 70 per cent of the remaining guidelines, which originate in the EMA independently from ICH guidelines, contain references to ICH guidelines. Therefore, ICH guidelines form an important part of the scientific guidance provided by the EMA.

In addition to the implementation of the ICH guidelines through the EMA, references to ICH guidelines can also be found in Commission guidelines and, at least in one instance, the ICH guidelines have been shown to exert influence on Commission guidelines, leading to amendments. Moreover, in the case of the Good Manufacturing Practice and the Good Clinical Practice, the analysis has shown that there has been influence on European legislation, sometimes even literal transposition of ICH standards into binding EU law. Moreover, the potential use of the ICH guidelines in the Court of Justice as an interpretative aid has been pointed out. Therefore, the ICH guidelines, which originate as soft law on the global level, deeply permeate the European pharmaceuticals regulation and it has become increasingly difficult to identify the borderline between global standards and the EU risk regulation framework.

II. THE LEGITIMACY OF GLOBAL PHARMACEUTICAL STANDARDS

While this book has demonstrated the interplay between ICH standards and EU pharmaceutical law, which influence the regulation of the whole pharmaceutical lifecycle, it has also shown that the ICH procedure does not live up to the procedural standards applied to comparable measures in the EU. The ICH guidelines are adopted by the EMA in the CHMP, but they do not undergo the usual guideline adoption procedure. In the true spirit of harmonisation, the guidelines, once they are adopted by the ICH, can only be implemented into the framework of the EU without undergoing further changes. Thus, where the procedure of the adoption of ICH guidelines does not live up to the procedural standards as set by EU administrative law, these flaws are carried over into the European regulatory framework. In this regard, first of all flaws in terms of the participation of stakeholders in the decision-making process were identified. In the ICH, representatives of the pharmaceutical industry have obtained full membership status and have become co-regulators of their own products. This partnership between regulators and industry is not counterbalanced with an equal institutionalised role of other stakeholders in the ICH process. Moreover, the transparency of the guideline adoption process is limited and the institutional structure and decision-making process is irreconcilable with the principle of independence of expertise as applicable in the EU.

The analysis of the ICH's institutional structure and procedure shares the same characteristics as the EU's risk regulation in the food safety area prior to the BSE (bovine spongiform encephalopathy) crisis: with an industry-focused regulatory body operating under conditions of secrecy and advice given within small closed groups of experts.[1] In essence, the ICH standard-setting is the epitome of a mode of governance that the EU has aimed to overcome for the sake of good governance since the beginning of this millennium.[2] It is remarkable that while the EU increasingly aims at improving the legitimacy of its own decision-making by means of increased transparency and participation, global standards are being absorbed into the legal framework of the EU without being measured against the same benchmarks of good governance.

One could, therefore, argue that the legitimacy flaws identified – the most pronounced being lack of independence due to industry influence at ICH

[1] See: E Millstone and P van Zwanenberg, 'The Evolution of Food Safety Policy-Making Institutions in the UK, EU and Codex Alimentarius' (2002) 36 *Social Policy & Administration* 59: E Vos, *Institutional Frameworks of Community Health and Safety Regulation – Committees, Agencies and Private Bodies* (Oxford: Hart Publishing, 1999).

[2] European Commission, European Governance – A White Paper, COM(2001) 428 final, [2001] OJ C287/1.

level – would best be resolved if either the ICH was again radically reformed, this time to mitigate industry influence, or, alternatively, if the EU were to leave the ICH and halt the implementation of ICH standards. With regard to the first option, given that the ICH has only recently undergone reform, precisely to curb industry influence, it can be assumed that the current status of its institutional structure and procedural rules represents the common denominator of the ICH members, and further changes are not to be expected in the near future.

The second option – the EU leaving the ICH – also has fundamental problems. First, the benefits achieved by the ICH harmonisation should not be forgotten: standards create a level playing field for global trade, and thus relieve producers from the duty of either having to adapt their products or (where applicable) their marketing authorisation application to every single constituency in which they want to sell their products. In terms of pharmaceuticals, this also shortens the time patients have to wait for a drug to be authorised. Moreover, it facilitates better accessibility, given that where the costs of adjusting to a regulatory system are high, companies might choose not to make medicines available at all. Furthermore, through regulatory cooperation, regulators benefit from the sharing of resources with their foreign counterparts. In the case of standard-setting with the participation of private parties, they benefit from the expertise that the private parties have in these very technical and scientific regulatory fields, with experts from pharmaceutical companies being involved in the research and development of innovative medicines. In addition, leaving the ICH would mean that the EU would also leave its seat at the table, losing any say in the development of standards that have become globally accepted. It would become a mere recipient of these norms,[3] or would have to develop its own standards, constantly in competition with the globally accepted ICH standards. Thus, overall, the market pressures with regard to pharmaceuticals seem to prohibit attempting to resolve the legitimacy problems highlighted in this research by leaving the ICH altogether.

While this research has shown that the ICH standards raise several concerns where they are measured against the benchmark of EU administrative law, it should be remembered that on the global level analogous general principles also arise. The global administrative law scholarship has identified a tendency in global administrative practice for bodies to subject themselves to administrative law principles like transparency and participation, regardless of their public, private or hybrid nature. This research has shown that the ICH, like other global administrative bodies, has indeed in the recent past undergone procedural changes in order to better define the different roles of regulators and industry in the decision-making procedure. Moreover, it has taken several measures to increase the transparency of its processes. Thus, the tendency towards the

[3] For a similar argument concerning the UK's ICH membership post-Brexit: M Flear, 'Charting a roadmap towards membership and formal voice in global bioethics standard-setting: Health research and the case of the International Council on Harmonisation' (2018) *Medical Law International* 157.

development of certain best practices on the global level that has been observed by the global administrative law (GAL) scholarship can also be confirmed for the ICH. These procedural changes to a certain degree originated in concerns about how the ICH process would be evaluated in a domestic context. For the European actors in the ICH process, the debates in the EU on transparency and independence in the area of pharmaceutical regulation also led to a re-thinking of whether the ICH harmonisation process can be justified.

Thus, what this book has proposed is to upload certain practices based on EU administrative law and its sector-specific practices in the area of pharmaceuticals, while acknowledging that this has to be done in dialogue with the other ICH members. It also been argued that this would serve as a valuable source of inspiration for the evolving global administrative law. Moreover, given the interaction between the European and the global level, in terms of European actors participating in global standard-setting and the standards finding their way back into the EU, the question of compatibility of global standard-setting with European administrative law procedural standards cannot be avoided. What can be learned from the analysis of the implementation of ICH standards into the pharmaceutical regulation of the EU is that global administrative law could be further defined through 'uploading' certain EU administrative law norms and practices, in order to ensure a more balanced participation of stakeholders, more transparency with regard to conflicts of interest, and also the decision-making procedures. Moreover, beyond the specific case of pharmaceuticals, the administrative law applicable in other regulatory areas in the EU could also provide insights that could valuably contribute to the formation of an administrative law applicable to global standard-setting bodies. Further research on this is certainly required. This also holds true from a European perspective, as the implementation of global standards is a phenomenon that spans over a multitude of regulatory areas in the EU's risk regulation framework.

III. LESSONS LEARNED FROM 'UPLOADING' EU LAW TO THE ICH

With regard to the ICH, the lessons from the comparison with EU administrative law concerned the principles of participation, independence of expertise and transparency. While the pharmaceutical industry is represented as members in the ICH process, other stakeholders can only become observers. The only other possibility to provide input into the ICH standard setting-process for other stakeholders remains the public consultation procedure carried out in the adoption process of the guidelines. However, the consultation takes place after the scientific consensus has been formed and, furthermore, no feedback is provided on how the comments have been used. Therefore, in the ICH harmonisation process, the industry has become a privileged stakeholder, while this pronounced status is not counterbalanced with similar roles for other stakeholders such as doctors' or patients' associations. In this regard, the comparison with participatory mechanisms in EU administrative law and the procedural norms applicable to the adoption of post-legislative guidance by the EMA specifically allowed for suggesting some improvements to the ICH process.

The EMA has institutionalised the participation of patients as well as doctors' associations in its Management Committee, as well as in some of its scientific committees and through special working parties. Similar specialised fora could be integrated into the institutional structure of the ICH, potentially also offering financial support to NGOs to lower the hurdle to participate in the ICH activities. Subsequently, the created stakeholder bodies could be integrated into the guideline adoption process to provide input into the guideline development at various steps of the procedure. Still, a core concern identified is that currently the ICH participation mechanisms are insufficiently balanced, making the pharmaceutical industry a co-regulator while limiting the influence of other stakeholders from providing comments in the public consultation procedure. This could be resolved by giving all interested NGOs access to full membership, which has been denied currently due to efficiency concerns. The other option would be to radically rethink the institutional structure of the ICH, creating specific stakeholder working groups including one for industry stakeholders, while cancelling the current membership and observer status of industry representatives. This would mean that the ICH would become a body with purely regulatory members and only allow the industry – together with other stakeholders – a place in the institutional structure and procedure in stakeholder working groups.

This also aligns with the concerns regarding the independence of expertise. The ICH has not undertaken any measures to address the conflicts of interest which are inherent in its institutional structure as regulator-industry partnership. In the EU, however, the independence of the administration and the prevention of conflicts of interest has become an important procedural standard, especially in the risk-regulation process. The role of the industry in the ICH process fundamentally counteracts the independence of expertise, and consequently applying EU administrative law would require excluding the industry associations from membership. In practice, however, it is questionable whether such a fundamental restructuring of the ICH's 'institutional DNA' as public-private partnership is indeed a realistic option given the recent reform. Yet, while the inherent industry involvement in the ICH might not be changed, lessons can be learned from the EMA rules with regard to making conflicts of interest transparent. Here, the ICH could require the representatives in the ICH bodies and also the experts in the working groups to publish conflict of interest declarations; this would make such conflicts visible internally and externally, allowing increased accountability for undue influence. Moreover, it should be considered whether the personal and professional interests of an expert should be a factor to be considered in the nomination process.

Independently of the previous suggestions, the public consultation process could also be improved. Similar to the practice of the EMA, a two-step public consultation process could be introduced: first at the beginning of the drafting process for the development of the Concept Paper, and secondly after the adoption of the Draft Guideline. This would mean that stakeholders were involved in the early stages of the drafting process. In addition to that, the comments received should be published on the website, and a summary should be drafted by the rapporteur providing notes on how comments had been taken into account. This would undoubtedly increase the workload involved in adopting a guideline, but it would also contribute to better and more legitimate standards based on the meaningful input of a broad stakeholder base.

Both the observations about participation as well as independent expertise are closely linked to the overall transparency of the ICH process. While efforts have been undertaken to make the ICH process more transparent, it was shown that a lack of transparency persists with regard to the decision-making procedure and especially the membership of the expert working groups, as far as employment of the industry experts is concerned. Assessed against the transparency commitment enshrined in European administrative law and the practice of the European Medicines Agency, several advantages of the EMA approach have been identified which could be transferred to the ICH process. This includes that the identity of experts in the guideline adoption process should be made public and conflict of interest declarations published. Moreover, by adjusting the public consultation procedure in the way suggested above, the decision-making process would become more visible and it would become possible to evaluate the influences exerted by stakeholders from the summary of the comments received.

IV. THE IMPLEMENTATION OF GLOBAL STANDARDS AS A LEGITIMACY CHALLENGE FOR THE EU

Finally, what became clear in this book is that the implementation of global standards in EU risk regulation also raises challenges for EU constitutional, institutional and administrative law. Developing an administrative law framework for the external activities of European administrative bodies will be an important task of the legal scholarship and also the European institutions in the face of an ever-globalising regulatory reality. It was proposed to use the opportunity provided by the discussions surrounding an EU law of administrative procedure to subject the participation of EU administrative actors in global standard-setting bodies, and the implementation of global standards in the EU to general juridification. This can also strengthen the political accountability mechanisms for the global regulatory activities of the EU administration. Furthermore, when it comes to judicial review, it was pleaded that the *de facto* legal effect of administrative guidance should be acknowledged. This would enable the administrative measures which are implementing global standards to be subjected to legal accountability.

It has to be concluded that, given the increasing importance of global standards, a commitment in the EU towards democracy and good governance will remain incomplete as long as it does not address questions of global standards. A transfer of regulatory power to the global level opens the door to the implementation into the regulatory framework of the EU of global standards that fall short of respecting essential procedural requirements for administrative action in the EU. It is essential that the EU critically examines the global standards it integrates into its regulatory framework with regard to the core criteria of EU administrative law, as otherwise these general principles are 'hollowed out'.[4] This requires research beyond the case of pharmaceuticals and one specific global standard-setting body. The questions asked in this book will also apply to other fields of risk regulation, and a broader discussion is needed in order to ensure that the EU can continue to maintain and improve the high level of health protection it promises its citizens in a globalised world.

[4] J Mendes, 'EU Law and Global Regulatory Regimes: Hollowing Out Procedural Standards?' (2012) 10 *International Journal of Constitutional Law* 988.

Bibliography

Abbott K, Keohane R, Moravcsik A, Slaughter A and Snidal D, 'The Concept of Legalization' (2000) 54 *International Organization* 401.

Abbott K and Snidal D, 'Hard and Soft Law in International Governance' (2000) 54 *International Organization* 421.

Abbott K and Snidal D, 'International "Standards" and International Governance' (2001) 8 *Journal of European Public Policy* 345.

Abbott K, 'Public Private Partnership', in R Wolfrum (ed), *The Max Planck Encyclopedia of Public International Law* (Oxford: University Press Oxford, 2016), article last updated February 2008, available via: opil.ouplaw.com/home/EPIL.

Abraham J and Lewis G, *Regulating Medicines in Europe: Competition, Expertise and Public Health* (London: Routledge, 2000).

Abraham J and Reed T, 'Trading Risks for Markets: The International Harmonization of Pharmaceuticals Regulation' (2001) 1 *Health, Risk and Society* 113.

Abraham J, 'The Pharmaceutical Industry as a Political Player' (2002) 360 *The Lancet* 1498.

Abraham J and Reed T, 'Progress, Innovation and Regulatory Science in Drug Development: The Politics of International Standard-Setting' (2002) 32 *Social Studies of Science* 337.

Alemanno A, 'The Shaping of European Risk Regulation by Community Courts', Jean Monnet Working Paper 18/2008, (2008).

Alemanno A, 'A Meeting of Minds on Impact Assessment – When Ex Ante Evaluation Meets Ex Post Judicial Control' (2011)17 *European Public Law* 485.

Alemanno A, 'Unpacking the Principle of Openness in EU Law: Transparency, Participation and Democracy' (2014) 39 *European Law Review* 72.

Arnold R, 'Objectives and Preparation of the Conference and the Role of the Workshops', in P D'Arcy and D Harron (eds), *Proceedings of the First International Conference on Harmonisation – Brussels 1991* (Belfast: The Queen's University Belfast, 1992) 7–11.

Arnull A, 'Private Applicants and the Action for Annulment since *Codorniu*' (2001) 38 *Common Market Law Review* 7.

Aust A, *Handbook of International Law*, 2nd edn (Cambridge: Cambridge University Press, 2010).

Aziz D, 'Global Public-Private Partnerships in International Law' (2012) 2 *Asian Journal of International Law* 339.

Bach D and Newman A, 'The European Regulatory State and Global Public Policy: Micro-institutions, Macro-influence' (2007) 14 *Journal of European Public Policy* 827.

Bach D and Newman A, 'Governing Lipitor and Listerine: The Domestic Roots of International Pharmaceutical and Cosmetics Regulation', IE Business School Working Paper, WP08-17, (11 March 2008).

Bache G, Flear M and Hervey T, 'The Defining Features of the European Union's Approach to Regulating New Health Technologies', in M Flear, A Farrell, T Hervey and T Murphy (eds), *European Law and New Health Technologies* (Oxford: Oxford University Press, 2013) 7–45.

Bahri P and Tsintis P, 'Pharmacovigilance-related topics at the level of the International Conference on Harmonisation (ICH)' (2005) 14 *Pharmacoepidemiology and Drug Safety* 377.

Baldwin J and Davis G, 'Empirical Research in Law', in P Cane and M Tushnet (eds), *The Oxford Handbook of Legal Studies* (Oxford: Oxford University Press, 2003) 880–900.

Bangemann M, 'Welcome Address by Mr Martin Bangemann', in P D'Arcy and D Harron (eds), *Proceedings of the First International Conference on Harmonisation – Brussels 1991* (Belfast: The Queen's University Belfast, 1992) 1–5.

Bast J, 'Internationalisierung und De-Internationalisierung der Migrationsverwaltung', in C Möllers, A Vosskuhle and C Walter (eds), *Internationales Verwaltungsrecht – Eine Analyse Anhand von Referenzgebieten* (Tübingen: Mohr Siebeck, 2007) 279–312.

Batory A, 'Uploading as Political Strategy: the European Parliament and the Hungarian Media Law Debate' (2014) 30 *East European Politics* 230.

Beck U, *Risk Society: Towards a New Modernity* (London: Sage, 1992).

Berman A, 'The Public-Private Nature of Harmonisation Networks' (2011) CTEI Working Paper, CTEI-2011-06.

Berman A, 'Public-Private Harmonization Networks: The Case of the International Conference on Harmonization (ICH)', in S Cassese, B Carotti, L Casini, E Cavalieri and E MacDonald (eds), *Global Administrative Law: The Casebook*, 3rd edn (2012a, IRPA-IILJ, ebook) 228–34.

Berman A, 'The Distributional Effects of Transnational Pharmaceutical Regulation' (2012b) CTEI Working Paper, CTEI-2012-01.

Berman A, 'Informal International Lawmaking in Medical Products Regulation', in A Berman, S Duquet, J Pauwelyn, R Wessel and J Wouters (eds), *Informal International Lawmaking: Case Studies* (The Hague: Torkel Opsahl Academic Publishers, 2012c) 353–93.

Berman A, 'Accordion Governance' (2019) 13 *Vienna Journal on International* Constitutional Law 203.

Bevilaqua D, 'The Codex Alimentarius Commission and its Influence on European and National Food Policy' (2006) 1 *European Food and Feed Law Review* 3.

Bevilaqua D, 'Global Food Safety Regulation and the Interplay between Global Standards and WTO Law: How to Close the Legitimacy Gap?', in M Eliantonio and C Cauffman (eds), *The Legitimacy of Standardisation as a Regulatory Technique: A Cross-Disciplinary and Multi-Level Analysis* (Cheltenham: Edward Elgar, 2020) 243–64.

Bignami F, 'Three Generations of Participation Rights Before the European Commission' (2004) 68 *Law and Contemporary Problems* 61.

Black J, 'Critical Reflections on Regulation', Centre for Analysis of Risk and Regulation, CARR Discussion Papers DP 4, London School of Economics and Political Science (London, 2002).

Black J, 'Constructing and Contesting Legitimacy and Accountability in Polycentric Regulatory Regimes' (2008) 2 *Regulation & Governance* 137.

Black J, 'The Role of Risk in Regulatory Processes', in R Baldwin, M Cave and M Lodge (eds), *The Oxford Handbook of Regulation* (Oxford: Oxford University Press, 2010) 302–48.

Blichner L and Molander A, 'Mapping Juridification' (2008) 14 *European Law Journal* 36.

Börzel T, 'Organizing Babylon – On the Different Conceptions of Policy Networks' (1998) 76 *Public Administration* 253.

Börzel T and Risse T, 'Public-Private Partnerships: Effective and Legitimate Tools of International Governance?', in E Grande and L Pauly (eds), *Complex Sovereignty: On the Reconstruction of Political Authority in the 21st Century* (Toronto: University of Toronto Press, 2007) 195–216.

Bodansky D, 'The Legitimacy of International Governance: A Coming Challenge for International Environmental Law?' (1999) 93 *The American Journal of International Law* 596.

Bodansky D, 'Legitimacy in International Law and International Relations', in J Dunoff and M Pollack (eds), *Interdisciplinary Perspectives on International Law and International Relations – The State of the Art* (Cambridge: Cambridge University Press, 2013) 321–41.

Borrás S, Koutalakis C and Wendler F, 'European Agencies and Input Legitimacy: EFSA, EMEA and EPO in the Post-Delegation Phase' (2007) 29 *Journal of European Integration* 583.

Borrás S, 'Three Tensions in the Governance of Science and Technology', in D Levi-Faur (ed), *The Oxford Handbook of Governance* (Oxford: Oxford University Press, 2012) 429–40.

Bothe M, 'Legal and Non-Legal Norms – A Meaningful Distinction in International Relations?' (1980) 11 *Netherlands Yearbook of International Law* 65.

Bovens M, 'Analysing and Assessing Accountability: A Conceptual Framework' (2007) 13 *European Law Journal* 447.

Bovens M, Curtin D and 't Hart P, 'Studying the Real World of EU Accountability: Framework and Design', in M Bovens, D Curtin and 't Hart P (eds), *The Real World of EU Accountability – What Deficit?* (Oxford: Oxford University Press, 2010) 31–62.

Boyle A, 'Some Reflections on the Relationship of Treaties and Soft Law', (1999) 48 *International and Comparative Law Quarterly* 901.

Bretherton C and Vogler J, *The European Union as Global Actor*, 2nd edn Edition (Oxon: Routledge, 2006).

Buchanan A and Keohane R, 'The Legitimacy of Global Governance Institutions' (2006) 20 *Ethics and International Affairs* 405.

Büthe T and Mattli W (eds), *The New Global Rulers: The Privatization of Regulation in the World Economy* (Princeton: Princeton University Press, 2011).

Burci G, 'Public/Private Partnerships in the Public Health Sector' (2009) 6 *International Organizations Law Review* 359.

Busuioc M, *European Agencies: Law and Practice of Accountability* (Oxford: Oxford University Press, 2013).

Cafaggi F, 'Rethinking Private Regulation in the European Regulatory Space', European University Institute Department of Law, EUI Working Papers Law No. 2006/13, (2006).

Cafaggi F and Renda A, 'Public and Private Regulation – Mapping the Labyrinth', Centre for European Policy Studies, CEPS Working Document No 370, (October 2012).

Cantero Gamito M and Micklitz H (eds), *The Role of the EU in Transnational Legal Ordering – Standards, Contracts and Codes* (Cheltenham: Edward Elgar, 2020).

Casini L, 'Global Hybrid Public-Private Bodies: The World Anti-Doping Agency (WADA)' (2009) 6 *International Organizations Law Review* 421.

Casini L, 'Beyond drip-painting? Ten years of GAL and the emergence of a global administration' (2015) 13 *International Journal of Constitutional Law* 473.

Cassese S, 'Administrative Law without the State? The Challenge of Global Regulation' (2005) 37 *International Law and Politics* 663.

Cassese S (ed), *Research Handbook on Global Administrative Law* (Cheltenham: Edward Elgar, 2016).

Castle G and Kelly B, 'Global Harmonization Is Not All That Global: Divergent Approaches in Drug Safety' (2008) 63 *Food and Drug Law Journal* 601.

Cecchini P, *The European Challenge 1992 – Benefits of a Single Market* (Aldershot: Wildwood House, 1988).

Chamon M, *European Agencies – Legal and Political Limits to the Transformation of the EU Administration* (Oxford: Oxford University Press, 2016).

Chamon M and Wirtz S, 'Complex procedures as hurdle to accountability: verticalization of pharmaceutical enforcement', in M Luchtman and M Scholten, *Law Enforcement by EU Authorities – Political and judicial accountability in a shared legal order* (Cheltenham: Edward Elgar, 2017) 141–67.

Chamon M, 'A Constitutional Twilight Zone: EU Decentralized Agencies' External Relations' (2019) 56 *Common Market Law Review* 1509.

Chamon M and Demedts V, 'Constitutional Limits to EU agencies' external relations', in H Hofmann, E Vos and M Chamon (eds), *The External Dimension of EU Agencies and Bodies – Law and Policy* (Cheltenham: Edward Elgar, 2019) 12–33.

Charnovitz S, 'International Standards and the WTO', GW Law Faculty Publications & Other Works, Paper 394, (2005).

Chinkin C, 'The Challenge of Soft Law: Development and Change in International Law' (1989) 38 *International and Comparative Law Quarterly* 850.

Chiti E, 'EU and Global Administrative Organizations', in E Chiti and B Mattarella (eds), *Global Administrative Law and EU Administrative Law* (Heidelberg: Springer, 2011) 13–39.

Chiti E and Mattarella B (eds), *Global Administrative Law and EU Administrative Law* (Heidelberg: Springer, 2011).

Chiti E, 'European Agencies' Rulemaking: Powers, Procedures and Assessment' (2013) 19 *European Law Journal* 93.

Clarke L, 'The Exercise of Public Power over Global Health through Public-Private Partnerships and the Question of Responsibility Under International Law' (2011) 105 *Proceedings of the Annual Meeting of the American Society of International Law* 96.

Collatz B, *Die neuen europäischen Zulassungsverfahren für Arzneimittel* (Aulendorf: Editio-Cantor-Verlag, 1996).

Coman-Kund F, *European Union Agencies as Global Actors – A Legal Study of the European Aviation Safety Agency, Frontex and Europol* (London: Routledge, 2018).

Connolly J, 'Europeanization, Uploading and Downloading – The Case of Defra and Avian Influenza' (2008) 23 *Public Policy and Administration* 7.

Contrera J, 'The Food and Drug Administration and the International Conference on Harmonisation: How Harmonious Will International Pharmaceutical Regulations Become?' (1994–1995) 8 *The Administrative Law Journal* 927.

Craig P, 'Legality, Standing and Substantive Review in Community Law' (1994) 14 *Oxford Journal of Legal Studies* 507.

Craig P, *EU Administrative Law* (Oxford: Oxford University Press, 2012).

Craig P, 'A General Law on Administrative Procedure, Legislative Competence and Judicial Competence' (2013) 19 *European Public Law* 503.

Craig P, Hofmann H, Schneider J and Ziller J (eds), *ReNEUAL Model Rules on EU Administrative Procedure* (Oxford: Oxford University Press, 2017).

Cremona M, 'The Union as Global Actor: Roles, Models and Identity' (2004) 4 *Common Market Law Review* 553.

Curtin D, 'Delegation to EU Non-Majoritarian Agencies and Emerging Practices of Public Accountability', in D Geradin, R Munoz and N Petit (eds), *Regulation Through Agencies in the EU: A New Paradigm of European Governance* (Cheltenham: Edward Elgar, 2006) 88–119.

Curtin D and Meijer A, 'Does Transparency Strengthen Legitimacy?' (2006) 11 *Information Polity* 109.

Curtin D and Eckes C, 'The *Kadi* Case: Mapping the Boundaries between the Executive and the Judiciary in Europe' (2008) 5 *International Organizations Law Review* 365.

Curtin D, *Executive Power of the European Union – Law, Practice and the Living Constitution* (Oxford: Oxford University Press, 2009).

Curtin D, Hofmann H and Mendes J, 'Constitutionalising EU Executive Rule-Making Procedures: A Research Agenda' (2013) 19 *European Law Journal* 1.

Cutler C, Haufler V and Porter T (eds), *Private Authority and International Affairs* (Albany: State University of New York Press, 1995).

Cutler C, 'The Legitimacy of Private Transnational Governance: Experts and the Transnational Market for Force' (2010) 8 *Socio-Economic Review* 157.

Cuvillier A, 'The role of the European Medicines Evaluation Agency in the harmonization of pharmaceutical regulation', in R Goldberg and J Lonbay, *Pharmaceutical Medicine, Biotechnoloy and European Law* (Cambridge: Cambridge University Press, 2001) 137–54.

D'Arcy P and Harron D (eds), *Proceedings of the First International Conference on Harmonisation – Brussels 1991* (Belfast: The Queen's University Belfast, 1992).

Dagron S, 'Global Harmonization through Public-Private Partnership: The Case of Pharmaceuticals', Instituto di Ricerche sulla Pubblica Amministrazione, Global Administrative Law Working Papers (2012), IRPA GAL Working Paper 2012/2.

Dagron S, 'Die International Conference on Harmonization of Technical Requirements for Registration of Pharmaceuticals for Human Use (ICH)', in C Lenk, G Duttge, H Gangerau, *Handbuch Ethik und Recht der Forschung am Menschen* (Heidelberg: Springer, 2014) 541–45.

Dahl R, 'Can International Organizations be Democratic? A Skeptic's View', in I Shapiro and C Hacker-Cordón (eds), *Democracy's Edges* (Cambridge: Cambridge University Press, 1999) 19–36.

Dawson M, *New Governance and the Transformation of European Law: Coordinating EU Social Law and Policy* (Cambridge: Cambridge University Press, 2011).

de Bellis M, 'The Legitimacy of Banking and Financial Standards: Representation, Due Process and Regulatory Capture', in M Eliantonio and C Cauffman (eds), *The legitimacy of standardisation as a regulatory technique: A cross-disciplinary and multi-level analysis* (Cheltenham: Edward Elgar, 2020) 180–202.

de Búrca G and Scott J (eds), *Law and New Governance in the EU and the US* (Oxford: Hart Publishing, 2006).

de Búrca G, 'Developing Democracy Beyond the State' (2008) 46 *Columbia Journal of Transnational Law* 221.

de Búrca G, 'The European Court of Justice and the International Legal Order after *Kadi*' (2010) 51 *Harvard International Law Journal* 1.

Dehousse R, 'Regulation by Networks in the European Community: The Role of European Agencies' (1997) 4 *Journal of European Public Policy* 246.

Delimatsis P (ed), *The Law, Economics and Politics of International Standardization* (Cambridge: Cambridge University Press, 2015a).

Delimatsis P, 'Introduction: Continuity and Change in International Standardization', in P Delimatsis (eds), *The Law, Economics and Politics of International Standardization* (Cambridge: Cambridge University Press, 2015b).

Derderer H, *Korporative Staatsgewalt – Integration Privat Organisierter Interessen in die Ausübung von Staatsfunktionen. Zugleich eine Rekonstruktion der Legitimationsdogmatik* (Tübingen: Mohr Siebeck, 2004).

de Ruijter A, 'The impediment of health law's values in the constitutional setting of the EU', in T Hervey, C Young, and L Bishop (eds), *Research Handbook on EU Health Law and Policy* (Cheltenham: Edward Elgar, 2017) 479–95.

de Ruijter A, *EU Health Law & Policy: The Expansion of EU Power in Public Health and Health Care* (Oxford: Oxford University Press, 2019).

Devaux C, 'The Experts in the Elaboration of the Cape Town Convention: Between Authority and Legitimacy' (2013) 19 *European Law Journal* 843.

DiMasi J, Grabowski H and Hansen R, 'Innovation in the pharmaceutical industry: New estimates of R&D costs' (2016) 47 *Journal of Health Economics* 20.

Doi O, 'Role and Public Health Responsibilities of the Authorities', in P D'Arcy and D Harron (eds), *Proceedings of the First International Conference on Harmonisation – Brussels 1991* (Belfast: The Queen's University Belfast, 1992) 18–26.

Dorbeck-Jung B, 'Challenges to the Legitimacy of International Regulation: The Case of Pharmaceuticals Standardisation', in A Føllesdal, R Wessel and J Wouters (eds), *Multilevel Regulation and the EU: The Interplay between Global, European and National Normative Processes* (Leiden: Martinus Nijhoff Publishers, 2008) 51–71.

Durner W, 'Internationales Umweltverwaltungsrecht', in C Möllers, A Vosskuhle and C Walter (eds), *Internationales Verwaltungsrecht – Eine Analyse Anhand von Referenzgebieten* (Tübingen: Mohr Siebeck, 2007) 121–64.

Eeckhout P, *EU External Relations Law*, 2nd edn (Oxford: Oxford University Press, 2011).

Eifert M, '§19 Regulierungsstrategien', in W Hoffmann-Riem, E Schmidt-Aßmann and A Voßkuhle (eds), *Grundlagen des Verwaltungsrechts Band I* (München: Beck, 2012) 1319–94.

Eliantonio M, 'Judicial Review in an Integrated Administration: the Case of "Composite Procedures"' (2014) 7 *Review of Administrative Law Journal* 65.

Eliantonio M and Stefan O (eds), 'Soft Law in the EU Legal Order: Reflections and Contemporary Trends' [Special Issue] (2017) 37 *Yearbook of European Law* 457.

Eliantonio M and Cauffman C (eds), *The legitimacy of standardisation as a regulatory technique: A cross-disciplinary and multi-level analysis* (Cheltenham: Edward Elgar, 2020).

Esty D, 'Good Governance at the Supranational Scale: Globalizing Administrative Law' (2005–2006) 115 *Yale Law Journal* 1490.

Everson M and Vos E, 'European Risk Governance in a Global Context', in E Vos (ed), *European Risk Governance – Its Science, its Inclusiveness and its Effectiveness*, Connex Report Series No 6 (2008) 7–36.

Everson M and Vos E, 'The Scientification of Politics and the Politicization of Science', in Everson M and Vos E (eds), *Uncertain Risks Regulated* (Oxon: Routledge/Cavendish, 2009) 1–18.

Everson M, Monda C and Vos E (eds), *European Agencies in between Institutions and Member States* (Alphen aan den Rijn: Kluwer Law International, 2014).

Feick J, 'Learning and Interest Accommodation in Policy and Institutional Change: EC Risk Regulation in the Pharmaceutical Sector', ESCR Centre for Analysis of Risk and Regulation (CARR) Discussion Paper 25, (January 2005).

Fisher E, 'Drowning by Numbers: Standard-Setting in Risk Regulation and the Pursuit of Accountable Public Administration' (2000) 20 *Oxford Journal of Legal Studies* 109.

Fisher E, 'Unpacking the Toolbox: Or Why the Public/Private Divide is Important in EC Environmental Law', Florida State University College of Law – Public Law and Legal Theory Working Paper No 35, (August 2001).

Fisher E, *Risk Regulation and Administrative Constitutionalism* (Oxford: Hart, 2010).

Fisher E, 'Expert Executive Power, Administrative Constitutionalism and Co-production: Why They Matter', in M Weimer and A de Ruijter, *Regulating Risks in the European Union – The Co-production of Expert and Executive Power* (Oxford: Hart, 2017) 37–56.

Flear M, *Governing Public Health: EU Law, Regulation and Biopolitics* (Oxford: Hart Publishing, 2015).

Flear M, 'Charting a roadmap towards membership and formal voice in global bioethics standard-setting: Health research and the case of the International Council on Harmonisation' (2018) *Medical Law International* 157.

Føllesdal A, Wessel R and Wouters J (eds), *Multilevel Regulation and the EU: The Interplay between Global, European and National Normative Processes* (Leiden: Martinus Nijhoff Publishers, 2008).

Gehring T and Krapohl S, 'Supranational Regulatory Agencies between Independence and Control. The EMEA and the Authorisation of Pharmaceuticals in the European Single Market' (2007) 14 *Journal of European Public Policy* 208.

Geradin D, Muñoz R and Petit N (eds), *Regulation Through Agencies in the EU – A New Paradigm of European Governance* (Cheltenham: Edward Elgar, 2006).

Goldmann M, 'Inside Relative Normativity: From Sources to Standard Instruments for the Exercise of International Public Authority', in A von Bogdandy, R Wolfrum, J von Bernstorff, P Dann and M Goldmann (eds), *The Exercise of Public Authority by International Institutions: Advancing International Institutional Law* (Heidelberg: Springer, 2010) 661–711.

Goldmann M, *Internationale öffentliche Gewalt – Handlungsformen internationaler Institutionen im Zeitalter der Globalisierung* (Heidelberg: Springer, 2015).

Grant R and Keohane R, 'Accountability and Abuses of Power in World Politics' (2005) 99 *American Political Science Review* 29.

Groenleer M, *The Autonomy of European Union Agencies – A Comparative Study of Institutional Developments* (Delft: Eburon, 2009).

Groenleer M, 'Linking Up Levels of Governance: Agencies of the European Union and International Institutions', in O Costa and K Joergensen (eds), *The Influence of International Institutions on the European Union: When Multilateralism Hits Brussels* (Basingstoke: Palgrave Macmillan, 2012) 135–54.

Groenleer M and Gabbi S, 'Regulatory Agencies of the European Union as International Actors: Legal Framework, Development over Time and Strategic Motives in the Case of the European Food Safety Authority' (2013) 4 *European Journal of Risk Regulation* 479.

Guy M and Sauter W, 'The history and scope of EU health law and policy', in T Hervey, C Young and L Bishop (eds), *Research Handbook on EU Health Law and Policy* (Cheltenham: Edward Elgar, 2017) 17–35.

Haas P, 'Introduction: Epistemic Communities and International Policy Coordination' (1992) 46 *International Organization* 1.
Habermas J, *The Theory of Communicative Action – Volume 2* (Boston: Beacon Press, 1987).
Habermas J, 'Die Postnationale Konstellation und die Zukunft der Demokratie', in J Habermas, *Die Postnationale Konstellation – Politische Essays* (Frankfurt am Main: Suhrkamp Verlag, 1998) 91–169.
Hachez N and Wouters J, 'A Glimpse at the Democratic Legitimacy of Private Standards: Assessing the Public Accountability of Global G.A.P.' (2011) 14 *Journal of International Economic Law* 677.
Hancher L, *Regulating for Competition – Government, Law and the Pharmaceutical Industry in the United Kingdom and France* (Alblasserdam: Haveka, 1989).
Hancher L, 'Creating the Internal Market for Pharmaceutical Medicines – An Echternach Jumping Procession?' (1991) 28 *Common Market Law Review* 821.
Hancher L, 'The EU Pharmaceuticals Market: Parameters and Pathways', in E Mossialos, M Mrazek and T Walley (eds), *Regulating Pharmaceuticals in Europe: Striving for Efficiency, Equity and Quality* (Maidenhead: Open University Press, 2004) 635–82.
Harlow C, 'Towards a Theory of Access for the European Court of Justice' (1992) 12 *Yearbook of European Law* 213.
Harlow C, 'Global Administrative Law: The Quest for Principles and Values' (2006) 17 *European Journal of International Law* 187.
Harlow C, 'Composite Decision-Making and Accountability Networks: Some Deductions from a Saga' (2013) 32 *Yearbook of European Law* 3.
Herberg M, 'Global Governance Networks in Action: The Development of Toxicological Test Methods at the OECD', in O Dilling, M Herberg and G Winter (eds), *Transnational Administrative Rule-Making – Performance, Legal Effects and Legitimacy* (Oxford: Hart Publishing, 2011) 77–108.
Hervey T and McHale J, *Health Law and the European Union* (Cambridge: Cambridge University Press, 2004).
Hervey T and Vanhercke B, 'Health Care and the EU: The Law and Policy Patchwork', in E Mossialos, M Mrazek and T Walley (eds), *Regulating Pharmaceuticals in Europe: Striving for Efficiency, Equity and Quality* (Maidenhead: Open University Press, 2004) 84–133.
Hervey T and McHale J, *European Union Health Law – Themes and Implications* (Cambridge: Cambridge University Press, 2015).
Hervey T, 'The EU's (Emergent) Global Health Law', in T Hervey, C Young and L Bishop (eds), *Research Handbook on EU Health Law and Policy* (Cheltenham: Edward Elgar, 2017) 453–76.
Hervey T, Young C and Bishop L, 'Introduction', in T Hervey, C Young and L Bishop (eds), *Research Handbook on EU Health Law and Policy* (Cheltenham: Edward Elgar, 2017) 1–13.
Hervey T, Young C and Bishop L (eds), *Research Handbook on EU Health Law and Policy* (Cheltenham: Edward Elgar, 2017).
Hervey T and de Ruijter A, 'The Dynamic Potential of European Union Health Law' (2020) *European Journal of Risk Regulation*, First View doi:10.1017/err.2020.70.
Herwig A, 'The Contribution of Global Administrative Law to Enhancing the Legitimacy of the Codex Alimentarius Commission', in O Dilling, M Herberg and G Winter (eds), *Transnational Administrative Rule-Making –Performance, Legal Effects and Legitimacy* (Oxford: Hart Publishing, 2011) 171–212.
Hodgkin C, 'International Harmonisation – The Need for Transparency' (1996) 9 *International Journal of Risk & Safety in Medicine* 195.
Hofmann H and Türk A, 'An Introduction to EU Administrative Governance', in H Hofmann and A Türk (eds), *EU Administrative Governance* (Cheltenham: Edward Elgar, 2006) 1–10.
Hofmann H, 'Seven Challenges for EU Administrative Law' (2009) 2 *Review of European Administrative Law* 37.

Hofmann H, Rowe G and Türk A, *Administrative Law and Policy of the European Union* (Oxford: Oxford University Press, 2011).
Hofmann H, 'Dealing with Trans-Territorial Executive Rule-Making' (2013) 78 *Missouri Law Review* 423.
Hofmann H and Mihaescu B, 'The Relation between the Charter's Fundamental Rights and the Unwritten General Principles of EU Law: Good Administration as the Test Case' (2013) 9 *European Constitutional Law Review* 73.
Hofmann H, Schneider J and Ziller J, 'The Research Network on European Administrative Law's Project on EU Administrative Procedure – Its Concepts, Approaches and Results' (2014) 7 *Review of European Administrative Law* 45.
Hofmann H, 'European Regulatory Union? The Role of Agencies and Standards', in P Koutrakos and J Snell, *Research Handbook on the Law of the EU's Internal Market* (Cheltenham: Edward Elgar, 2017) 460–76.
Hofmann H, Vos E and Chamon M (eds), *The External Dimension of EU Agencies and Bodies – Law and Policy* (Cheltenham: Edward Elgar, 2019).
Hood C, Rothstein H and Baldwin R, *The Government of Risk: Understanding Risk Regulation Regimes* (Oxford: Oxford University Press, 2003).
Howell K, 'Uploading, Downloading and European Integration: Assessing the Europeanisation of UK Financial Services Regulation' (2004) 6 *Journal of International Banking Regulation* 53.
Howorth J, 'The EU as a Global Actor: Grand Strategy for a Global Grand Bargain?' (2010) 48 *Journal of Common Market Studies* 455.
Hurd I, 'Legitimacy and Authority in International Politics' (1999) 53 *International Organization* 379.
Jackson E, *Law and the Regulation of Medicines* (Oxford: Hart, 2012).
Jackson E, *Medical Law – Text, Cases, and Materials*, 5th edn (Oxford: Oxford University Press, 2019).
Jasanoff S, 'Epistemic Subsidiarity – Coexistence, Cosmopolitanism, Constitutionalism' (2013) 4 *European Journal of Risk Regulation* 133.
Jasanoff S, 'Constitutions of Modernity: Science, Risk and Governable Subjects', in M Weimer and A de Ruijter, Regulating Risks in the European Union – The Co-production of Expert and Executive Power (Oxford: Hart, 2017) 19–36.
Joerges C, 'Law, Science and the Management of Risks to Health at the National, European and International Level: Stories on Baby Dummies, Mad Cows and Hormones in Beef' (2001) 7 *Columbia Journal of European Law* 1.
Jordan D, 'International Regulatory Harmonization: A New Era in Prescription Drug Approval' (1992) 25 *Vanderbilt Journal of Transnational Law* 471.
Julliet Y, 'CTD – A Tool for Global Development and Assessment' (2011) 3 *Drug Information Association Global Forum* 25.
Kadelbach S, 'EU Administrative Law and the Law of the Europeanized Administration', in C Joerges and R Dehousse (eds), *Good Governance in Europe's Integrated Market* (Oxford: Oxford University Press, 2002) 167–206.
Kalberg S (ed), *Max Weber – Readings and Commentary on Modernity* (Malden: Blackwell, 2005).
Kanusky R, 'Pharmaceutical Harmonization: Standardizing Regulations among the United States, the European Economic Community, and Japan' (1994) 16 *Houston Journal of International Law* 665.
Katsikas D, 'International Conference on Harmonization of Technical Requirements for the Registration of Pharmaceutical Products', in T Hale and D Held (eds), *Handbook of Transnational Governance – Institutions & Innovations* (Cambridge: Polity Press, 2011) 88–94.
Kaul I, 'Exploring the Space between Markets and States: Global Public-Private Partnerships', in I Kaul and P Conceicao (eds), *The New Public Finance: Responding to Global Challenges* (Oxford: Oxford University Press, 2006) 219–68.

Keohane R and Nye J, 'Transgovernmental Relations and International Organizations' (1974) 27 *World Politics* 39.

Keohane R, 'Global Governance and Legitimacy' (2011) 18 *Review of International Political Economy* 99.

Kerwer D, 'Standardising as Governance: The case of credit rating agencies', MPI Collective Goods Preprint, No. 2001/3, (2001).

Kerwer D, 'Rules that Many Use: Standards and Global Regulation' (2005) 18 *Governance* 611.

Kica E and Bowman D, 'Transnational Governance Arrangements: Legitimate Alternatives to Regulating Nanotechnologie?' (2013) 7 *NanoEthics* 69.

Kidd D, 'The International Conference on Harmonization of Pharmaceutical Regulations, the European Medicines Evaluation Agency, and the FDA: Who's Zooming Who?' (1996) 4 *Indiana Journal of Global Legal Studies* 183.

Kingsbury B, 'The Administrative Law Frontier in Global Governance' (2005) 99 *Proceedings of the Annual Meeting of the American Society of International Law* 143.

Kingsbury B, Krisch N and Stewart R, 'The Emergence of Global Administrative Law' (2005) 68 *Law and Contemporary Problems* 15.

Kingsbury B and Stewart R, 'Legitimacy and Accountability in Global Regulatory Governance: The Emerging Global Administrative Law and the Design and Operation of Administrative Tribunals of International Organizations', in K Papanikolaou and M Hiskaki (eds), *International Administrative Tribunals in a Changing World* (London: Esperia, 2008) 193–220.

Kingsbury B and Casini L, 'Global Administrative Law Dimensions of International Organizations Law' (2009) 6 *International Organizations Law Review* 319.

Klabbers J, 'The Redundancy of Soft Law' (1996) 65 *Nordic Journal of International Law* 167.

Klabbers J, 'The Undesirability of Soft Law' (1998) 67 *Nordic Journal of International Law* 381.

Klabbers J, *An Introduction to International Institutional Law*, 3rd edn (Cambridge: Cambridge University Press, 2015) 46–50.

Knauff M, *Der Regelungsverbund: Recht und Soft Law im Mehrebenensystem* (Tübingen: Mohr Siebeck, 2010).

Koechlin L and Calland R, 'Standard Setting at the Cutting Edge: An Evidence-Based Typology for Multi-stakeholder Initiatives', in A Peters, L Koechlin, T Förster and G Fenner Zinkernagel (eds), *Non-State Actors as Standard-Setters* (Cambridge: Cambridge University Press, 2009) 84–112.

Kohler-Koch B and Eising R (eds), *The Transformation of Governance in the European Union* (London: Routledge, 1999).

Kohler-Koch B and Quittkat C (eds), *De-Mystification of Participatory Democracy* (Oxford: Oxford University Press, 2013).

Kooiman J (ed), *Modern Governance: New Government – Society Interactions* (London: Sage, 1993).

Korkea-aho E, 'Better Judicial Review? EU Courts and the Smart Regulation Agenda in Implementing Chemicals Regulation' (2012) 6 *Legisprudence* 397.

Korkea-aho E, 'Legal Interpretation of EU Framework Directives: A Soft Law Approach' (2015) 40 *European Law Review* 70.

Korkea-aho E, 'National Courts and European Soft Law: Is Grimaldi Still Good Law?' (2018) *Yearbook of European Law* 470.

Krapohl S, 'Thalidomide, BSE and the Single Market: An Historical-Institutionalist Approach to Regulatory Regimes in the EU' (2007) 46 *European Journal of Political Research* 25.

Krapohl S, *Risk Regulation in the Single European Market – The Governance of Pharmaceuticals and Foodstuffs in the European Union* (Basingstoke: Palgrave 2008).

Krisch N, 'The Pluralism of Global Administrative Law' (2006) 17 *European Journal of International Law* 247.

Krisch N and Kingsbury B, 'Introduction: Global Governance and Global Administrative Law in the International Legal Order' (2006) 17 *The European Journal of International Law* 1.

Krisch N, 'Das Migrationsrecht und die Internationalisierung des Verwaltungsrechts', in C Möllers, A Vosskuhle and C Walter (eds), *Internationales Verwaltungsrecht – Eine Analyse Anhand von Referenzgebieten* (Tübingen: Mohr Siebeck, 2007) 313–18.

Kuhnert B, 'ICH at 20: An overview' (2011) 3 *Drug Information Association Global Forum* 17.

Ladeur K, 'Towards a Legal Theory of Supranationality – The Viability of the Network Concept' (1997) 3 *European Law Journal* 3.

Ladeur K, 'Die Internationalisierung des Verwaltungsrechts: Versuch einer Synthese', in C Möllers, A Vosskuhle and C Walter (eds), *Internationales Verwaltungsrecht – Eine Analyse Anhand von Referenzgebieten* (Tübingen: Mohr Siebeck, 2007) 375–94.

Lee J, 'What is Past is Prologue: The International Conference on Harmonization and Lessons Learned from European Drug Regulations Harmonization' (2005) 26 *University of Pennsylvania Journal of International Economic Law* 151.

Legrand P, 'The Impossibility of Legal Transplants' (1997) 4 *Maastricht Journal of European and Comparative Law* 111.

Lezotre P, *International Cooperation, Convergence and Harmonization of Pharmaceutical Regulations – A Global Perspective* (Oxford: Academic Press Elsevier, 2014).

Lin C, 'Public-Private Regime Interactions in Global Food Safety Governance' (2014a) 69 *Food and Drug Law Journal* 143.

Lin C, 'The European Food Safety Authority in Global Food Safety Governance: A Participant, a Benchmark, and a Model', in A Alemanno and S Gabbi (eds), *Foundations of EU Food Law and Policy* (Farnham: Ashgate, 2014b) 347–62.

Lindström-Gommers L and Mullin T, 'International Conference on Harmonization: Recent Reforms as a Driver of Global Regulatory Harmonization and Innovation in Medical Products' (2019) 105 *Clinical Pharmacology & Therapeutics* 926.

Lisman J and Lekkerkerker J, 'Four Decades of European Medicines Regulation: What Have They Brought Us?' (2005) 17 *International Journal of Risk & Safety in Medicine* 73.

Livermore M, 'Authority and Legitimacy of Global Governance: Deliberation, Institutional Differentiation, and the Codex Alimentarius' (2006) 81 *New York University Law Review* 766.

Lourenco C, Orphanos N and Parker C, 'The International Council for Harmonisation: Positioning for the future with its recent reform and over 25 years of harmonisation work' (2016) *Pharmaceuticals Policy and Law* 79.

Majone G, 'Science and Trans-Science in Standard Setting' (1984) 9 *Science, Technology, & Human Values* 15.

Majone G, 'The Rise of the Regulatory State in Europe' (1994) 17 *West European Politics* 77.

Majone G, 'Europe's "Democratic Deficit": The Question of Standards' (1998) 4 *European Law Journal* 5.

Majone G, 'The Regulatory State and Its Legitimacy Problems' (1999) 22 *West European Politics* 1.

Manley M and Vickers M (eds), *Navigating European Pharmaceutical Law* (Oxford: Oxford University Press, 2015).

Marx A, Maertens M, Swinnen J and Wouters J, *Private Standards and Global Governance – Economic, Legal and Political Perspectives* (Cheltenham: Edward Elgar Publishing Ltd, 2012).

Mayntz R, 'Legitimacy and Compliance in Transnational Governance', MPIfG Working Paper 10/5 (2010).

Masson-Matthee M, *The Codex Alimentarius Commission and Its Standards* (The Hague: TMC Asser Press, 2007).

Mataija M, 'Private standard setting in the TBT Agreement: control and recognition', in M Cantero Gamito and H Micklitz (eds), *The Role of the EU in Transnational Legal Ordering – Standards, Contracts and Codes* (Cheltenham: Edward Elgar, 2020) 135–54.

Mattli W, 'The Politics and Economics of Institutional Standards Setting: An Introduction' (2001) 8 *Journal of European Public Policy* 328.

Mattli W and Büthe T, 'Setting International Standards: Technological Rationality or Primacy of Power?' (2003) 56 *World Politics* 1.

Meidinger E, 'The Administrative Law of Global Private-Public Regulation: the Case of Forestry' (2006) 17 *European Journal of International Law* 47.

Mendes J, *Participation in EU Rule-Making – A Rights-Based Approach* (Oxford: Oxford University Press, 2011a).

Mendes J, 'Participation and the Role of Law After Lisbon: A Legal View on Article 11 TEU' (2011b) 48 *Common Market Law Review* 1849.

Mendes J, 'Administrative Law Beyond the State: Participation at the Intersection of Legal Systems', in E Chiti and B Mattarella (eds), *Global Administrative Law and EU Administrative Law* (Heidelberg: Springer, 2011c) 111–132.

Mendes J, 'EU Law and Global Regulatory Regimes: Hollowing Out Procedural Standards?' (2012) 10 *International Journal of Constitutional Law* 988.

Mendes J, 'Rule of Law and Participation: A Normative Analysis of Internationalized Rulemaking as Composite Procedures' (2014) 12 *International Journal of Constitutional Law* 370.

Menon A and Weatherill S, 'Transnational Legitimacy in a Globalising World: How the European Union Rescues its States' (2008) 31 *West European Politics* 397.

Meuwese A, Schuurmans Y and Voermans W, 'Towards a European Administrative Procedure Act' (2009) 2 *Review of European Administrative Law* 3.

Millstone E and van Zwanenberg P, 'The Evolution of Food Safety Policy-Making Institutions in the UK, EU and Codex Alimentarius' (2002) 36 *Social Policy & Administration* 59.

Möllers C, 'Transnationale Behördenkooperation – Verfassungs- und Völkerrechtliche Probleme Transnationaler Administrativer Standardsetzung' (2005) 65 *Zeitschrift für ausländisches öffentliches Recht und Völkerrecht* 351.

Möllers C, 'European Governance: Meaning and Value of a Concept' (2006), 43 *Common Market Law Review* 313.

Möllers C, 'Internationales Verwaltungsrecht – Eine Einführung in die Referenzanalyse', in C Möllers, A Vosskuhle and C Walter (eds), *Internationales Verwaltungsrecht – Eine Analyse Anhand von Referenzgebieten* (Tübingen: Mohr Siebeck, 2007) 1–6.

Möllers C and Terhechte J, '§40 Europäisches Verwaltungsrecht und Internationales Verwaltungsrecht', in J Terhechte (ed), *Verwaltungsrecht der Europäischen Union* (Baden-Baden: Nomos, 2011) 1437–52.

Möllers C, 'Ten Years of Global Administrative Law' (2015) 13 *International Journal of Constitutional Law* 469.

Molzon J, 'The International Conference on Harmonization Common Technical Document – Global Submission Format?' (2005) 60 *Food and Drug Law Journal* 447.

Molzon J, Giaquinto A, Lindström L, Tominaga T, Ward M, Doerr P, Hunt L and Rago L, 'The Value and Benefits of the International Conference on Harmonisation to Drug Regulatory Authorities: Advancing Harmonization for Better Public Health' (2011) 89 *Clinical Pharmacology & Therapeutics* 503.

Molzon J, 'The Value and Benefit of the International Conference on Harmonisation (ICH) to Drug Regulatory Authorities: Advancing Harmonization for Better Public Health', in J van de Laan and J DeGeorge (eds), *Global Approach in Safety Testing – ICH Guidelines Explained* (New York: Springer, 2013) 23–28.

Morais H, 'The Quest for International Standards: Global Governance vs. Sovereignty' (2001-2002) 50 *University of Kansas Law Review* 779.

Moravcsik A, 'In Defence of the "Democratic Deficit": Reassessing Legitimacy in the European Union' (2002) 40 *Journal of Common Market Studies* 603.

Mossialos E, Mrazek M and Walley T, 'Regulating Pharmaceuticals in Europe: An Overview', in E Mossialos, M Mrazek and T Walley (eds), *Regulating Pharmaceuticals in Europe: Striving for Efficiency, Equity and Quality* (Maidenhead: Open University Press, 2004) 1–37.

Müller-Graff P, 'Das "Soft Law" der Europäischen Organisationen' (2012) 1 *Europarecht* 18.

Mulberg A and Cripps T, 'Global Harmonization of Pediatric Drug Development: Critical for Progress for Developing Safe and Effective Therapeutic Agents for Children' (2019) *Current Therapeutic Research* 109.

Nadvi K and Wältring F, 'Making Sense of Global Standards', INEF Report Heft 58/2002 (2002).

Nanz P and Steffek J,' Global governance, Participation and the Public Sphere' (2004) 39 *Government and Opposition* 314.

National Institute for Public Health and the Environment (RVIM), 'Minds Open – Sustainability of the European Regulatory System for Medicinal Products', RVIM-Report 2014-0033.

Nelken D, 'The Meaning of Success in Transnational Legal Transfers' (2001) 19 *Windsor Yearbook of Access to Justice* 349.

Neumeyer K, *Internationales Verwaltungsrecht – Vol. IV: Allgemeiner Teil* (Zürich: Verlag für Recht und Gesellschaft, 1936).

Orzack L, Kaitin K and Lasagna L, 'Pharmaceutical Regulation in the European Community: Barriers to Single Market Integration' (1992) 17 *Journal of Health Politics, Policy and Law* 847.

Ott A, 'EU Regulatory Agencies in EU External Relations: trapped in a Legal Minefield Between European and International Law' (2008) 13 *European Foreign Affairs Review* 515.

Ott A, Vos E and Coman-Kund F, 'European Agencies on the Global Scene: EU and International Law Perspectives', in M Everson, C Monda and E Vos (eds), *European Agencies In Between Institutions And Member States* (Alphen aan den Rijn: Kluwer Law International, 2014) 87–122.

Ott A and Bartelt S, 'The Administrative Cooperation of the European Commission with Third Countries and International Organisations' (2016) 29 *Europarecht* 143.

Ott A, 'Informalization of EU Bilateral Instruments: Categorization, Contestation, and Challenges' (2020) 28 *Yearbook of European Law*.

Pammolli F, Magazzini L and Riccaboni M, 'The Productivity Crisis in Pharmaceutical R&D' (2011) 10 *Nature Reviews Drug Discovery* 428.

Pauwelyn J, 'Informal International Lawmaking: Framing the Concept and Research Questions', in J Pauwelyn, R Wessel and J Wouters (eds), *Informal International Lawmaking* (Oxford: Oxford University Press, 2012) 13–34.

Pelkmans J, 'The New Approach to Technical Harmonization and Standardisation' (1987) 25 *Journal of Common Market Studies* 249.

Pereira R, 'Why Would International Administrative Activity Be Any Less Legitimate? – A Study of the Codex Alimentarius Commission', in A von Bogdandy, R Wolfrum, J von Bernstorff, P Dann and M Goldmann (eds), *The Exercise of Public Authority by International Institutions: Advancing International Institutional Law* (Heidelberg: Springer, 2010) 541–71.

Permanand G, *EU Pharmaceutical Regulation: The Politics of Policy-Making* (Manchester: Manchester University Press, 2006).

Peters A and Pagotto I, 'Soft Law as a New Mode of Governance: A Legal Perspective', New Modes of Governance Project Paper 04/D11 (2006).

Peters A, Koechlin L and Fenner Zinkernagel G, 'Non-state Actors as Standard Setters: Framing the Issue in an Interdisciplinary Fashion', in A Peters, L Koechlin, T Förster and G Fenner Zinkernagel (eds), *Non-State Actors as Standard-Setters* (Cambridge: Cambridge University Press, 2009) 1–32.

Pilgerstorfer M, 'EU law and policy on pharmaceuticals marketing and post-market control including product liability', in T Hervey, C Young, and L Bishop (eds), *Research Handbook on EU Health Law and Policy* (Cheltenham: Edward Elgar, 2017) 156–198.

Ponce Solé J, 'The History of Legitimate Administration in Europe', in M Ruffert (ed), *Legitimacy in European Administrative Law: Reform and Reconstruction* (Groningen: European Law Publishing, 2011a) 155–73.

Ponce Solé J, 'EU Law, Global Law and the Right to Good Administration', in E Chiti and B Mattarella (eds), *Global Administrative Law and EU Administrative Law* (Heidelberg: Springer, 2011b) 133–45.

Pound R, 'Law in Books and Law in Action' (1910) 44 *American Law Review* 12.

Prechal S and Widdershoven R, 'Principle of effective judicial protection', in M Scholten and A Brenninkmeijer, *Controlling EU Agencies – The Rule of Law in a Multi-jurisdictional Legal Order* (Cheltenham: Edward Elgar, 2020) 80–97.

Purnhagen K, 'The Challenge of Globalization in Pharmaceutical Law – Is an International Drug Approval System Modeled after the European System Worth Considering?' (2008) 63 *Food and Drug Law Journal* 623.

Quack S, 'Law, Expertise and Legitimacy in Transnational Economic Governance: An Introduction' (2010) 8 *Socio-Economic Review* 3.

Raustiala K, 'The Architecture of International Cooperation: Transgovernmental Networks and the Future of International Law' (2002-2003) 43 *Virginia Journal of International Law* 1.

Renn O, *Risk Governance: Coping with Uncertainty in a Complex World* (London: Routledge, 2008).

Risse T, 'Transnational Governance and Legitimacy', in A Benz and Y Papadopoulos (eds), *Governance and Democracy – Comparing National, European and International Experiences* (Oxon: Routledge, 2006) 179–99.

Rizzi M, 'Simple, Safe and Transparent (?): Preliminary Reflections on the Proposal for a New EU Regulation of Clinical Trials' (2013) 4 *European Journal of Risk Regulation* 534.

Rizzi M, 'Non-Measurable Negotiations: The EU between Transnational Regulation of Pharmaceuticals and Private Law', in M Cremona and H Micklitz, *Private Law in the External Relations of the EU* (Oxford: Oxford University Press, 2016) 273–95.

Rockhold F, 'Industry Perspectives on ICH Guidelines' (2002) 21 *Statistics in Medicine* 2949.

Röhl H, 'Internationale Standardsetzung', in C Möllers, A Vosskuhle and C Walter (eds), *Internationales Verwaltungsrecht – Eine Analyse Anhand von Referenzgebieten* (Tübingen: Mohr Siebeck, 2007) 319–43.

Röttger-Wirtz S, 'Independence under threat – the role of private actors in the setting of global pharmaceutical standards and resulting challenges for European public law' (2018a) 24 *European Public Law* 433.

Röttger-Wirtz S, 'Delegated and implementing acts in the regulation of pharmaceuticals – an analysis through the lens of subsidiarity', in E Tauschinsky and W Weiß (eds), *The Legislative Choice Between Delegated and Implementing Acts: Walking a Labyrinth* (Cheltenham: Edward Elgar, 2018b) 117–44.

Röttger-Wirtz S and Eliantonio M, 'From integration to exclusion – EU composite administration and gaps in judicial accountability in the authorisation of pharmaceuticals' (2019) 10 *European Journal of Risk Regulation* 393.

Röttger-Wirtz S, 'Mutual Recognition and the Ever-incomplete Internal Market for Pharmaceuticals' (2020a) 13 *Review of European Administrative Law* 61.

Röttger-Wirtz S, 'Standardisation of health products in search of legitimacy: rethinking judicial review?', in M Eliantonio and Cauffman, *The Legitimacy of Standardization as a Regulatory Technique in the EU* (Cheltenham: Edward Elgar, 2020b) 266–91.

Rhodes R, *Understanding Governance: Policy Networks, Reflexivity and Accountability* (Buckingham: Open University Press, 1997).

Rosenau J, 'Governance, Order and Change in World Politics', in J Rosenau and E Czempiel (eds), *Governance without Government: Order and Change in World Politics* (Cambridge: Cambridge University Press, 1992) 1–29.

Rosenau J and Czempiel E (eds), *Governance without Government: Order and Change in World Politics* (Cambridge: Cambridge University Press, 1992).

Rossi M, 'Europäisiertes internationales Umweltverwaltungsrecht', in C Möllers, A Vosskuhle and C Walter (eds), *Internationales Verwaltungsrecht – Eine Analyse Anhand von Referenzgebieten* (Tübingen: Mohr Siebeck, 2007) 165–80.

Ruffert M, *Die Globalisierung als Herausforderung an das Öffentliche Recht* (Stuttgart: Boorberg, 2004).

Ruffert M, 'Perspektiven des Internationalen Verwaltungsrechts', in C Möllers, A Vosskuhle and C Walter (eds), *Internationales Verwaltungsrecht – Eine Analyse Anhand von Referenzgebieten* (Tübingen: Mohr Siebeck, 2007) 395–419.

Ruffert M, '§17 Rechtsquellen und Rechtsschichten des Verwaltungsrechts', in W Hoffmann-Riem, E Schmidt-Aßmann and A Voßkuhle (eds), *Grundlagen des Verwaltungsrechts Band I* (München: Beck, 2012) 1163–255.

Ruffert M and Steinecke S, *The Global Administrative Law of Science* (Heidelberg: Springer, 2011).

Sauer F, 'Preface', in J van de Laan and J DeGeorge (eds), *Global Approach in Safety Testing – ICH Guidelines Explained* (New York: Springer, 2013) v–viii.

Savino M, 'EU "Procedural" Supranationalism: On Models for Global Administrative Law', paper presented at NYU Global Forum on 13 December 2006, available via: http://www.law.nyu.edu/sites/default/files/upload_documents/gffsavinopaper.pdf.

Schachter O, 'The Twilight Existence of Nonbinding International Agreements' (1977) 71 *The American Journal of International Law* 296.

Schäferhoff M, Campe S and Kaan C, 'Transnational Public-Private Partnerships in International Relations: Making Sense of Concepts, Research Frameworks, and Results' (2009) 11 *International Studies Review* 451.

Scharpf F, *Demokratietheorie Zwischen Utopie und Anpassung* (Konstanz: Universitätsverlag Konstanz, 1970).

Scharpf F, *Governing in Europe – Effective and Democratic?* (Oxford: Oxford University Press, 1999).

Schepel H, *The Constitution of Private Governance – Product Standards in the Regulation of Integrating Markets* (Oxford: Hart, 2005).

Schepel H, 'The New Approach to the New Approach: The Juridification of Harmonized Standards in EU Law' (2013) 20 *Maastricht Journal of European and Comparative Law* 521.

Schmidt V, 'Democracy and Legitimacy in the European Union Revisited: Input, Output *and* "Throughput"' (2013) 61 *Political Studies* 2.

Schmidt-Aßmann E, *Das allgemeine Verwaltungsrecht als Ordnungsidee – Grundlagen und Aufgaben der verwaltungsrechtlichen Systembildung*, 2nd edn (Heidelberg: Springer, 2006).

Schmidt-Aßmann E, 'The Internationalization of Administrative Relationships as a Challenge for Administrative Law Scholarship', in A von Bogdandy, R Wolfrum, J von Bernstorff, P Dann and M Goldmann (eds), *The Exercise of Public Authority by International Institutions: Advancing International Institutional Law* (Heidelberg: Springer, 2010) 943–63.

Schneider I, *Das Kooperationsprinzip im Vorfeld der Arzneimittelzulassung – Zum national und Europarechtlichen Rahmen des Zusammenwirken von Potentiellen Antragsstellern und Zulassungsbehörden* (Frankfurt am Main: Peter Lang Europäischer Verlag der Wissenschaften, 2003).

Scholten M, *The Political Accountability of EU and US Independent Regulatory Agencies* (Leiden: Brill Nijhoff, 2014).

Scholten M and Brenninkmeijer A, *Controlling EU Agencies – The Rule of Law in a Multi-jurisdictional Legal Order* (Cheltenham: Edward Elgar, 2020).

Scholten M, Maggetti M and Papadopoulos Y, 'Towards a comprehensive system of controls for EU agencies', in M Scholten and A Brenninkmeijer, *Controlling EU Agencies – The Rule of Law in a Multi-jurisdictional Legal Order* (Cheltenham: Edward Elgar, 2020).

Schwarze J, *EU Administrative Law* (London: Sweet and Maxwell, 2006).

Schwarze J, 'Soft Law im Recht der Europäischen Union' (2011) 1 *Europarecht* 3.

Scott C, 'Standard-Setting in Regulatory Regimes', in R Baldwin, M Cave and M Lodge (eds), *The Oxford Handbook of Regulation* (Oxford: Oxford University Press, 2010) 104–19.

Scott J and Trubek D, 'Mind the Gap: Law and New Approaches to Governance in the European Union' (2003) 8 *European Law Journal* 1.

Scott J, 'International Trade and Environmental Governance: Relating Rules (and Standards) in the EU and WTO' (2004) 15 *European Journal of International Law* 307.

Scott J and Sturm S, 'Courts as Catalysts: Rethinking The Judicial Role in New Governance' (2007) 13 *The Columbia Journal of European Law* 565.

Scott J, 'In Legal Limbo: Post-Legislative Guidance as a Challenge for Administrative Law' (2011) 48 *Common Market Law Review* 329.

Scott J, 'The New EU "Extraterritoriality"' (2014a) 51 *Common Market Law Review* 1343.

Scott J, 'Extraterritoriality and Territorial Extension in EU Law' (2014b) 62 *American Journal of Comparative Law* 87.

Senden L, *Soft Law in European Community Law: Its Relationship to Legislation* (Nijmegen: Wolf Legal Publishers, 2003).

Senden L and van den Brink A, 'Checks and Balances of Soft EU Rule-Making', European Parliament – Directorate General for Internal Policies Study (2012) PE 462.433.

Senden L, 'Soft Post-Legislative Rulemaking: A Time for More Stringent Control' (2013) 19 *European Law Journal* 57.

Seuba X, 'International Harmonization of Pharmaceutical Standards: Trade, Ethics and Power', in G Burci and B Toebes, *Research Handbook in Global Health Law* (Cheltenham: Edward Elgar, 2018) 460–84.

Seyett K, 'Looking After the Orphans? Treatments for Rare Diseases, EU Law, and the Ethics of Costly Healthcare', in M Flear, A Farrell, T Hervey, and T Murphy (eds), *European Law and New Health Technologies* (Oxford: Oxford University Press, 2013) 125–47.

Shaffer G and Pollack M, 'Hard and Soft Law', in J Dunoff and M Pollack (eds), *Interdisciplinary Perspectives on International Law and International Relations –The State of the Art* (Cambridge: Cambridge University Press, 2013) 197–222.

Shamir-Borer E, 'Legitimacy without Authority in Global Standardization Governance: The Case of the International Organization for Standardization (ISO)', in S Cassese, B Carotti, L Casini, E Cavalieri and E MacDonald (eds), *Global Administrative Law: The Casebook*, 3rd edn (2012, IRPA-IILJ, ebook) 162–83.

Shapiro M, 'Administrative Law Unbounded: Reflections on Government and Governance' (2001) 8 *Indiana Journal of Legal Studies* 369.

Shelton D, 'Soft Law', in D Armstrong (ed), *Routledge Handbook of International Law* (Oxon: Routledge, 2009) 68–80.

Shorthose S, *Guide to European Pharmaceutical Regulatory Law* (Alphen aan den Rijn: Kluwer, 2013).

Simonati A, 'The Principles of Administrative Procedure and the EU Courts: An Evolution in Progress?' (2011) 4 *Review of European Administrative Law* 45.

Sindbjerg Martisen D, 'Governing EU health law and policy – on governance and legislative politics', in T Hervey, C Young and L Bishop (eds), *Research Handbook on EU Health Law and Policy* (Cheltenham: Edward Elgar, 2017) 36–59.

Slaughter A, 'The Real New World Order' (1997) 76 *Foreign Affairs* 183.

Slaughter A, 'The Accountability of Government Networks' (2001) 8 *Indiana Journal of Global Legal Studies* 347.

Slaughter A, *A New World Order* (Princeton: Princeton University Press, 2004).

Slaughter A and Zaring D, 'Networking Goes International: An Update' (2006) 2 *Annual Review of Law and Social Science* 211.

Snyder F, 'Soft Law and the Institutional Practice in the European Community', in S Martin (ed), *The Construction of Europe – Essays in Order of Emile Noel* (Dordrecht: Kluwer, 1994) 197–225.

Spagnuolo F, 'Diversity and pluralism in earth system governance: Contemplating the role for global administrative law' (2011) 70 *Ecological Economics* 1875.

Spina A, 'The Regulation of Pharmaceuticals Beyond the State: EU and Global Administrative Systems', in E Chiti and B Mattarella (eds), *Global Administrative Law and EU Administrative Law* (Heidelberg: Springer, 2011) 249–68.

Stefan O, 'European Union Soft Law: New Developments Concerning the Divide Between Legally Binding Force and Legal Effects' (2012) 75 *The Modern Law Review* 865.

Stefan O, Soft Law in Court: Competition Law, State Aid, and the Court of Justice of the European Union (Alphen aan den Rijn: Kluwer, 2013).

Stefan O, 'Helping Loose Ends Meet? The Judicial Acknowledgement of Soft Law as a Tool of Multi-Level Governance' (2014) 21 *Maastricht Journal of European and Comparative Law* 359.

Steffek J and Ferretti M, 'Accountability or "Good Decision"? The Competing Goals of Civil Society Participation in International Governance' (2009) 23 *Global Society* 37.

Stewart R, 'The Reformation of American Administrative Law' (1975) 88 *Harvard Law Review* 1669.

Stewart R, 'Administrative Law In The Twenty-First Century' (2003) 78 *New York University Law Review* 437.
Stewart R, 'U.S. Administrative Law: A Model For Global Administrative Law?' (2005) 68 *Law and Contemporary Problems* 63.
Tallberg J, 'Delegation to Supranational Institutions: Why, How, and With What Consequence' (2002) 25 *West European Politics* 23.
Terpan F, 'Soft Law in the European Union – The Changing Nature of EU Law' (2015) 21 *European Law Journal* 68.
Tietje C, *Internationalisiertes Verwaltungshandeln* (Berlin: Duncker & Humblot GmbH, 2001).
Timmermans K, 'Harmonization, Regulation, and Trade: Interactions in the Pharmaceutical Field' (2004) 34 *International Journal of Health Services* 651.
Trute H, '§6 Die demokratische Legitimation der Verwaltung', in W Hoffmann-Riem, E Schmidt-Aßmann and A Voßkuhle (eds), *Grundlagen des Verwaltungsrechts Band I* (München: Beck, 2012) 341–435.
Turner M, Catapano M, Hirschfeld S and Giaquinto C, 'Global Research in Paediatrics. Paediatric drug development: the impact of evolving regulations' (2014) 73 *Advanced Drug Delivery Reviews* 2.
Valverde J, 'The Globalization of Medicines as a Challenge for Governments' (2016) 18 *Pharmaceuticals Policy and Law* 19.
Vamvakas S, 'EU Perspectives on ICH', in J van de Laan and J DeGeorge (eds), *Global Approach in Safety Testing – ICH Guidelines Explained* (New York: Springer, 2013) 13–22.
van Asselt M, Everson M and Vos E, 'The European Union Put to the Test: The Quest for Politics', in M van Asselt, M Everson and E Vos (eds), *Trade, Health and the Environment – The European Union Put to the Test* (Oxon: Routledge/Earthscan, 2014) 9–21.
van Gestel R and Micklitz H, 'European Integration through Standardization: How Judicial Review is Breaking Down the Club House of Private Standardization Bodies' (2013) 50 *Common Market Law Review* 145.
van Kersbergen K and van Waarden F, '"Governance" as a Bridge between Disciplines: Cross-Disciplinary Inspiration Regarding Shifts in Governance and Problems of Governability, Accountability and Legitimacy' (2004) 43 *European Journal of Political Research* 143.
van Vooren B, Blockmans S and Wouters J (eds), *The EU's Role in Global Governance – The Legal Dimension* (Oxford: Oxford University Press, 2013).
van Vooren B and Wessel R, 'The EU as Global Legal Actor', in B van Vooren and R Wessel (eds), *EU External Relations Law – Text, Cases and Materials* (Cambridge: Cambridge University Press, 2014) 1–34.
van Waarden F, 'Dimensions and Types of Policy Networks' (1992) 21 *European Journal of Political Research* 29.
Vaillancourt Rosenau P (ed), *Public-Private Policy Partnerships* (Cambridge: MIT Press, 2000).
Vaughan S, 'Differentiation and Dysfunction: An Exploration of Post-Legislative Guidance Practices in 14 EU Agencies' (2015) 17 *Cambridge Yearbook of European Legal Studies* 66.
Vogel D, 'The Globalization of Pharmaceutical Regulation' (1998) 11 *Governance* 1.
Vogel D, *The Politics of Precaution- Regulating Health, Safety and Environmental Risks in Europe and the United States* (Princeton: Princeton University Press, 2012).
Volpato A and Eliantonio M, 'The contradictory approach of the CJEU to the judicial review of standards: a love-hate relationship?', in M Eliantonio and C Cauffman (eds), *The Legitimacy of Standardisation as a Regulatory Technique: A Cross-disciplinary and Multi-level Analysis* (Cheltenham: Edward Elgar Publishing, 2020) 91–110.
von Bogdandy A, Wolfrum R, von Bernstorff J, Dann P and Goldmann M (eds), *The Exercise of Public Authority by International Institutions: Advancing International Institutional Law* (Heidelberg: Springer, 2010).
von Bogdandy A, Dann P and Goldmann M, 'Developing the Publicness of Public International Law', in A von Bogdandy, R Wolfrum, J von Bernstorff, P Dann and M Goldmann (eds), *The Exercise of Public Authority by International Institutions: Advancing International Institutional Law* (Heidelberg: Springer, 2010) 3–32.

von Bogdandy A, 'The European Lesson for International Democracy – The Significance of Articles 9 to 12 EU Treaty for International Organizations' (2012) 23 *European Journal of International Law* 315.

Vos E, *Institutional Frameworks of Community Health and Safety Regulation – Committees, Agencies and Private Bodies* (Oxford: Hart Publishing, 1999).

Vos E and Joerges C, 'Structures of Transnational Governance and their Legitimacy', in J Vervaele (ed), *Compliance and Enforcement of European Union Law* (London: Kluwer, 1999) 71–93.

Vos E, 'European Agencies and the Composite EU Executive', in M Everson, C Monda and E Vos (eds), *European Agencies In Between Institutions and Member States* (Alphen aan den Rijn: Kluwer Law International, 2014) 11–47.

Vos E, 'EU Agencies and Independence', in D Ritleng (ed), *Independence and Legitimacy in the Institutional System of the European Union* (Oxford: Oxford University Press, 2016) 206–28.

Vos E and Röttger-Wirtz S, 'EU Food Law and the WTO: Trade, Science and Politics', in D Prévost, I Alexovičová and J Hillebrand Pohl (eds), *Restoring Trust in Trade: Liber Amicorum in Honour of Peter Van den Bossche* (Oxford: Hart Publishers, 2018) 219–34.

Wallach L, 'Accountable Governance in the Era of Globalization – The WTO, NAFTA and International Harmonization of Standards' (2001-2002) 50 *Kansas Law Review* 823.

Weber M, *Wirtschaft und Gesellschaft – Grundriss der Verstehenden Soziologie*, 5th Edition, (Tübingen: Mohr Siebeck, 1972).

Weil P, 'Towards Relative Normativity in International Law?' (1983) 77 *American Journal of International Law* 413.

Weiler J, Haltern U and Mayer F, 'European Democracy and its Critique' (1995) 18 *West European Politics* 4.

Weiler J, 'The Geology of International Law – Governance, Democracy and Legitimacy' (2004) 64 *Zeitschrift für ausländisches öffentliches Recht und Völkerrecht* 547.

Weimer M and de Ruijter A, *Regulating Risks in the European Union – The Co-production of Expert and Executive Power* (Oxford: Hart Publishing, 2017).

Wessel R, 'The Legal Framework for the Participation of the European Union in International Institutions' (2011) 33 *European Integration* 621.

Wheatley S, 'Democratic Governance beyond the State: The Legitimacy of Non-State Actors as Standard-Setters', in A Peters, L Koechlin, T Förster and G Fenner Zinkernagel (eds), *Non-State Actors as Standard-Setters* (Cambridge: Cambridge University Press, 2009) 215–40.

Wolfrum R, 'Legitimacy in International Law', in R Wolfrum (ed), *The Max Planck Encyclopedia of Public International Law* (Oxford: University Press Oxford, 2016), article last updated March 2011, available via: opil.ouplaw.com/home/EPIL.

Wouters J and Verhoeven S, 'Regulation and Globalization: Interaction between International Standard-Setting Agencies and the European Union', in D Geradin, R Muñoz and N Petit (eds), *Regulation Through Agencies in the EU: A New Paradigm of European Governance* (Cheltenham: Edward Elgar, 2006) 246–73.

Wouters J and van Kerckhoven S, 'The OECD and the G20: An Ever Closer Relationship?' (2011) Leuven Centre for Global Governance Studies Working Paper No 71.

Wouters J, Odermatt J and Ramopoulos T, 'The EU in the World of International Organizations: Diplomatic Aspirations, Legal Hurdles and Political Realities', Leuven Centre for Global Governance Studies, Working Paper 121, September 2013.

Zisowsky J, Krause A and Dingemanse J, 'Drug Development for Pediatric Populations Regulatory Aspects' (2010) 2 *Pharmaceutics* 364.

Zürn M, 'Global Governance and Legitimacy Problems' (2004) 39 *Government and Opposition* 260.

Index

www.ingramcontent.com/pod-product-compliance
Lightning Source LLC
Chambersburg PA
CBHW071258180926
51613CB00001B/67
* 9 7 8 1 5 0 9 9 4 2 9 9 2 *